Courtiers of the Marble Palace

Courtiers of the Marble Palace

The Rise and Influence
of the Supreme Court Law Clerk

TODD C. PEPPERS

Stanford Law and Politics
An Imprint of Stanford University Press
Stanford, California 2006

Stanford University Press
Stanford, California

Printed in the United States of America on acid-free,
archival-quality paper

Library of Congress Cataloging-in-Publication Data

Peppers, Todd C.
  Courtiers of the Marble Palace : the rise and influence of the
Supreme Court law clerk / Todd C. Peppers.
      p. cm.
  Includes bibliographical references and index.
  ISBN 0-8047-5381-4 (cloth : alk. paper)--ISBN 0-8047-5382-2 (pbk.
: alk. paper)
  1. United States. Supreme Court--Employees. 2. Law clerks--United
States. I. Title.

KF8742.P3356 2006
347.73'2636--dc22   2006004887

Original Printing 2006
Last figure below indicates year of this printing:
15   14   13   12   11   10   09   08   07   06

Typeset by Bruce Lundquist in 10/12.5 Bembo

Special discounts for bulk quantities of Stanford Law and Politics
are available to corporations, professional associations, and other
organizations. For details and discount information, contact the special
sales department of Stanford University Press. Tel: (650) 736-1783,
Fax: (650) 736-1784

To Michele

Contents

Foreword

AMONG SEVERAL OFTEN BAFFLING ASPECTS of the American legal system, one that evokes as much mystery—and misunderstanding—as any is the role of Supreme Court law clerks. Yet remarkably little is reliably known about this dimension of the judicial process. Those of us who have served as clerks to a justice of the High Court are sworn to secrecy, constrained both by the injunctions imposed during our service and by an abiding lifelong sense of self-restraint. With a very few notable exceptions, we do not disclose what occurred within a justice's chambers, or between chambers, even when nothing more is sought than confirmation (or refutation) on matters of public record.

Meanwhile, those in the news media and elsewhere who have no inside knowledge of the Court and its workings speculate endlessly about what may or may not have happened behind the marble pillars and walls that physically separate an institution that must remain isolated in intangible ways as well from the rest of society. Perceptions range all the way from attributing to law clerks not only the writing of virtually all opinions but also the decision of major cases as well, to regarding them as near-clerical functionaries who may be responsible for cite checking, spelling, and grammar but little more. (There is, as it turns out, some basis in fact for views approaching both extremes.)

At long last, the critical need for an inside view is being met through *Courtiers of the Marble Palace,* a remarkably thorough and thoughtful study of the Supreme Court clerkship. Todd Peppers brings to this task a rare blend of legal knowledge about and understanding of the Supreme Court's role and mission on the one hand, and on the other hand a political scientist's critical skills at placing this singular institution in the broader perspective essential to such a study. He has, quite simply, entered previously uncharted (indeed, in part presumptively forbidden) territory with a tenacity and insistence that yielded answers to questions that have been unrequited for nearly a century.

Thanks to this book, we now know a great deal about the Supreme Court clerkship in all its fascinating dimensions. Even those of us who have been there learn vast amounts from this study—indeed, in some respects, it may be we who stand to learn the most from Peppers' insights.

Predictably, what the reader learns is not always what one would have expected or assumed. There are many surprises along the way—about individual justices, about individual clerks (including one who became chief justice later in life), about important decisions and how opinions may have been shaped, and most of all about the High Court as an institution. In most respects what we learn is reassuring, if only to the degree that the tribunal that emerges seems more human and approachable than conventional wisdom usually posits. Throughout the book, one is reminded of the wisdom behind Chief Justice Charles Evans Hughes' explanation for the High Court's eminence: "We are not final because we are infallible; rather we are infallible because we are final."

Four dimensions of this book are especially valuable. For the first time, we not only have a clear sense of the antecedents (indeed the origins) of the current clerkship, but also can trace its evolution in ways that previous histories of the Supreme Court or biographies of individual justices only hinted at—and even then not always accurately. Striking is the recency of the clerkship model as we know it today, even though one cannot mark a catalytic event or precise date that explains such a metamorphosis. The changing personality of the justices over the years affords some insight, but falls far short of providing complete answers to questions that remain even after Peppers' exhaustive chronology of an evolving institution.

Mention of judicial personalities underscores a second striking quality of *Courtiers of the Marble Palace.* As one might expect, the relationship between particular justices and their law clerks have varied vastly from one chamber to another—more so than prior fragmentary accounts have suggested and substantially more, in fact, than those of us who served in this role might recall. Most of us tend to assume that the dynamics of other chambers roughly resembled our own, even when faced with evidence of a greater diversity or dissonance. Perhaps we have been lulled into such a comfortable sense of symmetry because the justice next door tended to relate to clerks other than his or her own in a manner that seemed to befit the adjacent chamber, and not necessarily the way things happened back home.

This book illuminates another, very different, contrast between perception and reality. The public image of a given justice turns out to be remarkably unhelpful in defining the dynamics of judge-clerk relationships behind the marble pillars and heavy oak doors. In short, "Mr. or Ms. Nice Justice" (as seen by the media and even the Supreme Court bar) may sometimes turn out to be a very different, less benign person within the intense and demanding relationship inside chambers. Conventional wisdom in this regard turns out to be even less helpful than the wary Court observer would have assumed until Todd Peppers probed actual day-to-day relationships to an unprecedented degree. Not surprisingly, some justices benefit from such scrutiny while others suffer—and a few, like Justice William J. Brennan, Jr., turn out to have been remarkably consistent as public figures and private mentors.

The final dimension that merits encomia for this book is the enhanced understanding it provides of the Supreme Court as an institution. Whether or not it is viewed as the "least dangerous branch," the nation's highest tribunal evokes a remarkable and varied range of images and perceptions. Until now, those images have been strikingly incomplete in one vital respect. Whatever view of the law clerk's role one brings to this book, that perception will surely change as a result of intense immersion in the realities of the Supreme Court clerkship. Those who claim or believe that clerks write all the opinions and negotiate judgments as well are bound to be surprised and disappointed, as are those at the other extreme who view a clerkship as a ministerial extension of law school. Whatever we may have believed or assumed about the clerkship—even those of us who spent a year or more in that challenging role—we will take away from this book a new level of understanding and appreciation.

Robert M. O'Neil
Charlottesville, Virginia
August 2005

After graduating from Harvard
Law School, Robert M. O'Neil
clerked for Associate Justice
William J. Brennan, Jr., during
October Term 1962.

Preface

THE SPARK FOR THIS PROJECT was struck during a graduate school semi-
nar on judicial behavior at Emory University, when the proverbial scales
fell from my eyes and I finally accepted the heretofore heretical idea that
Supreme Court opinions can be explained not only by applying the relevant
case facts to controlling legal principles, but also by examining the goals and
preferences of the individual justices. While hardly an insight to many social
scientists or legal theorists, the idea that the traditional legal model (*facts* +
law = *outcome*) was not the only theoretical framework by which to explain
and predict judicial decision making was revolutionary to me—a former
law student and law clerk who rejected legal realism and swallowed without
question the old chestnut that judges do not make law, but rather discover
and apply it with a mathematical precision that precludes the impact of discretion or personal ideology.

   This new appreciation for extralegal theories of judicial decision making
was quickly wed to a second interest of mine, law clerks. Every year, thousands of law school graduates spend one to two years clerking for federal
and state court judges across the country. I was no different. After attending
the University of Virginia School of Law, I clerked for a federal district court
judge in Omaha, Nebraska, and a federal magistrate judge in Roanoke, Virginia. During those two years, I became intrigued by the wide variation
in how judges used and related to their law clerks. In graduate school I
remained interested in the role that law clerks played in the judicial system,
and suddenly I grew aware of the possibility that the preferences of law
clerks themselves might impact the judicial process. The spark turned into
a flame.

   My decision to examine U.S. Supreme Court law clerks was driven by
two factors—the higher profile enjoyed by these clerks (and thus the greater
amount of existing data), and the fact that extralegal explanations of judicial behavior tend to be more applicable to appellate courts, where judges

struggle with issues that cannot be neatly answered by turning to controlling legal precedent or unambiguous constitutional principles. What I quickly discovered is that while the issue of law clerk influence on judicial decision making was a favorite topic of former law clerks, journalists, Supreme Court historians, and a few conspiracy theorists, the relevant literature failed to ask what I ultimately came to consider the more important and interesting questions—what are the institutional roles and norms surrounding the hiring and utilization of law clerks (what I will hereafter refer to as the "clerkship institution"), how have these rules evolved over time, and do these institutional structures allow law clerks to leave their own fingerprints on constitutional doctrine? In other words, what conditions must exist to create the environment in which law clerks might influence judicial outcomes?

At first, I doubted whether the question could be answered. Current and former Supreme Court clerks are bound by rules of confidentiality, and in recent decades those rules have been codified into a formal, written code of conduct that stifles discussion about the clerkship institution. While I did not believe that questions about how a justice selected or utilized his or her law clerks infringed on the duty of confidentiality, I suspected that law clerks—fearful of a backlash from their former employers—would broadly interpret the duty to include even the most mundane information about their clerkship. My initial data collection efforts, however, revealed a more complex situation.

I discovered that as law clerks aged and their justices retired, the former clerks were more willing to talk about their clerkship experiences. While the older law clerks were hesitant to divulge information about specific cases, constitutional issues, or personality quirks of the justices (topics not relevant to my project), they were willing to discuss how they were selected and what job duties they held. Despite the difficulties in gathering information from former clerks of current Supreme Court justices, the "flame" became a five-year research project. The fruits of these labors you hold before you now.

I must confess, however, that I do not consider my research to be complete, and I am not ready to end my pursuit of the elusive law clerk. Although this book contains what I believe to be the most definitive examination to date of the evolution of the clerkship institution, more data sources remain to be discovered and mined. There are still former clerks and their family members who have untold stories, forgotten diaries, and dusty photographs of Supreme Court justices and the young men and women who served in their chambers. Given these untapped veins of history, I hope that readers view this book as an invitation to contact me, share their stories and photographs, and thereby help complete the captivating tale of the courtiers who have toiled away within the walls of the Marble Palace.

Acknowledgments

WITHOUT THE ASSISTANCE of many different people and organizations, this project would not have been possible. Trips to the Library of Congress and Harvard Law School as well as student assistant salaries and copyright fees were funded through generous research grants from the Roanoke College Faculty Development Committee and dean of the College John T. Day. Anyone who subscribes to the myth that research is not supported and funded at small, liberal arts colleges is simply not familiar with wonderful institutions like Roanoke College.

I was the beneficiary of outstanding research assistance provided by a number of dedicated Roanoke College students, including Andrew Crowder, Shontia Echols, Kelli Goad, Carrie Harris, John Hull, Aaron Kahn, Jessica Swanson, Beth See, and Amanda Tolley, by departmental secretaries Karen Harris and Judi Pinckney, and by Rebecca Heller, Jeffrey Martin, and Patricia Scott at Roanoke College's Fintel Library. Further research assistance was provided by John Jacob, Curator of the Powell Archives at Washington and Lee University School of Law; Ted E. Aaberg, Assistant Director of Research at Harvard Law School; Lesley Schoenfield, Special Collections Access Service Coordinator at Harvard Law School; Coleen McFarland, Whitman College Special Collections, and the staff of the Manuscript Reading Room in the James Madison Building at the Library of Congress.

I am indebted to an endless number of former law clerks who took the time to talk repeatedly with me about their clerkship experiences and complete my surveys. Moreover, a number of individuals reviewed sections of my book manuscript and offered valuable feedback. They include Hugo L. Black, Jr.; Clare Cushman of the Supreme Court History Society; Professor Eugene Gressman of the University of North Carolina School of Law; Professor Andrew Kaufman of Harvard Law School; James Marsh; Wanda Martinson; Professor Chad Oldfather of Marquette University Law School; Professor Robert O'Neil of the University of Virginia School of

Law; Josephine Black Pesaresi; Professor Charles Reich; and Dr. Christopher Zorn of the University of South Carolina. My former dissertation committee chair, Dr. Micheal W. Giles of Emory University, warrants a special thank you. After assisting with the difficult birth of my dissertation, Dr. Giles again answered the call to arms and willingly read through multiple versions of my book manuscript as well as fielded an endless stream of questions by e-mail. I can think of no better example of a mentor than Mike Giles. I also want to thank Anne Coughlin, Charlotte Crane, Alan Dershowitz, Ashton Embry, C. David Ginsburg, Raymond Gray, Roderick Hills, Thomas Jorde, Hans Linde, Vincent McKusick, Judith McMorrow, Nancy Mott, Thomas O'Neill, Josephine Black Pesaresi, E. Barrett Prettyman, Jr., Charles Reich, Deborah Rhode, Ernest Rubenstein, Margo Schlanger, Arthur Seder, and Jonathan Varat for sharing their personal law clerk photographs with me. Finally, thanks to Jennie Berry for letting me take an advance peek at her book manuscript on Lucile Lomen, the first woman to clerk at the Supreme Court.

This project would not have been possible without the love of my family. My generous parents provided both emotional and financial support to a son who decided to attend both law school and graduate school. Thank you for the endless sacrifices you have made for your children. My sister Susan, a fellow academic, always supplied a needed boost to my spirits when my "quest" lost momentum. My children, Gabrielle and Sam, demonstrated their enthusiasm for Daddy's project by incorporating the phrase "law clerk" into their two-year-old vocabularies and waiting (somewhat) patiently when I had to visit the library before going to the park. The greatest thanks go to my wife, Michele. Because of her love, energy, enthusiasm, and understanding, over the last seven years I have been able to experience the adventure and joy of being a husband, a father, a student, a researcher, a lawyer, a professor, and an author. To her this book is dedicated.

"The reason why the public thinks so much of the Justices is that they are almost the only people in Washington who do their own work."
—Associate Justice Louis Brandeis

CHAPTER 1

In Search of the Elusive
Supreme Court Law Clerk

"I would have our game this evening be this, that one of
this company be chosen and given the task of forming in
words a perfect Courtier, setting forth all the conditions and
particular qualities that are required of anyone who deserves
this name."
> —Baldassare Castiglione, *The Book of the Courtier*

FIVE SUPREME COURT JUSTICES. Two secretaries of state. Two U.S.
attorney generals—one of whom also served as the secretary of defense, secretary of commerce, and ambassador to Great Britain. The solicitor general
of the United States. Two commissioners of the Federal Communications
Commission. A member of the Quorum of Twelve Apostles of the Mormon Church. The chairman of U.S. Steel. The head of the Department of
Transportation. The secretary of the Department of Homeland Security. The
publisher of the *Washington Post*. The president of ABC News. The governor
of the New York Federal Reserve Bank. The presidents of Brigham Young,
Columbia, Cornell, New York, and Yale Universities. Two chairmen of the
Securities and Exchange Commission. A presidential campaign manager.
The governor of Illinois. Two members of the U.S. House of Representatives. The secretary of the Smithsonian Institution. A lead character in a
major Hollywood film. The secretary of the U.S. Air Force. White House
counsel. And an accused spy.

No other internship program in the history of the United States has
produced as impressive and diverse a collection of individuals as the U.S.
Supreme Court law clerk corps. Following a tradition begun in 1882 by
Associate Justice Horace Gray, over the last 120 years the best and brightest law school students have postponed the riches of private practice or the
studied leisure of a teaching career for the opportunity to anonymously toil

away for low government wages within the marble walls of the Supreme Court. The rewards for such devotion include an insider's view of judicial decision making in our nation's highest court, the opportunity to form lifelong relationships with Supreme Court justices, access to tenure-track positions on the faculties of elite law schools, up to $150,000 in signing bonuses at top law firms,[1] and, some say, the opportunity to write their own policy preferences into the Constitution of the United States. Those selected for a Supreme Court clerkship are acutely aware of the pressures and privileges attendant with the position. Former Powell law clerk Andrew Leipold recalls standing outside of the Supreme Court, ready to enter the Marble Palace for his first day of work. "Before going in, I said two things to myself: First, 'You are the luckiest man in the world,' and second, 'Please, Dear God, don't screw this up' . . . I felt a combination of excitement and pure trepidation."[2]

Throughout the twentieth century, Supreme Court watchers have been fascinated with this elite fraternity of law clerks. They represent, to some, the penultimate example of a secret society, a chosen few who have been tapped to jealously guard the secrets of the Marble Palace and burnish the judicial legacies of its black-robed sovereigns. While the subsequent professional achievements of these former clerks is often dazzling, this enduring intrigue and interest about Supreme Court law clerks has stemmed primarily from one central debate—do law clerks wield an inappropriate amount of influence over their justices? While this is an interesting and important question, the debate has blinded legal scholars, political scientists, and journalists to the more fundamental questions about the institutional rules and norms surrounding the hiring and use of law clerks. Americans love a good conspiracy theory, and the idea that unelected, unaccountable, young law school graduates are the puppet masters of infirm and elderly justices is too irresistible to ignore. Thus the body of knowledge we possess about Supreme Court law clerks is distorted and limited by the debate over influence.

In a delicious twist of historical irony, it would be a future U.S. Supreme Court chief justice who helped spark the first great debate about law clerks and their influence. In the summer of 1957, *U.S. News & World Report* published an article titled "The Bright Young Men Behind the Bench."[3] Touting the article as the first to present "the story of the 18 young men who make up the 'second team' on the U.S. Supreme Court," the magazine provided the first public vetting of the clerkship institution. The article as a whole was rather uncontroversial. It provided the names and biographical information of the October Term (hereinafter "OT") 1956 clerks, discussed the subsequent professional achievements of former law clerks, and supplied quotations from anonymous clerks about their job duties. Yet the last paragraph left the reader with a tantalizing and thus far unanswered question:

"[W]hether the influence of these young law clerks—some not yet admitted to the bar—is reflected in Court opinions."

This question was too irresistible to ignore, especially in a time when the Supreme Court was playing a more active role in American life, and it opened the floodgates to a stream of articles on U.S. Supreme Court law clerks. Three months later the *New York Times* published its own feature on Supreme Court law clerks.[4] Bearing the subtitle "Recent Law Graduates Aid Justices With Their Facts But Not Their Decisions," the article refuted the suggestion that law clerks exercised undue influence. The front page featured pictures of Justice William J. Brennan, Jr., and his law clerks at work—images that clearly could not have been obtained without the justice's permission—and the article contained quotations from more anonymous sources who strenuously disavowed the idea of law clerk influence. "It has been suggested that the clerks have an important influence on the court," notes the article, "but former clerks say in persuasive language, that nothing could be further from the truth." Reading the article, one suspects that the justices themselves were answering the allegations raised in the earlier *U.S. News & World Report* piece.

In December of 1957, a young Arizona attorney named William Rehnquist entered the fray. In an article titled "Who Writes Decisions of the Supreme Court?"[5] Rehnquist discussed his clerkship with the late Justice Robert H. Jackson and summarized the role that law clerks played on the U.S. Supreme Court during the 1952 term. While initially conceding that "[s]ome of the mystery and rumor which shroud their work so far as the general public is concerned must necessarily remain," Rehnquist nevertheless offered an insider's analysis of a duty common to many Court clerks—reviewing petitions of certiorari.

According to Rehnquist, law clerks during OT 1952 had the "substantial responsibility" of reviewing all cert. petitions and drafting memoranda for their justices. Each memorandum summarized case facts, lower court holdings, and precedent. Additionally, the memorandum included the clerk's recommendation as to the disposition of the petition. Rehnquist professed concern that inadequate legal research by the law clerk, as well as the "*unconscious* slanting" of the memorandum, might result in a justice's decision-making process being influenced. If such unconscious influence existed, then Rehnquist feared that the justices would be pushed in a more liberal direction because "the political cast of the clerks as a group was to the 'left' of either the nation or the Court." Rehnquist disavowed knowledge of any law clerk consciously manipulating his justice, but the author's tone left the impression that manipulation was not impossible. In short, the former Jackson clerk wrecked the *New York Times'* carefully crafted rebuttal of eight weeks prior. It should be noted that Attorney Rehnquist was not troubled by Justice Jackson's practice of permitting his law clerks to assist in opinion drafting, noting that "the end product was unquestionably the Justice's own, both in form and in substance."

Rehnquist's suggestion that liberal clerks might influence the review of cert. petitions triggered an immediate backlash from his law clerk peers. For the first time, a Court insider had suggested that law clerks might be the culprits of the Supreme Court's liberal stance. The gloves were off, and no longer did defenders of the Supreme Court rely on quotations from anonymous clerks. Spearheading the response were former Felix Frankfurter clerk Alexander M. Bickel and former Stanley Reed clerk William D. Rogers.

For Yale Law School professor Bickel, the influence debate was simply a smoke screen for a larger attack: "Given the current agitation about the Supreme Court of the United States and the condition of sputtering rage that grips the court's more excitable critics, it was to be expected that the justices of the court would not long be spared the fate of many another public man: that is, a flanking attack intended to strike at them through their entourage."[6] In other words, Bickel believed that the spotlight trained on the law clerks was the product of political forces angered by the Supreme Court's recent, controversial decisions in such areas as civil rights and criminal procedure.

Bickel quickly dismissed the claims that law clerks were radical liberals bent on manipulating their justices to rewrite their own preferences into constitutional law. Not only did Bickel challenge the "hysterical assumption" that law clerks were uniformly liberal, but his description of the clerks' typical duties—including legal research, reviewing opinion drafts, serving as sounding boards—also made the idea of influence appear silly.[7] If law clerks were checking legal citations and listening to their bosses drone on about old cases, then what mechanism existed through which they wielded influence?

Bickel conceded only one point, namely, that law clerks were a conduit through which new legal theories migrated from law school classrooms to the Supreme Court. As with the more formal, carefully reasoned law review articles, law clerks exposed the justices to "ideas and arguments and puzzlements that fill the classrooms of any university worthy of the name." Bickel concluded that law clerks performed a valuable service by keeping the justices abreast of the newest legal theories. "[I]t serves to enhance the intellectual integrity of the judicial process, and is in its modest way one of the influences that keep judicial law rationally responsive to the needs of the day."

Interestingly, Bickel did not directly address the charges that law clerks drafted legal opinions and reviewed the cert. petitions filed with the Supreme Court. At most, he obliquely referred to law clerks "present[ing] the fruits of their searches to their justices along with their recommendations." Moreover, Bickel did not mention the fact that one of the individuals making the "half-baked" argument that clerks had influence was William

Rehnquist, a former law clerk. Anyone unaware of Rehnquist's prior article might assume that Bickel's ire had been triggered by the comments of un-informed Court outsiders.

Joining Bickel, former law clerk William Rogers, by then an associate at the prestigious Washington, D.C., law firm of Arnold & Porter, directly challenged Rehnquist's claim that law clerks "exercise[d] a quietly effective and pernicious power over the Court" and scornfully dismissed the sugges-tion that young, inexperienced law school graduates could consciously or unconsciously influence their older, wiser employers—even if a "flaming liberal or hidebound conservative" clerk vowed to do so.[8] Rogers pointed out that most of the clerks' job responsibilities included researching "apoliti-cal" issues, and even in politically charged cases clerks were given mundane, inconsequential duties.

In the same 1958 magazine, Rehnquist responded to Rogers' criticism.[9] While disavowing the heretical "thought that a clerk could exercise any sway over the views of a Justice," Rehnquist repeated his early theory that a law clerk might "unconsciously" write his own views into work assign-ments.[10] Rehnquist closed with the following observation: "The resolution of these disagreements must await a thorough, impartial study of the matter by someone who is not personally involved."

The storm had yet to pass. On May 6, 1958, Senator John C. Stennis of Mississippi took the Senate floor and added his voice to the furor over law clerk influence. Quoting liberally from Rehnquist's 1957 article, Senator Stennis raised the specter of unqualified, liberal law clerks "deciding vital questions of national effect."[11] Not only did Stennis call into question the clerks' political ideology, but he also challenged their competence. "[T]he American people have no reason to assume that the professional assistance available to Supreme Court justices is characterized by experience, achieve-ment, or distinguished judicial service. What evidence there is available leads to a contrary conclusion." As further evidence that the best and brightest were not applying for judicial clerkships, Stennis noted that the modest sal-ary of Supreme Court law clerks—ranging from approximately $5,500 to $6,500 per year—was "not designed to attract attorneys of top legal talent and experience." Stennis failed to acknowledge, however, that the modest salary suffered by law clerks was dramatically offset by the professional and financial riches awaiting them.

While Stennis was neither the first nor last to criticize the selection and utilization of law clerks, his comments remain unique insofar as calling into question the clerks' basic *competence*. By the 1950s, justices were uniformly picking law clerks from the best law schools, and the OT 1957 clerks were selected from Harvard, Yale, University of Chicago, Notre Dame, Univer-sity of California, University of Pennsylvania, Washington University, and

Southern Methodist University. These were not young men hamstrung by a mediocre legal education. One suspects that Stennis was either simply ignorant of or indifferent to the clerks' legal pedigrees.

In concluding his remarks, Stennis recommended that minimal professional qualifications be established for law clerks. "The American people have a right to expect that some safeguards are provided to assure that professional assistants for Supreme Court Justices are of the highest level of competence." Stennis' second major recommendation, however, is arguably less concerned about clerk competency than about clerk ideology: Congress should debate whether to subject law clerks to Senate confirmation hearings.[12]

While the first great debate over influence helped introduce the American public to the Supreme Court law clerk, it lacked the one piece of information critical to reaching a reasoned conclusion as to whether law clerks did, in fact, wield undue power—an accurate and complete list of their job duties. The thrusts and parries between the former law clerks had the feel of an intimate family feud, where outsiders were not privy to the whole story and therefore could not make an informed judgment as to who was right. If people outside the Marble Palace did not know what law clerks did, then how could they decide whether they were doing too much?

With the exception of a couple of minor articles, the topic of law clerks and influence died away until the 1970s. And once again it was William Rehnquist who pulled law clerks into the media spotlight. In October of 1971, President Richard M. Nixon nominated Assistant U.S. Attorney General William Rehnquist for the position of associate justice on the Supreme Court. Rehnquist had been nominated to replace the ailing John Marshall Harlan, who retired in September 1971. Nixon simultaneously announced the nomination of Lewis F. Powell, Jr., to replace the late Hugo Black.

According to former White House counsel John W. Dean, the Nixon administration originally believed that Rehnquist would be quickly confirmed by the Senate.[13] This assessment changed on December 13, 1971, when *Newsweek* published an article that discussed a memorandum written by Rehnquist while he was a law clerk for Justice Jackson.[14] Drafted regarding the pending case of *Brown v. Board of Education* and bearing the title "A Random Thought on the Segregation Cases," the memo stated, in part: "I realize that it is an unpopular and unhumanitarian position, for which I have been excoriated by 'liberal' colleagues but I think *Plessy v. Ferguson* was right and should be re-affirmed."

Dean writes that Rehnquist's memo "created a buzz in the Senate that was heard all the way down Pennsylvania Avenue ... not only was there a real debate on Rehnquist's nomination, there was concern by his handlers."[15]

Dean observes that Rehnquist was forced to respond to the 1952 memo in order to save the nomination. Rehnquist's explanation came in a letter sent to Senate Judiciary Committee chairman James Estland, who read the letter on the Senate floor. Rehnquist wrote:

As best I can reconstruct the circumstances after some nineteen years, the memorandum was prepared by me at Justice Jackson's request; it was intended as a rough draft of a statement of *his* views . . . He expressed concern that the conference should have the benefit of all of the arguments in support of the constitutionality of the "separate but equal" doctrine, as well as those against its constitutionality.

I am satisfied that the memorandum was not designed to be a statement of *my* views on these cases. . . . I am fortified in this conclusion because the bald, simplistic conclusion that "*Plessy v. Ferguson* was right and should be re-affirmed" is not an accurate statement of my own views at the time.[16]

Although Rehnquist was subsequently confirmed by a mollified Senate, some—including former White House counsel John Dean[17] and Justice Jackson's former Supreme Court secretary, Elsie Douglas[18]—concluded that Rehnquist lied about the memorandum's true author in order to bolster his chances at confirmation.[19] While the controversy did not directly focus on the powers and responsibilities of Supreme Court law clerks, it served to place the clerkship institution in the public spotlight—courtesy, once again, of William Rehnquist.

In 1979 the Supreme Court was rocked with the publication of *The Brethren*,[20] the first book to contain explicit details of the relationships between law clerks and Burger Court justices. *The Brethren* provided tantalizing, if unsubstantiated, glimpses of the varied roles of the law clerk across chambers. Besides enraging many justices, the book guaranteed that Supreme Court law clerks, and the question of their influence, would never again leave the public eye.

While *The Brethren* was first and foremost a story about the individual justices, the tale could not be told without repeated references to the justices' attitudes toward, and reliance on, their clerks—nor, some argued, without the participation of many former law clerks as well. Bob Woodward and Scott Armstrong's book revealed that the level of law clerk influence varied by justice and legal task. At one end of the spectrum was the crusty William O. Douglas, whose opinions were crafted without law clerk assistance, review, or editing. Although Douglas' law clerks reviewed cert. petitions and prepared memoranda for his review,[21] Douglas did not rely on them in either decision making or opinion writing. At the opposite end of the spectrum was Thurgood Marshall, who Woodward and Armstrong portrayed as a tired, disillusioned old man who depended on his clerks to shoulder his workload.[22] Between these two extremes lay the other justices, who utilized their law clerks to review petitions of certiorari and prepare memoranda summarizing the petitions, draft bench memoranda, lobby clerks in other chambers for changes in circulating opinions, and write the first drafts of majority and dissenting opinions.

The fallout over the book was immediate and fierce. It was evident that former clerks had talked to Woodward and Armstrong, and Court insiders bemoaned the breach of the duty of confidentiality owed by clerk to justice and the casting of the Supreme Court as a politically polarized body. The justices themselves were shocked at the amount of confidential information leaked in the book, and incoming law clerks were warned of the dire consequences of any future leaks. The justices were unaware, however, that the chief culprit was not their former law clerks but Associate Justice Potter Stewart. As for the public, the waters remained muddy. While *The Brethren* offered some details about the job duties of law clerks, the information on the nine chambers was not systematically presented. Moreover, the authors' reliance on anonymous, possibly self-interested sources rendered the data suspect.

The introduction of the law clerk to a broader audience resulted in popular culture taking an interest in law clerks and their alleged influence. In the 1980s and 1990s, law clerks began appearing as major and minor characters in works of popular fiction. In Margaret Truman's 1982 mystery *Murder in the Supreme Court*, a young, philandering law clerk ("a dedicated swinger, broads all over the place") plays the role of corpse in a murder mystery in which fellow clerks and Supreme Court justices are all suspects.[23] In the late 1990s, law clerks were prominent characters in a trio of books: *The Tenth Justice, 9 Scorpions*, and *The Simple Truth*.[24] All three books offer characters and story lines far more compelling than reality: a law clerk investigating the murder of a fellow clerk and a military cover-up (*The Simple Truth*), a former exotic dancer turned law clerk trying to sway a justice's vote via her brilliant legal mind and her nonlegal assets (*9 Scorpions*), and law clerks (with the aid of their well-placed, non–law clerk friends) racing to undo the catastrophic financial results of an inadvertent leak about an upcoming decision (*The Tenth Justice*).

Whether the law clerks are perpetrating or solving crimes, these three books feature clerks who revel in the heady rush of power. As a court clerk explains to the newest batch of clerks:

> This is an important job—probably more important than any job you'll ever have . . . Alongside the justices, you will draft decisions that change lives. Your input will be constantly sought, and your ideas will certainly be implemented. In many instances, the justices will rely entirely on your analysis. They'll base their opinions on your research. That means you affect what they see and what they know. There are nine justices on this Court. But your influence, the power that you hold, makes you the tenth justice.[25]

Popular culture's interest in the law clerk, however, produced the same distorted, inaccurate image of law clerks as that spawned by the mainstream media's hand-wringing over law clerks and influence.[26]

The high-water mark in the influence debate was the publication of *Closed Chambers* in 1998.[27] Authored by a former Blackmun law clerk, *Closed Chambers* offered gossipy stories of conservative law clerks—determined to undo the "excesses" of the Warren Court—manipulating their gullible justices and pushing the Court to the political far right. At various points in his tell-all tale, former law clerk Edward Lazarus claimed that law clerks in the late 1980s tried to impose their personal policy preferences on all aspects of the High Court's docket, including cert. petitions, death penalty stays, and legal opinions.

Lazarus did not assert that clerk influence completely pervaded the judicial chambers. Skeptical about the efforts of both liberal and conservative law clerks to manipulate the review of cert. petitions, he concluded that "[t]he danger of clerk bias and the potential for real mischief was much more intense and dramatic in the emergency death penalty stays." While Lazarus stated that the law clerks for Justices Blackmun and Stevens were bound by "exacting instructions" regarding these stays, he revealed that conservative law clerks were less constrained:

> Quite a different attitude pervaded the cabal. Its members considered expediting executions a central part of their collective mission, and they pursued that goal passionately in both the argued cases and the emergency stay process. Their resolve reflected a powerful philosophical commitment to the right of states to execute vicious murderers, but it manifested itself in an amazing blood thirst, a revelry in execution reminiscent of the celebratory crowds that years ago thronged to public hangings.

According to Lazarus, this "blood thirst" drove the conservative law clerks to lobby, pressure, and manipulate their justices to reject stays.[28]

Lazarus concluded that the practice of letting law clerks prepare opinion drafts presented the greatest opportunity for clerk influence to seep into the decision-making process:[29]

> In the endlessly ongoing interpretation of Supreme Court opinions, the devil is in these details. How the facts of a case are characterized, how the Court's standard of review is phrased, which precedents and principles are marshaled to support the ruling . . . it is here, in wielding the enormous power of the first draft and, specifically, in the selection of words, structure, and materials, that clerks may exercise their greatest influence.[30]

Lazarus conceded that justices have the ultimate editorial power over the clerk's written draft. However, because the justice/editor adopted a more deferential stance while editing, as opposed to drafting, justices did not fully consider a case and its hidden complications. "[W]hile everything they write passes through the filter of their Justices' scrutiny, this scrutiny is directed at an essentially complete product and often amounts to little more than a surface polish."

According to Lazarus, the siren song of clerk power was the most irresistible in the chambers of Justices Anthony Kennedy and Sandra Day O'Connor, where the law clerks were intoxicated by the enormous power of the swing vote. Lazarus wrote that both justices were "susceptible to clerks' arguments and delegate to them almost all the opinion drafting and doctrine crunching," adding that the justices are "targets of every form of clerk machination."[31] Lazarus' book generated a swirl of controversy, as much for its thesis of clerk influence as for the author's alleged breach of confidentiality. Subsequent reviews blasted Lazarus for his disloyalty to the Court, adding—for good measure—that his legal analysis was subpar, his writing clumsy, and his intellect suspect.[32]

Considered together, the Rehnquist and Lazarus contributions serve as useful bookends for the influence debate. Both men suggested that clerks, at a minimum, might wield influence for their own ideological purposes. The difference is that Rehnquist pronounced the liberal law clerks guilty of such misadventure, while Lazarus pointed an accusatory finger toward conservative clerks. Neither Lazarus nor Rehnquist, however, place the influence debate in the larger context of institutional evolution.

Lazarus and Rehnquist are not alone in this omission. While a significant number of former law clerks have provided limited accounts of their clerkships,[33] the data have not been woven together to provide a historical overview of the clerkship institution. Nor have Supreme Court scholars looked to existing theories of institutional development to explain the evolution of the clerkship institution. Drawing upon both original and existing data, my goal is both to provide the missing comprehensive historical treatment of the clerkship institution and to place the influence debate within the framework of principal agent theory.

Principal Agent Theory

The law clerk is not an autonomous actor. He or she arrives at the Supreme Court as a green, inexperienced attorney who stands in a special hierarchical relationship with his or her justice. Additionally, the law clerk is immediately thrust into a thicket of preexisting rules, norms, and expectations. The Supreme Court as an organization has developed written and unwritten rules on the proper role of a law clerk, and the individual justices have unique expectations regarding their new staff members. In short, a law clerk must negotiate a maze of institutional norms and dictates to carry out his or her daily tasks. The failure to appreciate this fundamental reality of the clerkship institution underlies many of the wildly exaggerated claims of law clerk influence.

Political scientist Douglass C. North defines institutions as "the rules of the game in a society or, more formally . . . the humanly devised constraints that shape interaction."[34] Institutions are distinct from organizations, which are instead "groups of individuals bound by some common purpose to achieve objectives."[35] North uses the analogy of a game to flesh out the distinction between the two, with organizations as the players and institutions as the rules that players must follow to win the game. Stated differently—opposing players may have different goals, but they are bound by the same rules in the pursuit of these goals. It is North's basic definition of an institution that I adopt when discussing the clerkship institution.

Unlike a traditional game of golf or football, however, the players can sometimes change the rules of the game to better achieve their goals. Hence, institutions (the rules) affect the players, and the players reshape and amend the rules. North also defines pressures outside the "game," or institution, that affect the rules—forces beyond the control of the players.[36] Our study of institutions, however, is not complete. We must still consider why the players select the particular rules of a game. Regarding the clerkship institution, I believe that the answer lies in principal agent theory.

A Micro-theory of Institutional Growth

The picture of a young subordinate straining against the restrictions imposed by an older superior is not unique to the Supreme Court. Indeed, this dynamic is an example of the fundamental relationship between a principal and an agent, according to the following definition:

> The principal agent model is an analytic expression of the agency relationship, in which one party, the principal, considers entering into a contractual agreement with another, the agent, in the expectation that the agent will subsequently choose actions that produce outcomes desired by the principal.[37]

Political scientists have applied P-A theory to a number of different topics, including the development and evolution of the clerkship institution.[38]

In selecting an agent the principal is faced with two distinct problems: incomplete information about the agent and a conflict of interest between the parties.[39] The agent, not the principal, possesses the most accurate information about his or her own skills and abilities (information that is highly important when the principal is intent on selecting the most qualified agent). Because the agent does not have the incentive to share this information with the principal, the principal's "recruitment effort will tend to suffer from adverse selection; he will attract a disproportionate number of low-quality applicants."[40]

Moreover, agents possess the most accurate information about their own activities once they have been hired by the principal. As author Terry Moe observes, "there is no guarantee that the agent, once hired, will in fact choose to pursue the principal's best interests or to do so efficiently. The agent has his own interests at heart." This is referred to as "moral hazard," which "arises from the unobservability of actual behavior in the ex post contracting situation." To protect against the wayward agent, a principal must monitor the agent and create contractual and noncontractual incentives so that the agent will not violate his fiduciary responsibilities.

Thus, "[t]he central concern is how the principal can best motivate the agent to perform as the principal would prefer, taking into account the difficulties in monitoring the agent's activities."[41] When the duties delegated to the agent are insignificant, the risks attendant with a defecting agent are minimal. Thus, the principal will not vest significant resources in monitoring and incentive structures. When the agent, however, is vested with major responsibility, the consequences of an agent "shirking" his job duties are severe. Here the principal will commit significant resources to creating a contract "that, in mitigating the informational asymmetries and structuring rewards, prompts the agent to behave as the principal would under whatever conditions might prevail."[42]

The principal-agent model is readily applicable to the clerkship institution. The justice, as principal, employs a law clerk/agent to assist the principal in achieving his or her goals. Traditionally, justices have hired law clerks to reduce their workload. There are, however, many different aspects of a justice's workload. The law clerk can be employed to answer correspondence, to write speeches, to perform legal or non-legal research, to "cite check" a draft opinion, to review cert. petitions, to prepare bench memoranda, or to draft opinions. Some justices have employed law clerks for such reasons as patronage, companionship, or mentorship, while others have had multiple goals in hiring clerks. Finally, the applicant will have his or her own goals in pursuing a clerkship. While some view a clerkship as an opportunity to assist the nine justices in administering justice, others view it as the capstone on their résumé or even the chance to write their own preferences into law.

In the bountiful literature on law clerks, the phenomenon of shirking or defection has been given a different label—influence. Alas, those who debate law clerk influence often neglect to agree on a common definition. Influence has both a stylistic and substantive dimension. Let's first consider "stylistic influence." One can imagine a scenario in which a justice herself writes the first draft of an opinion without requesting *any* assistance from a law clerk. After completing the first draft, she hands the opinion to her law clerk and requests a careful review of spelling and grammar. The justice is uninterested in the clerk's views of the substantive content of the draft.

The law clerk subjects the draft to a rigorous edit. During his review, the clerk finds multiple spelling mistakes, corrects three cites to conform to the *Harvard Blue Book*, and modifies the justice's improper and repeated use of the semicolon. Assuming that the justice adopts each suggested revision, it would be improper to conclude that the law clerk has influenced the justice's decision-making process or affected the substantive development of the law. Instead, the clerk has marginally influenced the justice's style of writing and her propensity for spelling errors. This is hardly the form of influence that incites the wrath of judicial conspiracy theorists.

Stylistic influence, as in the example above, differs from substantive influence. At its extreme, substantive influence can be defined as complete control over the appeals process. For example, rather than making an independent judgment based on the information and arguments provided by a law clerk, a justice could simply permit the clerk to decide the winners or losers in an appeal. A variation of this strain of influence would be a justice who reserves the power to determine the outcome, but vests the law clerk with sole discretion for providing the rationale or doctrinal basis for the case holding.

The definition of substantive influence, however, is broader. It can be defined as a *"but for"* proposition—that is, absent the law clerk's input, a justice would vote in a different direction. Consider one example. Before the weekly conference, a justice announces to his law clerk that he will find in favor of the government in a search and seizure case of first impression. The law clerk disagrees with the justice's decision, arguing that the logical extension of precedent mandates that the Court find the government's action to be unconstitutional. The justice reflects on his law clerk's reasoning and subsequently decides that it is sound. Accordingly, the justice changes his vote to find that the government violated the Fourth Amendment. The law clerk has substantively influenced the justice's behavior. *But for* the clerk's input, the justice would have voted to uphold the search. The justice, however, remains the ultimate decision maker.

Substantive influence does not always involve a justice changing his or her vote because of a law clerk's input. One can imagine a case in which the outcome remains the same but a justice rests the decision on a new legal doctrine after consulting with a law clerk—for instance, a justice follows his clerk's recommendation that a specific right be classified as "fundamental" and worthy of a higher level of judicial protection when it is the target of state legislation. The impact of the clerk's influence might be difficult to measure in the case before the Court; however, the new doctrinal test, standard of review, or jurisprudential lens affect the litigation of future cases in federal courts throughout the land.

Substantive influence does not always involve the interpretation of statutory or constitutional principles. We can imagine a scenario in which a justice's vote is changed not because of a compelling legal argument by a bright young clerk, but because an observant law clerk pointed out a dispositive fact that the justice overlooked. Many former Supreme Court law clerks have commented that the most important aspect of their job was to familiarize their justice with the factual record, conceding that the justices possessed a greater appreciation of the controlling legal principles than the inexperienced law clerk.

Although the debate over influence generally focuses on the drafting of legal opinions, clerks' other judicial duties also involve the potential for influence. Throughout the latter part of the twentieth century, law clerks have reviewed petitions of certiorari and prepared memoranda summarizing the factual record, the lower courts' rulings, and the relevant legal arguments— often concluding with a recommendation whether to grant or deny certiorari. Bench memoranda present a third major method by which law clerks could exercise substantive influence. Most justices require their law clerks to prepare bench memoranda before oral argument, briefs that summarize the factual record, the lower court record, and the salient legal arguments. Besides these duties, law clerks also assist with the review of emergency death penalty stays and their justice's circuit duties. In this book, I will focus on their more typical job duties.

One can imagine a scenario in which a law clerk might use either the cert. or bench memoranda to highlight certain facts, downplay aspects of the lower court ruling, or "punch up" a specific legal argument to influence the justice's view of the case and, ultimately, his or her vote. Undoubtedly, the justice is presented with additional sources of information on the case—amicus briefs, oral argument, and the weekly conference—and the law clerk's manipulation might be undermined or exposed. One can, however, also envision a situation in which an infirm, disinterested, or weak-minded justice is substantively affected by the "spin" generated by the law clerk's memoranda and votes accordingly.

In short, the contractual relationship between a justice/principal and his or her clerk/agent varies with the clerk's job duties. If a clerk is limited to checking cites, then there is only a slight chance that his or her policy preferences diverge from the justice's in regards to this mundane task, and the consequences of clerk shirking are inconsequential. In such a scenario, we would not expect a justice to dedicate time and energy to selecting and monitoring a clerk or creating sanctions for shirking. But if a justice is forced to delegate substantive duties to the clerk, the probability of divergent clerk/justice interests increases and the risks associated with clerk shirking loom large. Now the justice is forced to devote significant resources to (1) reducing the likelihood of divergent preferences, (2) monitoring the law clerks' job duties, and (3) increasing the incentive structure.[43]

A Macro-theory of Institutional Growth

While the existing literature has discussed the law clerk as a rational actor who attempts to pursue his or her own goals (to wit, influence judicial decision making), the literature has failed to recognize that justices are also rational actors with the institutional resources necessary to counter the shifting relationship. Of course, the principal is not unconstrained in the creation of the agency relationship. There are realities, rules, and pressures external to the agency relationship that affect the delegation of authority among principal and agent. In fashioning the contractual arrangement at the heart of the principal-agent relationship, the justice is constrained by external realities and pressures regarding incentive and sanctioning structures. The law clerk/agent is also constrained by external forces.

Judge Richard Posner argues that one external, macro-level force that impacts the principal-agent relationship is the Supreme Court's rising workload; Posner writes that the justices have hired more law clerks and delegated more duties to the clerks as the workload has increased.[44] Other macro-level forces might include shifts in the external political environment (for example, the increased political polarization found in all levels of government and in society) as well as changes in other political institutions, in legal education, and in the legal profession. For example, the movement away from the professional law clerk to the one-year, rotating clerkship might have less to do with the changing preferences of the justices and more to do with the tempting career opportunities facing the modern law clerk. Moreover, in recent years the justices' hiring decisions undoubtedly have been affected by the claims of discriminatory hiring practices raised by civil rights organizations.

In conclusion, the rules and norms that undergird the clerkship institution are the product of micro- and macro-level forces. The individual justices fashion rules in order to achieve goals. The law clerks pursue their own goals within the net of rules, and in so doing they manipulate and change the existing rules. Individual justices amend the rules in order to minimize law clerk mischief. Finally, forces beyond the control of either the justices or law clerks can constrain both agents and principals in altering the rules of the game and pursuing their own goals.

Application of P-A Theory to the Clerkship Institution

In applying P-A theory to the clerkship institution, I will assume that both the justice and the law clerk are self-interested actors with multiple goals regarding the agency relationship. While the justice has the primary goal of hiring a clerk to reduce his or her workload, additional goals could include using the law clerk to effectuate the justice's political agenda, acting as a mentor/teacher to the clerk, and (although rare in the modern clerkship) relying on the clerk for companionship. A law clerk's potential goals in entering into the principal/agent relationship include using the clerkship as a professional stepping-stone, as an educational experience, and as a method of enacting his or her own policy preferences. Of course, the law clerk—like any other agent—possesses an informational advantage in terms of his or her skills, policy preferences, and degree of compliance with the justice/principal's instructions and rules.

Based on the following assumptions, I hypothesize that justices create rules and informal norms designed to constrain law clerks from pursuing their own self-interests. The justices will modify these rules and norms as rising workload levels force them to hire more law clerks and delegate more substantive job responsibilities, such as reviewing cert. petitions and drafting cert. memoranda, preparing bench memoranda, and preparing first drafts of majority, concurring, and dissenting opinions. If P-A theory does not explain the creation and evolution of the clerkship institution, then what picture of the institution will emerge? We will find evidence of justices striving to find quality law clerks, but no evidence of internal structures designed to minimize law clerk defection. Now we turn to the question of collecting data to test these hypotheses.

CHAPTER 2

A Portrait of the Supreme Court Law Clerk

"In these books we shall not follow any set order or rule
of distinct precepts, as is most often the custom in teaching
anything whatever, but, following the manner of many
ancient writers, and to revive a pleasant memory, we shall
rehearse some discussions which took place among men
singularly qualified in such matters."
—Baldassare Castiglione, *The Book of the Courtier*

OVER THE LAST HUNDRED YEARS, former Supreme Court law clerks have enjoyed unparalleled professional success. Often their tour of duty at the Supreme Court is immediately followed by employment at top law firms, on the staffs of the U.S. attorney general or solicitor general, or at prestigious law schools. At the zenith of their careers, former law clerks have held cabinet-level positions in presidential administrations, authored textbooks read by generations of law school students, assumed the stewardship of our nation's oldest law schools, and donned the black robes of a Supreme Court justice. While undoubtedly these men and women would have achieved acclaim regardless of their clerkship, one cannot challenge the fact that a Supreme Court clerkship is an invaluable stepping-stone to future glory.

The professional accomplishments of former law clerks alone demands that we assess their academic backgrounds and qualifications. Are only the best and brightest tapped to receive the brass ring of law clerk fame, and is the hiring process free of academic, gender, and racial bias? The personal characteristics of the young men and women who toil away as law clerks takes on an added importance when we factor in the ongoing debate over law clerk influence. If law clerks wield influence and affect policy decisions, then the gender, racial and socioeconomic backgrounds, legal training, and ideology of the law clerks become relevant.

In this chapter, I will discuss my efforts in collecting data on law clerks and the clerkship institution. I will also analyze the data regarding the racial, gender, and academic makeup of the law clerk corps. Subsequent chapters will summarize the clerkship institution itself and the evolution of the institution over time.

Collecting Data on Law Clerks and the Clerkship Institution

Due mainly to confidentiality rules, neither legal historians nor social scientists have provided a comprehensive summary of the clerkship institution. Thus my first task was to review all existing data on law clerks and determine what new data needed to be collected. Once I ascertained what scholars did and did not know about the clerkship institution, I attempted to fill in the missing information with the gathering of original data.

The logical sources of data are past and present Supreme Court justices and law clerks. Time and confidentiality rules, however, have limited my reliance on these primary sources. There were no living former Supreme Court justices when I completed my research in the spring of 2004, and only two current Supreme Court justices—John Paul Stevens and Antonin Scalia—agreed to speak with me about their clerkship hiring practices. Justice Stevens gave an "on the record" interview, while Justice Scalia provided "off the record" background information. For the six justices who officially declined my request for a personal interview, I followed up with a letter asking them to review written questions regarding their clerkship practices. All six declined the second request as well. Only one justice failed to respond to any of my requests.

The U.S. Supreme Court Public Information Office proved to be the best source for basic information regarding law clerks. It provided a list containing the following data:

1. Names of former clerks from 1886 to 2004
2. Initial term clerked
3. Justice(s) for whom the clerks worked
4. Law school attended
5. Prior lower court clerkships.

Working from this list, I used legal databases (such as *Martindale-Hubbell*) to collect mailing addresses for former clerks. To the approximately 1,000 clerks whose addresses were available, I originally mailed a one-page survey. The survey asked basic information about the former clerk, including academic background, membership in law school organizations, justice(s) for whom the clerk was employed, year(s) of the clerkship, subsequent professional accomplishments, and political ideology of the clerk. The survey did not ask any questions about the clerkship itself due to concerns that such questions would dramatically reduce my response rate. Approximately 40 percent of those surveyed responded, and a second round of surveys was mailed to nonrespondents. Admittedly, some of the data collected by the survey replicated data provided by the Public Information Office. This was a deliberate decision, based on my discovery that the aforementioned list contained inaccurate information for late-nineteenth- and early-twentieth-century law clerks.

After reviewing the results of my survey efforts, I wrote approximately 100 former clerks and requested personal interviews regarding their clerkships. In my letter, I stated that the interview would not touch upon any potentially confidential topics—such as communications between a justice and a clerk about cases or a justice's views on specific constitutional issues. I explained that the interview questions focused on how the specific justice selected and used their clerks, and I gave the former clerks the option of speaking with me anonymously—although I conveyed my preference that their remarks be attributable. Appendix One contains a list of all former law clerks ultimately interviewed for this book either in person or by telephone. I also spoke with a limited number of individuals who were not former law clerks but who were familiar with the Supreme Court's clerkship practices. Their names are listed in Appendix Two.

Because of the high rejection rate for interviews, I subsequently tried a different tactic—writing former law clerks and attaching the written interview questions. The difference between my interview script and the written questions was insignificant, but I hypothesized that the rejection rate might fall if the former clerks could see the benign nature of the interview questions. This second approach was moderately successful in obtaining additional data. Appendix Three contains a list of all former law clerks who answered written questions about their clerkship, as opposed to speaking with me about it. Appendix Four contains a list of all men and women who have clerked on the Supreme Court from 1882 to 2004.

While I tried to interview a representative sample of law clerks from across the span of the clerkship institution, certain realities shaped the distribution of respondents interviewed. Of course, most clerks from the early twentieth century are deceased. The oldest clerk interviewed was Wilbur Friedman, who clerked for Associate Justice Harlan Fiske Stone during OT 1930. In total, I interviewed five men who clerked in the 1930s, three of whom (Wilbur Friedman, Warner Gardner, and Louis Lusky) clerked for Associate Justice Harlan Fiske Stone. I interviewed approximately ten former law clerks from the 1940s. Together, these fifteen former clerks provided invaluable information regarding the clerkship hiring and utilization practices of eight former Supreme Court justices.

My reliance on law clerk interviews increased for individuals who clerked in the 1950s through the 1970s, due to the combination of a larger pool of former clerks from which to select and a decreased concern by the former clerks about confidentiality rules. To be blunt, former clerks evidenced a greater willingness to discuss their clerkship if their former employer was deceased. As for former law clerks from the 1980s and 1990s, the even larger pool of former clerks was offset by a general unwillingness to be interviewed. Most of my written interview requests were answered and declined, with the ongoing duty of law clerk confidentiality cited as the reason.

To supplement data collected by law clerk interviews, I turned to information found in the personal papers of former justices, judicial biographies, law review and periodical articles, oral histories, and publicly available interviews.[1] The quality and quantity of data regarding the justices' clerkship hiring and utilization practices varied by both the individual justice and by year.

Female Law Clerks

From 1882 to 2004, 66 U.S. Supreme Court justices have employed approximately 1,800 law clerks. The clerks come from all regions of the United States and represent a rich variety of ethnic and academic backgrounds. The justices have drawn their law clerks from 81 different law schools, and many of the clerks first trained with one of 240 different lower court judges. Thus, at first glance it seems that the men and women selected for clerkship positions represent a diverse range of backgrounds and experiences.

Critics of the Supreme Court's hiring practices, however, charge that the justices have historically selected white male law clerks from a handful of elite American law schools. Over the last 100 years, it is undeniable that women have been underrepresented in the clerkship corps. Of the 1,870 law clerks for whom I have collected data, 85 percent have been male and 15 percent have been female. The first female law clerk—Lucile Lomen— was hired in 1944 by Justice William O. Douglas, a decision motivated less by concerns over equitable hiring practices than by the shortage of male law students due to the Second World War.[2] Before hiring Lomen, Douglas wrote former law clerk Vern Countryman, who had attended law school with Lomen, and asked, "how [do] you think a girl would fare as a law clerk in these surroundings which you now know so well?"[3] Countryman's response is not found in the Douglas papers.

The second female law clerk—Margaret Corcoran—was not hired until 1966. She was selected by Hugo Black,[4] a choice that both Justice and Mrs. Black came to regret. Margaret "Peggy" Corcoran was the daughter of New Dealer and Washington insider Tommy "the Cork" Corcoran, himself a former law clerk for Oliver Wendell Holmes, Jr.[5] As the second female law clerk in the Court's history, Margaret Corcoran did not distinguish herself. In their joint memoirs, Elizabeth Black makes repeated references to

Corcoran's subpar performance. In one instance, Mrs. Black recounts that Justice Black was "still upset because Margaret flew off the handle and said she could not do thirty-five *certs.* on the weekend. She had to go to parties with her daddy."[6] Despite several lectures by Justice Black, Corcoran's performance did not improve.

The assessment of Corcoran's performance is echoed by co-clerk Stephen Susman. "I did all of her work that year, and I didn't complain one iota because Margaret provided my wife and I with a wonderful social life in Washington."[7] Susman recalled that Corcoran often arrived late to Black's chambers and "slept all day" in an upstairs office. As for how Black handled the situation, Susman stated "very well. He understood as soon as he appointed Margaret that it was a mistake and that he wasn't going to change Margaret." Thomas Corcoran biographer McKean writes that Tommy Corcoran knew that his daughter was floundering in the clerkship, and he tried to mitigate the damage by apologizing for her behavior and—more remarkably—"assisting her in writing legal briefs for the justice."[8]

During OT 1968, the third female law clerk—Martha F. Alschuler[9]—served in Justice Fortas' chambers. Thurgood Marshall hired Barbara Underwood[10] as a law clerk for OT 1971. Slowly, the number of female law clerks at the Supreme Court has risen. Ten percent of all law clerks hired in the 1970s were women (33 in all), a percentage that rose to 23 percent in the 1980s (78 women) and 30 percent in the 1990s (111 women). During OT 2004, 14 of the 35 law clerks (40 percent) working at the Supreme Court were women.

The number of women hired by the Rehnquist Court justices varied across chambers. As of 2005, at least 40 percent of the law clerks hired by Justices Sandra Day O'Connor, Ruth Bader Ginsburg, and Stephen Breyer were women, as were 36 percent of the clerks employed by Justice John Paul Stevens and 30 percent of those employed by Justice Clarence Thomas. At the other end of the spectrum is Justice Antonin Scalia, who has employed 66 male law clerks (87 percent) and only 10 female law clerks (13 percent). Chief Justice Rehnquist and Associate Justice Anthony Kennedy's clerkship ranks were also predominantly male (84 percent). Justice David Souter has hired 14 female law clerks (23 percent).

Of the former Supreme Court justices, Harry Blackmun hired the most female law clerks—33 of the 93 clerks who worked in the Blackmun chambers were women. Gender diversity also flourished in the chambers of Justices Thurgood Marshall and Lewis F. Powell, Jr. Twenty-four of the 89 law clerks who worked for Justice Marshall were women (27 percent), as were 12 of the 67 clerks hired by Justice Powell (18 percent). Chief Justice Earl Warren never hired a female law clerk, and only 5 percent of Chief Justice Warren E. Burger's law clerks were women.

Minority Law Clerks

While few claim that the selection of Supreme Court law clerks remains riddled with gender bias,[11] the modern Supreme Court has been repeatedly challenged regarding its minority hiring practices. I have been able to collect data on the ethnic backgrounds of 1,507 former Supreme Court law clerks from the years 1882 to 2004. Of those, 1,424 (94 percent) are Caucasian, 42 (2.7 percent) Asian, 27 (1.8 percent) African American, and 10 (.6 percent) Hispanic.

William T. Coleman, Jr., was the first African American hired as a Supreme Court law clerk. Coleman graduated summa cum laude from the University of Pennsylvania in 1941 and magna cum laude from Harvard Law School in 1946, where he served as an editor of the *Harvard Law Review*. Selected to clerk for Justice Felix Frankfurter during OT 1948, his hiring was sufficiently noteworthy to merit mention in the *New York Times* and *Washington Post*.[12] It would be almost twenty years before Chief Justice Earl Warren selected the second African American law clerk, Tyrone Brown (OT 1967).[13] The third African American law clerk, and the first female African American clerk, Karen Hastie Williams, clerked for Justice Thurgood Marshall during OT 1974.

I have been unable to determine the precise number of African Americans or other minorities hired in the 1970s and 1980s, but it is clear that racial parity among Supreme Court law clerks proved more elusive than gender parity. In 1998, *USA Today* ran two articles on the Supreme Court by journalist Tony Mauro. He reported that Chief Justice Rehnquist and Associate Justices Scalia, Kennedy, and Souter had never hired an African American law clerk. Collectively, the four justices had hired 218 law clerks while on the Supreme Court. Mauro further reported that Justices O'Connor, Thomas, Ginsburg, and Breyer had each hired only a single African American law clerk since taking the bench.[14] Of all the sitting justices, John Paul Stevens had hired the largest number of African American clerks—three out of sixty-one total clerks employed.

The Rehnquist Court's hiring record for other minority groups was slightly better. Mauro reported that Chief Justice Rehnquist and Associate Justice Scalia had never hired an Asian law clerk, while Justices Stevens, Scalia, Thomas, and Ginsburg had never hired a Hispanic clerk. In total, approximately 4 percent of all law clerks hired by the Rehnquist Court were Asian, and 1 percent were Hispanic. None of the sitting justices had ever hired a Native American law clerk. At the time of the reports, approximately 24,000 minority students (roughly 19 percent of all law students) were enrolled in ABA-accredited law schools. Given the historically high number of minorities attending law schools, Court critics were not moved by the justices' claims that qualified minority candidates were difficult to find and hire.

Mauro's articles ignited a controversy over law clerk diversity.[15] Legal scholars now turned their attention to the lack of racial diversity among Supreme Court law clerks.[16] The *USA Today* series sparked NAACP protests on the Supreme Court steps,[17] the grilling of Justices David Souter and Clarence Thomas by congressional subcommittees,[18] the introduction of the Judicial Branch Employment Non-Discrimination Act of 1999 (H.R. 1048) by Congressman Jesse Jackson, Jr., the creation of endless clerkship diversity task forces by various national and state bar associations, and a February 2000 symposium on law clerk diversity at Howard University Law School.

Chief Justice Rehnquist finally entered the debate. In a November 17, 1998, letter in which he declined to meet with congressional and bar association representatives to discuss the lack of minority law clerks, the chief justice responded for the High Court. Rehnquist emphasized that none of the justices screened out candidates "because of race, religion, gender, nationality, or any other impermissible reason." Chief Justice Rehnquist acknowledged the lack of minorities among the clerkship corps, but blamed larger social trends:

> We agree that the statistics set forth in your letter identify concerns which all of us share, but you must realize that many factors entirely unrelated to the hiring of law clerks are responsible for this situation. We select as clerks those who have very strong academic backgrounds, and have had previously successful law clerk experience, most often in the federal courts. As the demographic makeup of this pool changes, it seems entirely likely that the underrepresentation of minorities to which you refer in your letter will also change.[19]

From 1999 to 2004, the Rehnquist Court made some modest changes in the diversity of its law clerk corps. Through OT 2004, the demographic characteristics of law clerks hired by the Rehnquist Court justices are as shown in Table 2.1.

As a point of comparison to the number of minority law clerks—8,367 minorities graduated from 188 accredited law schools in 2004.[20]

Academic Diversity

The diversity debate has expanded to include academic diversity among law clerks. Pointing to the dominance of the "elite" law schools among High Court clerks, law school deans and professors called upon the justices to look beyond Harvard and Yale for bright young applicants.[21] As for the charges that the justices were also guilty of academic elitism during the selection process, the numbers, in general, support the allegations. I have

TABLE 2.1. Minority Hiring Practices of the Rehnquist Court, 1986–2004

	Caucasian	African American	Asian	Hispanic	Native Indian	Missing Data
Breyer	30	4	5	2	0	3
Ginsburg	35	1	5	1	0	6
Kennedy	62	2	5	1	0	3
O'Connor	80	2	6	2	0	7
Rehnquist	93	0	2	1	0	3
Scalia	70	1	1	0	0	4
Souter	49	1	5	1	0	4
Stevens	67	5	5	2	0	4
Thomas	46	1	4	0	0	6

NOTE: Justices Blackmun, Brennan, Marshall, Powell, and White are not included.

collected data on academic background for all but approximately 76 former law clerks from the years 1882 to 2004. Many of the clerks for whom information is not available clerked in the late nineteenth century and likely did not attend law school, instead either "reading the law" or being stenographers rather than lawyers.

From 1882 to 2004, 81 law schools sent their graduates on to Supreme Court clerkships. The majority of Supreme Court law clerks have been drawn from the august halls of Harvard Law School. Approximately 29 percent of the clerkship corps is composed of Harvard Law School graduates, followed by Yale (16 percent), University of Chicago (8 percent), Columbia (7 percent), Stanford (6 percent), the Universities of Michigan and Virginia (4 percent each), the University of Pennsylvania (3 percent), the Georgetown Law Center (2 percent), and New York University (2 percent).

Harvard Law School's dominance at the Supreme Court has diminished over time. Undoubtedly due to the early hiring norms established by Justices Horace Gray, Oliver Wendell Holmes, Jr., Louis Brandeis, and Felix Frankfurter,[22] from 1882 to 1940 approximately 62 percent of all law clerks for whom we have academic background data (138 clerks) held Harvard Law School diplomas. Columbia Law School trailed Harvard with 10 percent, and Harvard's future rival, Yale, contributed to only 3 percent of the law clerk corps. In fact, from 1882 to 1910, the only law schools other than Harvard who contributed law clerks were George Washington, Detroit College of Law, Columbian University (not to be confused with Columbia University in New York City), and Georgetown. The number of law clerks hired from elite universities over the last century is shown in Table 2.2.

While the traditional law schools have retained their dominance over the clerkship corps, the *number* of law schools contributing graduates to the

TABLE 2.2. Number of Law Clerks Selected from Elite Law Schools, 1882–2000

Years	Harvard	Yale	Columbia	University of Chicago	Stanford
1882–1920	39	0	1	0	0
1921–1940	54	8	11	0	0
1941–1960	88	48	19	18	9
1961–1980	131	85	29	25	31
1981–2000	169	120	49	77	53

Supreme Court has increased over time. From 1882 to 1940, only twelve law schools placed graduates at the Supreme Court: Harvard, Columbia, Yale, George Washington, Georgetown, University of Pennsylvania, University of Washington, Detroit College of Law, Catholic University, University of Texas, Columbian University, and National Law School. During the 1950s the number increased to thirty (with University of Chicago, Northwestern, University of Pennsylvania, and Stanford joining Harvard and Yale as substantial contributors), and during the 1970s the justices drew their clerks from forty-eight different schools (with the Universities of Michigan and Virginia becoming repeat players).

Looking across the entire law clerk alumni rolls, eighty-one law schools are represented—including one-time contributors Dickinson School of Law (Justice Harry Blackmun), Yeshiva (Justice William Brennan), Case Western Reserve (Justice Harold Burton), Drake University, South Texas College of Law, and Washburn University School of Law (Justice Tom Clark), and University of Puget Sound and Howard University (Justice Thurgood Marshall).

The increasing number of law schools represented among the ranks of Supreme Court clerks, however, does not undercut the argument that the justices return again and again to the same schools for the majority of their law clerks. If we examine the selection practices of those justices from the early twentieth century, we find that most justices looked to a slowly widening range of schools. Looking at twenty-year blocks over the last century, the number of law schools represented in the corps of law clerks was 4 through 1920, 10 through 1940, 37 through 1960, 54 through 1980, and 56 through 2000. Yet Table 2.3 presents a truer measure of the narrow range of law schools represented by the law clerks of justices who served the Court more than ten years (this table does not include Rehnquist Court justices).

From 1986 to 2004, the nine justices of the Rehnquist Court followed traditional, if slightly more inclusive, selection practices. Seven law schools (Harvard, Yale, University of Chicago, New York University, Stanford, and the Universities of Michigan and Virginia) contributed approximately 80

TABLE 2.3. Number of Law Clerks Selected from Elite Law Schools, per Justice, 1902–1969

Justice	Harvard	Yale	Stanford	Chicago	Columbia	NYU	Michigan	Virginia
Black	14	19	0	3	4	2	0	3
Brandeis	18	2	0	0	0	0	0	0
Burton	9	1	0	3	0	0	0	0
Clark	7	6	0	3	2	1	2	1
Douglas	6	2	9	0	0	0	0	0
Frankfurter	35	0	0	1	0	0	0	0
Harlan	25	3	1	0	6	0	1	2
Holmes	28	0	0	0	0	0	0	0
Jackson	3	1	1	1	0	0	0	1
Reed	17	10	1	2	7	0	0	2
Stone	3	0	0	0	14	0	0	0
Warren	5	10	4	2	1	1	5	1

NOTE: Only those justices have been selected who served for more than ten years on the U.S. Supreme Court and for whom information is available on the academic backgrounds of the majority of their law clerks.

percent of all the High Court's law clerks. Add the University of Pennsylvania, Georgetown, University of Texas, Northwestern, and University of California-Berkeley, and the country's remaining 178 ABA-accredited law schools have filled a mere 10 percent of the clerkship slots.

As for the individual Rehnquist Court justices, the emphasis remained on selecting clerks from the most prestigious law schools. Seventy-four percent of Justice Souter's, 71 percent of Justice Scalia's, 66 percent of Justice Kennedy's, and 57 percent of Justice Thomas' law clerks were selected from just three schools: Harvard, Yale, and the University of Chicago. All in all, these four justices turned to only 8, 13, 16, and 15 law schools, respectively, for their law clerks.

The more conservative members of the Rehnquist Court were not the only justices to follow familiar, "safe" selection practices. Justice Ruth Bader Ginsburg selected 65 percent of her law clerks from three law schools: 29 percent from Columbia University (her alma mater), 19 percent from Yale, and 17 percent from Harvard. Of all the Rehnquist Court justices, Justice Stephen Breyer depends the most on a single law school for his clerks. Since taking the bench, Breyer has selected 43 percent of his clerks from Harvard Law School. Both Justices Ginsburg and Breyer have looked to a total of eleven law schools for their clerks. (See Table 2.4 for a breakdown of law schools represented by the clerks of the Rehnquist Court.)

Chief Justice Rehnquist is one of the few justices to have selected clerks from a broad range of schools. Not only were his law clerks picked from thirty-four different law schools, but less emphasis also was placed on selecting the majority of clerks from a handful of the elite law schools. Chief Justice Rehnquist selected only 9 percent of his law clerks from Harvard, 7.1 percent from Yale, and 10 percent from the University of Chicago. In fact, his favorite source of law clerks was the University of Virginia—from 1972 to 2004, Rehnquist selected thirteen law clerks from Virginia. Over all, he selected at least two law clerks from twenty different law schools—including Brigham Young University, the University of Illinois, Boston University, Duke University, the University of Missouri, Notre Dame, Washington and Lee University, and the University of Arizona.

The historical data indicate that while the chief justices turn to a slightly broader range of law schools for their law clerks, no modern chief justice has selected clerks from as many different law schools as Chief Justice Rehnquist. This is not to say that former chief justices did not look to the perennial favorites, but that top law schools tend not to play as dominant a role. For example, Chief Justice Earl Warren selected 20 percent of his law clerks from Yale, and Chief Justice Warren E. Burger picked 23 percent of his law clerks from Harvard, but both men demonstrated a willingness to look beyond the top ten law schools.

TABLE 2.4. Number of Law Clerks Selected from Elite Law Schools by the Rehnquist Court Justices, 1986–2004

Justice	Harvard	Yale	Stanford	Chicago	Columbia	NYU	Michigan	Virginia
Blackmun	20	24	5	7	5	3	3	5
Brennan	35	12	6	10	4	3	3	4
Breyer	19	9	4	2	2	2	1	0
Ginsburg	8	9	4	2	14	1	0	3
Kennedy	20	16	6	12	1	0	2	4
Marshall	35	14	7	1	8	1	4	4
O'Connor	12	15	15	9	10	4	8	2
Powell	9	11	5	6	2	2	4	15
Rehnquist	9	7	5	10	4	0	3	13
Scalia	29	9	4	15	4	2	1	2
Souter	23	18	4	4	4	2	4	0
Stevens	17	12	6	10	4	4	8	2
Thomas	12	10	1	15	1	1	1	4
White	16	19	6	7	5	4	6	1

Justice O'Connor is the only other Rehnquist Court justice to come close to Chief Justice Rehnquist's more diversified selection practices. From 1981 to 2004, O'Connor looked to 22 different law schools for her clerks. While the bulk of her clerk selections come from the same familiar names (Harvard, Yale, Stanford, University of Chicago, and Columbia University), Justice O'Connor also turned to less traditional law schools (Tulane, William & Mary, University of Miami, Arizona State, Ohio State, and Vanderbilt) for a few clerks.

Some have suggested that the justices not only favor the elite law schools, but that within that select group they also favor their own alma mater or region of birth. Certainly there is evidence that some justices prefer selecting law clerks from their old "stomping grounds," although this effect is difficult to measure when the justice has graduated from a top law school— for example, it is impossible to determine whether the fact that 43 percent of Justice Breyer's law clerks hail from Harvard Law School is due to the school's sterling reputation or due to his personal bonds with the school (Harvard Law School class of 1964).

Nevertheless, we find some interesting selection practices for some justices. Justice Frank Murphy selected six of his seven law clerks from his alma mater, the University of Michigan School of Law. Murphy was raised in Michigan and served both as mayor of Detroit and as governor. Justice William O. Douglas, who grew up in the Pacific Northwest, selected 45 of his 54 law clerks from law schools sitting in the Ninth Circuit. Douglas made no secret of his preference for West Coast law school graduates. Hoosier Sherman Minton looked to his alma mater of Indiana University for 7 of his 15 law clerks, and he selected 3 other clerks from law schools within the Seventh Circuit—where he once sat as a federal appeals court judge.

Ohio native Justice Harold H. Burton also attempted to bring native sons into his law clerk corps. During his first year on the Supreme Court, Burton asked the dean of Harvard Law School to recommend a student from Ohio to serve as his law clerk.[23] While Burton selected only a single law clerk from an Ohio school (Case Western Reserve), he showed an affinity for Midwestern law schools—picking clerks from the University of Nebraska, Indiana University, and the University of Chicago.

Of all the pre-Rehnquist Court justices, the most eclectic selection record belongs to Tom C. Clark, the bow tie–wearing Texan. While Justice Clark turned to Harvard and Yale for 13 of his 44 clerks, he also picked a law clerk from each of the following schools: Drake University, Fordham University, Loyola Los Angeles, South Texas College of Law, Southern Methodist University, St. Mary's University of San Antonio, University of Mississippi, Villanova, and Washburn University. It has been said that Justice Clark's selection practices were driven not only by regional considerations (four additional law clerks graduated from the University of Texas), but also by political and social bonds.

Modern Supreme Court justices also have demonstrated some favoritism to region and alma mater. Justice Powell drew 17 of his law clerks from his home state of Virginia—15 from the University of Virginia School of Law, and 2 from his alma mater Washington and Lee. Justice Ginsburg has evidenced a preference for clerks from where she completed her education, Columbia Law School, over Harvard Law School, where she began her legal studies. Justice Ginsburg has selected 14 of her 48 law clerks from Columbia, twice the number she has selected from Harvard. No other Rehnquist Court justice has picked as many Columbia Law School graduates as Ginsburg. While Justice O'Connor has selected 15 law clerks from her alma mater, Stanford University, Chief Justice Rehnquist looked to Stanford University for only five of his clerks.

Undeniably, the justices depend on the graduates of a few elite law schools to fill the clerkship ranks. When pressed to answer charges of academic elitism, they have publicly and privately bemoaned the lack of qualified candidates at less prestigious schools and the risks attendant with making such picks. Yet consider the names of a few law schools that did not contribute candidates to the Rehnquist Court: Brooklyn Law School; American, Baylor, Cardozo-Yeshiva, Florida State, George Mason, Northeastern, Southern Methodist, Tennessee–Knoxville, Wake Forest, and Washington Universities; Universities of Connecticut, Florida, Illinois–Champaign Urbana, Louisville, Nebraska–Lincoln, Richmond, South Carolina, St. John's, Washington, and Wisconsin–Madison. While the number of talented students per class at these law schools is arguably less than at a Harvard or Yale, one wonders if the difference between the top law student at the University of Chicago versus the University of Illinois or Northeastern is that significant, given a clerk's Supreme Court duties.

Supreme Court justices pick from not only the best law schools but also the best students from these schools. From 1950 to 2004, data regarding law review membership were collected for 910 out of 1,568 law clerks. Of these 910 clerks, approximately 221 (24 percent) were former heads of their respective school's law review, another 577 (63 percent) were on the management or editorial board, and 61 (7 percent) were members of law review. Only 51 out of the 910 law clerks (6 percent) were not members of law review, and the majority of these 51 clerks held management positions on other law school journals.

Emphasis on law review experience has remained constant over time. While the percentage of law clerks who served as editors-in-chief of their law reviews dipped from a high of 34 percent in the 1960s to 24 percent in the 1980s and 12 percent in the 1990s, the percentage of former clerks who served on the editorial boards of law reviews climbed from 34 percent in the 1950s to 66 percent in the 1980s and 69 percent in the 1990s. What explains the drop in the number of law review editors-in-chief is not that the justices place less importance on the position, but that the number of editors-in-chief at elite law schools has remained constant while the number of law clerk positions per justice has increased from two to four over the last fifty years.

Feeder Court Judges and Political Ideology

Not only are Supreme Court law clerks selected from the best law schools, but they also are expected to have trained for their clerkship by first clerking with well-known and trusted federal appellate court judges. The rise of the "feeder court" judge is a relatively new phenomenon for the clerkship institution. From 1940 to 1950, 18 of the 44 law clerks surveyed clerked for a federal appeals court judge prior to arriving at the Supreme Court. Of this number, six clerks worked for Judge Learned Hand, five for Judge Calvert Magruder, two for Judge Augustus Hand, and two for Judge Herbert Goodrich. Justice Frankfurter was the only justice from this time period who consistently hired law clerks with prior clerkship experience.

During the following decades, the number of Supreme Court law clerks who first clerked on lower courts remained fairly constant. In the 1950s, 30 of the 58 law clerks surveyed clerked for a lower court judge (popular feeder court judges remained Judges Learned Hand, Herbert Goodrich, and Calvert Magruder), and in the 1960s, 49 out of the 101 clerks surveyed had lower court clerkship experience. Thus, in this thirty-year span, less than one-half of all surveyed law clerks had worked for a lower court judge prior to their Supreme Court clerkship.

As discussed later, the arrival of Chief Justice Warren E. Burger triggered a dramatic change in the institutional norms regarding lower court clerkships. Chief Justice Burger wanted law clerks who had previously clerked in the federal judiciary, and the other Burger Court justices quickly took notice. During the first five years of the Burger Court, 68 percent of law clerks surveyed had clerked for a federal or state court judge. From 1980 to 1985 that percentage had swelled to 95 percent of clerks surveyed.

A lower court clerkship remains an informal prerequisite for today's Supreme Court law clerks. From 1994 to 2004 approximately 99 percent of all Supreme Court law clerks had previously clerked with federal and state court judges. While most clerkships were with federal appeals court judges, some clerks worked for federal district court judges and at least one state supreme court justice.[24]

Over the last hundred years, 245 federal and state court judges have trained future Supreme Court law clerks. Despite these diverse sources of clerks, modern Supreme Court justices have favored a handful of feeder court judges. The list of preferred judges from 1882 to 2004 includes U.S. Court of Appeals for the District of Columbia Circuit judges J. Skelly Wright (34 clerks), Harry T. Edwards (33), Laurence H. Silberman (31), Abner Mikva (24), David L. Bazelon and Stephen F. Williams (21), Carl Mc-Gowan (20), and David S. Tatel (18); Second Circuit judges Guido Calabresi (19), Wilfred Feinberg (19), Henry J. Friendly (19), and James L. Oakes (18); Fourth Circuit judges J. Michael Luttig (36) and J. Harvie Wilkinson III (26); Seventh Circuit judge Richard Posner (19); and Ninth Circuit judge Alex Kozinski (33). Occasionally, the justices also have looked to federal district courts for their law clerks. The most popular judges have been Louis H. Pollak of the Eastern District of Pennsylvania (13 clerks), Edward Weinfeld of the Southern District of New York (10 clerks), and Louis F. Oberdorfer of the District of Columbia (8 clerks). Interestingly, both Pollak and Ober-dorfer were themselves former Supreme Court law clerks (for Justices Wiley Rutledge and Hugo Black, respectively).

As demonstrated by political scientists Corey Ditslear and Larry Baum, Supreme Court justices often turn to those feeder court judges with whom they share a similar political ideology. For example, the majority of Justices Thomas, Scalia, and Kennedy's law clerks have previously clerked for Judges Alex Kozinski, J. Michael Luttig, Laurence Silberman, J. Harvie Wilkinson, or Stephen F. Williams—all judges who were appointed by conservative presidents. While similar patterns are not as clear for the more moderate members of the Rehnquist Court, there is evidence from early Courts that liberal justices followed similar strategies. During their tenure on the Supreme Court bench, Justices William J. Brennan, Jr., and Thurgood Marshall hired forty-six clerks who had trained in the chambers of Judges David Bazelon, Harry T. Edwards, Abner Mikva, and J. Skelly Wright. Tables 2.5 and 2.6 present statistics on the most popular feeder court judges.

One new wrinkle to the hiring process—law clerks who work in top law firms or elite government posts between their clerkships with lower federal court judges and Supreme Court justices. "The justices themselves are encouraging this trend," writes Supreme Court reporter Tony Mauro, "in an apparent desire to recruit a more seasoned and varied mix of clerks— including minorities and applicants from schools other than Harvard and Yale, whose résumés might gain luster from an extra year or so of post-appeals court, post-law school work." Often these clerks do not apply for Supreme Court clerkship positions until they have completed their lower court clerkship. While this new clerkship model provides the justices with more mature assistants, there is an unintended consequence for this principal-agent relationship—an older, wiser clerk may be less deferential and loyal to his or her justice.[25]

TABLE 2.5. Number of Law Clerks Selected from the Top Feeder Court Judges by the Rehnquist Court Justices, 1986–2004

Justice/Feeder Court Judge	David Bazelon	Guido Calabresi	Harry Edwards	Wilfred Feinberg	Alex Kozinski	J. Michael Luttig	Carl McGowan	Abner Mikva	Laurence Silberman	Richard Posner	J. Harvie Wilkinson III	J. Skelly Wright
Blackmun	2	0	2	4	0	0	2	6	0	2	0	1
Brennan	12	0	3	2	0	0	0	5	0	1	0	11
Breyer	0	8	2	0	0	0	0	0	3	3	0	0
Ginsburg	0	3	2	1	3	0	0	0	0	0	2	0
Kennedy	0	0	0	0	15	6	0	1	4	3	7	0
Marshall	3	0	5	6	0	0	2	4	0	0	0	9
O'Connor	0	1	6	0	10	1	1	2	4	2	5	3
Powell	2	0	0	0	1	0	5	2	0	0	1	2
Rehnquist	0	0	0	2	1	2	0	1	3	1	2	0
Scalia	0	1	0	0	4	13	0	0	8	4	1	0
Souter	0	2	6	0	0	0	0	1	0	0	1	0
Stevens	0	4	5	1	0	0	0	2	0	1	0	3
Thomas	0	0	0	0	0	14	0	0	9	1	7	0
White	0	0	2	1	0	0	1	0	0	1	0	2

TABLE 2.6. "Second String" of Feeder Court Judges

First Circuit	Second Circuit	Ninth Circuit	D.C. Circuit
Michael Boudin (15)	Henry J. Friendly (20)	William A. Norris (14)	Ruth B. Ginsburg (18)
Stephen G. Breyer (10)	James L. Oakes (18)	J. Clifford Wallace (13)	David S. Tatel (18)
Frank M. Coffin (10)	Learned Hand (10)	Diarmund O'Scannlain (9)	David M. Sentelle (14)
Calvert Magruder (9)	J. Edward Lumbard (8)	Dorothy W. Nelson (8)	Patricia M. Wald (14)

Ditslear and Baum argue that lower court clerkships can be used to maximize the likelihood that a law clerk and a justice share the same political ideology. Using surveys of former law clerks, I have attempted to gauge the law clerk's political ideology by asking which political party—Democratic or Republican—more closely reflected the law clerk's own personal beliefs during his or her clerkship. While this is an imperfect measure of personal political ideology, I decided that any survey with the emotionally charged words "conservative" and "liberal" would more likely be tossed in a garbage can.

I was able to collect ideology measures for 491 out of 1,524 former law clerks from the years 1940 to 2000. Of those, 368 (75 percent) described their political beliefs at the time of their clerkship as more closely affiliated with the Democratic party and 117 (24 percent) more closely affiliated with the Republican party. Approximately 6 (1 percent) of the respondents described themselves as "Independent"—despite not being given this option by the survey. An additional 95 refused to answer the question (often indignantly challenging the relevance of my inquiry).

I cannot conclude, however, that the completed surveys from 1940 to 2000 constitute a representative sample of former law clerks. The survey responses are biased because former clerks whose justices are deceased were more likely to return the survey with the party affiliation question completed than clerks whose justices currently sit on the Supreme Court. I believe that concerns about violating the ongoing duty of confidentiality owed a sitting justice explain the lower response rates (in fact, many law clerks cited this duty in refusing to answer the question).

Although any conclusions about law clerk political preferences must be tentative, some interesting findings emerge. Of the eighteen individuals who clerked for Chief Justice Fred Vinson, seven described themselves as Democrats and two as Republicans. I was unable to gather data for the other nine

Vinson clerks. The pattern of Democrat versus Republican law clerks holds for Chief Justice Warren as well. Party affiliation scores were gathered for 22 of the 50 men who clerked for Warren. All but three former clerks reported that they more closely associated with the Democratic party.

The pattern of employing more Democrat than Republican law clerks appears to cease with Chief Justices Burger and Rehnquist, but the small number of party affiliation scores caution against any firm conclusions. Data were gathered from 24 out of 76 former Burger law clerks and from 24 out of 99 former Rehnquist clerks. For both sets of clerks, the number of law clerks whose political beliefs more closely mirrored the Republican party was equal to (Burger) or slightly outweighed (Rehnquist) the number of Democratic party affiliated clerks. Table 2.7 presents the party affiliations of clerks for the four prior chief justices.

Assuming that I obtained a representative sample and can properly conclude that liberal chief justices are more likely to hire liberal law clerks than are conservative justices, two different problems remain. First of all, I cannot control for the pool from which the law clerks were selected. The counterfactual remains unanswered, namely, whether earlier chief justices (Vinson and Warren) hired more liberal law clerks than conservative justices (Burger and Rehnquist) because law school students in the 1940s to 1960s tended to be more liberal than their counterparts in the 1970s and 1980s.

Additionally, a second problem involves self-selection. If law clerks are more likely to apply to like-minded justices, then the pool of applicants is again skewed. Today, it is considered poor form for clerkship candidates to target specific justices, and some justices ask candidates if they have applied to all nine justices. Most of the law clerks that I interviewed from earlier decades, however, reported that they applied to only two or three of the nine justices. Moreover, it appears that the decision whether to apply to a specific justice was often driven by ideological or jurisprudential considerations.

Keeping these two problems in mind, the aforementioned pattern repeats itself for liberal justices Brennan and Marshall. Of the 45 out of 107 former Brennan law clerks who answered the party affiliation question, 40 stated that at the time of their clerkship they more closely associated with

TABLE 2.7. Law Clerk Party Affiliation by Chief Justice

	Republican	Democrat	Independent	Refused to Answer	Missing Data
Vinson	2	7	0	0	9
Warren	3	19	0	2	26
Burger	12	12	0	6	46
Rehnquist	14	10	0	8	67

the Democratic party; of the 29 out of 89 former Marshall law clerks surveyed, all but 3 more closely associated with the Democratic party. While it is slightly more difficult to place Hugo Black, Harry Blackmun, and Byron White in the same, neat ideological category as Marshall and Brennan, their law clerks were also overwhelmingly affiliated with the Democratic party. Table 2.8 presents the party affiliations of clerks for eleven former associate justices.

These findings can be contrasted with the law clerks of more conservative justices like Harold Burton and John Harlan. Twelve out of 27 former Burton law clerks responded to my survey, with 5 clerks listing themselves as Republican and 7 as Democrats. As for Justice Harlan's law clerks, 4 out of the 18 respondents more closely identified with the Republican party, and 7 with the Democratic party. An additional 7 clerks refused to answer the ideology question. At best, one might tentatively conclude that these two justices had more of an ideological balance among their clerks.

Finally, Justices Douglas and Frankfurter provided two instances in which the self-selection problem is not present. As I discuss later, potential law clerks did not apply specifically for Douglas or Frankfurter clerkships; law clerks were tapped by individual professors or clerkship committees. Given that fact, we again find some interesting party affiliation patterns among these two sets of clerks. Of the twenty-four former Douglas law clerks who completely answered my survey, all but one more closely affiliated with the Democratic party. The same results are found with Frankfurter law clerks.

I am hesitant to draw any dramatic conclusions about the ideological makeup of the law clerk corps. There is evidence suggesting that law clerks historically have associated more closely with the Democratic than with the Republican party, and that they tend to share the ideological beliefs of their justices. Given the difficulty in collecting data from more recent law clerks, however, combined with concerns about the ideological composition of the applicant pool and a self-selection effect, no additional conclusions can be reached.

Conclusion

The allegations of elitism among the law clerk corps have mixed support. In the first half of the twentieth century, Supreme Court law clerks were—with the single exception of Lucile Lomen and William T. Coleman, Jr.—white males from a small handful of elite law schools. Most of the justices looked no farther than the staff of the *Harvard Law Review* for their law clerks, although justices such as William O. Douglas, Robert H. Jackson, and Tom C. Clark did search beyond the Ivy League. While the 1980s and 1990s witnessed solid gains in the hiring of female law clerks, minorities continued to

TABLE 2.8. Law Clerk Party Affiliation by Associate Justice

	Republican	Democrat	Independent	Refused to Answer	Missing Data
Black	2	19	0	2	29
Blackmun	2	26	1	3	61
Brennan	5	40	0	10	52
Burton	5	7	0	0	15
Clark	5	13	0	1	25
Douglas	1	23	2	2	27
Frankfurter	2	12	0	0	23
Harlan	4	7	0	7	22
Marshall	3	26	0	5	52
Stewart	1	21	0	4	44
White	8	25	1	12	54

be dramatically underrepresented in the clerkship corps. While the justices publicly announce their commitment to diversity, the number of minority hires has not increased.

As for the issue of academic diversity, it is undeniable that more and more law schools have placed graduates in the chambers of the modern Supreme Court. What has not changed, however, is the dominance of the top law schools. Given the justices' public statements about their unwillingness to take chances, it is unlikely that law schools such as Harvard, Yale, and Stanford will lose their beachhead at the Supreme Court.

CHAPTER 3

The Law Clerk as Stenographer

"But those men who, even when they think they will not
be observed or seen or recognized by anyone, show courage
and are not careless of anything, however slight, for which
they could be blamed, such have the quality of spirit we are
seeking in our Courtier."
—Baldassare Castiglione, *The Book of the Courtier*

DURING THE FIRST FIFTY YEARS of its existence, the Supreme Court was
a relatively small institution with a limited number of employees. When
it moved from Philadelphia to Washington, D.C., in the fall of 1800, the
Court had no official home and initially took up residence in an unfin-
ished committee room in the U.S. Capitol.[1] The Supreme Court remained
in the committee room until 1808, spent the 1809 term in a local tavern
while the Capitol was renovated, and moved into its new chambers in the
basement of the Capitol in 1810. While the justices undoubtedly appreciated having a permanent home, their new court was "small, damp, and
poorly lighted."[2]

Befitting the Court's humble beginnings, the Supreme Court justices
were served by only a small handful of support personnel. Besides the justices themselves, the Court's original support staff consisted of the clerk
of the Supreme Court, the official Court reporter, and the marshal of the
Court. The Court created the position of clerk in February of 1790. The
first clerk of the Court, John Tucker, had a number of different duties, including "responsibility for the Court's library, courtroom, and employees,
as well as for collecting justices' salaries and finding local lodgings for the
justices."[3] Court historian Carl B. Swisher describes the original clerk of the
Court as "a kind of business manager and errand boy for the Justices."[4] Fifty
years after its creation, the clerk's staff remained small in size, employing less
than five deputies or assistants.

As opposed to the clerk of the Court, the Court reporter's role evolved
more informally[5] and was originally filled by an enterprising volunteer. It

was not until 1816 that Congress formally recognized the need for a re-porter of Supreme Court decisions and authorized a salary. The Supreme Court staff was rounded out with the appointment of a Supreme Court marshal, a post filled by the marshal of the District of Columbia until a for-mal position was created in 1867.[6] In subsequent decades, the staff of the Su-preme Court was supplemented with what Chief Justice Roger Taney called "servants about the Court."[7] Little is known about these additional Court employees. Political scientist Chester A. Newland writes that although Con-gress first appropriated funds for the hiring of messengers in 1867, individual justices employed messengers before that date.[8] Newland states that messen-gers were given a number of different job responsibilities, including serving as barbers, waiters, and chauffeurs.

In 1850 Congress debated whether to increase the size of the Court's support staff. On February 12, 1850, Senator Arthur P. Butler of South Caro-lina introduced the following joint resolution[9]:

> That the Chief Justice of the Supreme Court of the United States be and he is hereby authorized to appoint a special clerk to attend said Chief Justice and the Associate Justices of said Supreme Court during the time it is in session each year, and it shall be the duty of said clerk to do such copying of opinions and other mat-ters, and to make such researches, as the Chief Justice or either of his associates may require in the progress of the business of the said court.

In his introduction, Senator Butler pointed to the fact that the Supreme Court was faced with cases that "depend mainly upon proofs contained in papers in the Spanish language, correspondence, and otherwise; and it is im-possible for the Court to act upon those cases satisfactorily without the aid of an officer such as here proposed."

While the joint resolution generated little discussion in the Senate and was subsequently passed, it faced stiff opposition in the House chamber. In introducing the joint resolution, Representative Thomas Henry Bayly of Virginia, a lawyer, characterized the bill as one that would relieve the over-worked justices from having to transcribe their opinions personally:

> The Judges of the Supreme Court were required to record their opinions of course. In writing their opinions they frequently interlined them very much. Some of them wrote in bad hands. It was impossible for men of their age to do this copying for themselves; and if they could do it it would be very false economy to require them to do it, because their time might be much better employed. A clerk to copy these opinions must be a man who understood technical terms, who understood the abbreviations which the judges made. He must be a lawyer. But in addition to that, the resolution contemplated additional duty upon his part. It was to make investigation, to aid the Court in investigations, which would save much mere drudgery of labor on their part, and enable them to dispatch their business more expeditiously.

In explaining the rationale behind the joint resolution, Bayly added that it was the justices themselves who requested the aid.

Representative David K. Cartter of Ohio, also a lawyer, rose to heap scorn on the joint resolution. He characterized the request as "extraordinary" given the fact that the Court already possessed a "competent clerk" who employed three deputies. Cartter suggested that if the justices had become too infirm to copy their own opinions, then the solution was not to provide them with "a supplemental judge" but to strip the justices of lifetime tenure. Apparently enjoying the opportunity to needle the Supreme Court, Cartter added that the justices were asking Congress "that they might be furnished with auxiliary brains, to do their thinking ... which now, God knows, they did not do." Despite being subsequently chastised by his fellow representatives for his impertinent denouncement of the Supreme Court, Cartter refused to be cowed and later mockingly referred to the joint resolution as providing a "thinking machine for the Bench!"[10]

The majority of the House was not swayed by Representative Cartter's heated remarks, and the joint resolution was passed on February 13, 1850. The next day, however, Representative Lucius B. Peck of Vermont requested that the vote be reconsidered since he had subsequently learned that "the Judges were not unanimously in favor of the project—that they were divided in opinion as to its expediency—a majority, however, desiring its adoption."[11] In rising to announce his support of Representative Peck's request, Representative William Strong of Pennsylvania attacked the bill in language that echoes current criticisms of law clerks:

> [The Supreme Court's] usefulness will continue only while it retains the confidence of the people. Now what, think you, would more directly and cogently tend to impair that confidence which it has enjoyed, and which is essential to its continued usefulness, than a resolution declaring that its members need an officer to aid them in legal research ... [moreover] the proposed additional clerk would inevitably give character to the opinions emanating from the Court. Judges are but men. With an officer under their control, whose duty it would be to investigate the questions referred to him, it is too much to hope that they would not roll off upon him the labor from which all naturally shrink. *His researches would give tone to the opinions, and, doubtless, in many cases control the judgments of all the Court. His particular opinions would tinge all the opinions of the Court. His mind, his hand, would be visible in them all.*[12]

While at least one House member stood up to support the bill, the die was cast. The motion to reconsider the joint resolution easily passed and, after some minor procedural wrangling, the resolution was "laid on the table" and quietly died. Summarizing the peculiar life and death of this joint resolution, Swisher concludes that thus "[t]he Court was thereby saved from the threat of subversion by an investigating clerk."[13] As noted above, Congress, however, would throw the justices a few crumbs by authorizing the hiring of messengers in 1867.[14]

After the Civil War, the Supreme Court faced unprecedented caseload pressures. Frankfurter and Landis write that in the decade before the Civil War, the Supreme Court's docket hovered around 250 to 300 cases per term. After the Civil War, however, the Court witnessed "the beginning of vast extensions of federal jurisdiction."[15] Frankfurter and Landis cite numerous examples of specific Congressional acts in the 1860s and 1870s that increased the scope of the Supreme Court's appellate review. This legislation, combined with increased numbers of case filings in the Court's traditional areas of review as well as litigation related to the Reconstruction amendments, resulted in a dramatic increase in workload for the justices. Between 1860 and 1870 the Supreme Court's docket doubled in size, from 310 to 636 cases. By 1880 the Court's docket had swelled to 1,212 cases, and by the close of the decade justices were faced with approximately 1,800 cases.[16] "The court was like a man with a shovel trying to empty a grain elevator with the new grain flowing in and engulfing him."[17]

By this time the Supreme Court had moved to its new home, located in the former Senate chamber of the U.S. Capitol. Although visually impressive,[18] its physical limitations added to the general discomfort imposed on the justices by their expanding docket:

> The courtroom was badly ventilated and ill-lit. The Clerk's quarters were inadequate. There was no room provided for the bar. The library and conference room, in the basement, was small, cluttered, and extremely ill-ventilated....At this time, no office space at all was made available to the Justices in Washington. They all had to maintain chambers in their homes, the government providing for a $2,000 furniture allowance, as well as the rudiments of a working law library, for each Justice.[19]

While individual members of Congress were not unsympathetic to the Supreme Court's plight, judicial reform proved an elusive goal. Congress had debated various plans for judicial reorganization as early as 1848,[20] but "political passions . . . [and] conflicting conceptions about the role of the federal court in the national polity" repeatedly blocked efforts to reorganize the federal courts, narrow the Supreme Court's jurisdiction, and reduce the justices' caseload. Frankfurter and Landis characterized the struggle over the contours of judicial reform as "a story of strife between those who sought to curtail the jurisdiction of the federal courts and those who aimed merely to increase the judicial force to cope with the increase of judicial business."[21]

Individual justices periodically lent their own voices to the demand for judicial reform. In 1872 Justice Samuel F. Miller painted a dismal picture of a Supreme Court docket, remarking "it may be fairly and safely affirmed, that an average period of three years elapses in cases appealed to the Supreme Court . . . This does not look like speedy justice."[22] Justice Miller warned that the Court would continue to fall behind. In September of 1887, Chief Justice Morrison R. Waite echoed Justice Miller's assessment of the Supreme Court's workload and called upon Congress to reduce the High Court's appellate jurisdiction lest litigants continue to suffer "the ruinous consequences of the tedious and oppressive delays" in justice.[23] Three years later Justice Stephen J. Field joined in the demand for judicial reform, observing that the High Court "has a right to call upon the country to give it assistance and relief" from what the justice characterized as "the immense burden now cast upon it."[24]

While real reform would not take place until the signing into law of the 1891 Evarts Act, in 1885 the Supreme Court was the beneficiary of more modest forms of relief and assistance. In the *Annual Report of the Attorney General of the United States for the Year 1885*, Attorney General Augustus H. Garland made the following recommendation:

> I believe it would greatly facilitate the business of the Supreme Court if each justice *was provided by law with a secretary or law clerk, to be a stenographer,* to be paid an annual salary sufficient to obtain the requisite qualifications, whose duties shall be to assist in such clerical work as might be assigned to him. The labor of the judges of the court in investigating questions and preparing their opinions is immense, and while the heads of Departments and Senators have this assistance, I do not think there is any good reason that the judges of this court should not also have it, and I therefore recommend that such provisions be made.[25]

Note the curious language of Garland's recommendation, that either a law clerk or a secretary should be hired as a stenographer.[26] Did the attorney general believe that the role of stenographer would be the same, whether it was filled by a secretary or a trained attorney?

In a small book that Garland later published on the Supreme Court, he briefly addresses his proposal. Garland writes: "I was satisfied this was . . . a much needed measure, and the pressure of business upon the judges would never, in all probability, lessen the importance of it." Garland adds that his modest assistance to the Court prompted "the thanks and good wishes of nine very prominent officials."[27] Garland does not indicate whether he intended that men possessing both legal and stenographic skills would be hired by the justices.

There is no evidence that this newest request for judicial assistants sparked outrage in the House or Senate. In fact, Congress swiftly acted upon Garland's recommendation. In 1886, Congress authorized funds for the hiring of a "stenographic clerk for the Chief Justice and for each associate justice of the Supreme Court, at not exceeding one thousand six hundred dollars each."[28]

One Supreme Court justice, however, had beaten Attorney General Garland to the punch. When Horace Gray was appointed to the U.S. Supreme Court in 1882, he began hiring Harvard Law School graduates to serve one- or two-year appointments as his assistants. Gray had previously been chief judge of the Massachusetts Supreme Judicial Court, and in that role he first started employing clerks. While no historical evidence exists that Garland knew of this unique practice, it is not unreasonable to assume that the attorney general was aware of, if not inspired by, Gray's staffing arrangement. Perhaps cognizant of earlier criticisms regarding "thinking machines" for the justices, neither Garland nor Congress made any mention of substantive job duties.

Justice Horace Gray and the Birth of an Institution

It is generally undisputed that Horace Gray was the first U.S. Supreme Court justice to hire a law clerk, and it is the judgment of most historians that Gray was also the first U.S. judge—state or federal—to hire a law clerk, during his tenure on the Massachusetts Supreme Judicial Court. "Some other judges, both state and federal, had hired secretaries before Gray, but they had always gotten professional secretarial help. Gray is believed to have been the first to take for his clerical, a young law school graduate."[29] Despite Gray's service on both state and federal Supreme Courts and his contributions to judicial administration, he is not listed among the giants of the Supreme Court. Gray has not been the subject of modern scholarly writings, and the only biography about the late jurist is a 1961 doctoral dissertation.[30]

In his later years, Horace Gray was a large, balding man with "mutton chop" whiskers and a stern countenance. Former Gray law clerk Samuel Williston describes him thusly:

In appearance Judge Gray was one of the most striking men of his time. He was six feet and four inches tall in his stockings. Unlike most very tall men, all the proportions of his body were on the same large scale. His massive head, his large but finely shaped hands, and the great bulk of his frame, all seemed to mark him as one of a larger race than his fellows.[31]

Gray's contemporaries viewed him as a man "possessed of great physical as well as great mental vigor," an individual blessed with "abounding vitality and a delightful flow of animal spirits," a jurist endowed with a "extraordinary" memory, a strong work ethic, and heightened awareness of "the dignity of the court and the position of judge."[32] Attorney Jack B. Warner painted a picture of a man who was more deity than mortal. "His great stature and commanding figure heightened the impression of a presence never to be trifled with, and suggested the classic demi-god walking on the earth with his head reaching among the clouds."[33] Given Gray's status as the creator of the modern law clerk, perhaps it is only fitting to describe him in biblical terms.

Gray was born in Boston on March 24, 1828, to a wealthy shipping family. He received both his undergraduate and law degrees from Harvard University, graduating from Harvard Law School in 1849. Gray's decision to attend law school and earn a professional degree was motivated by a dramatic reversal in his family's financial fortunes after he earned his undergraduate degree. "[I]t is partly due to accidental circumstances that he became eminent as a judge, rather than as an ornithologist or botanist," comments former legal secretary Samuel Williston, who believes that Gray was contemplating "a life of studious leisure" before the aforementioned financial crisis.[34]

After five years of private practice, Gray became the reporter of decisions for the Supreme Judicial Court of Massachusetts. He remained in this position until 1860 and also practiced law with future U.S. attorney general Ebenezer Rockwood Hoar. As an attorney, Gray's practice was described as "considerable, though not very large; the cases which he argued were more important than numerous."[35]

On August 23, 1864, Horace Gray was appointed to the Massachusetts Supreme Judicial Court. He was thirty-six years old and the youngest judge ever to sit on the Massachusetts high court. On September 5, 1873, Gray was appointed chief judge of the Supreme Judicial Court, a position he held until 1882.[36] Gray was nominated to be an associate justice of the U.S. Supreme Court by President Chester A. Arthur in 1881. He took the bench on January 9, 1882, and remained on the Supreme Court until a stroke forced his resignation in 1902.

As a jurist, Gray's considerable energies were focused on legal opinions that modern scholars have found to be "heavy-handed" and "drawn out." Gray's peers took a slightly different view of the justice's work product. They commented that he "delighted to go to the fountains of the law and trace its growth from the beginning," adding that Gray "believed that an exhaustive collection of authorities should be the foundation of every judicial opinion on an important question."[37] Gray's indefatigability in legal research might well explain his motivation in seeking out legal assistance. On the bench, Gray displayed a grim, cold demeanor, and his judicial energies extended not only to cases before the Court but also "to the color of the clothes worn by some members of the bar in court."[38]

Legal Secretaries and the Massachusetts Supreme Judicial Court, 1875–1882

During the summer of 1875, Chief Judge Gray began hiring recent Harvard Law School graduates to serve as his legal secretaries.[39] The secretaries were selected by Harvard Law School professor John Chipman Gray, Horace Gray's half-brother.[40] Horace Gray's motivations for hiring clerks are unknown, although some suggest that he started the practice to handle the increased workload of the chief judge position.[41]

While on the Massachusetts bench, Gray personally paid his young assistants' salaries.[42] From the start, he treated his assistants as more than mere secretaries. From 1879 to 1881, future Supreme Court associate justice Louis Brandeis clerked for Gray. In a July 12, 1879, letter, Brandeis described his job duties as follows:

> Our mode of working is this. He takes out the record and briefs in any case, we read them over, talk about the points raised, examine the authorities and arguments, then he makes up his mind if he can, marks out the line of argument for his opinion, writes it, and then dictates to me. But I am treated in every respect as a person of co-ordinate position. He asks me what I think of his line of argument and I answer candidly. If I think other reasons better, I give them; if I think his language obscure, I tell him so; if I have any doubts, I express them. And he is very fair in acknowledging a correct suggestion or disabusing one of an erroneous idea.[43]

Francis Lowell provides a similar summary of his job duties as a legal secretary during Gray's tenure on the Massachusetts court. Lowell writes that Gray discussed the pending cases with his secretaries. As with Brandeis, Lowell did not feel constrained in these discussions, describing himself as "ready to argue with a good deal of confidence any legal point whatsoever, and not inclined to drop the argument when he had before him so lively and open-minded a disputant as the chief judge."[44] Again, Lowell provides evidence of Gray's meticulous examination of cases. "As his secretary during his last twenty months in Massachusetts, I observed that he examined literally every case cited in every brief, unless the case cited was already familiar to him."[45] Finally, Gray dictated his opinions to his secretaries, who wrote out his comments in longhand.

In short, while on the Massachusetts court Horace Gray did not utilize his young charges as simple secretaries. The young men performed some secretarial duties, but both Brandeis and Lowell reviewed case files, read the parties' briefs, and discussed the merits of the pending cases with Gray. These were not eager, young law school graduates forcing their views upon a disinterested, single-minded judge; Gray sought his clerks' input and advice. While Gray would maintain this clerkship model when elevated to the U.S. Supreme Court, it would be decades before his fellow justices followed his lead.

The Waite and Fuller Courts, 1874–1910

Understanding how stenographic clerks were hired and utilized in the 1880s and 1890s requires the researcher to draw conclusions from limited and incomplete historical data. Obviously, the eyewitnesses to history—the justices and their clerks—are not available for interviews. Moreover, many Waite and Fuller Court justices did not donate their personal papers to the Library of Congress, major universities, or private organizations.[46] Of the justices who did preserve their personal papers, many donated materials are incomplete or lack any reference to the justices' personal assistants. Judicial biographies of the Waite and Fuller Court justices are also scarce, and the few existing biographies do not contain a substantive discussion about clerks nor depend on former clerks to provide historical data. Finally, the stenographic clerks themselves remained silent. While many modern law clerks do not hesitate to discuss their clerkship experience in law review articles and television interviews, the clerks who served during the Waite and Fuller Courts remain—with a very few exceptions—silent, forever shrouded by the passage of time.

The picture, thankfully, is not completely bleak. The National Archives has incomplete records on the appointment of stenographic clerks in the 1880s and 1890s. These records contain minimal information regarding the hiring and resignation of clerks from the Waite and Fuller eras. Specifically, the records include the stenographic clerk's official appointment form, notification from the clerk of the Supreme Court to the "disbursing clerk" at the Department of Justice and the "first auditor" at the Treasury Department as to the clerk's appointment and resignation dates, and, infrequently, the clerk's resignation letter.

Any conclusions we draw from the records, however, must be cautiously made. For example, a significant number of stenographic clerks from the Waite and Fuller Courts do not have personnel records in the National Archives collections, while only incomplete records exist for other clerks. Thus we cannot conclude that the absence of records signals the nonuse of stenographic clerks.[47]

Not surprisingly, the most complete set of appointment records belongs to Justice Gray. When Gray was appointed to the Supreme Court in 1882, he continued his practice of hiring recent Harvard Law School graduates as his legal secretaries for a single, one-year term on the Court. Neither the National Archives records nor information provided by the Supreme Court Public Information Office include the names of the original legal secretaries hired by Justice Gray. I obtained the names of Gray's first assistants from a silver loving cup that his law clerks presented to him, upon which all the names of his clerks are engraved. Thanks to the loving cup, we now know the name of the very first man to have clerked on the U.S. Supreme Court, Harvard Law School graduate Thomas A. Russell. A complete list of Horace Gray's nineteen clerks is listed in Table 3.1.

As discussed earlier, Gray's work habits, previous use of secretaries, and the Supreme Court's increasing workload are likely explanations for his de-

TABLE 3.1. Legal Secretaries of Associate Justice Horace Gray, 1882–1902

Name	Legal Education	Years of Service
Thomas A. Russell	Harvard Law School	1882–1883
William Schofield	Harvard Law School	1883–1885
Henry Eldridge Warner	Harvard Law School	1885–1886
William H. Dunbar	Harvard Law School	1886–1887
Edward Twisleton Cabot	Harvard Law School	1887–1888
Samuel Williston	Harvard Law School	1888–1889
Blewett Lee	Harvard Law School	1889–1890
Francis Richard Jones	Harvard Law School	1890–1891
Ezra R. Thayer	Harvard Law School	1891–1892
Moses D. Kimball	Harvard Law School	1892–1893
James M. Newell	Harvard Law School	1893–1894
Gordon T. Hughes	Harvard Law School	1894–1895
Jeremiah Smith	Harvard Law School	1895–1896
Charles L. Barlow	Harvard Law School	1896–1897
Robert Romans	Harvard Law School	1897–1898
Roland Gray	Harvard Law School	1898–1899
John Gorham Palfrey	Harvard Law School	1899–1900
Joseph Warren	Harvard Law School	1900–1901
Langdon Parker Marvin	Harvard Law School	1901–1902

cision to hire legal secretaries once he arrived at the Supreme Court. As for his practice of rotating secretaries on a yearly basis, Williston simply remarks that it was Gray's custom to do so.[48]

Determining the professional training of the clerks hired by Gray's fellow justices becomes more difficult. When I first began researching the educational background of the early clerks, I assumed that most were not attorneys—the law clerk list created by the Supreme Court Public Information Office did not provide law school affiliations for many of the individuals listed, which is not surprising given the nonlegal aspects (shorthand and typing) of their job duties.

Ascertaining the clerks' professional training also proved difficult because some clerks attended law school during or after their clerkships while others may have worked as *both* professional stenographers and attorneys. For example, Noble E. Dawson was an Iowa native who worked as a stenographer and private secretary in Washington, D.C., at the end of the nineteenth century. His business card claimed that he was an attorney and "sometimes confidential secretary" to Army commander-in-chief General Nelson Appleton Miles, director of the "World's Columbian Exposition," Associate

Justice Samuel Miller, and "Other Men of Affairs,"[49] and Dawson also ran a stenography business with his son, William.[50]

Dawson was fired from his position in the War Department after publicly criticizing President McKinley's foreign policy in official correspondence with the postmaster general. In a letter of apology to the secretary of the War Department, Dawson claimed that mental anguish stemming from the service of his three sons in the Spanish-American War triggered the outburst. After being fired he commented to the *Washington Post*: "The trouble with me was that I could not bring myself to follow the old Persian proverb which says, 'Should the prince at noonday say it is night, declare that you behold the moon and stars.'"[51] I have not been able to locate any public comments by Justice Miller on his stenographic clerk's misadventure.

Subsequent research, however, has convinced me that many of the early clerks were either lawyers or law students at the time of their clerkship. Based on information found in the 1890 *City of Washington, D.C., Directory*, the *Washington Post*, and early editions of *Martindale's American Law Dictionary*, I believe that the following clerks who have been previously identified as having no law school affiliation were *most likely* law students or practicing attorneys at the time of their employment with the Supreme Court: Brown law clerk Charles F. Wilson (Columbian), Field law clerks George O'Doherty (Georgetown) and Irwin B. Linton (Columbian), Fuller law clerk Thomas H. Fitnam (Georgetown), and Harlan law clerks Blewitt Lee (Harvard), William Lewis (Georgetown), and William Harr (Georgetown). In fact, some early clerks were prominent members of the Washington legal and political community. From 1899 to 1909, Edwin P. Hanna (clerk to Justice Harlan) served as the solicitor general of the U.S. Navy, a job requiring him to argue at least one recorded case before the U.S. Supreme Court. Irwin B. Linton (clerk to Justice Field) appears repeatedly in the "Legal Record" section of the *Washington Post*, sat on the board of directors of the American National Bank, and served as the choir director (and occasional soloist) of the Eckington Presbyterian Church.[52]

While Justice Stephen Field's first clerk (George O'Doherty) was an attorney, his second clerk (George B. Edwards) was listed in the 1890 *City of Washington, D.C., Directory* (hereinafter referred to as the *D.C. Directory*) as a stenographer. Justice Field's clerk during the 1890 term (E. D. York) is listed simply as a secretary. In 1888, Justice Harlan hired his son, John Maynard Harlan, as his first clerk upon the latter's graduation from Columbia Law School.[53] Harlan's second clerk was Benjamin Hanna, who is listed in the 1890 *D.C. Directory* as a private secretary and stenographer to the secretary of war. Justice David J. Brewer's first clerk was H. A. Jetmore, likely the same "Harry Jetmore" listed in the 1890 *D.C. Directory* as a clerk. Brewer appears to have employed Frederick J. Haig throughout the 1890s, identified in the January 13, 1896, edition of the Decatur, Illinois, *Evening Bulletin* as the justice's "private secretary" but in other records as an attorney.[54] Finally, Justice Samuel Miller's clerk during the 1889 term was stenographer Noble E. Dawson.[55]

Chief Justice Melville Fuller appears to have hired attorneys as his assistants, although I cannot determine whether all of his secretaries were attorneys at the time of their clerkships. The aforementioned Thomas H. Fitnam and H. A. Jetmore clerked for Fuller in 1888 and 1898, respectively. In the same year Chief Justice Fuller hired another Harlan son—James S. Harlan—to work briefly in his chambers.

From 1890 to 1906, Clarence Melville York served as Fuller's private secretary.[56] York appears to have enjoyed some prominence in Washington in both political and social circles, and in 1905 the *Washington Post* profiled Benjamin F. Barnes, John W. Crawford, and Clarence M. York—three friends from Vineland, N.J., who came to Washington and quickly obtained posts in the offices of high government officials. Barnes,[57] a graduate of Georgetown Law School, served as assistant secretary to President Theodore Roosevelt, and Crawford was a graduate of National Law School and a secretary to Admiral George Dewey. As for York, a graduate from National Law School and the son of a school principal, he subsequently obtained his position with Chief Justice Fuller through the efforts of Justice Miller. Noting that the three men "are sometimes called 'The Inseparables' in the secretary corps of Washington," the articles painted a picture of three lads whose rise to fame and fortune was celebrated with "deep admiration and wonder" by the "simple folk of the quiet New Jersey hamlet" of Vineland.[58]

Within two years, this story of "hometown boys made good" lay in ruins with the mysterious deaths of York and Crawford. On June 20, 1906, York fell to his death from a second-floor window at the Garfield Hospital in Washington, D.C. Earlier, York had been taken to another hospital and been treated for a head injury after falling out of a street car, perhaps while drinking, but returned home that same day. After awakening and finding that the head wound suffered in the accident was bleeding, York checked into the Garfield Hospital for treatment.[59] Early the next morning, York's nurse discovered that her patient was missing, and the resulting search found York's body twenty feet below his hospital room window. As for how he came to fall out of his window, the *Post* reported: "Dr. Frank Leech thinks that Mr. York woke a few hours after retiring and, after being dazed by new surroundings, walked to the window to look out, and lost his balance."[60]

A year later York's story was cast in a different, more ominous light when the *Washington Post* published a series of articles on the disappearance and suicide of his boyhood friend John W. Crawford.[61] Apparently despondent over financial difficulties, Crawford jumped off the Alexandria ferry *Lackawanna* and drowned in the Potomac River. Initially police believed that Crawford staged a fake suicide, perhaps to collect on insurance money, but six weeks later his body was found on the Maryland shore. As for boyhood friend Clarence York, the *Post* provided a slightly new version of his death: York became "demented, jumped from a second-story window and was killed."[62] Thus the later account of the death of Clarence York becomes more macabre, shifting from an accidental fall to possible insanity and suicide.

I could find no official reaction of Chief Justice Fuller to the death of young York. At least one observant father, however, rushed to fill the vacancy left by York's death. In a June 28, 1906, letter to Fuller, Associate Justice William Rufus Day nominated his son, Stephen Day, for the position. Noting that Stephen had worked as his private secretary for two years, Justice Day wrote that his son was "industrious and reliable" and possessed stenographic skills. "If you can see your way to give him a trial I shall esteem the favor highly and can say for Stephen that he will do his best to meet your approval of the work."[63]

Stephen Day subsequently worked for Fuller during OT 1906. Day had not attended law school when he clerked for the chief justice but had "read the law" for two years. The experience must have been satisfactory, because a 1907 letter from Stephen Day to Chief Justice Fuller announced that the young man would "resist the temptation to return to Washington for a longer period of great pleasure and to enjoy its inestimable advantages" and instead take "the path beset with a young lawyer's trials and tribulations at the Cleveland, Ohio, law firm of Solders, Thayer, Mansfield & Day."[64] Fuller's law clerk in 1907 was Colley W. Bell. I cannot conclude that Bell was an attorney during his clerkship, but by 1914 he was practicing law.[65]

The appointment practices of the other justices varied. Perhaps in keeping with his legendary temper, Justice Stephen Field was hard-pressed to keep a stenographic clerk for longer than one year, and the appointment records indicate erratic appointment and resignation periods. In fact, one clerk—the aforementioned Irwin B. Linton—initially worked for Justice Field from May 28 to June 21, 1889, before signing on for a second tour of duty in November 1891. Linton continued to work for Justice Field until November 11, 1895, at which time he penned the following, terse letter to the justice: "I have just received your letter of the 9th . . . and in view of my inability to render greater services than I have, I hereby tender my resignation as your stenographic clerk." While the Treasury Department was immediately notified of Linton's resignation, fences were apparently mended because Justice Field reappointed Linton as his stenographic clerk on November 15, 1895. The appointment records do not indicate whether Linton survived the remainder of Justice Field's time on the bench, but Linton was at Field's side when the former justice died on April 9, 1899.[66]

Other justices on the Waite and Fuller Courts appointed their steno-graphic clerks to longer terms. Justice Henry Billings Brown's first clerk, Albert B. Hall, served from January of 1891 to 1896, and his successor, Frederick E. Chaplin, remained with the justice for eight years (despite initially describing his position in an October 2, 1896, letter as "temporary").[67] Charles F. Wilson, a graduate of the Virginia Military Institute and the Columbian University Law School, was Brown's final clerk and subsequently worked for Justice William H. Moody.[68] After first employing his son, John Maynard Harlan, as his first stenographic clerk, Justice Harlan hired brothers Benjamin W. Hanna and Edwin P. Hanna as clerks during portions of the 1888 and 1889 Terms. Justice Harlan first adopted a one-year hiring system before settling on a series of three stenographic clerks—Perry Allen, William Harr, and Julius Baldwin—who each served a minimum of three years.

Justice Harlan must have become dependent on the assistance provided by a secretary, because shortly before his retirement Harlan requested that Congress continue to provide a secretary after he left the bench. Noting that these private secretaries become "almost indispensable" during their years of service to the same justice, the *Washington Post* observed that Harlan wanted a private secretary "who would assist him in the preparation of the doubtless interesting story of his experiences in public life."[69] Members of Congress were not impressed with Harlan's plea, responding that such staff support might set an alarming precedent.

When it comes to the job duties of clerks of the Waite and Fuller Courts, the historical record becomes even sparser. With the exception of Horace Gray and Oliver Wendell Holmes, Jr., there is no evidence in the personal papers or biographies of the justices as to how they employed their clerks. Once on the Supreme Court, Gray continued to treat his young assistants as more than mere stenographers. Former Gray law clerk Samuel Williston writes: "The secretary was asked to do the highest work demanded of a member of the legal profession—that is the same work which a judge of the Supreme Court is called upon to perform." After oral argument, Gray would give his young secretary the applicable briefs and legal pleadings and ask him to review the "novelettes" and report back to the justice with his independent thoughts. Gray did not share his own opinion of the case with his secretary, but "[i]t was then the duty of the secretary to study the papers submitted to him and to form such opinion as he could." Since Gray "liked best to do his thinking aloud and to develop his own views by discussion," Gray and his secretary would then sit down prior to the Court's Saturday conference and discuss the pending cases—first Gray would ask his secretary to "state the points of the case as best he could," with Gray closely examining and challenging the secretary's "conclusions."[70] When he made the reports, Williston writes, "the Judge would question me to bring out the essential points, and I rarely learned what he thought of a case until I had been thoroughly cross-examined."[71]

As with his state court assistants, Gray permitted his clerks to offer opinions as well as case recitations. Williston writes that Gray "invited the frankest expression of any fresh idea of his secretary . . . and welcomed any doubt or criticism of his own views."[72] Former Supreme Court law clerk Ezra Thayer echoes Williston's comments about the intellectual give-and-take between Gray and his young charges. Thayer writes that Gray "liked best to do his thinking aloud, and develop his own views by discussion." During these discussions Gray "would patiently and courteously listen to the crudest deliverances of youth fresh from the Law School."[73] In his memoirs, Williston is careful not to give the impression of undue influence. "I do not wish, however, to give the impression that my work served for more than a stimulus for the judge's mind . . . my work served only as a suggestion."[74] Other clerks do not comment on whether their efforts went beyond mere suggestion.

Gray would then adjourn to the Saturday conference.

> When . . . the Judge returned, he would tell the conclusions reached and what cases had been assigned to him for opinions. *Often he would ask his secretary to write opinions in these cases*, and though the ultimate destiny of such opinions was the waste-paper basket, the chance that some suggestion in them might be approved by the master and adopted by him, was sufficient to incite the secretary to his best endeavor.[75]

In short, the secretaries took part in all aspects of the decision-making process. They not only culled the records and briefs in order to distill the relevant facts and legal arguments for Justice Gray, but they also then debated and argued their conclusions and suggested holding with the justice. Once Gray was assigned an opinion, the secretaries often prepared the first draft of an opinion; and while that draft may have landed in the trash can, it provided the secretaries with the critical chance to frame the issues and shape the legal analysis necessary to reach the Court's position. Finally, Gray asked Williston to review the opinions written by the other chambers.[76] Interestingly, neither Gray nor Thayer mention reviewing cert. petitions or preparing cert. memoranda—a duty that has become the bane of the modern law clerk's existence.

Finally, as a brief aside on the role of Horace Gray as the father of the clerkship institution, there is the curious case of Raphael Hayden. While Supreme Court records do not list any staff members for Chief Justice Morrison R. Waite, the July 21, 1904, edition of the *Bluefield Daily Telegraph* reported that a "brilliant young attorney" named Raphael Hayden (his full name was Eldwin Raphael Hayden) died after mysteriously falling out of his office window in Fairmont, West Virginia. The paper reported that Hayden was thirty-five years old when he died, and that he served for several years "as private secretary to Chief Justice Waite, of the United States Supreme Court."

I have found no other Supreme Court records showing any details of Hayden's employment with Waite. No mention of Hayden appears in Waite's personal papers at the Library of Congress, although there are several letters of application to Chief Justice Waite for stenographic positions[77] (Waite replied that no such position existed at the Supreme Court) and a clipping of an undated newspaper article, which notes that the seventy-two-year-old justice "is the only one of the justices who has not availed himself of the act of Congress giving him a private secretary at $1,800 a year." According to the newspaper account, Waite commented that a private secretary would "only be in the way."

The 1890 *D.C. Directory* lists a Raphael Hayden as a local clerk, yet Hayden became a member of the West Virginia bar on June 20, 1893, and worked for Justice George Shiras in 1893 and Justice Joseph P. Bradley in 1898. Thus, at most we can conclude that a Raphael Hayden—who later practiced as a West Virginia lawyer—likely worked for Chief Justice Waite in an unknown capacity for an unspecified period of time in the 1880s. It is unlikely that Hayden would have been an attorney while employed by Waite, since Hayden was approximately eighteen years old during the chief justice's final year on the Supreme Court.[78] Is this enough evidence to suggest that Horace Gray should not claim the undisputed title as father of the federal clerkship institution?

Unfortunately, Williston's detailed summary of his clerkship does not include any discussion of the job duties of the stenographic assistants for the other justices. With the exception of Oliver Wendell Holmes, Jr. (discussed below), the only other Fuller Court justice for whom we have any information regarding the hiring and utilization of a stenographic clerk is the first John Marshall Harlan. The information is found in the family memoirs of former "private secretary" Edgar R. Rombauer, Sr.

After graduating from law school at Washington University, Rombauer took a position with the Chicago law firm of Smith & Pence. Rombauer was seventeen years old at the time, and he could not be admitted to the local bar association until he was twenty-one. In 1889 Justice Harlan's son, John Maynard Harlan, also joined the law firm. It was through John Maynard Harlan that Rombauer learned that Justice Harlan needed a new secretary, and in December 1889 Rombauer moved to Washington, D.C., and accepted the position. He would remain with Justice Harlan until the Spring of 1892.

Rombauer writes that he worked with Justice Harlan at both his residence and at the Capitol, where the Supreme Court was still located. The justice required that his young secretary work extraordinarily long hours. Justice Harlan and Rombauer met each morning from 9:00 A.M. to 11:00 A.M., at which time the justice left for the afternoon Court session. In the wintertime, social events occupied Justice Harlan in the early evening. Yet when the justice returned home from a night of hobnobbing with the Washington elite, he met again with his private secretary. "It was not an infrequent occurrence that we began to work as late as midnight and many times we did not cease working until four or five o'clock in the morning. On these occasions, I seldom went to bed before breakfast."[79]

Rombauer's job duties proved to be a mix of secretarial and legal work. He writes: "My work consisted in part of taking letters for the Judge in shorthand and transcribing them on the typewriter, in part of reading records in cases and stating the facts from them, in part of examining authorities in briefs filed in cases pending before the court, and in doing the odds and ends always attendant upon a position involving close personal [sic] employer and employee."

Rombauer's account of his Harlan clerkship is fascinating because it shows that a justice other than Horace Gray used his young assistant as more than a stenographer. Rombauer undoubtedly reported his factual analysis of the cases to Harlan, and it is not implausible that the justice's decision-making process relied on these reports. Additionally, by "examining authorities in briefs," Rombauer performed legal research to determine the relative strength of the two parties' positions. In short, Rombauer was working as an attorney, not as a dictaphone.

Despite the long hours, Rombauer had time to take in Congressional debates and watch prominent attorneys, including Grover Cleveland and William Jennings Bryan, argue cases before the Supreme Court. Rombauer left his secretarial position in the spring of 1892, having "worked harder than I had ever before worked and harder than I have ever worked since."[80] His account of the strain associated with his clerkship is not an exaggeration; in the fall of 1892 he fell ill, and by the following December his personal physician recommended that the twenty-one-year-old take a six-month convalescence leave.

Thus, we have accounts of Gray's and, to a lesser extent, Harlan's clerkship models. What of the other law clerks from the 1880s and 1890s? Newland writes that the general job responsibilities of the first clerks included stenography, typing, and assisting with nonjudicial tasks (such as paying bills). Newland suggests that the personal duties given to the clerks was the function of the limited number of assistants provided to each justice as well as the fact that, before the construction of the modern Supreme Court building in the 1930s, the stenographic clerks worked in the justices' homes. Newland adds, however: "At the same time these men possessed legal training and were expected to assist with such legal work as their justices might require."[81]

The mystery remains, however, as to what "legal work" the justices required. While Newland concludes that "the duties of most of the clerks today are probably not much different in effect from those of their forerunners,"[82] there is no historical evidence—absent the Gray and Harlan accounts—to substantiate that claim. Conversely, Alexander Bickel writes that these young men "spent most of their time doing the chores of a personal secretary, which ranged from paying bills to reading proof. Others did some legal research for their Justices."[83] While Bickel does not cite any historical sources, his summary of duties makes more sense; if the early stenographic clerks were a mixture of lawyers, law students, and nonlawyers, it would be very unlikely that they had the time, education, or training to assist their justices in the same manner as the modern law clerk.

The existing judicial biographies of members of the Waite and Fuller Courts lack any substantive discussion of stenographic clerks. While Carl Brent Swisher's extensive biography on Justice Field reviews Field's senility during his final years on the bench, Swisher does not discuss any assistance the justice may have received from his staff.[84] In memorial proceedings published after the death of Justice Bradley, the following account of his work style is provided:

> After argument he retired to his library and examined the records and briefs patiently before arriving at a decision. He was accustomed oftentimes to prepare an outline of an opinion which he laid aside temporarily in order to return to it again after an interval, to criticise his own work and to see if he was still satisfied with the conclusion reached and the reasoning on which it was based. It is known to his associates that not infrequently after preparing this written outline, his own criticism thereon induced him to change his conclusions and rewrite a new opinion adverse to his first draft.[85]

Although Bradley employed two stenographic clerks during his last years on the Court, any contribution they made to the above process is not mentioned.

In those few cases in which clerks are mentioned, they play the roles of secretary and nonlegal assistant. Biographer Michael J. Brodhead writes that Justice Brewer dictated his opinions to a secretary and subsequently reviewed the dictation, but he provides no other information.[86] Biographer George Shiras III provides the following account of Justice Brown's work habits:

> Throughout his affliction [becoming blind], he continued to work, his secretary or clerk reading aloud slowly and with many pauses, while Brown memorized the material and gave directions for classifying the various points. After his notes were in shape, which often took days of patient labor, they were read and re-read to him until he could dictate the text of his opinion, fluently and without further reference to the written memoranda.[87]

The only other justice from either the Waite or Fuller Courts whose hiring and employment practices are well documented is Gray's successor, Oliver Wendell Holmes, Jr. The volume of articles and books written about Justice Holmes outstrips any of his fellow justices, and many of these articles are penned by former legal "secretaries."[88] The outpouring of analysis and affection by Holmes' secretaries is likely the product of two sources: Holmes' stature and his longevity as a justice. As former legal secretary and Holmes biographer Francis Biddle remarked: "His secretaries have perhaps done much to keep the Holmes tradition fresh and not inexact."[89]

Holmes' first legal secretary was Charles K. Poe, a graduate of George Washington University Law School. There is some confusion regarding when Poe clerked for Holmes; the Supreme Court records indicate that he started sometime during OT 1902 (Holmes took the bench on December 8, 1902), but the justice's personal papers show that Poe clerked in 1905. In short, I cannot determine whether Holmes hired a legal secretary during his initial years on the Court.

From 1906 to 1915, Harvard Law School professor John Chipman Gray selected a third-year law student to serve upon his graduation as Holmes' legal secretary. Biddle writes that Gray was well suited to the task: "Gray knew the kind of boys Holmes wanted—they must be able to deal with the *certiorari*, balance his checkbook, and listen to his tall talk. And they would have more chance of understanding it, thought Gray, if they also were honor men."[90] After Gray's death, Harvard Law School professor Felix Frankfurter assumed the responsibility of selecting Holmes' legal secretaries.[91] Given the fawning but calculating nature of Frankfurter's relationship with Holmes, one can imagine that it was a responsibility that Frankfurter seized quickly and guarded fiercely.[92] With the exception of Charles Poe, all legal secretaries came from Harvard Law School. Holmes maintained Horace Gray's tradition of rotating his secretaries annually, humorously suggesting that he did so because "he liked to continue to tell his fund of stories; this way, he could do so without being accused of repeating himself."[93]

There still remains some correspondence between Frankfurter and Holmes on the topic of the selection of legal secretaries. In a February 11, 1920, letter to then Professor Frankfurter, Holmes reminds him of the conditional nature of any secretarial position, namely, that the job offer was "subject to my right to die or resign, which I have mentioned since I was 70 but which I intend to do my best to avoid." In a January 6, 1925, letter to Frankfurter, Holmes references another stipulation of the position: the young men selected must be neither married nor engaged. Holmes writes that he would not have taken a previous secretary—Barton Leach—if he had known that Leach was married: "[H]e is a good worker and his wife does not interfere—indeed, is pleasant—but I want a free man, and one who may be a contribution to society."[94] Author John S. Monagan writes that the main reason for the no-marriage rule "was that one of the secretaries had got married before he began his service and . . . 'was a mess because he was moony and lovesick.'"[95]

One could be cynical and conclude that the legal secretaries also served as spies for the always-interested Professor Frankfurter. In a letter written during his 1926 clerkship, secretary Thomas Corcoran confides to Frankfurter that Holmes seems like "such a tired pitiable old man who rubs his eyes as he tries to work over cases after court . . . I almost feel rotten even for hoping that he'll stay with the Court while I'm with him—he's so so tired," and in an October 1, 1928, letter, secretary John E. Lockwood reports that the review of cert. petitions is "tiring" for the elderly Holmes, who "nearly fell asleep while I was giving him an outline of a case."[96] Clearly, the secretaries feel protective of their elderly master—but were they violating their duty of confidentiality by reporting such incidences to a Court outsider?

Augustin Derby worked for Justice Holmes during the 1906 term, and his account of the experience provides a window into the life of a legal secretary during the waning years of the Fuller Court. While Holmes would serve under three additional chief justices, the employment model described by Derby appears to remain fairly constant over time. Derby writes that Holmes worked in a second-floor library located in the back of the Holmes' residence at 1720 I Street in Washington, D.C. Holmes worked standing at his grandfather's desk, surrounded by floor-to-ceiling bookshelves and often smoking a Cuban cigar.[97] Writes former secretary Alger Hiss: "Aesthetically speaking, it was remarkable to see this beautiful man, with his heavy mane of completely snow white hair and handlebar mustache, his ruddy color, standing slightly stooped contemplating the surroundings . . . To see him at his writing desk, facing the garden, the clouds of white smoke as he puffed and worked resembled the halo of a sainted character."[98] The legal secretary's office was located in a room adjoining the library. Derby writes that no door separated justice and secretary, thus permitting Derby to "always see him at work, and respond to any call without the need of a signal or buzzer."[99]

Holmes' secretaries had both legal and nonlegal responsibilities. As Derby observes:

> The secretary read briefs, motion papers, petitions for *certiorari*, and reported on them. Perhaps he thought that he had given legal assistance; but the Justice read all the briefs and papers himself, and wrote his own opinions. He never asked me to find the law. He knew the law, at least as he believed it was or should be. He did direct me to find authorities to support a proposition in an opinion, but never asked me to find out whether the proposition was the law.[100]

Derby is dismissive of any contribution he made as a secretary. He concludes that Justice Holmes "really needed no secretary," adding that the secretaries merely "went through the form of rendering him legal aid." In regards to his minor contribution to legal analysis and decision making, Derby is not suffering from false modesty. Holmes "knew the law," and he did not require a green young attorney to remind him of the Supreme Court precedents that Holmes himself had shaped. At most, Holmes' secretaries assisted the justice by reviewing petitions for writ of certiorari.[101]

Derby's account of his clerkship duties mirrors accounts written by Charles Denby (OT 1925), Thomas Corcoran (OT 1926), Alger Hiss (OT 1929), and Robert Wales (OT 1930).[102] Both Derby and Denby state that Holmes wrote his own opinions in longhand, opinions that were concise and uncluttered with citations.[103] Typewriters were banned from the home by the justice himself.[104] While Derby and Wales recall performing limited legal research (usually finding cites from older Holmes opinions), Denby remarks that "[w]hat research was needed, he [Holmes] did it himself."[105] Neither Derby nor Denby comment upon reviewing drafts of Holmes' opinions, perhaps because the justice "made it a practice of writing his opinions over the week end when his Secretary was generally absent."[106] Wales, however, adds that at least some Holmes secretaries played a very minor role in the drafting process: "When the opinion was done, he liked to read it to his secretary. He was not seeking a critique or learned legal analysis from the young man but rather an indication of any point that seemed unclear. They read the opinion largely for his own consideration and as the final step in its preparation."[107] Denby and Wales write that the bulk of their legal duties entailed reviewing cert. petitions. Writes Denby: "My work . . . consisted mainly of reading applications for certiorari, preparing [written] summaries and recommendations thereon, and occasionally discussing my conclusions with the Justice."[108] Wales similarly reviewed the cert. petitions, although he gave an oral presentation of his review. Wales writes that during these presentations Holmes would take notes and inquire whether the federal circuit courts were "split" on the relevant issue of law. Holmes usually did not ask the clerk for a recommended ruling on the petition.[109] While the historical record is incomplete, Holmes appears to be the first justice to have his assistants review and summarize cert. petitions.

The main duties of a Holmes secretary were nonlegal in nature. "Secretaries, for Holmes, were primarily household staff members and intellectual and social companions."[110] Hiss adds that "the function of the secretary was rather that of a nineteenth-century private secretary in upper-class British life."[111] Some of these responsibilities were tedious. Derby lists his main, nonlegal duties as the following: "The secretary kept his check book, paid his bills, cut his coupons, left necessary calling cards for him . . . [and] ran errands for him not entrusted to his messenger."[112] The more unique dimension of the relationship lay in the role that clerks played as a companion of Holmes.

The most delightful part of my service was my afternoon walks with the Justice. There being in those days no traffic to speak of, it was possible to take leisurely strolls of an hour or so along the streets in the neighborhood . . . These walks were enlivened with Holmes' bantering comments and repartee, his reminiscences from the Civil War service, his years on the Court, his wide reading in all fields, and his experiences on his frequent trips to Europe in early days.[113]

These walks were not always relaxing. Monagan writes that Holmes did more than regale his legal secretaries with stories.

[Holmes] occasionally sought to test their minds and deepen their understanding of philosophy or ethics, history or religion . . . His method of exposition might be to pop a philosophical question at an unsuspecting young man—as he did one day with Donald Hiss: "Sonny, if you were at war and had your rifle raised and brought into your sights an enemy figure and God tapped you on the shoulder and said, 'If you let that man live, he'll be a great doctor some day,' what would you do?" Hiss replied that the question required thought and that he couldn't give a ready answer. "Don't be an idiot, boy," came the prompt response. "He's the enemy and you'd shoot him of course. You're not God, you are merely a soldier fighting a war."[114]

Another legal secretary—Thomas "Tommy the Cork" Corcoran—was assigned the task of reading and subsequently discussing and debating the Old Testament with Holmes.[115] Not all the conversations were so scholarly. Former law clerk Harvey Hollister Bundy states that Holmes "wanted some gaiety and youth around. He wanted his secretary to dine out every night and come back and tell him the latest gossip. That's right, it was one of the ways he had of keeping young."[116]

One change in the legal secretary model occurred late in Holmes' tenure on the Supreme Court. Holmes' wife, Fanny Dixwell Holmes, routinely read aloud to the justice. After her death in 1929, clerk Alger Hiss convinced a reluctant Holmes to permit him to assume her duties, and all subsequent secretaries adopted the practice. Hiss writes: "When he [Holmes] was in his usual high spirits a regular greeting on coming back from the Court was, 'Shall we have some culture,' or, perhaps, 'Will it be murder, or shall we improve our minds?' The reference to 'murder' was in recognition of his frequent indulgence in mystery stories."[117]

After Holmes retired from the Court, Felix Frankfurter kept selecting secretaries for the justice. Of course the secretaries no longer had any legal responsibilities, instead serving as companions and caretakers of the elderly, widowed Holmes. One of the postretirement secretaries was Mark De Wolfe Howe, who kept a diary of the experience. Howe's account is filled with small stories of Holmes in decline, with only the occasional spark of the justice's legendary wit and intellect. For example, Howe writes: "This morning when I was doing certain little duties for Holmes he suddenly said "Aren't you cold." I said I wasn't and why should I be. He replied, "Why, because you are so near to Heaven because of all your virtues.[118]

Howe records that he frequently read to the justice, supplied conversation when called upon, and drove Holmes to Arlington National Cemetery to visit the justice's burial spot. One might assume, in view of Howe's later role as biographer, that the diary would be permeated with a sense of awe. In fact, at various points Howe's writings reflect a mild disdain for his elderly charge. For example, a December 1933 entry reads: "One of Holmes' most pathetic little acts occurs often when I decide for him that he had better not take a drive because of the weather, etc. He will then acquiesce, but usually follows it up by saying that if I want to take [a] drive just go ahead—as if I should like to roll around Washington's environs alone."

Holmes' loyal assistants remained at his side to the end. Former secretaries visited the justice as he lay dying in March of 1935, and it was Howe that announced the justice's death to a waiting press corps. The secretaries, including Francis Biddle (then Chairman of the National Labor Relations Board), George Leslie Harrison (then Governor of the New York Federal Reserve Bank), and Thomas G. Corcoran served as ushers at the March 9, 1935, funeral ceremonies at All Souls Church in Washington, D.C.[119]

The only other Waite or Fuller Court justices for whom we have any information on clerkship hiring and utilization practices is Joseph McKenna, whose Court tenure stretched through the White and Taft Courts as well. Justice McKenna's first clerk, James Cecil Hooe, served from March 1889 until Hooe's death in 1910.[120] No information exists that conclusively demonstrates that Hooe was an attorney, although circumstantial evidence indicates that he graduated from Columbian University Law School.

Justice McKenna's second law clerk, Ashton Embry, was a Georgetown Law School graduate who clerked from 1911 to 1919. Embry had previously served as a stenographer to federal district court judge Edward T. Sanford and to the U.S. solicitor general. Doubtless Embry would have continued to serve in his clerkship position if not for a scandal involving his alleged role in leaking information on Supreme Court decisions.[121] Prosecutors alleged that the leaked information was used by confederates to speculate on the stock market. No convictions resulted from the matter, and Embry went on to open a successful chain of bakeries. Yet author John Owens believes that the scandal forever touched Embry: "Yet, his very successful business and family life apparently could not fill the void left by his resignation from the Court. Soon after Embry passed away in 1965, his son Lloyd, a prominent portrait artist . . . fulfilled one of his father's last requests. 'Carried out under the cover of darkness,' Lloyd scattered his father's ashes on the Court's grounds."[122] Embry's replacement was Robert F. Cogswell, a Harvard Law

School graduate who later worked for Chief Justice William Howard Taft and Associate Justice Harlan Fiske Stone.

The White Court, 1910–1921

In December of 1910, Edward White replaced Melville Fuller as chief justice. A veteran of the Confederate Army, White served on the Louisiana Supreme Court and as a U.S. senator before being appointed to the Supreme Court in 1894. Little information is known as to White's clerkship practices. In his autobiographical notes, Charles Evans Hughes states that White employed both a stenographer and a law clerk. Hughes adds that White himself paid the law clerk's salary.[123] Hughes doesn't define the role of "stenographer" versus "law clerk" in the White chambers. While the Supreme Court list contains the names of five men who worked for White during his chief justiceship—William Cullen Dennis,[124] James T. Ruiggold, Bertram Shipman,[125] Leonard Zeisler, and John J. Byrne—it is possible that some of these men were stenographic clerks authorized by Congress and not the law clerk hired and paid by Chief Justice White.

Charles Evans Hughes writes that he himself utilized stenographic clerks during his tenure as associate justice from 1910 to 1916:

> We had but a small allowance for clerical help; that is, $2000 a year, only enough to provide a secretary. Most of the Justices had secretaries who were lawyers, but these spent the greater part of their time in stenographic work and typewriting correspondence, memoranda and opinions. My secretaries [while Associate Justice I had three, in succession] were fine young men who had been admitted to the bar, *but as I kept them busy with dictation, hating to write in longhand, they had little or no time to devote to research* and whatever was necessary in that line I did myself.[126]

Although Hughes states that he employed three different clerks as associate justice, the Supreme Court records list only one stenographic clerk—Maurice M. Moore—during OT 1912.[127]

Hughes writes that the majority of the justices employed clerks who were lawyers, a statement that is supported by the Supreme Court's records. From 1910 to 1916, four justices—Holmes, Brandeis, Lamar, and Lurton—each hired at least one clerk who attended law school. Associate Justice John H. Clarke hired Detroit College of Law graduate S. Edward Widdifield in 1919. Widdifield was a Court veteran who had already clerked for Justices Peckham and Lamar. Widdifield would subsequently clerk for Justice Sutherland, thus clerking for four different Supreme Court justices over a span of twenty-one years.[128] In 1937 Widdifield contacted Hugo L. Black and offered his services as secretary and law clerk, commenting that "I am a stenographer, typewriter and lawyer—a member of the bar of the above [Supreme] Court—[and] familiar with the duties of the position."[129] While

Widdifield did not add another justice to his résumé, he would later serve for eighteen years as assistant clerk of the Supreme Court as well as mayor of North Beach, Maryland.[130]

Hughes writes that during his tenure as an associate justice, the idea of hiring law clerks in addition to stenographers was discussed. "Occasionally, the question of providing law clerks in addition to secretaries would be raised but nothing was done. Some suggested that if we had experienced law clerks, it might be thought that they were writing our opinions."[131] Hughes failed to acknowledge that two justices—Gray and Holmes—had already moved beyond the stenographic clerk model.

Besides Oliver Wendell Holmes, Jr., and Charles Evans Hughes, Louis Brandeis and James McReynolds are the only other justices who sat on the White Court for whom we have a fair amount of information on clerkship hiring and employment practices. Although Brandeis' assistant was classified as a stenographic clerk, the position required legal, not secretarial, skills. Hence, I will refer to Brandeis' young charges as law clerks. Like Gray and Holmes, Brandeis used his law clerks for legal research and other substantive duties.

As with Justice Holmes, Professor Felix Frankfurter selected Brandeis' clerks. In a December 1, 1916, letter to Frankfurter, Brandeis writes that he is pleased with Frankfurter's selection of Calvert Madgruder as his first law clerk—adding "I have added faith in your picking."[132] By 1920, Brandeis had given Frankfurter carte blanche to select law clerks: "I leave [the selection of a law clerk] wholly to you. Make the choice of the man & I shall obey."[133] Two years later Brandeis again refers to Frankfurter's grant of authority, commenting: "As to next year's secretary, I shall leave your discretion to act untrammeled. Wealth, ancestry, and marriage, of course, create presumptions; but they may be overcome."[134] Brandeis did provide Frankfurter with a few guidelines. In a January 28, 1928, letter to Frankfurter, he writes that "other things being equal, it is always preferable to take some one whom there is reason to believe will become a law teacher."[135]

The earliest account of life as a Brandeis clerk comes from former secretary of state Dean Acheson, a Harvard Law School graduate selected by Frankfurter to clerk for Brandeis. Acheson served for both OT 1919 and 1920, an apparent deviation from Brandeis' habit of rotating law clerks on a yearly basis.[136] Acheson professed some guilt at staying for another year, writing to Frankfurter: "I feel rather selfish taking someone's chance to be with the Justice for a year. It will have to go down on the debit side of my moral transactions to be justified perhaps some time in the future."[137]

Acheson worked at the justice's Stoneleigh Court apartment on Connecticut Avenue.[138] He writes:

> Each Justice was entitled to a set of federal court reports, a messenger, whom he inherited from the Justice whose place he took, and one other employee as desired.

Most of them chose a stenographer-typist. Justices Holmes and Brandeis chose differently . . . [and] supplemented their messengers by a June graduate of the Harvard Law School . . . They believed that these young men, fresh from the intellectual stimulation of the law school, brought them constant refreshment and challenge, perhaps more useful in their work than the usual office aides.[139]

Hence, Acheson writes that in 1919 he and Justice Holmes' law clerk [Stanley Morrison] were "pioneering . . . a wholly new and unique institution," namely, the modern law clerk.[140] While Acheson erroneously assumes that no other justices hired young law school graduates—in the previous decade Justices Lamar, Lurton, and Hughes had all done so—he is correct in asserting that the clerkship institution was being shaped by Justices Holmes and Brandeis.

The role of all Brandeis law clerks was forever defined as the result of a blunder committed by the young Dean Acheson. After discovering that there were two incorrect legal cites in an opinion he was preparing to announce from the bench, Brandeis returned to his home office and sternly announced to Acheson: "Please remember that your function is to correct my errors, not to introduce errors of your own."[141] James Landis,[142] who clerked for Brandeis during OT 1925, received a similar lecture from Brandeis after failing to correct some erroneous legal citations: "Sonny [said Brandeis], we are in this together. You must never assume that I know everything or that I am even correct in what I may say. That is why you are here."[143]

Regarding his substantive duties, Acheson writes:

> In two respects my work with Justice Brandeis was different from the current work of many law clerks with their chiefs. This is sometimes closely concerned with the function of deciding. The Justice wanted no help or suggestions in making up his mind. So I had nothing to do with petitions for certiorari . . . the Justice was inflexible in holding that the duty of decision must be performed by him unaided . . . He was equally emphatic in refusing to permit what many of the Justices today require, a bench memorandum or précis of the case from their law clerks to give them the gist of the matter before the argument. To Justice Brandeis . . . this was a profanation of advocacy. He owed it to counsel—who he always hoped . . . would be advocates also—to present them with a judicial mind unscratched by the scribblings of clerks.[144]

Acheson's two primary job duties were the drafting and preparation of opinions and legal research. Given Justice Brandeis' edict about the proper roles of clerk and justice, one might be surprised that the justice trusted a clerk with the substantial responsibility of preparing the first draft of a judicial opinion. On close reflection, however, there is no inconsistency. Brandeis exercised the "function of deciding" with his conference vote, and opinion writing—under his close supervision—was merely the fleshing out of that decision.

Acheson writes that Brandeis divided up his assigned opinions between himself and his clerk and provided the necessary instructions. Brandeis would start writing his opinion drafts in longhand while Acheson typed. When Brandeis was ready for Acheson to review his draft, they swapped opinions. Brandeis did not want either himself or his clerk to treat the other's work as gospel.

> My instructions regarding his work were to look with suspicion on every state-ment of fact until it was proved from the record of the case, and on every statement of law until I had exhausted the authorities. If additional points should be made, I was to develop them thoroughly. Sometimes my work took the form of a revision of his; sometimes of a memorandum of suggestions to him.[145]

Conversely, Acheson adds that Brandeis might use portions of his clerk's original draft opinion or instead begin anew.[146]

It is apparent that Brandeis considered his clerk a partner (although not an equal one) in a joint task. This partnership extended through the opinion-drafting process. Former law clerk Paul A. Freund writes that both Justice Brandeis and his law clerk received copies of revised opinions from the Supreme Court printing office.[147] In describing the final editing process, Acheson comments: "A touching part of our relationship was the Justice's insistence that nothing should go out unless we were *both* satisfied with the product. His patience and generosity were inexhaustible."[148] Landis felt the same, referring to himself as being in "a junior partnership with the greatest Justice of the Supreme Court."[149] This "partnership" placed tremendous stress on the clerk. "The illusion was carefully fostered that the Justice was relying, indeed depending, on the criticism and collaboration of his law clerk. How could one fail to miss the moral implications of [that] responsibility?"[150]

The other main responsibility for a Brandeis clerk was legal research. Not surprisingly, the inventor of "the Brandeis brief" gave his clerks daunting research assignments. While Justice Brandeis expected his clerks to provide "the most exacting, professional, and imaginative search of the legal authori-ties," Acheson states that successful legal research "was more often than not the beginning, not the end, of our research."[151] Thus Acheson's research time was spent equally in the Supreme Court Library as in the Library of Con-gress, "with civil servants whose only recompense for hours of patient help to me was to see an uncatalogued report of theirs cited in a footnote to a dissenting opinion."[152]

Acheson assures the reader that Brandeis—nicknamed "Isaiah" by subse-quent law clerks due to his "prophetic, if not intimidating aura"[153]—was not an unrelenting, severe taskmaster. Law clerk and justice discussed the current events of the day, and Acheson and his wife were often drafted to help host the weekly teas that Washington society expected Mrs. Brandeis to hold.[154]

Moreover, the daily grind was often interrupted with trips between the Brandeis and Holmes residences. Because Justices Brandeis and Holmes did not like the telephone, Acheson's responsibilities included carrying materials between the two justices' homes. This purely secretarial responsibility gave Acheson the opportunity to know Holmes. "One rarely got away from 1720 I Street [Holmes' residence] without what was then called there 'a chin.'" As with most young men who encountered Oliver Wendell Holmes, Jr., Acheson is extravagant in his description of the "Great Dissenter." Holmes was "possessed of a grandeur and beauty rarely met among men . . . his presence entered a room with him as a pervading force; and left with him, too, like a strong light put out." As for his conversations with Holmes, Acheson writes: "In these he gave the young a sense of great community of interest by his joy, eagerness, and delight in the beauty of life."[155]

Thanks to the personal papers of Louis Brandeis, we get a glimpse of the other side of the Brandeis-Acheson relationship. Although Brandeis requested that Acheson remain his assistant for a second year, Brandeis was not wholly impressed with his young clerk's abilities: in a November 25, 1920, letter to Professor Frankfurter, Brandeis writes:

> Acheson is doing much better work this year, no doubt mainly because of his greater experience; partly, perhaps, because I talked the situation over with him frankly. But for his own sake he ought to get out of this job next fall. I don't know just what his new job ought to be. It should be exacting. If I consulted my own convenience I might be tempted to ask him to stay.[156]

There is no indication in Acheson's memoirs as to "the situation" that was the subject of a discussion between the two men.

Acheson was not the only law clerk to receive sharp comments from the justice. During OT 1928, Professor Frankfurter's vaunted track record of selecting perfect assistants was single-handedly ended by the antics of incoming clerk Irving B. Goldsmith. One week into Goldsmith's clerkship, Brandeis wrote Frankfurter that Goldsmith had arrived hours late to work on two different days, making excuses about being "poisoned by seafood," the hotel failing to provide a requested wake-up call, and fatigue from his first week of the clerkship. Brandeis is unconvinced, writing: "His excuses are barely plausible. I suspect his habits are bad—the victim of drink or worse vices. I have a sense of his being untrustworthy; and something of the sense of uncleanness about him."[157]

While Frankfurter made arrangements for an immediate replacement, Brandeis hesitates—worried that Goldsmith's abrupt firing "would be a severe blow to G. and might impair his future success for an appreciable time." After having a frank discussion with Goldsmith—during which the young man promised "total abstinence from drink" and maintaining a lifestyle that "will give him his maximum working capacity," Goldsmith was permitted to remain in his position.[158] Brandeis, however, never regained confidence in Goldsmith. In an October 13, 1929, letter praising a subsequent clerk as "too good in mind, temper, and aspirations to waste on a New York or other law offices," Brandeis cites Goldsmith as a counterexample: "he lacked the qualities which would have made him desirable in a law school, or in any important public service."[159]

As the justices began assigning their assistants substantive duties, it became more important that the incoming clerks receive some training from their departing counterparts. Brandeis is the earliest justice for whom there is evidence of this training period. In a June 17, 1923, letter to Felix Frankfurter, Brandeis comments that he wants outgoing law clerk William McCurdy to remain in his clerkship position long enough to "show . . . the ropes" to incoming law clerk Samuel H. Mason.[160] Brandeis also had his outgoing clerks prepare written instructions for the new hires—further evidence that guidelines and instructions became more important as the young agents were given substantive duties.[161]

Justice James McReynolds was appointed to the Supreme Court in 1914 by Woodrow Wilson. An unapologetic grouch and anti-Semite, McReynolds' tenure on the bench is recalled less for his judicial opinions than his stormy relations with Justices Brandeis and Benjamin Cardozo. Not surprisingly, McReynolds' dour disposition would affect the lives of his law clerks.

From the beginning, McReynolds hired law students and lawyers as his law clerks. His first law clerk was Leroy E. Reed, who served during OT 1914. The *Washington Post* reports that Reed left his position as "confidential secretary" in the Department of Justice to work for Justice McReynolds, adding that Reed also had served as the private secretary of former attorney general George W. Wickersham.[162] While I have not ascertained where Reed attended law school, he became a member of the District of Columbia Bar in 1913.[163] S. Milton Simpson clerked for Justice McReynolds during OT 1915. A graduate of Georgetown University Law School, Simpson later served in the Department of Justice.[164]

T. Ellis Allison served during OT 1916. A former librarian of the District of Columbia Bar Association and secretary to a U.S. Court of Appeals judge, Allison managed to juggle a clerkship with the difficult and temperamental McReynolds while simultaneously attending Georgetown University Law School. After graduating from law school in 1918, Allison spent his professional career in government service—primarily with the Internal Revenue Service. Another Georgetown University Law School student, Norman B. Frost, also managed to work for McReynolds during OT 1920 while finishing his legal studies.[165]

A fascinating window into the life of the McReynolds law clerks is found in the diary of former clerk John Knox. Knox was a graduate of Northwestern University and Harvard University law schools who, as a teenager, began corresponding with many Supreme Court justices, including Oliver Wendell Holmes, Jr., Willis Van Devanter, and Benjamin Cardozo. After Knox graduated from Northwestern University Law School, "he would write Van Devanter from time to time, notifying him of his academic progress, asking questions for advice on beginning a career, and even seeking views on social questions." It is through Van Devanter that Knox's name was suggested to Justice McReynolds as a candidate for a clerkship.[166]

After an initial interview with Justice Van Devanter, John Knox traveled to Washington, D.C., in June 1936 and interviewed with Justice McReynolds. Interview questions included whether Knox smoked (McReynolds forbid his clerks to smoke), typed, and took dictation.[167] Knox also provided a handwriting sample. Although McReynolds was a rabid (and vocal) opponent of Franklin Delano Roosevelt, Knox writes that neither McReynolds nor Van Devanter asked about his own political ideology. When McReynolds offered Knox the job, it was conditioned upon Knox renting an apartment in McReynolds' building—McReynolds wanted his law clerk to be available at any time his services might be required.[168]

McReynolds explained that Knox's job duties would include reviewing cert. petitions. According to Knox, McReynolds stated:

> There will be hundreds of petitions for certiorari coming in during the summer, and I want you to read each one. Then summarize each petition in one page of typing, single spaced. Give me the facts of each case, the question of law presented, the holding of the lower courts, and your own personal recommendation whether you think the petition should or should not be allowed.[169]

After interviewing with McReynolds, Knox met with Harry Parker, Justice McReynolds' messenger. Knox arranged the meeting upon the advice of the clerk of the Supreme Court, who warned Knox that Parker was McReynolds' "alter ego" and whose advice would help Knox survive his clerkship. Parker provided Knox with some additional, sobering details about the unspoken job requirements:

> You can't smoke or drink, and you can't have no dates with girlfriends during the year. If anybody is going to do any dating, it will be the Justice and nobody else. You will also be fired if the Justice ever calls upon his apartment during the day and finds out you are not there. You cannot eat at the Justice's, and you will have to walk six or seven blocks to a restaurant . . . Remember, the Justice is a bachelor and has a number of prominent lady friends, and don't you get too friendly with any of them. That is, if you want to keep your job.[170]

Throughout his clerkship, Parker and Mary Diggs, McReynolds' cook and

maid, helped Knox navigate around the hidden landmines in the McReynolds household. They warned Knox of the justice's endless quirks and his
hatred of Justices Brandeis and Cardozo, and they taught him the hidden
code phrases that they used to talk about the Justice (code-named "Pussy
willow") and his extracurricular activities while he was in the apartment.[171]

In August of 1936, Knox again traveled to Washington, D.C., to begin
his clerkship. At McReynolds' apartment, he found a room supplied with a
small desk and a typewriter and filled with over 500 cert. petitions. Reviewing cert. petitions would prove to be the largest part of Knox's law clerk duties. During his first week of employment, however, Knox also learned that
he would be acting as both law clerk and secretary since Justice McReynolds had "no use for women secretaries and always prefer[red] my law clerk
to do secretarial work, too."[172] Thus Knox's job duties included answering
the justice's telephone and correspondence, acting as occasional traveling
companion, writing checks for household expenses, answering the endless
number of dining invitations and calling cards received by McReynolds,
maintaining the notebook in which McReynolds recorded the Court's conference votes, taking draft opinions to the Supreme Court printer, and even
supplying McReynolds with the occasional weather forecast.

Except for preparing cert. memoranda, Knox was not given any additional, substantive legal responsibilities. Knox recounts a single occasion when
McReynolds asked him to prepare a draft opinion.[173] Knox threw himself
into the task, recalling that he approached the assignment as "a fire horse
waiting to start running to the nearest conflagration." Despite being warned
by Parker that it was simply a trick that McReynolds played on all of his
clerks to keep them busy and that McReynolds would junk the opinion,
Knox slaved away at four different drafts. When McReynolds returned from a
short trip and was given Knox's draft, he tossed away the opinion while commenting: "We will now start writing the opinion as it should be written!"
Thinking back on that incident, Knox writes: "I experienced a terrible sink-
ing feeling in the pit of my stomach—as if something had just died that I had
once very much believed in." Knox himself was fired shortly before the end
of his clerkship, when he requested time off to study for the bar exam.[174]

As for the remaining justices on the White Court who hired law school
graduates, we have very little information. In 1910 Justice Horace H. Lurton appointed Harvey D. "Harry" Jacob as his stenographic clerk. What is
unusual about the appointment is that Jacob was in his first year of law
school at Georgetown when selected.[175] He served as Justice Lurton's clerk
until the justice's death in July of 1914. The circumstantial evidence is that
Jacob was more than a mere clerical worker—he accompanied the body
of the late justice back to Clarksville, Tennessee, for burial, and he was later
involved in the probate of Justice Lurton's handwritten will.[176]

Both Justices Joseph Rucker Lamar and John H. Clarke employed Detroit Law School graduate S. Edward Widdifield. We don't know how Justice Lamar utilized his law clerk, and there is no mention of his law clerks
in Lamar's personal papers. Clarke biographer Hoyt Landon Warner writes
that Justice Clarke composed a rough draft of his opinions by longhand and
revised the draft by dictating it to his law clerk.[177] Other than taking dictation, Warner does not provide any additional information on Widdifield's
job duties.[178]

Little information can be found regarding Justice Willis Van Devanter's
clerkship practices. Appointed by President William Howard Taft in 1910, Van
Devanter remained on the Supreme Court for twenty-six years. While Van
Devanter enjoyed a lengthy tenure on the Court, he employed only eight assistants. It is simply impossible to determine whether his early hires were even
attorneys, although during Van Devanter's first years on the Court both attorneys and law students were applying for the stenographic clerk position.

Van Devanter's clerk from OT 1910—Richard E. Repath—is likely a
secretary from the justice's days on the U.S. Court of Appeals for the Eighth
Circuit. Repath remained with Justice Van Devanter for only one term, but
upon his return to Wyoming he continued to perform services and favors
for the justice—paying dues owed to a local Masonic lodge, cleaning out the
justice's old Eighth Circuit chambers, and closing bank accounts.[179] In later
years, Justice Van Devanter employed both a law clerk and a stenographer,
and at least one clerk—John T. McHale—held the position of stenographer
for several years before being appointed law clerk in August of 1929. McHale
was elevated to law clerk despite the fact that on April 18, 1929, Justice Van
Devanter received a letter from The Hecht Company, stating that McHale
owed them $78.48 for "wearing apparel." Noting that they could not "in-
duce" Mr. McHale to settle the debt, the letter concluded as follows: "Any
assistance that you call [*sic*] give us that may bring about a settlement of this
obligation will be very much appreciated."[180]

The only summary of the clerkship experience is found in a letter from
former clerk J. Arthur Mattson, who worked for Justice Van Devanter from
1924 to 1929. Penned shortly before he formally resigned as law clerk, Mattson is lavish in his praise of his employer:

> You have been so good to me during the nearly five years I have been in your
> employment, and my association with you has been such a fine thing in my life, that
> I would be ungrateful not to tell you of my deep appreciation. Your uniform kind-
> ness, consideration, and patience is something I shall never forget. You have been at
> once a kind and just employer and a good father to me. Perhaps I can best show my
> appreciation by striving always in the years to come to reflect your kind manner and
> sweet disposition, your noble character and your profound knowledge of law and
> men. They will be treasured memories of mine always.[181]

One wonders, however, if some of the sentiment expressed by Mattson is partially due to the fact that one month earlier he wrote Justice Van Devanter, divulged his plans of moving to New York, and asked for a $200 loan.[182] None of Mattson's correspondence contains details of his job duties with Van Devanter.

In March of 1912, Mahlon Pitney joined the White Court. During his ten years on the bench, Justice Pitney employed two law clerks: Horatio Stonier and William Dike. I have not been able to find any information on Justice Pitney's clerkship practices. Horatio Stonier later worked as an assistant clerk in the Supreme Court clerk's office.[183] Stonier was appointed a deputy clerk in February of 1928.[184] I do not know the educational background of either Horatio Stonier or William Dike.

Conclusion

Any study of the hiring and utilization of stenographic clerks in the late nineteenth and early twentieth centuries must depend on both direct and circumstantial evidence. No witnesses are available to interview, and the historical record—personal accounts, judicial biographies, personal papers—is scant. It is this very lack of information, however, that supports the conclusion that the Waite, Fuller, and White Court justices (with the exception of Gray, Harlan, Holmes, and Brandeis) used their assistants primarily as stenographers. Compare the absence of stenographic clerk data for the majority of the justices with the wealth of data regarding clerks for three justices from the same era—Gray, Holmes, and Brandeis. The fact that these three justices depended on their clerks to perform legal duties required them to select outstanding graduates of top law schools. The strong academic backgrounds of the former clerks, combined with their important job duties and subsequent professional successes, meant that these men would be called upon to tell their stories—whether at funerals, to judicial biographers, or in law review articles; the former stenographers, however, likely lacked both the prominence to be selected as an eyewitness to history as well as the insider's view of the justices' decision-making process.

As the era of the White Court drew to a close, the majority of justices maintained the clerk-as-stenographer model. Simply put, the justices needed stenographers/secretaries to get opinions published and the office work processed. When Congress authorized a position for a second assistant in 1920, the justices had the luxury of selecting an assistant whose time could be devoted to other matters. Now, the institutional resources existed for the justices to hire a true legal assistant.

Associate Justice Horace Gray, the first Supreme Court justice to hire law clerks. Used with permission by Harvard Law School.

A graduate of Detroit College of Law, S. Edward Widdifield holds the distinction of clerking for four different Supreme Court justices. Photograph provided by Nancy Mott.

Oliver Wendell Holmes, Jr., with legal secretary Alger Hiss on September 16, 1930, at Holmes' summer home in Beverly Farms, Mass. Photograph by John Knox. Used with permission by Harvard Law School.

Legal secretary James Rowe, Jr., at work in the secretary's office on the second floor of Justice Oliver Wendell Holmes, Jr.'s Washington, D.C., residence. Photograph, Harris & Ewing.

William T. Coleman, Jr. and Elliot L. Richardson, standing in front of Justice Felix Frankfurter's chambers. Coleman was the first African American law clerk. Photograph by Arthur Seder. Used with permission.

Justice William O. Douglas with secretary Edith Waters and his first law clerk, C. David Ginsburg. Both Waters and Ginsburg previously worked with Douglas at the SEC. Used with permission by C. David Ginsburg.

Lucile Lomen, working in the chambers of William O. Douglas in October 1944. Lomen was the first female law clerk. Copyrighted by Bettman/CORBIS.

The law clerks from October Term 1947. This group includes future Supreme Court justice John Paul Stevens (second row, second from right). Photograph by Arthur Seder. Used with permission.

Justice Felix Frankfurter with October Term 1951 law clerks Vincent McKusick and Abram J. Chayes. McKusick went on to serve as chief justice of the Maine Supreme Court, Chayes as the Felix Frankfurter Professor of Law at Harvard Law School. Photograph by C. Sam Daniels.

Felix Frankfurter's legacy: former Frankfurter law clerks who returned to Harvard Law School as faculty members. *Front row*: James Vorenberg and Abram Chayes. *Back row*: Albert Sacks, John H. Mansfield, Andrew Kaufman, Donald J. Trautman, and Frank A. E. Sander. Used with permission by Harvard Law School.

Byron White, on the steps of the Supreme Court. A law clerk to Chief Justice Fred
Vinson during October Term 1946, White would return to the Court in 1962 as a
Supreme Court justice. Used with permission by AP/Wide World Photos.

Justice Byron White with law clerks Hal Scott, Jonathan Varat, and Pierce O'Donnell. Pick-up basketball games on the "highest court in the land" with Justice White often produced causalities among the law clerk corps. Used with permission by Jonathan Varat.

Justice Robert H. Jackson and chambers staff, October Term 1951. *Back row*: Harry N. Parker (messenger), William H. Rehnquist (law clerk), C. George Niebank, Jr. (law clerk), and Emerson R. Parker (messenger). *Front row*: Justice Jackson and Mrs. Elsie L. Douglas (secretary).

A reunion of Justice Hugo L. Black and his law clerks, held on the justice's 85th birthday. Used with permission by Josephine Black Pesaresi.

Former law clerk John P. Frank, Justice Hugo Black, and Cavett Roberts at the Racket Club, Phoenix, Arizona, 1957. Tennis matches were an important part of a Black clerkship. Used with permission by Elaine Frank.

Justice and Mrs. Goldberg joining former law clerk Alan Dershowitz and family for Yom Kippur, 1967. Used with permission by Alan Dershowitz.

Justice Harry Blackmun and his law clerks in the Supreme Court cafeteria, where they had breakfast every morning of the term. Used with permission by Jerry Colbert.

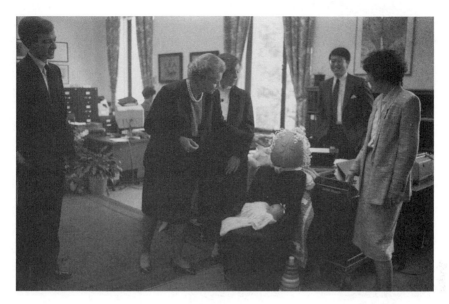

Justice O'Connor and her law clerks. To celebrate the birth of the justice's first grandchild, the law clerks incorporated the chamber's traditional Halloween pumpkin. Law clerks are Marci A. Hamilton, Ivan K. Fong, and Sandra S. Ikuta (left to right). Photograph, Paul Hosefros/New York Times. Used with permission.

Justice Ruth Bader Ginsburg and her law clerks at a 1995 reunion at the Supreme Court. Used with permission by Margo Schlanger.

Justice Clarence Thomas and his law clerks, June 25, 2002. Photograph, David Hume Kennerly/Getty Images. Used with permission by Getty Images

Former Rehnquist law clerks, including chief justice nominee John Roberts, carry the late chief justice's coffin into the Supreme Court. September 6, 2005. Photograph, Kevin Wolf/AP. Used with permission.

CHAPTER 4

The Law Clerk as Legal Assistant

"Another noble exercise and most suitable for a man at
court is the game of tennis which shows off the disposition
of the body, the quickness and litheness of every member,
and all qualities that are brought out by almost every other
exercise."
—Baldassare Castiglione, *The Book of the Courtier*

FROM 1886 TO 1919, Congress authorized each justice to hire one stenographic clerk. While the majority of the justices literally did so—hiring assistants to take dictation and run errands—a few used their young charges as
legal assistants, researchers, and sounding boards. In 1919 Congress authorized
the Supreme Court justices to each hire a law clerk. The new authorization
simply read: "For nine law clerks, one for the Chief Justice and one for each
Associate Justice, at not exceeding $3,600 each, $32,400."[1] Political scientist
Chester A. Newland writes that the congressional act surprised and confused
the Court, and the justices did not know whether Congress had intended to
replace or supplement the stenographic clerk position. "Whatever confusion
may have existed was settled in May 1920 when Congress expressly provided
for one law clerk at $3,600 and one stenographic clerk at $2,000."[2] Other
than the difference in salary, Congress provided no insight on how the two
positions differed in terms of job duties.

Many of the justices did not hire a second assistant but instead recatego-
rized their former stenographic clerks as law clerks so they could receive
the higher salary authorized by Congress. Newland concludes that Chief
Justice White and Associate Justices Brandeis, Clarke, Pitney, Sutherland, and
Sanford never hired a second assistant, while Justices McReynolds and Van
Devanter did not take advantage of the second staff position until the early
1920s. After his appointment in 1921, Chief Justice William Howard Taft
hired both a stenographic clerk—Wendell Mischler—and a law clerk.[3]

From 1886 to 1919, I have hesitantly concluded (due to the sketchy historical record) that all justices—save Gray, Harlan, Holmes, and Brandeis—

used their assistants as secretaries and stenographers. Accordingly, I have labeled that time period "The Law Clerk as Stenographer," as reflected in the title of the previous chapter. With the authorization of a second employment line in 1919, the justices had the resources to hire a second assistant whose energies could be devoted to more substantive job duties. The title of this chapter, "The Law Clerk as Legal Assistant," recognizes that the essential nature of the clerkship began to evolve.

In the modern legal community, a legal assistant (or "paralegal"; the terms are often synonymous) has a different status than an attorney. The American Bar Association (ABA) has defined the phrase "legal assistant" as follows:

> A legal assistant or paralegal is a person, qualified by education, training or experience who is employed or retained by a lawyer, law office, corporation, or governmental agency or other entity and who performs specifically delegated substantive legal work for which a lawyer is responsible.

Specifically, in most states a legal assistant or paralegal can perform legal research, draft pleadings and legal documents, interview witnesses, correspond with clients, conduct investigations, and summarize depositions and other official transcripts—all under the supervision of an attorney.[4] A legal assistant or paralegal *cannot* retain clients, provide legal advice to the public, sign court documents, or appear in court, and the line between the two occupations is typically drawn by state statute.

The ABA definition of legal assistant/paralegal captures the essential nature of the clerkship institution in the 1920s through 1940s. The young men (and one woman) assisting the Supreme Court justices were editing legal opinions, performing cite checks, Shepardizing cases, conducting legal research, and summarizing cert. petitions. With some exceptions, the law clerks were not called upon to provide sophisticated legal analysis—either in meetings with the justices, in bench memoranda, or in opinion drafts—and were not asked to give the type of legal advice that a client might call upon an attorney to provide. These job duties remained limited for the subsequent decades, and it was not until the Warren Court that a revolution occurred— not only in civil liberties but also in the clerkship institution.

The Taft Court, 1921–1930

On July 11, 1921, William Howard Taft assumed the mantle of chief justice. For Taft, the center seat on the Supreme Court provided the capstone to a career that had already seen the Ohio native serve as solicitor general, state and federal court judge, secretary of war, law school professor, and U.S. president. While Taft would demonstrate a facile skill at court administration, his clerkship practices vacillated between the competing models of clerk-as-stenographer and clerk-as–legal assistant.

The main source of information about Chief Justice Taft's use of law clerks comes from his personal papers and public comments as well as an article written by former clerk C. Dickerman Williams, a Yale College and Law School graduate who clerked during OT 1924.[5] Williams writes that Taft originally hired Chief Justice White's former law clerk, whom he implies served White throughout his time as chief justice. Williams does not name him or give his educational background, but the individual in question was John J. Byrne—first listed as clerking for Chief Justice White in OT 1918 and next as clerking for Chief Justice Taft in OT 1921. Upon Chief Justice White's death, Byrne wrote Taft and sought an interview for the position of law clerk. Somewhat immodestly, Byrne commented that "I have acquired a familiarity with the duties of that position [secretary to the chief justice] which I believe you would find of vast service were I permitted the high honor of serving you in a similar capacity."[6] As references, Byrne listed Justices Van Devanter and McKenna as well as the widow of the late chief justice. Byrne clerked for Taft for three years.[7]

Upon Byrne's resignation in favor of a position in the Prohibition Division of the Department of Justice, Williams states that Chief Justice Taft "decided to adopt the practice of Holmes and Brandeis in choosing a successor," to wit, selecting a newly graduated law student as a clerk. In a May 30, 1924, letter from Chief Justice Taft to Yale Law School dean Thomas W. Swan, Taft described the qualities he sought in a clerk: "It isn't exactly mental brilliancy that I need. What I need is plodding, thoroughness, and somewhat meticulous attention to details in the matter of jurisdiction."[8] As for the law clerk's responsibilities, in a May 17, 1924, letter to Dean Swan, Taft stated:

> The work which I would expect him to do would be to prepare for me a succinct statement of the briefs and record in every application for a certiorari, and to prepare, under my direction of course, the *per curiams*, which include nothing but references to authorities upon which the case is disposed of. There will be of course other things I shall need him for in the running down of a list of authorities and the finding of authorities where the briefs are insufficient in this regard. Then I would wish him to correct the proofs of my opinions and to keep track of my docket and keep it up to date.[9]

For his part, Dean Swan was "delighted" to receive Taft's request that Yale Law School provide law clerks to the chief justice. "It has been a fine thing for the Harvard Law School to have one or two of their brilliant men go down to Washington each year to serve under Justice Holmes and Justice Brandeis," Swan wrote. "I feel confident that we can supply you with men who will measure up to the standard of these Harvard graduates." He added this guarantee: "You may rest assured that I shall not recommend anyone on whom I am not willing to stake the reputation of the School."[10]

Dean Swan subsequently forwarded three names to Taft: Douglas Arant, William Dwight Whitney, and C. Dickerman Williams. Regarding Williams, Swan wrote that the young man was a top student, the editor-in-chief of the *Yale Law Journal*, and possessed "a charming personality and is in my judgment absolutely reliable."[11] Although Taft originally considered Arant to be the top candidate,[12] an interview with Arant convinced Taft that the young lawyer—who was working at the Birmingham, Alabama, law firm of Tillman, Bradley & Baldwin—would not be attracted to the lower pay and less glamorous work of a law clerk.[13] Williams was thereafter summoned to Washington, D.C., for an interview.

Williams writes that Taft "did not ask about either my politics or my religion" during his interview, instead talking about his course work and the duties of the new clerk position. Taft told Williams that his responsibilities would be to review the cert. petitions and prepare a summary of the "facts and issues" and assist Taft in legal research—a job description that tracks the one given to Dean Swan.[14] Shortly after the interview, Williams learned that he had been awarded the position.

Williams commenced his clerkship on August 1, 1924. He reported to the Supreme Court's conference room in the U.S. Capitol, secured a typewriter and an electric fan, and dove into the cert. petitions awaiting him.[15] All completed cert. memoranda were subsequently mailed to Chief Justice Taft's summer home in Murray Bay, Canada; Taft himself did not arrive in Washington, D.C., until early September.

The correspondence between Taft and Williams indicates that the new clerk initially struggled with the preparation of the cert. memoranda. Taft advised Williams to not be "too elaborate" in summarizing the cert. petitions,[16] but Williams worried that he had gone too far in the other extreme and been too brief in his analysis. "I have been aiming to present the facts necessary to an adequate comprehension of the issues, without necessarily commenting on the various points made nor giving any pretentious resume of the arguments," he wrote to the chief justice. "Please let me know if I have [been] going too far in my search for bare simplicity."[17] Taft, however, seemed pleased with the work product, responding that he had read Williams' first 35 cert. memoranda and they "seem to me to be all right."[18]

Once the term began, Williams worked in a small office in the attic of Taft's home located on Wyoming Avenue in Washington, D.C. Taft himself worked on the third floor, in a spacious, airy office that had formerly been a sleeping porch.[19] Williams shared the attic space with Wendell Mischler, who served as private secretary to Chief Justice Taft (and thereafter Chief Justice Hughes). At the time of Taft's elevation to the High Court, Mischler had already spent over a decade of service with Taft. He worked at the Department of War as stenographer and private secretary to Taft, at the White House, and at Yale Law School and was described by the *Washington Post* as "one of the ablest and most reliable aids [*sic*] the President has ever had . . . it is because of his rare talents that Mr. Taft requested that Mr. Mischler accompany him to Yale."[20]

When Taft was elevated to the Supreme Court, the press again singled out the former president's personal secretary. The *Sandusky Star Journal* reported that Mischler—"a self-made man, having had no college training, but is considered one of the most efficient secretaries in the country"—would be returning to Washington with Taft.[21] Not to be outdone in the lavish praise of Mischler, the *Wichita Daily Times* chimed in:

> "Misch" [the nickname given to the venerable stenographer by Taft] is forever busy at the typewriter, the Dictaphone, the telephone, or what not, making Mr. Taft's engagements, keeping up with his correspondence, and performing all manners of service. "Misch" is no union man, for he works very often from sunrise until 10 and 11 o'clock at night . . . You could not pry "Misch" away from Taft. They are inseparable. "Misch" loves his job, and he loves Mr. Taft, and they will be faithful until death, for the reason that "Misch" believes in Mr. Taft, and believes also his own job as secretary is the most important job in all the world.[22]

Apparently, "Misch" was also good at press relations. It was Mischler who spent summers with the chief justice at Murray Bay, and it was Mischler, not a law clerk, who assisted Taft on "the work on the law."[23] Hence, it is not surprising that Williams writes that he suspected that Mischler "resented" him.[24] One can imagine how the devoted Mischler felt at the arrival of a young, interfering law school graduate.

Besides working on petitions for certiorari, Williams did legal research—including an "exhaustive" brief on President Andrew Johnson's impeachment—and occasionally reviewed drafts of Taft's opinions. Taft must have requested that Williams provide suggestions and feedback, because Williams recounts one instance in which Taft incorporated some minor changes (suggested by Williams) into a draft opinion.[25] Williams makes no mention of either drafting or redrafting any opinions for the chief justice.

Williams' article is important because it provides the first account of how a chief justice of the Supreme Court utilized his law clerks. Taft's experiment in hiring Yale Law School graduates,[26] however, met an unhappy end. In an October 13, 1929, letter to Felix Frankfurter, Justice Brandeis writes that the chief justice "has abandoned the practice of taking as a law clerk a Yale graduate."[27] Taft's decision is claimed to have been motivated by an unsatisfactory experience with his last law clerk (Yale Law School graduate John E. Parsons) and Taft's poor health, although there is no evidence in the Taft papers to indicate that Parsons was performing inadequately. In a letter dated August 17, 1928, Taft praises Parsons for his "satisfactory" work,[28] and at the end of his clerkship, Parsons wrote Taft that "I shall never forget my year in Washington and do not expect to have as pleasant and interesting a job for a long time. I cannot begin to thank you for the opportunity and your interest."[29] In response, Taft wrote: "It has been a very great pleasure to have you with me in this matter, John. You have done well . . . I shall always look back with pleasure upon our association."[30]

Whatever the reason, the rotating Yale law clerks were replaced with a permanent clerk, Reynolds Robertson, who had previously served as an assistant clerk of the U.S. Supreme Court. Robertson later authored a well-received book on Supreme Court procedural rules. After Taft's death, both Robertson and Mischler worked for Chief Justice Hughes.

The only other new member of the Taft Court for whom we have information regarding clerkship hiring and utilization practices is Harlan Fiske Stone.[31] Stone followed the practice of Holmes, Brandeis, and Taft of selecting a recent law school graduate as a clerk, although he usually turned to Columbia Law School for his young assistants.[32] When Stone took the bench in March 1925, he inherited longtime McKenna law clerk Roger Cogswell, a Harvard Law School graduate. The first law clerk Stone hired was Alfred McCormack, a Columbia Law School graduate who later assisted with the reorganization of the U.S. military intelligence apparatus during the Second World War.[33]

Former law clerk Warner Gardner (OT 1934) explains that Stone "gladly paid the high price . . . of breaking in a new clerk every fall. He seemed genuinely refreshed by a new face and a new outlook."[34] The "new outlook" that Stone sought included the new trends in legal thought bubbling up in the top law schools,[35] and the relationship that developed between the justice and the clerk "served as sort of an extension of [Stone's] teaching career."[36] Another former law clerk, Louis Lusky (OT 1937), adds that Stone rotated clerks because he thought a permanent position was not "a proper career for a young man."[37] In other words, after a year Stone believed that these young graduates should be blazing their own path in the legal community.[38]

Stone relied on various faculty members at Columbia—including dean of the law school Young B. Smith, constitutional law professor Noel T. Dowling,[39] and administrative law professor Walter Gellhorn (himself a former Stone law clerk)[40]—to forward several names of students to him.[41] According to Lusky, there was a peculiar twist to the selection process—the names forwarded to Stone would include the name of the Columbia Law School student with the highest grades. If, however, that student was Jewish, then Columbia would also send Stone the name of the non-Jewish student with the highest grades. Lusky believes that Stone was not anti-Semitic but rather that such practices simply were standard for the time.[42]

As for what Stone sought in a clerk, the justice wanted "a man who loves to work." More broadly, he required the following:

A man to be a good law clerk for me has to be a sort of paragon. . . . He should know more law than I do, be able to read proof and get stuff ready for the printer, which I am unable to do at all with any skill or success. He should also have sufficient command of English to get all the rough spots out of my opinions, to say nothing of supplying numerous other qualities which judges are supposed to possess and seldom do.[43]

As for law clerks' political beliefs, Stone informed Columbia Law School professor Dowling that he did not "object at all to having a man who has some of the so-called progressive ideas about law," assuming that such ideas did not prevent the clerk from possessing the "capacity to be receptive of my own ideas at least to the extent of being open-minded enough to ascertain whether they may possess some merit."[44] In the 1920s legal realism was gaining a foothold on a number of top law school campuses, and perhaps Stone feared that a true disciple of the movement might clash with him.

After the candidates' names were forwarded to Stone, a personal interview took place. Stone interviewed applicant Milton Handler at Columbia Law School in December 1925, and Handler vividly recalls "a gale raging in the room" throughout his interview because Stone had the office windows open to the cold winter winds. Handler writes that Stone had two requirements for the position: good typing skills and (like Holmes) bachelorhood. As for the latter requirement, Stone explained that "the work of a clerk was very exacting and time consuming, and he didn't feel that it would be fair to a young bride to spend a year in Washington, never seeing or having the company of her spouse." Since Handler "was very emphatic that there was no prospect whatsoever of my getting married that year," Stone offered him the position.[45]

Friedman interviewed in New York with Justice Stone and specifically recalled Stone asking two questions during the interview: the state of Friedman's health and whether Friedman typed quickly, which was a requirement for the position.[46] Apparently Stone had modified the "no marriage" clause. Given the passage of time, neither Gardner nor Lusky recalled any details of their interviews with Stone.[47] Boskey, however, is confident that Stone did not ask any questions about his personal political ideology—adding that he never heard of any justice from that era raising such questions.[48]

Of course, a justice who was determined to sniff out a candidate's political ideology had other sources—specifically, the law school professors who advanced the candidate's name. In other words, the fact that most of the law clerks from the 1930s and 1940s do not remember being asked such questions does not mean that their political preferences were not considered in the hiring process. Given the more limited job duties of the law clerks from that era, however, we would not expect that the justice/principal would be

concerned with minimizing law clerk shirking by investing his finite resources to select politically like-minded clerks.

The comments of former law clerks Alfred McCormack (OT 1925),
Milton Handler (OT 1926), Wilbur Friedman (OT 1930), Walter Gellhorn
(OT 1931), and Howard C. Westwood (OT 1933) provide a window into
Associate Justice Stone's employment practices in the 1920s and 1930s. As
was becoming the established practice among Supreme Court justices, the
law clerk's first responsibility was reviewing cert. petitions and preparing
cert. memoranda.[49] "The memorandum was typed on a plain sheet of paper
about six inches by nine inches and rarely did it cover more than that
page."[50] Friedman estimates that during his one-year clerkship he reviewed
and summarized approximately one thousand cert. petitions for the justice.
Subsequent law clerks Warner Gardner (OT 1934), Louis Lusky (OT 1937),
and Bennett Boskey (OT 1941 and 1942) confirm that their job duties included reviewing and summarizing all cert. petitions, so it is reasonable to
assume that Stone maintained this practice throughout his tenure as both
associate and chief justice.[51]

The cert. memoranda included not only a summary of the record but
also the clerk's recommended disposition[52]—a recommendation that Stone
often followed. "On certiorari applications he would, in almost every case,
accept the clerk's précis and share his conclusion. The same certiorari summary would ordinarily serve as his only introduction to a case prior to its
argument."[53] Stone's attitude toward law clerks and the review of cert. petitions is in direct contrast with that of Justice Brandeis, who maintained that
law clerks should play no role in decision making.

The law clerk's role in the opinion-drafting process changed slightly over
the years. Handler writes: "Stone did not welcome having his clerk prepare a
suggested opinion. He believed a Justice should do his own work."[54] After Justice Stone wrote out an opinion draft, the law clerk was summoned and "he
would turn it over to me for revision. That was the clerk's main role in the
process. I would then work on the opinion, chewing it up, tearing it to pieces
and reorganizing it. What I did constituted the second draft. Then the two of
us would sit together, sometimes for days, rewriting and reorganizing."[55]

Handler estimates that between six to eight drafts were required before
a finished opinion was produced. The other law clerks concur in Handler's
description of the care that went into drafting a Stone opinion. Gardner
states that Stone struggled as a writer, and that the law clerk was charged
with improving the text: "A major responsibility, tacitly delegated [to] the
clerk, was to improve the result. I should imagine that most years followed
a typical pattern: in the fall, 'ands' were replaced by periods[;] in the winter,
indisputable defects in sentence structure were corrected; in the spring, the
opinions began to take on some slight flavor of the law clerk's own style."[56]

Where the law clerks' accounts differ, however, is in whether their duties included preparing *any* opinion drafts. Friedman recalled that he worked on a single opinion draft during his clerkship, adding that Associate Justice Stone was always solicitous of clerks' comments regarding all draft opinions. Gardner recalls that he was assigned to do the first draft of three cases—the first two being "dreadfully dull" cases that Justice Stone didn't want to write, and the third case involving a legal issue about which Gardner had a special interest.[57] Lusky claims that he prepared several drafts that Stone used as a starting point and, moreover, takes credit for drafting a version of *Carolene Products* footnote no. 4. During the two terms that Boskey clerked for Stone, he could not recall a single instance in which a clerk prepared an opinion draft. These differing accounts could be attributable to Stone's workload, varying levels of confidence in his law clerks, exaggeration by former clerks, or faulty memories. Nevertheless, it is clear that it was not *standard* practice for Stone law clerks to draft opinions.

Stone law clerks did not draft bench memoranda, at least not during the 1920s. This was not because Stone thought such memoranda would be unhelpful, but because neither justice nor law clerk had access to the materials necessary to produce bench memoranda. In 1925 the Supreme Court justices did not receive briefs or other case materials before oral argument.[58]

Stone, like Gray and Brandeis before him, encouraged open conversation and debate between justice and law clerk. In a January 21, 1947, letter to Stone's former secretary, Walter Gellhorn writes:

Justice Stone . . . made one feel a co-worker—a very junior and subordinate co-worker, to be sure, but nevertheless one whose opinions counted and whose assistance was valued. He never seemed to regard it as an unnecessary expenditure of time to debate the questions or doubts which his clerk might entertain. And he solicited suggestion and comment upon his own work as well as upon the draft opinions of the other members of the Court.[59]

Milton Handler was unique among the Stone law clerks in regards to one dimension of his law clerk duties. In July 1926, Justice and Mrs. Stone began building a home on the corner of Wyoming Avenue and 24th Street in Washington, D.C. The Stones spent an inordinate amount of time personally designing every detail of their home. Stone biographer Alpheus Thomas Mason writes that the architects were given "a complete scale of drawings, including size and arrangement of rooms, location of windows, wardrobes, fireplaces and so on,"[60] and Handler assisted Justice and Mrs. Stone with their research regarding the construction of the new residence. Handler writes that "I was called upon to obtain literally hundreds of books from the Library of Congress on the design of fireplaces, mantle pieces, locks and hardware, paneling, trim and floors, etc."[61]

Once the home was finished, Justice Stone, his law clerk, and his secretary, Gertrude Jenkins, worked in one large wing of the Stone's personal residence. The new surroundings were a dramatic change from the justice's official chambers:

The library, a huge room occupying a wing of two stories, had been especially planned for the Justice's comfort. . . . Bookcases lined the lower walls. Above the level of the first floor, on four sides, were tall windows; favorite prints and portraits of famous jurists occupied the spaces in between. A balcony across the north end of the room over the secretary's office provided space for the law clerk. The Justice sat at a large desk below in full view . . . The Justice's secretary worked in a partitioned section at the north end of the room, and a messenger stood ready to dispatch messages to colleagues, fetch weighty tomes from the Library on the Hill, and rush copy to the printer.[62]

As with Justice Brandeis, Stone required his law clerks to perform extrajudicial duties at his wife's weekly receptions. Gardner comments that he was required to attend these teas and "be agreeable," behavior at which Gardner claims he did not excel.[63] Perhaps Gardner's reservations about Mrs. Stone's teas were triggered by the magnitude of a social faux pas that a young clerk might commit. Gardner jokes that the last thing a lowly law clerk wanted to do at the Stone teas was to unwittingly ask the Secretary of the Treasury "Oh, now what do you do?" Former law clerk Howard C. Westwood viewed the teas with less terror, referring to them as "a pleasant interlude in every week [that Mrs. Stone's] law clerks greatly enjoyed." Westwood agrees that the teas "were heavily attended by a most cosmopolitan group of people," although he wryly adds: "There were the usual number of those who betrayed some evidence of coming to 'worship' at the shrine."[64] When not performing legal duties or serving tea, the law clerks regularly joined Justice Stone on his traditional afternoon walk.[65]

Stone law clerks remained in regular contact with the justice after their clerkships. Stone's first clerk, Alfred McCormack, remarks that Stone monitored his former clerks' careers, wrote them on special occasions, and made time to visit with them when they returned to Washington.[66] Handler writes that the Stones maintained an "open house for all the former law clerks, each of whom was treated as though he was their son."[67] Every five years, Stone would reassemble his former clerks for a black-tie reunion dinner at his home.[68]

There is no evidence that Justice Stone created procedures to minimize law clerk defection (namely, rules to minimize the potential that clerks would pursue their own goals). Given the limited job duties performed by Stone's law clerks, this lack of evidence is not surprising. Additionally, informal mechanisms existed that maximized the probability that the clerk/agent would act in the justice's best interests. Stone employed only one law clerk, who worked with the justice in his private residence. The close quarters combined with the bond created between justice and clerk (all things being equal, it is easier to mentor one law clerk than four) served as informal monitoring devices.

I have been able to collect some limited data on Justice Pierce Butler and his law clerks. Appointed to the Supreme Court in 1922 by President Warren Harding, the Minnesota native received notoriety as one of the "Four Horsemen" who blocked Franklin D. Roosevelt's New Deal initiatives. John Francis Cotter of Catholic University served as Butler's law clerk from 1923 to 1939. I have been unable to locate any additional biographical information on Cotter.

From approximately 1928 to 1937, University of Minnesota Law School graduate William D. Donnelly held the stenographic clerk position. Donnelly, however, assumed many of the responsibilities of a law clerk. In an August 27, 1937, letter to Hugo Black (in which Donnelly applied to be Black's law clerk), Donnelly writes that his job duties in the Butler chambers included:

> [T]he preparation of notes on numerous petitions for certiorari and statements of jurisdiction, as well as on some of the argued cases prior to conferences of the Court. In addition, I have assisted in the writing of opinions in assigned cases in the following respects: Preparation of detailed statements of fact from the records; taking of dictation and transcription; analysis of briefs; research on points not briefed by the parties; preparation of citations; criticism of opinions with regard to content, form, grammar, etc; proofreading.[69]

Assuming that Donnelly was giving an accurate account of his job duties, and further assuming that law clerk Cotter was performing the same duties, Justice Butler was delegating substantially more responsibilities to his staff than most of his peers on the High Court. Donnelly worked in the Department of Justice from 1937 to 1940 before entering private practice in Washington, D.C.[70]

The Hughes Court, 1930–1941

In February of 1930, Charles Evans Hughes—having unsuccessfully run for the White House—returned to the Supreme Court as the chief justice. Hutchinson and Garrow write that by the mid-1930s: "There were thus two staff cultures at the Supreme Court . . . the elite, 'rotating' staffs from Harvard and Columbia, and the career secretaries used by the majority of the justices."[71] By the end of the Hughes Court in 1941, the career secretaries were no more. As the "four horsemen" retired and new justices joined the Court (Hugo Black in 1937, Stanley Reed in 1938, William O. Douglas and Felix Frankfurter in 1939, and Frank Murphy in 1940), they would all adopt variations of the legal assistant model.

When Hughes returned to the Supreme Court in 1930, he modified his use of law clerks. As an associate justice, his stenographic assistants were attorneys who primarily performed nonlegal tasks; as chief justice, Hughes now had two clerks at his disposal, and they were assigned more substantive duties:

> The law clerks of the Justices did the preliminary work in examining records and briefs [regarding cert. petitions and IFP's] and preparing copious memoranda. I had highly competent law clerks. . . . But, while availing myself of their memoranda, I made it a practice to check them by my own examination of the records and briefs and I made my own notes, which were as succinct as possible.[72]

Note that Hughes writes that the clerks for "the justices" (plural) prepared cert. memoranda. As discussed later, law clerks for Cardozo, Black, Reed, and Douglas all state that they reviewed and discussed cert. petitions with their justices. Accordingly, at least by the end of the Hughes Court, the practice of law clerk participation in cert. review had become institutionalized—save for Justice Brandeis.

Hughes' description of how he used his law clerks is confirmed by former clerk Edwin McElwain, a Harvard Law School graduate who clerked for the chief justice in 1938 and later was a partner at the Washington law firm of Covington & Burling. McElwain writes that Hughes required his law clerks to review cert. petitions and prepare memoranda for the upcoming Saturday conferences.[73] McElwain does not discuss the structure of the memorandum, namely, whether it simply included information on the parties and the basis of the appeal or whether it also included legal analysis and a recommended disposition. McElwain states that Hughes reviewed not only the memoranda but also the case records and parties' briefs—in other words, Hughes did not rely solely on his young charges' summary of the case.

After the Saturday conference, McElwain writes that Hughes and his law clerk would meet "to formulate the per curiam decisions and other orders to be handed down on the following Monday." While Hughes' law clerk spent Sunday preparing the first draft of the per curiam orders pursuant to the chief justice's direction, this job responsibility did not involve much discretion or effort by the clerk—McElwain writes that not only did Hughes have "several more or less standard forms of per curiam with standard citations designed to cover particular categories of cases," but also that on Monday Hughes carefully examined the drafted order and verified the accuracy of each case cite.[74]

McElwain discusses Hughes' careful preparation for both oral argument and the Court's Saturday conference, but he does not indicate whether the law clerk assisted Hughes in preparing for either activity. McElwain does write that Hughes met with his clerk after conference to make case assignments, but he doesn't state whether Hughes sought the law clerk's input on such assignments.

As for opinion writing, McElwain recalls that Hughes "approached his own opinions with his usual meticulous care, turning out innumerable drafts in order to be certain of the most correct and precise language."[75] If the law clerk assisted in preparing, polishing, researching, or proofreading the draft opinions, such contributions are not mentioned by McElwain or Hughes biographer Merlo Pusey and is unlikely to have occurred.[76] The only Hughes assistant who played a role in the opinion-writing process was the aforementioned Wendell W. Mischler, who took dictation. Hughes described Mischler as "a man of 'tact and discretion' who gave 'meticulous attention to every detail and never-failing devotion to duty.'"[77] Hughes (like Taft before him) must have considered Mischler to be an invaluable employee, because in 1937 Franklin Roosevelt signed an executive order that exempted Mischler from compulsory retirement.[78] Finally, in addition to the aforementioned law clerks and Mischler, Hughes also employed two stenographers—Albert W. Shupienis and Doris R. Williamson.[79]

The first justice to join the Hughes Court was Owen J. Roberts, an appointee of Herbert Hoover who served on the Supreme Court from 1930 to 1945. My research efforts have uncovered little about Roberts' clerkship practices. Political scientist David O'Brien writes that Roberts employed a husband and wife to work as his permanent law clerk and secretary, but he does not identify them by name. They were likely William R. and Carrie A. Loney; William Loney was a graduate of National University Law School who worked as a lawyer at the Department of Justice for twenty-five years before serving as a law clerk at the Supreme Court from 1928 to 1938.[80] The only other individual listed as clerking for Justice Roberts is Albert J. Schneider, who it appears subsequently worked for over thirty years as a reporter in the U.S. House of Representatives.[81] I have discovered no information on how Justice Roberts selected or used his law clerks.

The second justice to join the Hughes Court was Benjamin Cardozo, the famed New York state court judge. For the remainder of OT 1931, Cardozo employed his New York law clerk, Joseph Paley, as his Supreme Court clerk. When Paley resigned, Cardozo accepted the recommendation of Frankfurter and appointed Harvard Law School graduate Melvin Siegel. The same year Cardozo appointed a second Harvard Law School graduate, Percy Russell, to fill the position of secretary and de facto second law clerk.[82] While Cardozo rotated newly graduated law students on an annual or semiannual basis in the law clerk position,[83] only Russell (1932–1936) and Harvard Law School graduate Christopher Sargent (1936–1938) held the position of secretary/clerk.[84]

The individuals selected for the law clerk position attended one of three law schools: Columbia (Ambrose Doskow), Harvard (Melvin H. Siegel and

Joseph L. Rauh), or Yale (Alan M. Stroock).[85] Not surprisingly, the Harvard Law School clerks were selected by Frankfurter. Cardozo biographer Andrew Kaufman writes that Cardozo rejected Frankfurter's recommendation when it came time to replace Russell, selecting Christopher Sargent rather than Joseph Fanelli for the clerk/secretary position. There is no historical data available regarding any instructions Cardozo provided his screeners on the preferred type of clerk.

Cardozo interviewed the prospective clerks before formally hiring them, although the interview was a formality.[86] Former law clerk Joseph Rauh recalls that his interview lasted between three to five minutes, during which Rauh sweated heavily (from the Washington springtime heat and from nerves) as Cardozo praised Rauh's academic record and told him how lucky he, Cardozo, was to be getting such a fine clerk.[87] Clearly the interview was not used as a screening or selection tool by Justice Cardozo.

Cardozo and his two clerks worked in the justice's apartment on Connecticut Avenue. As for the law clerks' job duties, Kaufman writes:

> Cardozo's closest collaborator in the work of the Court was his law clerk. Since he had had no previous experience with a first-class clerk, he experimented with how to make best use of the able law school graduates who served him. He had the law clerk read and prepare brief memoranda on the facts and issues in all the petitions for certiorari. . . . The secretary-clerk would also work on a few of the petitions. Cardozo sometimes had the law clerk prepare memoranda for him in advance of argument on those difficult cases in which he thought that the law clerk could give some help. Before a case was argued, he read all the briefs himself and then discussed the cases with the clerks.[88]

Reviewing cert. petitions was not a responsibility left solely to the law clerks, however. Doskow states that if Cardozo had a lull in work, he would take some petitions and review them himself. While the clerks prepared bench memoranda, they differ in their accounts as to how often they prepared these materials. Doskow indicates that such memoranda were only occasionally written, but Stroock recalls that the clerks prepared thorough memoranda before oral argument—thus permitting Cardozo to quickly draft a subsequent opinion, if necessary.

Cardozo clerks did not draft opinions.[89] "Cardozo did not take the writing of his law clerks," observes Rauh. "He was just not congenitally able to take somebody else's writing." The former clerks recall that opinion assignments came out on either Saturday evening or Sunday morning, and by the time the clerks arrived to work on Monday morning Cardozo would have almost completed his opinion draft.

> [B]y Monday he had written so much of it that you really wouldn't affect the basic structure of it in any degree at all. You'd be affecting the minor aspects of it. His

relations to his clerk were not that of "How shall I write this opinion" or "Would you stand with this" or "Do you think this is the strong point?" He had it pretty well drafted before his clerk would see it.[90]

The only exception to the rule that law clerks did not prepare opinion drafts came during Cardozo's final illness. Rauh states that in the late fall of 1938, Cardozo was assigned to write the majority opinion in *Smyth v. United States* [302 U.S. 329 (1937)]. Cardozo prepared and circulated his draft opinion but fell ill before receiving a concurring opinion by Stone. Since the concurring opinion exposed a legal point not addressed by Cardozo, Rauh believed that Cardozo's original opinion needed to be amended. Cardozo's doctor put the law clerk in a difficult position—while he would not let the clerk discuss the case with Cardozo, the doctor also argued that the opinion needed to be issued to alleviate Cardozo's anxiety about the pending case. So Rauh drafted a couple of new sentences that addressed Stone's point (mimicking Cardozo's style of writing) and cleared his actions with Chief Justice Hughes. The opinion was subsequently published, containing the additional language neither reviewed nor approved by Cardozo.[91]

While law clerks reviewed drafts and performed legal research (checking citations and adding footnotes), and Cardozo would listen to any differing opinions offered by the clerks, Kaufman concludes that "in the main the law clerk's principal contribution was made before argument."[92] Yet Cardozo was lavish in his praise of the clerks' contributions to the opinion-writing process, commenting on one occasion that "I'd like to put in your name. It's really you who has written it and not I."[93] Former clerk Joseph Rauh recalls that Cardozo heaped "continuous, unbelievable, and incredible, and in a sense, ridiculous praise" on his clerks.[94] "When I found a few serviceable statutory precedents from colonial statutes for the Social Security case, the Justice acted as though I had just discovered nuclear fission."[95]

The secretary/clerk's job duties also included typical secretarial tasks, such as typing[96] and maintaining the case files.[97] Often the secretary/clerk would do typing not only for Justice Cardozo but for the full-time law clerk as well. While the law clerk and clerk/secretary would have different functions, Doskow states that Justice Cardozo was sensitive and treated the two assistants as equals. For example, Cardozo included both Doskow and Russell in lunch invitations.

According to Doskow, the most important and interesting aspect of the clerkship occurred after Court conferences, when Cardozo told his clerks how the votes came out on the different cases. "Like a child reporting to a parent on the day's activities at school, Justice Cardozo felt the need to unburden himself on the goings-on in the conference room." Cardozo's report would include not only the actual votes of the different justices, but also Chief Justice Hughes' summary of the cases and the comments of the other justices.[98]

While Cardozo did socialize with his clerks, Kaufman writes that "he was not on intimate terms with any of them. He was a private man, and the age difference was too great."[99] Cardozo's persistent health problems likely contributed to the distance between the justice and his clerks; Rauh recalls: "My earliest recollection is of watching the Justice take a little silver box from his vest pocket, remove a nitroglycerine tablet from the box and slide it delicately under his tongue." According to Rauh, "the principal thing that the law clerk supplied was ever-available companionship and reverential friendship," while Siegel adds that the clerks were "the intellectual companions that [Cardozo's] colleagues had been in Albany [at the New York Court of Appeals]."[100] The law clerks went to the theater with Cardozo and dined with him, both at his apartment as well as the law clerks' residences.[101] Additionally, the law clerks would bring their friends to meet and talk with Cardozo. Most of Cardozo's former law clerks viewed the justice in almost religious terms—the word "saint" is often used to describe his personality—but Stroock provides a more balanced description, commenting that Cardozo possessed his own unique quirks and vanities and was very vain about his hair style and dress.

The movement toward the modern clerkship model was furthered with the appointment of former solicitor general Stanley Reed to the Supreme Court in 1938 by Franklin Roosevelt. For the remainder of OT 1937, Reed used former Stone law clerk Harold Leventhal.[102] Reed's first full-time law clerk was John T. Sapienza, a Harvard Law School graduate who had previously clerked for Judge Augustus Hand[103] and had been selected by Frankfurter to clerk for Reed. This was the first and only time that Frankfurter assisted in the selection of a Reed clerk.[104] Reed's subsequent clerkship picks were often driven by recommendations by current law clerks, law school professors at Yale and Columbia, and federal judges.

Sapienza traveled to Washington, D.C., to interview with Reed, but the interview was a mere formality. Sapienza recalled that the justice asked him general questions about his prior educational background, his father's occupation, and his home state of New Jersey. Sapienza does not recall any questions about his personal political ideology.[105]

On one occasion, Justice Felix Frankfurter played a curious role in the selection of a Reed law clerk. While at Stanford Law School, Roderick Hills was selected to be a Douglas clerk. Since several Covington & Burling partners (Hills' future employers) believed that a clerkship with William O. Douglas would be a "joyless" experience, they encouraged Hills to pursue a position with Reed. Although surprised when contacted by Hills, Justice Reed interviewed him. The interview was interrupted by the arrival of one of Justice Frankfurter's law clerks, announcing that Justice Frankfurter was waiting for his chance to interview Hills. The interruption was a trick, per-petrated by Justice Frankfurter and Donald Hiss (a former Holmes law clerk and the hiring partner at Covington & Burling) and designed to convince Justice Reed that the young Hills was a hot commodity. Justice Reed there-after extended an employment offer. As for Justice Douglas, Hills observes: "I am sure that Justice Douglas could not have cared less. He probably did not even know that I had turned down the opportunity."[106]

Sapienza reviewed and summarized all cert. petitions in a one-page memorandum containing relevant facts, issues of law, and a recommenda-tion on whether to grant or deny certiorari. He subsequently discussed the memorandum with the justice. Sapienza did not draft bench memoranda for Justice Reed; instead, justice and law clerk reviewed the briefs and then chatted about the main issues of the case and the questions to ask during oral argument. Nor did Sapienza draft opinions. Instead, he edited, checked cites, and did any necessary legal research on drafts dictated by Justice Reed. The justice, however, "wanted all the thoughts and suggestions that I could give him" regarding the drafted opinion.[107] Thus Justice Reed adopted the newly emerging clerkship model—the law clerk prepared cert. memoranda, discussed pending cases before oral argument (but did not prepare bench memoranda), did legal research, and edited (but did not prepare) opinions.

Unlike prior generations of clerks, Sapienza worked in the new Supreme Court building. He had his own office in one corner of the three-room chambers with a desk and typewriter. Because the justices and their law clerks were beginning to slowly move into the Supreme Court, new op-portunities arose for social interaction (and more opportunities for law clerk defections). Sapienza and his roommate, Frankfurter law clerk Adrian S. Fischer, drove Frankfurter to the Court every morning. These drives, recall Sapienza, allowed Frankfurter the opportunity to "lobby" the law clerks. Additionally, Sapienza had the opportunity to debate pending cases when Justice Stone visited the chambers.

Although Justice Reed remained on the Court for two decades, his clerk-ship model did not drastically change. Thanks to the Stanley Forman Reed Oral History Project at the University of Kentucky, a wealth of informa-tion exists regarding Justice Reed and his clerks. In the 1980s approximately fifteen former Reed law clerks spoke with University of Kentucky inter-viewers about a wide range of topics involving their clerkships.[108] As with Sapienza, subsequent law clerks reviewed cert. petitions and prepared short, one-page memoranda that summarized the cases and provided recommen-dations on how the justice should vote.[109] Former Reed clerk Julian Burke suggests that Reed took a different approach to the cert. memoranda:

> Reed was not as interested in full-blown, thorough analyses of cert. petitions as some of the other justices were. . . . in effect, what he wanted you to do on cert. peti-

tions was . . . in as few words as possible tell him what the issues were and tell him . . . what the large issue or issues were, and what the main arguments were on both sides. . . . *He was more interested in learning how important the matter was than whether or not it had been decided correctly below.*[110]

Burke adds that Reed's approach to the cert. process resulted in the law clerks generating memoranda that "almost uniformly were significantly less long than almost any other clerk cert. petitions," thus permitting Reed to quickly review the memorandum as well as the cert. petition itself and spend more time on opinion writing.

Subsequent Reed law clerks, however, differ on the clerk's role in the opinion-writing process. Bayless Manning (OT 1949) first states that "Stanley Reed wrote his own opinions. It was just that simple." He then concedes that "once in a while" a law clerk "might write a draft of a part of something . . . and turn it in and he [Reed] would stitch it in somewhere in his own opinion if he thought he'd generally agree with it." Former Reed law clerk F. Aley Allan (OT 1946) recalled only a single instance when he prepared a draft opinion, and former Reed clerk Roderick Hills (OT 1955) commented that typically law clerks "were lucky to get a paragraph" of their own text into a Reed opinion.[111]

Former clerk Julian Burke (OT 1955) recalls a more nuanced role played by the clerks in the opinion-writing process. While observing that Reed "never wanted to be known as a justice whose opinions were written by his law clerks," Burke quickly adds: "That's not to say his law clerks didn't write some parts of each of his opinions." When Reed did rely on the clerks to draft sections of an opinion, he "would change some words to make it feel more like him to him."[112]

Other Reed clerks stated that they routinely prepared the first drafts of some—but not all—opinions.[113] Former clerk Von Mehren (OT 1947) commented:

> Another function we had was when the justice was assigned an opinion by the chief justice, he would ordinarily ask either John or myself to write a first draft of that opinion . . . [Justice Reed] felt this was very helpful because it allowed him to get . . . a structure of an opinion and get the ideas of somebody else as to what the issues were and how the issues should be considered and dealt with. He then, generally speaking, would . . . reorganize, rewrite, restructure . . . the opinion. There was . . . one case in which . . . I wrote an opinion for him. It was a very important case, but he . . . accepted it with, I think, very few changes at all.[114]

Von Mehren added that Reed occasionally had his law clerks draft dissenting opinions, too. Von Mehren recounted an occasion when he drafted a dissent that referred to an art metaphor, only to have Reed remove it to prevent an inquiry from Frankfurter as to which of Reed's law clerks wrote the dissent. Former Reed clerk William D. Rogers writes "I believe we first-drafted all the opinions assigned to Reed and, though not so uniformly, his dissents and concurrences."[115] Von Mehren was not the only law clerk to have his opinion draft be accepted without substantial changes. Barbash (OT 1949) states that Reed "hated" to discard his law clerks' drafts, and Zimmerman states that "there were occasions when we felt we made a dent, made an influence, wrote a first draft which he pretty much adopted."[116]

Why the variation in the Reed clerks' regarding opinion writing? In approximately 1947, the associate justices started hiring two law clerks as well as a secretary.[117] Perhaps with the staff increase, Justice Reed felt comfortable delegating more of the opinion writing duties to his clerks. Alternatively, the amount of writing assigned to a law clerk may have been a function of Justice Reed's confidence in the clerk or even of his age and health. More pragmatically, the variation may be due to some former clerks being unduly modest or self-congratulatory.

Finally, Reed occasionally asked his law clerks to prepare bench memoranda and perform legal research. For Reed, the bench memoranda were a "fact sheet-reference tool" for the justice during oral argument. They would include questions to ask and citations to the parties' briefs.[118] As for legal research, "it was a shared task. [Reed] loved to pore through the statues [*sic*] books and the cases himself, and he expected his law clerks to do the same thing."[119]

According to former Reed law clerks, the justice also used his law clerks as sounding boards. Von Mehren commented that Reed had difficulty deciding cases, and would "like to talk at considerable length" with his law clerks regarding "the problems and the approach he was taking to it."[120] Reed encouraged his law clerks to be frank and open in these discussions and not simply parrot back the justice's own position. Former law clerk Joseph Barbash recounts an instance when Reed decided not to extend a clerkship offer to a bright applicant because, according to Reed, the young man "kept agreeing with me" during the interview. Reed, concluded Barbash, "didn't want a 'yes man.'"[121]

Reed was not the only justice who used the Reed clerks as sounding boards. Several of the former Reed law clerks recall that Justice Frankfurter would also talk with them, trying to find any means of influencing the justice. Hills comments that Frankfurter was "quite fond of using Justice Reed's law clerks as an avenue to the justice's opinions," adding that "Frankfurter was quite likely to walk into our chambers . . . and discuss issues with us that he never talked to the justice about."[122]

Edwin Zimmerman commented that "Frankfurter felt that Stanley Reed was an apt pupil, and Frankfurter . . . was forever trying to seduce Reed's law clerks in the expectation that they would help seduce Stanley Reed."[123] The practice of the justices lobbying the law clerks of other justices ended in the 1960s. As justices asserted tighter control over their law clerks, such interactions were considered inappropriate.

Like many modern justices, Reed held annual reunion dinners with his former law clerks. Typically they would be held on a Saturday night at the Army-Navy Club in Washington, D.C., with Reed's "senior" law clerk, Harold Leventhal, serving as the master of ceremonies.[124] A brunch the following morning was hosted by the Reeds at their Mayflower Hotel apartment.[125] Looking back on the reunions, former Reed law clerk David Schwartz commented that "it became clearer and clearer that he thought the world of his law clerks." The reunions were well attended, and Reed's law clerks shared a universal affection for the justice. While they did not have the type of close, personal relationship enjoyed by the Frankfurter or Black clerks, it is clear that Reed's former clerks looked back on their clerkships with gratitude. Writes former law clerk Roderick Hills: "Justice Reed's fondness for his clerks was enormous. We had annual reunions for several years after he retired and for each year that he sat. For many years clerks contributed to a book fund at the University of Kentucky and near the end of his life we commissioned a grand plaque with his likeness, which hangs in the Law School of the University."[126]

Many clerks secretly referred to Reed as "Uncle Stanley," and Bayless Manning described Reed as "the single most serene, courtly, gracious, old-school gentleman I had ever met before that or I have met since then."

In sum, Stanley Reed's own model of the clerkship institution was a combination of the older and newer clerkship models. At least one Court insider would have preferred Reed to have leaned more heavily on his clerks. In explaining how Reed used his clerks in comparison to the other justices, former law clerk F. Aley Allan recalled a quote from Felix Frankfurter: "The trouble with Stanley is that he doesn't let his law clerks do enough of the work. The trouble with [Justice Frank] Murphy is that he lets his law clerk do too much."

Four other justices joined the Supreme Court toward the last years of Chief Justice Hughes' tenure—Hugo Black, Felix Frankfurter, William O. Douglas, and Frank Murphy. Douglas enjoyed the longest tenure of the four new justices, serving as an associate justice for an astonishing thirty-six years, while Black followed close behind with thirty-four years on the bench. Frankfurter remained on the Supreme Court through the first decade of the Warren Court, while Frank Murphy served less than a decade as a Supreme Court justice.

No longer selecting law clerks for other justices, Frankfurter relied on his own set of Harvard Law School professors to choose clerks—primarily Henry M. Hart, Jr. (himself a former Brandeis law clerk) and, in later years, Albert

M. Sacks.[127] Former law clerk Andrew Kaufman (OT 1955 and 1956) writes that Frankfurter gave the professors "carte blanche" to select law clerks,[128] an assessment echoed in Frankfurter's letters to Henry M. Hart, Jr. Frankfurter did not interview candidates, joking that he had "resolved to take law clerks, unlike houses, sight unseen."[129] Frankfurter, however, did provide the selectors with some minimal instructions. In a December 27, 1946, letter to Professor Henry Hart, Frankfurter writes: "I now write merely to suggest that if you could manage to 'channel'—I think it is a loathsome word—people like Bill Bundy and [Elliot] Richardson . . . to Calvert and one of the Hands, so that they could have had the experience of work in the Circuits before they come down here, it would greatly enhance their usefulness to me."[130]

Frankfurter professed no preference for a law clerk's ethnic or religious background.[131] Frankfurter hired the first African American law clerk— William T. Coleman, Jr. In a December 18, 1947, letter to Harvard Law School professor Paul Freund, Frankfurter discusses his feelings about hiring a minority. "I don't have to tell you that I don't care what color a man has, any more than I care what religion he professes or doesn't."[132]

This is not to say that the significance of Coleman's hiring escaped notice. In a March 29, 1948, letter from Harry Mansfield to Justice Frankfurter, the former clerk applauds the hiring decision. "He is a first rate choice in every respect. His mind is brilliant and with brilliance he combined judgment. . . . In addition, it is gratifying to me that you can be the first to give someone like Bill his opportunity without relaxing in any measure the standards ordinarily applied."[133] Persons outside the Frankfurter family also wrote to praise the choice. The Frankfurter files contain congratulatory letters from the General Alliance of Unitarian and Other Liberal Christian Women, the Race Relations Committee of the American Friends Service Committee, the Christian Friends for Racial Equality, and at least one member of Congress. If Frankfurter received letters condemning his selection, they are not found in his personal papers.

By the 1940s, the law was no longer a jealous mistress who forced her young charges to forgo marriage before entry into the Marble Palace. In short, the institutional norm that clerks be bachelors had been abandoned. Katharine Graham writes that her late husband, Philip Graham, however, did discuss his marriage plans with Justice Frankfurter. "[H]e drove the justice home from the Court one night and told him of our decision to be married and even asked his permission, for there had been an unwritten rule that the law clerks remain single, so as to be at the complete service of the justice, day or night. By this time that tradition had broken down, but Phil still felt the need to ask."[134]

Curiously, Frankfurter did not require his law clerks to have served as the editor-in chief of a law review—a de facto requirement when Professor

Frankfurter was selecting clerks for others. Kaufman points out that Frankfurter's clerks typically were not former presidents of the *Harvard Law Review*. Frankfurter did not formally interview clerks prior to hiring them, and
there was no mandatory meeting with Frankfurter prior to the start of the
clerkship—although many clerks had already met the justice through Harvard Law School classmates or during *Harvard Law Review* dinners.

Upon his arrival at the Supreme Court, Frankfurter asked former Cardozo law clerk Joseph L. Rauh, Jr., to serve as his clerk for the remainder
of OT 1938. For OT 1939, Frankfurter hired his former protégé at Harvard
Law School, student Edward F. Prichard, Jr. Prichard was a brilliant, larger-
than-life Kentuckian whose subsequent political career would be destroyed
by a ballot-box stuffing scandal.[135] Prichard, in turn, would be succeeded by
the aforementioned Philip Graham, a close friend of Prichard's at Harvard
Law School.

Frankfurter himself described the relationship between justice and law
clerk as a partnership:

> They are, as it were, my junior partners—junior only in years. In the realm of the
> mind there is no hierarchy. I take them fully into my confidence so that the relation
> is free and easy. However, I am, they will tell you, a very exacting task-master; no
> nonsense, intellectually speaking, is tolerated, no short-cuts, no deference to posi-
> tion is permitted, no yes-sing, however much some of them in the beginning be
> awed.[136]

In fact, the relationship between Frankfurter and his law clerks was the intellectual equivalent of a rugby match between teams of unequal ability.[137]
Former Frankfurter law clerk Alexander Bickel describes debates during
which Frankfurter "gave it to you with both barrels . . . there were no holds
barred."[138] These exchanges extended beyond Frankfurter's chambers to
social engagements and the justice's daily car rides with his clerks.

> He often tested his clerks' intellectual mettle by goading them into long argu-
> ments over legal history, current events, constitutional doctrine, and music: Name
> ten milestones in Anglo-American law and defend your choices. Who was Home
> Secretary in the Atlee government? Who was the greater composer, Bartok or
> Bruch? To win these debates, he did not hesitate to intimidate his young opponents
> by invoking his seniority or his intimate knowledge of the persons and events un-
> der discussion. Sometimes sensing defeat, he would bolt from the office in disgust,
> leaving a shaken law clerk behind. But by next morning, within earshot of the same
> clerk he would tell his secretary: "Wasn't that a terrific argument last night? Wasn't
> Al just great? Did you hear what he said to me?"[139]

His law clerks returned Frankfurter's honesty and tenacity in kind.
Frankfurter biographer Baker recounts an occasion when the justice asked
his clerks to select the worst opinion issued by the Supreme Court during

its prior term. Then current law clerk Andrew Kaufman selected one of Frankfurter's opinions, resulting in an argument between the two men.[140] Baker quotes another Frankfurter clerk as commenting that "[w]e regarded it as part of our job when we disagreed with him,"[141] and former law clerk Harry Wellington (OT 1955) recalls that, while driving Frankfurter home, a heated debate ended when the justice ordered Wellington to stop the car, exited, and caught a taxicab. Wellington drove home, believing that he would be fired, and returned to work the next day to find that Frankfurter had drafted an opinion that contained the very changes the young man advocated. "That was the nature of the relationship," concluded Wellington, "one argued about everything."[142]

The candor between justice and law clerk, however, was always tempered with awareness of status and position. "You were careful," observes Kaufman, "but you were encouraged to speak up." The exchanges were "entirely professional and intellectual" but could also be rather loud. "The shouts of the Justice and his law clerks could often be heard through closed doors in the hallways of the Supreme Court."[143]

In carrying out their duties, the Frankfurter law clerks followed a set of chamber rules that evolved over time. Originally, one of Justice Frankfurter's law clerks took a few yellow pages of notebook paper and typed out some basic instructions regarding how the justice ran his chambers. In subsequent terms, the new clerks reviewed the sheets and amended the notes to reflect changes in the justice's rules.[144] In essence, each new set of Frankfurter law clerks drew upon the collective wisdom of past law clerks as they carried out their assignments.[145] These notes are the equivalent of a time capsule, with the original typed comments crossed out, amended, and fleshed out by subsequent groups of Frankfurter clerks.

Since Frankfurter—like Brandeis—believed that his most important responsibility was monitoring the activities of the lower courts and deciding which cases to hear, Frankfurter normally did not have his law clerks review cert. petitions.[146] Kaufman estimates that he reviewed no more than a half dozen cert. petitions in the two terms of his clerkship, explaining that Frankfurter regarded such assignments as an "inefficient use of his law clerks' time." Occasionally, Frankfurter had his law clerks write bench memos in cases that interested him. When asked to quantify the number of bench memoranda he drafted, Kaufman replied "I wouldn't say it was a steady diet."[147] Other former law clerks do not mention bench memoranda as part of their job duties.[148]

Before I discovered the Frankfurter chamber notes, I concluded that the main responsibilities of his clerks were legal research (such projects included reading all the Supreme Court opinions of Justices Holmes, Brandeis, and Cardozo regarding their views on methods of statutory interpretation, or studying the origins of the word "sacrilegious") and editing Frankfurter's opinion drafts.[149] Based on my interviews and research, I initially felt that, while law clerks may have assisted the justice in drafting *portions* of an opinion, Frankfurter usually wrote the first draft himself; any original writing would involve the clerks "filling in" incomplete sections of drafts rather than writing an entire first draft.[150]

The in-chamber rules discovered in the Frankfurter papers, however, paint a different picture. They state, in relevant part:

> Normally, one of you will write a memorandum on each case assigned to the Justice, as well as on many of his concurrences and dissents. A memorandum is a memorandum is a memorandum. Usually, it should be in the form of an opinion, and in the form in which you would be willing to see it go down. Sometimes, a more discursive and perhaps introspective essay is in order . . . Most frequently, however, when the Justice writes, he will dictate with your memorandum in hand. You may recognize much of yourself in the final, or nothing. Don't let either get you down. . . . As to both substance and style, feel free to suggest and to argue; on the other hand, remember that it is the Justice who is responsible for the opinion and everything in it (except with your fellow law clerks) and use your discretion as to when you've done all you could to make him see the light.[151]

There is no indication in the notes themselves that this system was ever modified in subsequent Court terms, although former law clerk Andrew Kaufman points out that the notes did not represent inflexible rules.[152] If the notes are accurate, they provide new and startling evidence of the larger role that Frankfurter clerks played in opinion drafting; such law clerk responsibilities are not unusual on the modern Supreme Court, but they counter the typical account of the Frankfurter clerkship.

Finally, Frankfurter's preference for law clerk candor extended to the opinion-writing process. In a 1949 note to law clerks Fred N. Fishman and Albert M. Sacks, Frankfurter states: "When I ask you lads to read a draft of mine, I expect you to read it critically—i.e., to deal with substance and style unmercifully and put your questions and objections to me."[153] Overall, the Frankfurter law clerks had great latitude to help Justice Frankfurter "see the light."

Justice Frankfurter did not have any formal, written rules regarding law clerk confidentiality, but his law clerks were aware of the duty owed to their justice.[154] Comments former clerk Kaufman: "The day I got there it was crystal clear to me that this was a confidential relationship." Lest the clerks forget this duty, in later terms Frankfurter circulated a December 1955 memorandum written by former Brandeis law clerk William Graham Claytor, Jr.[155] In part, Claytor bemoaned what he viewed as "the diminishing strength of one of the oldest and most basic traditions of the office of law clerk . . . the tradition that gossip about or any discussion of the Court's work with outsiders is absolutely not to be tolerated." Characterizing the duty of confidentiality as a "moral obligation" rather than a rule of employment, Claytor hypothesized that this duty once drew its strength from "the particular working conditions which existed when many of the Justices had their Chambers and their residences in different parts of the City, and when the relatively few law clerks as a group seldom met except on an occasional opinion day." Claytor rejected the idea that a formal code of law clerk conduct was the solution, a protection in fact implemented by the Rehnquist Court. Instead, Claytor called for "a revival of a more intense feeling of individual responsibility in the law clerk himself."[156]

Claytor's comments contain fascinating insights as to the unintended consequences flowing from the evolution of the clerkship institution. Claytor argued that the combination of the placement of law clerks within the relatively new Supreme Court building, together with the increased number of clerks, had weakened the bonds between clerk and justice and the attendant duty owed by the clerk to his or her employer. Moreover, Claytor further asserted that the increase in law clerks per chambers had reduced a law clerk's accountability or ownership in the work product. "It is hard to see how the same feeling of personal responsibility for a recommendation [to a justice] can exist when it is made after extensive discussion and exchange of views with eight or nine others who have been working on the same problem."[157] If Claytor is correct, then we should find (and we do) a further decline in the duty of confidentiality as well as a sense of accountability for memoranda and opinion drafts as the clerkship institution swells to four law clerks per chambers.

The most unique aspect of a Frankfurter clerkship: it was a lifetime appointment.[158] Former law clerk Andrew Kaufman observes:

[Frankfurter] was loyal to his friends. Once he admitted you to that circle—and the circle was very large—you were his friend for life. There was one group that was admitted en masse: his law clerks. Frankfurter treated us like colleagues; he was interested in our lives; he included our families in his interest; and he kept his clerks as his friends and as his colleagues forever. It is hard not to reciprocate the affection of someone who cares passionately for you.[159]

Kaufman adds that the law clerks uniformly returned this affection, although the affection was tempered with "a current of tolerant criticism about his personal foibles and professional missteps."[160]

As with most Frankfurter law clerks, Kaufman or his co-clerk would arrive at the Frankfurter's Georgetown residence and discuss the morning news as the justice ate his breakfast. "Justice Frankfurter expected us to have read the morning newspaper," remarks Kaufman, and law clerk and justice would have an "animated conversation" about current events. Conversation did not cease when the clerks delivered Justice Frankfurter to his chambers. "There were also random conversations and a stream of questions at any time of day, and sometimes at night, about history, the law, philosophy, politics, personalities, the Harvard Law School, music—in short, any subject whatever." [161] The law clerks drove the justice home at night, and Kaufman recalls "often sitting in the driveway and talking for a half-hour."

To be fair, Frankfurter himself was tolerant of his law clerks' foibles and mistakes as well. During OT 1939, Edward F. Prichard, Jr.—a law clerk whose intellect was not matched by an eye for detail—failed to Shepardize all the case cites contained in a Frankfurter opinion draft, resulting in the case being set for rehearing. Despondent over the error, Prichard left Washington, hid in New York City, and did not return to the Supreme Court until he learned that Frankfurter had forgiven his error. Writes Tracy Campbell: "Within a few days, the justice was at work in his chambers when a tearful Prichard appeared at the door. The bulky figure was soon on his knees crawling on all fours to Frankfurter, begging forgiveness. The two embraced in a scene that has probably never been re-created at any time in the history of the U.S. Supreme Court." [162]

Frankfurter's law clerks worked five-day weeks but would receive weekend calls or visits from the justice. Kaufman remembers occasionally dining at the justice's residence on weekends and taking long walks with him in a local park. "I spent many happy hours with Justice Frankfurter," characterizing the time as both "social and intellectual." [163] Kaufman's experiences were not unique to his clerkship; by all accounts, the former Harvard Law School professor joyfully embraced all of his young charges.

> What law clerk will forget listening to the sextet from *Lucia* being whistled somewhat off key in the corridor of the Court, followed by the Justice bursting in the door of the law clerks' room fresh from conference or a court session with the news of the day? What Supreme Court page will forget the constant procession to the Frankfurter law clerks whenever the Court was in session with notes requesting information or merely informing the clerk of some interesting repartee in the courtroom . . . There also comes to mind an occasional whole day spent on some such topic as selecting the ten or fifteen milestones in the history of private law and defending and discussing the choices. [164]

The conversations and work assignments did not cease after the clerks left the Supreme Court. "You never stop being a Frankfurter law clerk," writes former clerk Irving J. Helman (OT 1947). While he was a new associate at the law firm of Dewey Ballantine, Fishman received notes from Frankfurter asking that he "run down the elusive legislative history of the New Jersey escheat law" or "find time to put on paper what you would deem the proper content for such a phrase [as institutional awareness]." [165] Helman was requested to research why some states had abolished the death penalty. As an inducement to Helman, Frankfurter writes that the project "also might still your conscience for spending most of your time in saving the ogres of Big Business from just punishment."[166]

The most powerful examples of the bond between Justice Frankfurter and his law clerks are found in the personal papers of E. Barrett Prettyman, Jr. Here we find letters regarding reunion dinners,[167] the 1959 purchase of an automatic stair lift for the ailing justice, and the 1972 creation of the "Marion Frankfurter Trust" to care for his ailing widow (the $10,000 annuity received by Mrs. Frankfurter as the widow of a Supreme Court justice failed to cover her considerable medical expenses). In Justice Frankfurter's later years, his former law clerks also held a sherry party in the justice's chambers to celebrate his birthday.

The lasting effects of the Frankfurter clerkship are reflected in Paul Freund's (a former Brandeis law clerk) comments at Justice Frankfurter's February 24, 1965, funeral service. Freund poignantly remarks: "Who of us will not continue to feel that iron grip on the arm, to hear the full-throated greeting, to be rocked with the explosive laughter, and to be moved by those solicitous inquires [*sic*] about ourselves and our dear ones that seemed to emanate from some miraculous telepathic power on his part."[168] Based on my interviews with former Frankfurter clerks, Freund's comments are prophetic even forty years later in the vivid memories that former clerks hold of the unique man that was Felix Frankfurter.

Of all the Hughes Court justices, Frank Murphy adopted the most modern clerkship model. As discussed below, Justice Murphy provides the first historical evidence of a justice who purposefully considered an applicant's political ideology in making selection decisions. Moreover, he is arguably the first justice to completely delegate to his clerks the preparation of judicial opinions as well as the responsibility of reviewing and summarizing cert. petitions.

Because Justice Murphy was appointed during the 1939 term, his first law clerk was a Harvard Law School graduate—Edwin E. Huddleston—selected by Felix Frankfurter[169] and viewed by Murphy as a Frankfurter "plant."[170] All subsequent Murphy clerks were selected from the University of Michigan School of Law. An original list of six potential law clerks was prepared for Justice Murphy by Michigan Law School dean E. Blythe Stason. From the list, Justice Murphy selected John Adams to be his law clerk for OT 1940, and Murphy subsequently returned to the same list to pick later law clerks John Pickering (1941 and 1942 terms) and Eugene Gressman (1943–1948 terms).[171]

Biographer Sidney Fine writes that Justice Murphy's selection process originally focused on the applicant's personal character as well as his intellectual abilities. Fine adds, however, that in subsequent years Murphy considered the applicant's ideological orientations: "[Murphy] was also concerned that his clerk share his 'legal philosophy,' regarding that attribute as second only to character among the qualifications of a potential clerk."[172]

What is unclear, however, is whether Murphy preferred law clerks who did not run afoul of his personal religious biases. What is known is that Murphy law clerk John Adams wrote Michigan Law School dean Stason that the justice preferred non-Jewish clerks over Jewish clerks, "partially because of the social responsibility of the position but also because the justice, Adams thought, did not wish to have a Jew 'representing the school.'"[173] Even if Adams was not accurately reflecting Murphy's own preferences— and, in fact, former law clerk Eugene Gressman writes "I can't believe that Murphy would have expressed such anti-Jewishness in his selection of law clerks"[174]—the statement about Murphy's preferences may have skewed later names submitted to the justice.

It is a commonly shared opinion among observers both within and outside the Court that Frank Murphy depended heavily upon his law clerks to draft his opinions.[175] Based on a review of Frank Murphy's personal papers, Fine concludes: "Although the final decision in cases was definitely his own, the Murphy Papers and other evidence leave absolutely no doubt that the justice delegated extraordinary responsibilities to his clerks."[176] Former clerk Eugene Gressman does not challenge this assessment of the opinion-writing process, instead emphasizing that "none of us clerks ever got involved in suggesting how to vote on the merits of an argued case . . . Murphy made his own judgments in every argued case, usually after hearing the views of other Justices during those conferences."[177]

> The extent of the justice's own involvement in the writing of opinions varied from case to case depending on the importance he attached to the opinion. . . . *it is doubtful if the justice drafted a single opinion in its entirety.* Sometimes he instructed his clerks how he wanted an opinion to be written but then permitted them to do the drafting, the resulting product being subjected to his scrutiny and criticism. Sometimes he drafted portions of an opinion, and the clerk drafted the remainder. Frequently, the clerks wrote the opinion with very little if any guidance from the justice, and Murphy then revised the draft or perhaps accepted it without change.[178]

Fine admits that Murphy was not completely divorced from the drafting process. The justice required his law clerks to follow a specific opinion outline, preferred the minimal use of footnotes and citations, and "instructed his clerks to stress 'simplicity' and 'readability' in drafting opinion since he wished them 'to be understandable to every American.'"[179] In short, Murphy retained a form of stylistic control over the opinion-writing process.

In keeping with their important role, Murphy's law clerks were not shy about offering their candid assessment of the justice's rare contributions to the opinion-writing process. In the case of *Royal Indemnity Co. v. United States* [313 U.S. 289 (1941)], Justice Murphy prepared a dissenting opinion.

After reviewing Murphy's efforts, law clerk John Adams penned a note to Murphy that read as follows: "Seems like this is briefly and rather well done. But if you are going to dissent, I suggest that you do a little better job." [180]

The law clerks were not the only nonjudicial actors to arguably wield influence over the decision-making process. Throughout his tenure on the Court, Justice Murphy shared a hotel suite at the Hotel Washington with Edward Kemp. Murphy and Kemp first met while undergraduates at the University of Michigan, and they subsequently attended law school at Michigan. After studying abroad in England, the two men returned to the United States and Kemp began a lifelong career as Murphy's personal assistant and political adviser. It has been suggested by authors Joyce Murdoch and Deb Price that Kemp and Murphy were possibly romantically and emotionally linked. [181] What is clear to one Murphy biographer, however, is that Kemp did play a limited role in the decision-making process:

> [A]fter discussing the case in conference and with his clerk, [Murphy] would set the clerk to writing on the basis of general directions in notes and memoranda prepared by himself. After soliciting criticism from the clerks, other Justices, and occasionally Kemp, Murphy would circulate the usual draft opinion among the Justices for the same process to begin again. His major opinions thus were collegial in a double sense. The clerks were chiefly responsible for research and the details of writing under his supervision. Kemp was used . . . as a conservative foil and as a guard against his own impulsiveness. Rarely, if ever, did Kemp's views influence the outcome. [182]

On the one hand, evidence that a sitting justice was reviewing circulating opinions with a Court outsider is extraordinary, [183] even if former law clerk Eugene Gressman is correct that Kemp's memoranda "never had any effect. We law clerks usually put them in the waste paper basket." [184] Alternatively, assume that Murphy and Kemp were a couple. Would a husband seeking advice on a pending opinion from his wife be unheard of—especially a spouse who had also attended law school? [185]

Reflecting the practice of the newer justices, Murphy also assigned his law clerks the duties of reviewing and summarizing cert. petitions. Justice Murphy, however, did not ask his clerks to draft bench memoranda. The cert. memoranda included a statement of facts, the lower court holding, analysis of the grounds for appeal asserted by the petitioner, and a recommended disposition. [186] At the end of each week, the memoranda would be attached to the cert. petitions and given to Murphy. Unlike opinion writing, however, it is unclear how much reliance Murphy placed on the memoranda. Fine quotes one anonymous clerk as boasting that "[m]y factual presentation—and comments . . . can make or break a case so far as [Murphy] is concerned," but Fine observes that the unnamed clerk later realized that Murphy exercised his own discretion in voting to grant or deny cert. petitions. [187]

Given the limited number of Murphy law clerks (John J. Adams, John H. Pickering, and Eugene Gressman) and the fact that Adams and Pickering are deceased, little evidence exists regarding the personal bonds between Murphy and his clerks. The law clerks referred to Murphy as "Boss," and Murphy's personal papers contain warm personal letters and holiday cards exchanged between the justice and his clerks. Perhaps the best measure of the depth of affection felt by the justice and his clerks is found in the $1 million gift from former clerk Pickering to the University of Michigan School of Law. Pickering instructed that the money be used to build the Justice Frank Murphy Seminar Room.[188]

In conclusion, Justice Murphy's clerkship model exceeds even the practices of the present Supreme Court justices as regards delegation of responsibility. P-A theory suggests that Murphy would create formal and informal institutional rules designed to maximize ideological compatibility between justice and clerk and minimize the likelihood of clerk defection. In fact, Murphy did so. He considered law clerk ideology, used a confidant (Kemp) to review work product, and hung on to those clerks whom he implicitly trusted (Eugene Gressman).

In 1939, President Franklin Roosevelt plucked William O. Douglas from the Security and Exchange Commission and appointed him to the Supreme Court. While Douglas flirted with the idea of seeking higher political office, he remained on the Court until a stroke drove him into retirement in 1975. His career on the bench, however, did not insulate him from the political fray. As a justice, Douglas would remain in the public eye and weather calls for his resignation as well as impeachment attempts.

Except at the beginning of his Court career, Douglas did not get involved in the selection of law clerks. Originally he attempted to personally select law clerks by reviewing applicants' files or granting short interviews, but he felt that the decision was being made "blindly" and that such a selection method prevented him from selecting the best candidate.[189] Douglas even questioned whether the problem lay in looking solely to western law schools but concluded that "probably my mistake has been in the method in which I've gone about it." Accordingly, Douglas began relying on others.

Typically, former law clerks as well as law school faculty would submit names to Douglas' clerkship committee, composed of one or more former Douglas law clerks. Berkeley Law School professor Max Radin originally served as a one-man selection committee after Douglas grew tired of relying on the dean and faculty of the University of Washington Law School, and after Radin's death the job went to California attorney and former Douglas law clerk Stanley Sparrowe. In the late 1960s, former clerk Thomas Klitgaard assumed Sparrowe's selection duties, and in later years a selection team—composed of individuals such as Arizona Law School dean Charles Ares,

Stanford Law School professor William Cohen, and Jerome Falk—made the choices.[190] After interviewing potential applicants, the selection committee would make its decision.[191]

At least in the early years, Douglas provided his selectors with some limited guidelines. In a May 27, 1946, letter to University of California–Berkeley law professor Max Radin, Douglas writes:

> I think you know exactly the kind of man I want. I need not only a bright chap, but also a hard-working fellow with a smell for facts as well as for law. I do not want a hide-bound, conservative fellow. What I want is a Max Radin—a fellow who can hold his own in these sophisticated circles and who is not going to end up a stodgy, hide-bound lawyer. I want the kind of fellow for whom this work would be an exhilaration, who will be going in to teaching or into the practice of law for the purpose of promoting the public good. I do not want to fill the big law offices of the country with my law clerks.[192]

It is unclear whether Douglas always instructed the selection committee on the appropriate selection criteria. While former clerk C. David Ginsburg considered factors such as scholastic record, personality (he wanted to pick a clerk who was outgoing and self-confident, somebody who would "speak out and take the consequences"), and a love of the outdoors, Ginsburg never discussed selection criteria with Douglas. When asked if he ever considered an applicant's political ideology, Ginsburg replied: "No . . . would never have occurred to me."[193]

Douglas' clerks were selected almost exclusively from law schools within the Ninth Circuit. In his autobiography, Douglas writes: "While each of the other Justices had his own circuit, no one else followed my practice of giving the patronage of their prized law clerkships to graduates of schools in their respective circuits."[194] When Douglas was appointed to the Supreme Court, he found that Harvard, Yale, and Columbia held a virtual stranglehold over the law clerk corps. Douglas wanted to break this monopoly and select western clerks. "I felt that there are some outstanding schools in the Ninth Circuit and that they deserve recognition and that their best men over the years will compare favorably with the best of the law schools in the east."[195]

In 1950, Douglas indicated to a member of his selection committee that he would start hiring two law clerks. Douglas had originally resisted the idea of two clerks, darkly joking that they would just talk to each other and ignore their work. Now Douglas was ready to make a change:

> I am not sure that the two law clerk idea will prove to be satisfactory. I am taking it merely on trial. But if it works out I will want to take both of the men from the law schools in the Ninth Circuit. So you would have two to select. But I think it would be desirable to spread them among different schools if possible.[196]

In experimenting with two clerks, Douglas wanted to try giving them different responsibilities. "It may be that the second law clerk should be someone who is an accomplished typist" and could assist Douglas' secretary. Douglas added that the second law clerk could be a female, didn't necessarily have to be a law clerk, and "might stay for more than one year. The regular law clerk would be changed annually as at present." The experiment with two law clerks lasted for one year. In the 1950s and 1960s, Douglas used the second law clerk allotment to hire a research assistant for the writing of his books. It was not until the late 1960s that he again employed two legally trained clerks.

In the early 1970s, Justice Douglas began hiring three law clerks. Although authors Woodward and Armstrong suggest that Douglas moved to three law clerks because he was dissatisfied with the quality of a specific clerk's work, former law clerk Carol Bruch (OT 1972) believes that it was due to his young wife's concern with the clerks' heavy workload.[197] While Douglas threatened to return to two law clerks, his clerkship committee urged the aging Justice to retain a larger staff. In a November 16, 1972, letter to Douglas, Jerome Falk writes:

> We [the clerkship selection committee] rather strongly hope that you will ultimately conclude that it would be desirable to have a third law clerk. We reached that conclusion notwithstanding the obvious advantages of a smaller staff because of the unhappy realities of the Burger court and the likelihood that you will want to continue leaving your footprints in the pages of the U.S. Reports at least as frequently as Brother Rehnquist leaves his on the back of the United States Constitution.[198]

William O. Douglas adopted a clerkship model that was quickly becoming the institutional norm in the 1930s and 1940s. During his entire time on the bench, law clerks never assisted in the drafting of important majority opinions, although they might be given a single, inconsequential opinion to draft.[199] The clerks, however, were given the responsibility for reviewing and summarizing all cert. petitions—although, unlike clerks in other chambers, the Douglas clerks did not discuss the memoranda with their boss.

The Douglas clerkship model remained fairly constant throughout his service on the Court—despite increases in caseload, myriad nonjudicial writing assignments,[200] the distractions of political battles, and the ravages of age. His first law clerk (C. David Ginsburg, OT 1939) and his final law clerks (Carol Bruch, OT 1972, and George Rutherglen, OT 1975) provide almost identical descriptions of their job duties: preparing short, one-page cert. memoranda and editing (not substantively) Douglas opinions.[201] The Douglas clerks did not routinely prepare bench memoranda, did not discuss their cert. memoranda with the justice, and typically did not provide any substantive review or revisions to draft opinions.

If any aspect of the clerkship model changed, it involved Douglas' willingness to listen to clerks' suggestions. Former clerk David Ginsburg writes:

As the years passed, argument with him on fundamental legal issues became more difficult. When a judge has been on a court long enough to cite himself and—as in Douglas' case—to see many of his dissents become majority opinions, the likelihood that a law clerk will persuade him to alter any of his basic views is remote. The clerk's contributions then fall more into the areas of style, analogies, clarification, and precision.[202]

The suggestion that a younger, less experienced Douglas was more willing to listen to his law clerks' suggestions is supported by the reflections of Stanley Sparrowe, the justice's OT 1947 clerk and longtime selector of subsequent law clerks. Sparrowe describes an editing process in which he and Douglas sat at a double desk, reviewing opinions "page by page, paragraph by paragraph, and line by line." While Sparrowe remarks that his labors were more akin to "a scrivener than an author," Sparrowe did feel that he was free to "make any suggestion I thought would improve the opinion and if he agreed, they would be made."[203]

Given the justice's extensive, nonlegal writings and involvements, it is not surprising to find that his law clerks were often given research questions that could not be answered by opening up the Constitution or the latest issue of *U.S. Reports.* Cohen writes that during his clerkship, questions posed by Douglas included "the height of a Himalayan peak, the reign of a Roman emperor or whether the Pennsylvania Constitution of 1776 had been ratified;"[204] former law clerk Charles Miller received the following questions during a single day of oral argument: "Find out the name of the chief of that Indian tribe in Nebraska. What's the score of the World Series game? What was the year of the Japanese invasion of Manchuria?"[205]

The combination of legal and nonlegal research assignments as well as the limited number of law clerks meant that the Douglas staff worked hard. "'He worked me like a goddamned dog,' recalled [former law clerk Vern] Countryman. 'But that seemed fair. I only had to do it for a year. He was doing it for life.'"[206] Douglas often began the workday by shouting "Work is energizing" at his staff, and in the evening would return to the office after initially departing to make sure that his staff was still working. Writes Douglas biographer Murphy: "The worst nights, though, were the ones when Douglas would leave the lights on in his office to make the staff think that he was still working and quietly sneak out. Since no one dared to peek in the Justice's office, that meant they all stayed well into the night." Needless to say, Douglas law clerks seldom ate lunch with their peers in the Court cafeteria.[207]

Because of the justice's remarkable tenure on the Court, approximately fifty-two men and three women had the opportunity to clerk in his chambers. The sheer number of clerks alone would account for the rich literature on the Douglas clerkship experience. The number of articles and portions of books relating to Douglas and his clerks, however, is undoubtedly increased by W.O.D.'s strained, often volatile relationship with some of his law clerks and staff. From these clashes Douglas gained the nickname "The Terror."[208]

No other justice since McReynolds fired more law clerks than Justice Douglas, although in the case of Douglas the firings were typically temporary. Nevertheless, the emotional turmoil a law clerk undoubtedly felt when such a death sentence was pronounced on his or her clerkship should not be discounted—if Douglas followed through on his brash announcement, the result would be personal and professional disgrace. While Douglas clerks are still loath to talk publicly about these faux firings, they could occur at any time—at least one law clerk was temporarily fired before he ever met Douglas.[209]

Firings aside, some Douglas law clerks have described their clerkships as one unending year of tension in which the law clerks dreaded the day when a simple mistake would unleash the legendary Douglas temper. Douglas was a curt, moody man who preferred the company of mountains and streams to the company of his staff. "A not atypical introduction to WOD's style was a summer memorandum informing the law clerk that other employment might better suit his inadequate legal talents."[210] For example, in an October 1, 1968, letter to law clerk Peter K. Westen, Douglas refers to his law clerk's "ignorance" and chastises him for not sending some requested documents to Douglas' vacation home. Douglas concludes:

> I do not desire to have a law clerk unless he is on the same team as I am on, and willing to run these errands for me from time to time, even though at the time they seem to him to be unimportant. You might think these things over, because the first case we have to dispose of when I get back is the case of P.K. Westen.[211]

Once the term was under way, flashes of Douglas' temper could stem from a clerk's editing suggestions,[212] the false perception that a law clerk had written in one of Douglas' case books,[213] an unfortunate clerk who dared to attend oral argument,[214] or the temerity of a clerk to use Douglas' personal shower (an offense that Douglas threatened to have the FBI investigate).[215] The aforementioned Westen remained the target of Douglas' venom during OT 1968: Douglas once asked Westen if the young man's law school was located "in the gutter," and Douglas pretended to fire Westen two days before his wedding reception was held at the Supreme Court.[216]

For Douglas, the ultimate offense may have been the law clerk with idle time on his hands. While this problem was effectively solved by Douglas rarely using the number of law clerks allocated by Congress, Douglas took further precautions by assigning his law clerks huge "term projects" that could not be completed. Any spare time would be dedicated to such vast research questions as creating a list of every Supreme Court decision that involved the 14th Amendment.[217]

The justice's ill temper extended to clerks in other chambers. Former Reed law clerk Adam Yarmolinsky referred to him as "a sadist" and remarked that the law clerks "used to have a pool to see who'd get him to say, 'Good Morning,' in the elevator if we met him coming up from the garage."[218] What also extended beyond the Douglas chambers was the justice's attitude toward women. Former Douglas law clerk Walter Dellinger has observed: "If Douglas saw a woman within thirty feet of the Court building, he'd hit on her instantly . . . we're not talking about just a case of infidelity here. He had a major problem with women."[219] Douglas' womanizing affected his staff, as current and former law clerks witnessed repeated acts of infidelity and a succession of younger and younger wives.[220]

Since Douglas' death, some modest efforts have been made to rehabilitate his reputation as "The Terror." Former law clerk David Ginsburg directly challenges these allegations, writing that "any suggestion that Douglas clerks were an unhappy group or left the Court unrewarded by their experience or relationship with the Justice is nonsense."[221] While Ginsburg is surely correct that even the most stressful clerkship still produced a unique and memorable experience, his conclusion that Douglas "charmed" all law clerks who encountered him seems astonishingly naïve.

Ginsburg's assessment of the bond between Justice Douglas and his law clerks, however, is echoed by former law clerk William Alsup. Now a federal judge, Alsup penned an article challenging the "flawed research" contained in Bruce Allen Murphy's recent biography on Douglas. Although Alsup primarily focuses on allegations that Douglas lied about his military service and childhood illnesses, Alsup does briefly address another consistent theme in the Murphy biography, namely, that Douglas was an abusive employer. Referring to Douglas as "demanding" but "fair," Alsup writes: "The sadistic impression left by Murphy and his chorus, who, after all, never actually served for the justice, is grotesquely unfair. Over the 30 years since, I have learned that the entire Douglas family of law clerks, with few exceptions, have respected and admired him, both as a justice and as a mentor."[222] To assert that the majority of the Douglas "family" of clerks admired the justice might be an exaggeration, but his personal papers do contain examples of warm bonds between Douglas and some former clerks. In a note written during yet another threat of impeachment proceedings against Douglas, former law clerk Warren Christopher—writing on behalf of himself and former clerks Walter Chaffee, William Cohen, Harvey Grossman, William Norris, William Reppy, and Charles Rickershauser—states: "The point of this note, however, is simply to let you know of our complete loyalty and unstinting support" and "our great and continuing admiration and affection."[223]

So why did Douglas subject a number of his law clerks to such abuse? Biographer Murphy offers a number of different explanations: Was Douglas simply trying to steel his young charges for the realities of the cold world? Was he a genius who did not suffer fools gladly? Did Douglas consider the law clerks punching bags? While not excusing his behavior, one more explanation comes to mind—the "terror" was Douglas' method of keeping his young agents in line; law clerks are more likely to defect and pursue their own goals if they conclude that, if discovered, their transgressions will be benignly forgiven.

The fourth justice to join the Hughes Court was Hugo LaFayette Black, a former police court judge and Alabama senator. Like Douglas, Black would serve on the Supreme Court for over thirty years and hire a remarkable fifty-four law clerks. Discussing the selection practices of Justice Black, former law clerk Daniel J. Meador wrote:

> Some Justices give preferences to particular law schools, some to regions, some to clerks among the lower federal judges, some to a combination of these. But Black has not set standards of this sort. He of course wants a man who has demonstrated a superior legal ability by his law school work or perhaps by clerking for a circuit judge . . . Beyond this he seems to put weight on the individual's interests and personality. After all, it is desirable that a Justice and his clerk get along well with each other, although it is not necessary that they agree on every question of law and policy.[224]

In fact, Black did look to a specific region for his clerks. While they didn't necessarily have to attend law school in the South, Black preferred clerks whose roots were southern.[225] Responding to an inquiry regarding a clerkship position, Black himself remarked: "In appointing clerks I give preference to applicants from the South."[226]

Why the preference for clerks with a southern heritage? Hugo Black, Jr., writes: "If he could, he would always hire young people from the South, who he believed might be persuaded to return there."[227] Justice Black not only wanted his law clerks to return to the South, he also wanted them to be messengers of his jurisprudence. Comments former law clerk David M. Clark (OT 1957): "Justice Black was interested in employing southern law clerks whom he hoped would carry some of his ideas back to the south."[228]

Black's selection criteria were not solely geographical. When interviewing Larry Hammond, Justice Black startled the young applicant by announcing that he preferred to hire law clerks that he could help. Black stated that he decided to interview Hammond because he knew that the young man stuttered. Black proceeded to show Hammond several books on the condition and hypothesized that stuttering was psychological. Hammond joked that he was literally "tongue-tied" during the interview, since he hadn't dreamed that his stuttering would be a topic of conversation.[229]

Hammond was not the only law clerk who was the recipient of Black's attentions. During Hammond's interview, Black commented that in previous terms he hired one young man in order to cure him of the pretentious practice of using a first initial as a name, and another to "clean up" his slovenly personal habits. Hugo Black, Jr., explains that his father loved to teach his clerks, took a personal interest in all of his assistants, and "attempted to change their lives."[230] Law clerks Charles Reich and David J.Vann lived with Justice Black after the death of his first wife, and Justice Black worked to encourage several behavioral changes in Vann—including weight loss and remembering to turn off the lights after leaving a room—while encouraging Reich to become a better driver and to have more fun.[231] Writes Reich: "How I gloried in that marvelous year. I knew it was one of the greatest experiences that any person could ever have. I never stopped marveling that there I was, sitting at dinner with Justice Black and talking about freedom of speech while the Justice divided a steak three ways, and we passed the corn sticks and greens."[232]

Justice Black never followed the selection model in which law professors had carte blanche to select law clerks. Former law clerk and Black biographer John P. Frank writes: "Not for him was the device of some of the Justices to delegate clerk choice to distinguished professors at law who would choose the best and the brightest. Black wanted talented young people, but also those with whom he could have a personal relationship."[233] In short, Black took great care in selecting his law clerks. He not only was assisted by letters of recommendation from trusted law professors and fellow judges, but he also relied on family, friends, and former clerks.[234] Justice Black selected law clerks pursuant to a mixture of different goals. Undoubtedly, Justice Black needed law clerks because of workload pressures. Yet Black also wanted to select young men whom he could help and, if possible, send back to the South.

Prospective clerks were required to interview with Black. The interviews were designed to measure compatibility between justice and clerk,[235] but a few interviews also had a substantive component. Former clerk William Joslin recalls that Justice Black asked a series of questions to determine whether the young man "was an out-and-out segregationist," while former clerk Daniel Meador stated that Justice Black wanted to be sure that Meador truly wanted the clerkship since the Supreme Court's decision to hear upcoming desegregation cases might damage Meador's prospects of getting subsequent employment in his home state of Alabama.[236]

With the exception of Joslin, none of the former law clerks recalled any interview questions designed to measure the applicant's personal political ideology. Howard commented that Justice Black was "not in the least bit worried that my philosophical bent matched his," explaining that the justices were simply looking for people who could do "first class" work, and Hammond—who was selected to clerk for Hugo Black during OT 1971—commented that Hugo Black "could have cared less" about his political beliefs. Yet there is evidence that recommendations were made to Black based on ideological considerations, regardless of whether the justice requested the information to be provided. In a November 26, 1947, letter to Justice Black, Yale Law School dean Wesley A. Sturges submitted the names of three law school students—Truman McGill Hobbes, Richard Lindsey Wharton, and Louis Heilprin Pollack—to the justice. After summarizing each candidate's individual merits, Sturges concludes as follows:

> I trust that you will understand with respect to all three of these boys that I believe them to be of liberal attitude, and I must say again that all three of them hold you and your work in the very highest regard. In other words, you would find each one of them, I believe, made happy by the environment in which they would find themselves with you and you would find them competent and happy in the service of the causes which you champion.[237]

In other words, the agents proposed by Sturges would be ideologically compatible with Black—thus promoting job satisfaction and minimizing shirking.

For years, Hugo Black hired only one law clerk per term, despite having the authorization to hire two. Black explained that he remained with a single clerk because he "did not want a bureaucracy." Echoing Justice Brandeis, Black further explained that a small staff reassured the public that "the justice did his own work."[238] In 1950, the justice began hiring two law clerks.[239] Black stated that he changed his mind because he felt that a clerkship was a valuable experience for a young person,[240] but one wonders if workload considerations also played a role in the change of heart.

Throughout Black's career on the Court, he remained constant in his clerkship model: law clerks prepared short, precise cert. memoranda and assisted in the drafting, revising, and editing of opinions. Black had specific rules regarding the cert. memoranda. They were one page in length and typed on a six-by-eight-inch piece of paper. The memoranda contained a summary of the appellate court's decision, the case facts, and a recommended disposition. Black would take the cert. memoranda to conference and make notes on the back of the memoranda regarding the justices' comments and votes. Because of the tight space limitations on the cert. memoranda, law clerks became "masters of abbreviation."[241]

Despite having his law clerks prepare cert. memoranda, Justice Black spent hours studying the cert. petitions. In a December 3, 1969, diary entry, Elizabeth Black writes that the justice "is absolutely swamped with *certs*. He conscientiously goes over every one of them and, as a result, he has done nothing today but read *certs*."[242] In other diary entries during the years 1965 and 1967, Elizabeth Black makes multiple references to the justice—then in his late seventies—working on cert. petitions until early in the morning. Hugo Black, Jr., confirms Elizabeth Black's claims. "Daddy used to keep up with his certiorari by reading them whenever he had a spare moment—at his desk, in the bathroom, on the tennis court, in the car or in bed when he had insomnia."[243] As for why Justice Black dedicated so much energy to the cert. process, his son explains: "My father recognized the process of selecting cases as the heart of a Justice's job, for he believed that whoever has the power to decide what cases will appear has the power of the Court and this was *therefore not a function to be relegated to clerks or anybody else*."[244] Louis Brandeis and Hugo Black served together only briefly on the Supreme Court, but it is intriguing to wonder whether the elderly Brandeis shared his views on cert. petitions with the Court's newest justice.

As for opinion drafting, Black's early law clerks—William Joslin (OT 1947) and Truman Hobbes (OT 1948) stated that Justice Black, not his law clerks, routinely prepared the first draft of an opinion, although Daniel Meador (OT 1954) added that each law clerk was given the opportunity to draft one opinion.[245] All three men described a time-consuming process of argument, revision, and editing:

> [Justice Black's] draft is then turned over to the clerks, and, with all the confidence of youth, they work it over. Then the fun begins. The two clerks and Black gather around his large desk and start through the draft, word by word, line by line. This may go on for hours . . . The discussion, often turning into lively debate, will sometimes be transferred to the study in his 18th century house in Alexandria and last until midnight. Often revisions result; sometimes a clerk can get a word or comma accepted, but the substance and decision are never anything but Black's alone.[246]

In his interview, Meador explained that the law clerks were "absolutely free" to make suggestions about the draft opinion, and that occasionally the justice and law clerk would get into rather heated debates. Often the editing process took place in Justice Black's second floor study in his home on 619 South Lee Street in old-town Alexandria, Virginia. During the years that Black was a widower, these editing sessions stretched into the early morning.[247]

Former law clerk A. E. Dick Howard, who clerked during OT 1962 and 1963, indicated that in later years Justice Black may have increased the number of first drafts assigned to his clerks. In such circumstances, Black and his law clerk first discussed the conference vote and outlined the result to be reached as well as the theory or theories to be used. Moreover, Black (by memory) provided cites to his prior, on-point opinions. When Howard wrote the first draft, he consciously adopted Black's writing style; Black had once instructed Howard that he should write an opinion in such a manner that he could take it home to his wife to read and understand.[248]

While law clerks rarely—if ever—prepared formal bench memoranda,[249] Black and his clerks had far-ranging discussions about the cases set for oral argument. Explains former clerk David M. Clark: "Bench memoranda would not be routinely drafted. The Judge used information he got from the cert. memoranda and his own personal review of the briefs."[250] Often these conversations quickly moved beyond the case at bar. "Black's clerks got discourses on the Constitution, on English history, on the history of civil rights, on the Greek wars, on Roman government, on seditious libel, on New Deal politics, on tyranny."[251] Black's home library was stocked with works by the best Greek and Roman writers, and one fortunate law clerk spent the evening listening to Black read Plato's *Phaedo* out loud![252]

By all accounts, Justice Black shared a tight bond with his law clerks. Hugo Black, Jr., writes that his father "genuinely cared" about his law clerks and "thought it was his duty to teach each clerk and build up any weaknesses in their intellectual ability, character, or personality."[253] The justice called his law clerks "the boys" and did not hesitate to dispense advice—whether requested or not. "[H]e was truly interested and concerned about the way they conducted their private lives as well as the way they performed in their professional lives," comments Josephine Black Pesaresi, daughter of the late Justice Black. "He always looked at the whole person and felt that strength of character, including most predominately kindness, integrity, and humility, must be part of every aspect of anyone's life." In Justice Black's eyes, the worst sin a law clerk could commit was becoming "puffed up" with self-importance. "He truly had equal respect for anyone who did a good job in any area, including menial work, and he was quite harsh in his judgment of people who treated people in lesser positions with a lack of respect and courtesy."[254]

One of the more well-known techniques that Black used to hone his clerks' intellects was requiring them to read Edith Hamilton's *The Greek Way*. Former clerk Meador claims that the book "held an extraordinary grip on [Black's] mind" and that "clerks over a span of many years recall having *The Greek Way* recommended by Black in their initial interview with him, or in the early days of the clerkship." Other books assigned to law clerks included Leon Whipple's *Our Ancient Liberties* and H. G. Wells' *The Outline of History*.[255]

Of course, the law clerks joined Justice Black on his own tennis court for vigorous games of doubles tennis. Even in his later years, Justice Black was a highly competitive player who hated to concede a single point. Hugo Black, Jr., recalls a match between his father and former law clerk George Treister, who was an outstanding tennis player in his own right. Hugo, Jr., recalls that one day Treister tired of the justice's competitiveness and hit a slice shot in such a manner that the only way it could be returned was for the justice to run into the garden wall (the assumption being that Justice Black would let the shot go). To his astonishment, Treister watched as Justice Black crashed into the wall again and again, and Treister was forced to abandon the strategy before the justice gravely injured himself.[256]

This warmth and caring was returned in kind. Howard refers to Black as a "mentor in every respect and a Dutch uncle," and Reich calls him "the grand old man." Biographer Howard Ball quotes a former law clerk as saying that "the overriding personal impression of the Judge was one of great humanity, love, warmth and youth."[257] The relationship between teacher and student continued after the clerkship. Letters flew back and forth between Justice Black and former law clerk John P. Frank[258] regarding recently issued Court opinions and members of the Court,[259] and on holidays former clerks gave Black gifts of Alabama pecans, sorghum, and tennis balls.

Black's law clerks held regular reunions, and on the Justice's eightieth birthday his former clerks threw a party at which all but six of his former and present "boys" attended. At the party, Black "arose and in a conversational tone told them how much he loved each one of them, of his pride in their records, and of his confidence in their integrity."[260] Hugo Black, Jr., himself refers to the law clerks "as my brothers," and he regularly joins the former clerks for reunion dinners at the U.S. Supreme Court. When Justice Black began his dramatic physical decline in the fall of 1971, it was a former law clerk—Louis Oberdorfer—who met with the justice to discuss whether he would stay on the Supreme Court and later helped Black draft his resignation letter.

As with the hero worship of Holmes and the fear of Douglas, the love felt by Black's law clerks toward their employer served multiple purposes. Hugo Black was a dynamic personality, and a clerkship with the former Alabama senator was an experience to be treasured. Like his nemesis, Frankfurter, Black inspired great loyalty from his law clerks. While a virtue unto itself, loyalty serves a different purpose in a principal-agent relationship—the more an agent embraces his fiduciary duty to a principal, the less likely the agent is to act in ways counter to the principal's goals. Hence, a principal can devote fewer resources to monitoring. Of course, as the number of law clerks increases other techniques must be adopted to monitor clerks and to minimize defection.

The Stone Court, 1941–1946

In July 1941, Harlan Fiske Stone was elevated to the Supreme Court's center chair. He remained chief justice until April 22, 1946, when he suffered a fatal cerebral hemorrhage while on the bench. While Chief Justice Stone's job duties expanded, there is no evidence that—absent having his law clerks review the *in forma pauperis* petitions—he delegated more substantive job duties to his clerks. Chief Justice Stone, however, employed additional staff. Upon being elevated to the center chair, Stone's chambers consisted of two law clerks, two female secretaries, and a messenger.[261] Newland writes that it was Stone's increased administrative responsibilities and his review of the IFP petitions that necessitated the staff increase.

Of the former Stone law clerks interviewed by this author, only Bennett Boskey clerked for him when he was chief justice (as opposed to associate justice). Boskey spent two terms with Chief Justice Stone, and he had some unique duties in keeping with Stone's elevated position. First of all, Boskey offered recommendations regarding opinion assignment. After the Court's conferences, Boskey would meet with Chief Justice Stone, discuss to whom Stone should assign opinions, and assist in the opinion-assignment process. Boskey stated that of the many factors considered in opinion assignment, three included (1) a justice's current workload, (2) a justice's areas of expertise, and (3) which justice could hold together the largest majority. Finally, Boskey sat in on the annual judicial conferences and helped Stone prepare conference reports.[262]

Of the four justices who joined the Stone Court—Harold Hitz Burton, James F. Byrnes, Robert H. Jackson, and Wiley Rutledge—Byrnes had the shortest stay. He was sworn in on July 8, 1941, resigned on October 3, 1942, and had a single law clerk—James E. Doyle.[263] According to an interview with the Wisconsin Historical Society, Doyle reported that Byrnes, who was unfamiliar with law clerk selection practices, asked Hugo Black to select two clerks for OT 1942 and give one to Byrnes. Doyle claims that he and another candidate interviewed with Byrnes and Black, and then the two justices flipped a coin. Given Hugo Black's careful selection of law clerks, Doyle's account should be taken with a grain of salt.[264]

In Byrnes' personal papers, there is a memorandum of unknown date and authorship summarizing the names and biographical information of what appear to be twelve candidates for the Byrnes' clerkship.[265] The memorandum is signed "Marx" (an indication that it was likely prepared by Marx Leva, Hugo Black's law clerk during OT 1940 and later assistant secretary of Defense) and addressed to "Judge," the title used by Black's clerks. Most of the background information is predictable—undergraduate and law school education, class rank, law review position, and current occupation. Interestingly, eight of the fourteen candidates—Charles Arendall, Marcus Cohn, John Costelloe, Charles Ewing, Robert Friedman, Maxwell Isenbergh, Frank Kaufman, and Hubert Nexon—have their religious affiliations noted (Arendall is Baptist; Costelloe and Ewing are Catholic; and Cohn, Friedman, Isenbergh, Kaufman, and Nexon are Jewish). Moreover, the author provides a brief assessment of the candidates' political ideology. For example, the list states that Costelloe is "moderately liberal except where the church is concerned," Ewing is "fairly conservative," and Friedman and Nexon are "very liberal."

What is fascinating about this memorandum is that it provides concrete evidence that in the 1940s a Supreme Court justice considered a law clerk candidate's political ideology to be, at the very least, relevant to the selection process. Other than wanting to award jobs to loyal members of a political party, the only other rationale for considering political preferences is to maximize ideological harmony between justice and clerk. It is possible, but not likely, that the individual who drafted the memorandum decided independently to research the candidates' religion and political ideology.

In fact, Byrnes himself expressed reservations about law clerk influence. In his autobiography, Byrnes writes that a justice who does not personally review all briefs and cases relevant to an appeal "may find himself influenced too much by the opinions of his clerk." Byrnes adds that he did not have such fears with law clerk Doyle. "Jim was an exceedingly capable lawyer whom I could trust to present a memorandum of the facts and the law without seeking to smuggle into it his own views and prejudices."[266] Given the time period in which Byrnes wrote the book (late 1950s), this is a remarkably candid remark about law clerks from a former Supreme Court justice.

There is only one document in the Byrnes papers that sheds light on how Justice Byrnes might have used his law clerk. In a 1941 memorandum to Doyle, Justice Byrnes *appears* to be responding to Justice Reed's dissent to Byrnes' circulating majority opinion in *United States v. Emory* [314 U.S. 423 (1941)]. At the very least, this memorandum is evidence that Justice Byrnes and Doyle had substantive legal conversations about Supreme Court cases.

Robert H. Jackson was named to the Supreme Court in 1941, having previously served as solicitor general and attorney general in the Roosevelt administration. During his thirteen years on the Court, Justice Jackson hired eleven law clerks—including future Supreme Court justice William Rehnquist. Unlike previous (and subsequent) justices, Jackson selected law clerks not only from top law schools like Harvard, Yale, and Stanford but also from "lesser" schools like Temple University, Albany University, Cornell, and SUNY-Buffalo. In a December 28, 1949, letter to Syracuse University College of Law dean Paul S. Andrews, Jackson summarized his more egalitarian hiring practices:

> Most of the Justices have pretty much settled on some school, the recommendation of whose dean they will accept as to a law clerk. I have not liked that system and have named my law clerks from various schools, including some of the smaller ones . . . I have never believed that a top mark in classes was always the final indication of a top man, either. I would not want a boy who could not get good marks, but we all know there are other things in the world that count besides marks, and good common sense and agreeable ways have their value.[267]

Jackson noted that his selection practices had a downside. "Word seems to have gotten around that mine is one of the open doors on the Court, and the volume of applications and correspondence has really become a burden." Since Jackson found most of the applications to be well-qualified, he found himself in a difficult position. "I would really rather take a horsewhipping than to tell any one of them that I can't open the doors and take him in and I am coming to appreciate Frankfurter's wisdom in simply saying that he will accept what is sent to him, without even an interview."[268]

Besides selecting his clerks from law schools not traditionally represented among the law clerk corps, Jackson occasionally relied on family members and friends to find law clerks. Former law clerk Philip C. Neal writes that he received an invitation to interview with Jackson after his name was suggested to the justice by William E. Jackson, the justice's son and Neal's law school classmate.[269] Neal would subsequently recommend Murray Gartner as his replacement, and Gartner clerked during OT 1945. In 1951, Neal—then a professor at Stanford Law School—arranged for Justice Jackson to interview Stanford Law School student William Rehnquist during the justice's visit to the school.[270]

The most fascinating clerkship application found in Justice Jackson's personal papers came from Alan Y. Cole, who subsequently clerked for Jackson during OT 1949. In a November 2, 1948, letter to Jackson, Cole wrote that he abandoned plans for a journalism career and instead attended Yale Law School after the U.S. Army assigned him to a military police unit that guarded prisoners during the Nuremberg trials. Cole writes: "My sojourn at Nurnberg [*sic*] wrought a considerable change, however—a change for which you are largely responsible. Your performance in the courtroom, your cogent opening and closing statements, and particularly your cross examination of the first defense witness, made very deep impressions upon me. My interest in law and lawyers was then awakened and this interest has since grown to considerable proportions." While admitting that his ultimate goal of clerking for Jackson was "somewhat sentimental," Cole added, "I can only borrow your words from another context, and say: 'If that is heresy, then I am guilty.'"[271]

Former law clerk James M. Marsh applied for a Jackson clerkship after originally arranging with Justice Jackson for the *Temple University Law School Law Review* to publish materials from the Nuremberg trials.[272] Marsh, like the young Robert Jackson, attended night law school and felt that Jackson was the only justice who would even agree to interview him. Jackson interviewed Marsh on two different occasions, and during the second interview expressed his reservations to the young man:

> You give me a problem. I have no doubt that you can handle the job. But if I hire you as my law clerk, we will be operating these chambers without even one college

degree. I do not have a degree. My secretary doesn't have a degree, and you do not have a degree. I have always felt that my writing has suffered because of my lack of formal education. So I would be compounding a weakness. What do you have to say about that?[273]

Marsh writes that he used his fledgling advocacy skills to persuade the justice that the lack of a college degree in the chambers should not play a deciding role in the hiring decision, and at Jackson's request Marsh ended up serving a second term as his law clerk.

Like Justice Black, Jackson's interviews were designed to judge personal, not ideological, compatibility. A former law clerk commented that Jackson "did not consider himself a political lawyer" and joked that Jackson's hiring of Rehnquist was sufficient evidence that the justice did not consider (or care about) his clerks' political beliefs. Rehnquist himself writes that Jackson asked only a few perfunctory questions about his education before telling war stories about his law practice in upstate New York,[274] and Marsh recalls Jackson's secretary commenting that Marsh got the position because Jackson felt comfortable with the young man.[275]

When Jackson was appointed to the Supreme Court in 1941, the associate justices were allowed to hire only one law clerk. This number was increased to two after Chief Justice Vinson's appointment, likely in response to Vinson's staff of seven (three law clerks, two secretaries, a messenger, and a stenographer).[276] Jackson took advantage of this new staff line, hiring two law clerks—Alan Y. Cole and Howard Buschman—during OT 1949. For OT 1953, however, Justice Jackson hired only one law clerk—E. Barrett Prettyman, Jr. Former law clerk James Marsh hypothesizes that Jackson's decision was due in part to friction between the justice and Rehnquist as well as tension between Rehnquist and co-clerk Donald Cronson during OT 1952.[277]

Given the limited job duties of the Jackson law clerks, it is not surprising that Justice Jackson was uninterested in scrutinizing his clerk's' political beliefs. As was the norm among Supreme Court justices, Jackson's clerks prepared cert. memoranda and reviewed judicial opinions.[278] Jackson had specific instructions as to the contents of a cert. memorandum: "[T]he Justice wanted a typed memorandum describing the legal questions presented by the petition for certiorari and giving the clerk's judgment as to whether the issues were serious and important ones. He then wanted the clerk's recommendation as to whether the petition for certiorari should be granted or denied by the Court."[279] Jackson also required law clerks to include the names of the Court of Appeals judges who heard the original appeal and whether any of said judges wrote any dissenting opinions.[280] In the opinion of clerk William Rehnquist: "This seems like a lot of responsibility for a brand-new law clerk." Rehnquist recalls reading his first set of cert. petitions and asking himself whether a recent law school graduate like himself should be drafting cert. memoranda and passing judgment on opinions written by more learned judges. Rehnquist's qualms, however, were put aside for the sake of expediency. "While the question may have been a good one, I rapidly realized that I must cast aside such modesty if I were to get through my share of the hundreds of cert. petitions that had to be processed."[281]

Jackson himself prepared the first draft of all opinions, with one exception. Justice Jackson "always tried to find some technical case, not involving any controversial social or political issues, on which he would allow the law clerk to draft an opinion delineating the court's reasons for an agreed result."[282] After Jackson wrote the first draft, a law clerk was responsible for thoroughly reviewing the opinion. In a memorandum given to the law clerks, the specific duties regarding the review of draft opinions were delineated as follows:

The clerk is expected to criticise [sic] the draft with utter candor and freedom, both as to form and substance. It is most helpful to consideration and discussion if he will put his criticisms in a brief typewritten memorandum and reduce any suggestion of substantial additions or substitutions to concrete typewritten form . . . Among service expected from the clerk in all opinions are a checking against the record (not briefs of parties, except as guides to the record) of every statement of fact made in the opinion to make sure that nothing is misstated; a study to see that no fact essential to the issue is omitted; verification of all citations included in the Justice's draft to determine that they fairly are authoritative on the point in question; a study for additional authorities appropriate for citation; preparation of foot notes at points indicated in the Justice's draft opinion or at points where the clerk thinks they might be appropriate; any editorial or literary criticism or correction of punctuation, spelling, form, etc.[283]

Jackson did not have his law clerks prepare bench memoranda.[284] Marsh explained that Jackson "knew the law, and the background of the issues; he read the briefs, and noted any questions he might want to raise at argument. He had lived the law a long time; didn't need my help."

The law clerks had more mundane duties in the Jackson chambers. "The law clerk shall maintain the office library; all advance sheets of statutes, supplements to Codes, and advance sheets will be delivered to him and he will be responsible for placing them with their series and maintaining the library in order."[285] Law clerks, however, were not to review written communications from other justices or circulating opinions, and the clerks could not access the locked office files without permission of secretary Elsie Douglas.

Unlike many of his contemporaries, Justice Jackson explicitly warned his law clerks of the duty of confidentiality, and his admonition foreshadows later descriptions of the Supreme Court as "nine little law firms":

At the Supreme Court the office of each Justice functions as a separate unit, so far as its work is concerned. Not only is all of the Court work highly confidential, but tentative plans or opinions are not to be prematurely disclosed, even to other offices. There have been scandals and trouble over "leaks" which have been embarrassing, not only to Justices, but to employees who happened to be so situated as to be subject to suspicion. Procedures to protect the office and each person in it, in event of leaks, conforming to the general practice of other offices should be carefully observed.[286]

Justice Jackson maintained contact with some of his former law clerks after they departed the Marble Palace, receiving not only notes about their personal lives but also their candid assessments of the Supreme Court's work. As for how the law clerks characterized the lessons learned during the clerkship, it varied by clerk. In an undated letter to Justice Jackson, William Rehnquist writes:

> I have occasionally reflected on the experience which I got while working for you; I think there is a tendency when one first leaves a job like that, and turns to the details of a general law practice, to feel "why, hell, that didn't teach me anything about practicing law." In a sense it didn't, and in that regard I am sure you would be the first to agree that there is no substitute for actually practicing. But I can't help feel that, in the addition to the enjoyment from the personal contacts, one does pick up from a clerkship some sort of intuition about the nature of the judicial process. It is so intangible I will not attempt to describe it further, but I think it is valuable especially in appellate brief-writing.[287]

There is no indication in Justice Jackson's personal papers as to how he responded to Rehnquist's lukewarm praise.

On February 15, 1943, Wiley B. Rutledge became the third new justice to join the Stone Court. A former dean of the University of Iowa College of Law and a federal appeals court judge, Rutledge served less than seven years on the Supreme Court. During that time, he hired six law clerks, the most well-known being future Supreme Court Justice John Paul Stevens.

Although William O. Douglas has the distinction of being the first Supreme Court justice to hire a female law clerk, Wiley Rutledge had an earlier opportunity to break the gender barrier. At the time of his elevation to the Supreme Court, Rutledge sat on the federal appellate bench and had extended a clerkship offer to Washington University Law School student Virginia Morsey. The Phi Beta Kappa graduate was the only female in her law school class, serving as editor-in-chief of the law review. While the newly confirmed justice "still felt an obligation to Morsey," John M. Ferren writes that instead he wrote her "an elaborate letter of explanation and apology" and selected Columbia Law School graduate Victor Brudney,[288] then working in the solicitor general's office, as his first law clerk.[289]

Information on Rutledge's hiring and employment practices comes from two different sources—Ferren's interview with Victor Brudney as well as this author's interview with Rutledge's most prominent former law clerk,

Justice John Paul Stevens. According to Justice Stevens, both Chief Justice Fred Vinson and Justice Rutledge had professional ties with Northwestern Law School professors Willard Wirtz and Willard Pedrick; Wirtz had clerked for Vinson on the Court of Appeals, and Pedrick had been on the faculty with Rutledge at the University of Iowa. The two professors convinced Vinson and Rutledge to each give one law clerk position to a Northwestern Law School graduate. Rutledge had a space available for OT 1947, and Vinson in OT 1948.[290]

The Northwestern law professors tapped Stevens and fellow classmate Arthur Seder for the two clerkship positions. Both students were at the top of their law school class and coeditors of the law review. Due to family considerations, both Stevens and Seder preferred to clerk during OT 1947 (the Rutledge spot) rather than OT 1948 (the Vinson spot). Stevens and Seder came up with a simple solution—a coin toss that took place in their law review office. Stevens won the toss (although he doesn't recall who tossed the coin or who called "heads or tails"), thus earning the Rutledge clerkship. During OT 1947, Stevens was joined by Stanley Temko, the justice's second clerk.[291]

As with many of the newer justices, Wiley Rutledge assigned his law clerks the principal job duty of reviewing cert. petitions and preparing cert. memoranda. Rutledge worked with his clerks to carefully review the pending cert. petitions before conference:

> Characteristic of the thoroughness with which he devoted himself . . . were the sessions on Friday nights before the regular Saturday conferences. It was his custom—until forbidden to do so by his doctor—to sit with his law clerk, into the following morning if necessary, and go over in detail the cases to be decided and the petitions for certiorari. Every memorandum on an *in forma pauperis* petition was read, underlined, and discussed, and if there were any doubts, the original, often ill-written papers were sent for and examined.[292]

At least during OT 1947, Rutledge had his law clerks prepare bench memoranda in approximately six cases that Rutledge deemed to require special attention. The clerks would also discuss cases with the justice prior to oral argument. Finally, Rutledge gave his law clerks the opportunity to prepare the first draft of one opinion during the term.[293] When Rutledge prepared opinion drafts, he often discussed the case with his law clerks before writing out his opinion in longhand and then giving it to his clerks for revisions and review.[294] Often Rutledge struggled to write his draft opinions and subjected them to endless rewrites.

According to Ferren, Rutledge encouraged intellectual debate and discussion in his chambers. While the give-and-take between justice and clerk did not rise to the fierce scrimmages seen in the Frankfurter chambers, they could become heated. Former law clerk Brudney recalled that "our voices occasionally rose" during these conversations, although the focus on the debates remained professional. Brudney, however, may have been the most vocal of the justice's assistants. Rutledge once commented in a letter that "I have never had a clerk who fought with me so hard when we differed as Vic did. More than once I threw him out of my office only to have him come back and reopen the argument," and Ferren writes that Brudney offered to resign in order to restore tranquility to the chambers (the justice refused to accept the proffered resignation).[295]

Harold Hitz Burton was the last justice to join the Stone Court. Burton was a Republican who practiced law before entering politics. After serving as mayor of Cleveland, Ohio, and as a U.S. Senator, Burton was selected by President Truman in 1945 to replace Owen J. Roberts. Burton remained on the Supreme Court bench for thirteen years, retiring in 1958.

Little is known about Burton's selection practices. Former law clerks Marvin Schwartz (OT 1950), Thomas O'Neill (OT 1954), and Carl Schneider (OT 1957) state that every term one of the two clerkship slots went to an individual who had first completed a federal appellate court clerkship with Judge Herbert Goodrich of the Third Circuit Court of Appeals, a judge with whom Burton had worked and developed a close friendship.[296] Occasionally, the second clerkship position went to former clerks from Second Circuit Court of Appeals judges Learned Hand and Sterry R. Waterman. As for why Justice Burton wanted law clerks with appellate experience, former law clerk Thomas N. O'Neill writes: "One of the reasons . . . was that when making a recommendation on the grant or denial of certiorari an experienced clerk would realize that most cases have to end in the Courts of Appeals."[297] Burton's preference for law clerks with prior experience represented a modification to the existing clerkship model, in which law clerks went directly from law school to the Supreme Court.

The justice drew his clerks from a fairly diverse group of law schools that included Catholic University, Harvard, the Universities of Chicago, Nebraska, Pennsylvania, and Yale. As noted earlier, the justice may have favored law clerks from his home state; during his first year on the Court, Burton asked the dean of Harvard Law School to recommend a student who was from Ohio to serve as his law clerk.[298] It isn't clear whether Justice Burton made similar requests when recruiting law clerks from other schools. Before hiring his law clerks, Burton required that they interview with him.[299]

Schwartz recounts that he interviewed with Justice Burton but that the meeting was not substantive in nature. As for the young candidate's political preferences, Schwartz writes that Justice Burton "certainly made no effort to assess my political ideology; to him, that would have been unthinkable."[300] Schwartz's comments are typical of law clerks that I have interviewed from the 1940s through 1960s; most are either amused or appalled at the suggestion that their justice would have based his selection decision upon ideological factors.

In a February 1947 letter to Dean C. M. Linfrock of Case Western Reserve Law School, Justice Burton described what he sought in a law clerk and what job duties said law clerk would be assigned:

> I believe it essential that . . . the man should have an "A" rating in law school and should have not only scholastic ability but real common sense and good judgment on matters in general. His work primarily consists of reading and summarizing briefs and records. He would be required to type his own summaries and he also would assist me in research work on pending cases and opinions on which I was working. He also would be expected to have some critical ability as to improving drafts of opinions.[301]

Burton biographer Mary Frances Berry writes that Burton depended greatly on law clerk W. Howard Mann (later a law professor at SUNY-Buffalo) during the justice's first year on the Court, but he then adopted a clerkship model that closely resembled that of the other newer justices. Berry writes:

> Because he was very uncertain during his first year on the Court, Burton relied heavily on his clerk, W. Howard Mann. . . . For the most part, the opinions of that first year represented a joint effort. Mann wrote a series of detailed memos on individual points in the cases and explained them to Burton. They worked almost every night in his chambers until Burton began to feel a surer grasp of the law, in the process developing procedures that Burton used throughout his years on the Court.[302]

In subsequent terms Burton grew more confident, did not rely on his clerks to draft opinions, and "never hesitated to reject his clerks' views concerning the outcome of a case. His vote was always his own."[303]

Interviews of former law clerks confirm that Burton assigned them the responsibility of preparing both cert. memoranda and bench memoranda in all opinions. What is less clear, however, is the function of the law clerks in the opinion-writing process. Former law clerk Harris K. Weston (OT 1946) only revised/edited the justice's opinion drafts,[304] and former clerk Schwartz (OT 1949) writes: "It was quite rare for Burton clerks to prepare first drafts of opinions."[305] Schwartz recalls only one instance in which he prepared the first draft of an opinion. He writes: "With respect to the one draft which I prepared, [Burton] told me what the decision should be. Incidentally, I thought the decision was wrong."[306]

Later Burton clerks, however, describe an opinion-writing process in which the law clerk prepared opinion drafts that Justice Burton either disregarded or adopted. Writes political scientist David N. Atkinson:

When Justice Burton was assigned to write the opinion of the Court, he would ask the clerk who had by then written two memoranda in the case to write a draft opinion. Knowing that Justice Burton would himself write a very long draft opinion, the clerks usually wrote a short opinion with the hope it would shorten the draft. "He prepared his own draft before looking at the clerk's draft and our efforts were therefore usually wasted," a clerk recalled. "On some occasion he would borrow a sentence or two (or maybe a paragraph) from the clerk's draft in preparing subsequent drafts of his own. . . . On the whole, the final official opinion he published was virtually entirely a product of his own pen."[307]

Correspondence with former law clerk Schneider (OT 1957) confirms the "draft swapping" technique used by Burton, although former law clerk O'Neill appears to state that Burton relied more heavily on the drafts: "We would discuss the case and the Justice would tell us the result at which we should arrive. I had no difference of opinion with Justice Burton as to the result on any case during the term. I do not remember if we prepared the first draft in all opinions or only in some opinions."[308]

At the very least, an argument can be made that Burton amended his clerkship model during his final years on the Court, although it is unusual for a justice to do so. One explanation for Justice Burton's increasing dependence upon his law clerks in drafting opinions is suggested by the justice's health. Atkinson writes that one of Burton's final clerks recalled him "having severe difficulty with his eyes and control of his hands, and he worked at a very slow pace"; in June of 1958 Burton was diagnosed with Parkinson's disease.[309] While Atkinson does not indicate when Justice Burton's condition first surfaced, one can hypothesize that the onset of early symptoms triggered a change in Burton's clerkship model.

Like Justice Rutledge, Burton held Friday night meetings with his law clerks to prepare for the Court's Saturday conference. Former law clerk Ray Troubh (OT 1953) writes that during these meetings "Justice Burton gave his clerks complete freedom of expression. . . . We were encouraged to suggest how we would vote. We could criticize his views—we were equals in shirtsleeves on those nights."[310]

Whether they clerked for Harold Burton or another justice, Supreme Court law clerks held Justice Burton in high regard. In comments made at a memorial service for Justice Burton, Troubh observed that the justice "was such a totally decent man. He was without guile and without deceit. When you use words to describe him as courageous, sincere, democratic, just, honorable, you say them without contradiction—because no one knew him otherwise."[311] Biographer Berry reports that during OT 1954 the law clerks in all nine chambers voted on which sitting justice they would like to effectively duplicate and fill all nine chairs on the Supreme Court bench. The winner by a landslide was Justice Burton.[312]

The Vinson Court, 1946 to 1953

Chief Justice Vinson was the first justice in the history of the Supreme Court to employ three law clerks, and it is with Vinson that the delegation of all major aspects of a justice's job duties—the review of cert. petitions and drafting of cert. memoranda, the preparation for oral argument via bench memoranda, and the drafting of opinions—became routine. The Vinson clerk was not a legal assistant but a full-blown junior partner. As P-A theory would lead us to expect, we also find the first evidence of careful attention paid by a sitting chief justice to the political ideology of clerkship applicants as well as the creation of a hierarchical office staff.

While Vinson originally selected law clerks from traditional sources like Harvard and Yale,[313] the chief justice became increasingly uncomfortable with the more liberal, Ivy League graduates.[314] Ultimately, Vinson turned to Northwestern for all of his law clerks. Many of the Northwestern law clerks were recommended to Vinson by Wilbur Pedrick, himself a former Vinson clerk and a tax professor at Northwestern Law School.[315] Pedrick used two criteria in selecting Vinson's clerks: the student must have been at the top of his class and served as the editor of the law review.[316] Vinson, however, looked beyond the recommendations of law professors and judges in selecting law clerks. Two former Vinson clerks recall that the chief justice consulted FBI files on applicants, and one law clerk received his clerkship offer after another candidate ran afoul of the background check.[317] "I know that Vinson reviewed FBI files on his prospective clerks in 1952. These were the awful years of the McCarthy hearings, and I believe that Vinson was especially sensitive to keep the Court and its personnel above suspicion."[318]

Vinson interviewed the law clerks recommended to him by Northwestern Law School. Former law clerk William Oliver (OT 1952) hesitated to define the interview as a mere "formality," characterizing it instead as an opportunity for Vinson to size up the potential hire.[319] Former law clerk Howard Trienens (OT 1951) shares Oliver's assessment of the nonsubstantive nature of the interview, remarking that "it really was a non-penetrating interview. You don't want to take a law clerk until you've seen him but it was obvious that if Pedrick said he was the guy, he was the guy."[320]

As noted above, Vinson was the first to employ three law clerks. The justification for the third law clerk lay in the fact that Vinson's assistants had the added responsibility of reviewing all *in forma pauperis* (IFP) petitions filed with the Supreme Court (the Vinson law clerks received the only copy of the IFP petitions, drafted memoranda, and circulated the memos to the associate justices), but this third position also provided continuity and structure in Vinson's chambers. One clerk always served for a second term and was designated the "senior clerk" or "chief clerk."[321] At least during the early years of Vinson's tenure, the senior clerk was responsible for determining which clerks worked on the bench and cert. memoranda.[322]

Additionally, Vinson initially employed former aide Paul Kelly as an administrative assistant. Kelly would occasionally get involved in the discussion of cases, however, and even wrote Vinson memoranda regarding the University of Texas and University of Oklahoma law school desegregation cases.[323] Vinson's staff was rounded out with a second secretary, a stenographic clerk, and a messenger.[324] With seven staff members, Vinson had the largest staff of any chief justice to date.

In a law review article collectively prepared by Vinson's law clerks after the chief justice's death, the former clerks write that they prepared cert. memoranda. The pressure to provide a highly accurate factual summary of the case was higher for Vinson's law clerks. "A correct statement of the facts was the most important function of a 'cert memo' from the Chief's point of view since it was his responsibility to state each case before discussion by the conference."[325] Depending on the level of preparation by the other justices, Vinson's law clerks faced the potential of misleading not only the chief justice with an incorrect summary of the facts but also the entire conference. Vinson's law clerks add, however, that the chief justice was less likely to rely on their recommended disposition of the cert. memoranda. Chief Justice Vinson had his secretary "keep a box score to determine the correlation between the clerk's recommendations and the Chief's actual vote and, in case of variation, to see whether the clerk or the Chief was consistent with the ultimate action of the Court."[326]

The Vinson clerks were also required to review and summarize the IFP petitions. Only the chief justice's law clerks prepared IFP memoranda, and their summaries were circulated to the other justices. In many cases only the memoranda and not the actual petition were sent to the other chambers, meaning that the other eight justices were relying on the chief justice's law clerks to accurately summarize the petitions. In short, the Vinson clerks "served in the capacity of law clerks to the entire Court."[327] Because of the extra burden imposed by the IFP petitions, the Vinson law clerks had the luxury of a secretary to type their memoranda.

Interestingly, in the 1954 law review article the Vinson law clerks do not discuss any involvement in opinion writing. Moreover, they either downplay or defend this role in interviews given for the Fred M. Vinson Oral History Project. Karl Price (OT 1946) glosses over this important job duty, blandly remarking that the clerks "did the writing that was required." Price defensively adds: "He did not use or rely on his law clerks in the sense of being dependent on them to make decisions for him."[328] Former law clerk William Oliver (OT 1952) argues that while political actors of the nineteenth century had the time to craft their own speeches and opinions, the pressures of the modern political arena force such actors to ask "whether or not the best expenditure of time and energy for any man in public life is to do more of his writing personally and turn less of it over to others under guidelines." Oliver is also quick to answer the charges that Vinson was overly dependent, adding that this myth was created by former clerks eager "to give the impression that they were the power behind the throne" and not by Vinson's actual practices.[329]

It is well established, however, that the chief justice's clerks prepared the first draft of opinions, a fact that his former law clerks now more readily concede.[330] So why the omission? The oversight by his former clerks is likely not the result of false modesty on the part of the former clerks but, instead, evidence that Vinson's practices hadn't achieved the status of an established Court norm—the ghosts of Holmes and Brandeis still loomed large. The Vinson law clerks' arguments track the arguments made by defenders' of today's court: rising caseload pressures dictate that the law clerks shoulder opinion-writing duties, but the decision-making process remains safely in the justices' hands.[331] What the Vinson clerks fail to acknowledge, however, is that in the late 1940s and early 1950s Vinson was the only justice, save Frank Murphy, to consistently use such a clerkship model. Surely the extra burdens of the center chair did not justify a total abdication of opinion-writing duties.

Vinson biographers James E. St. Clair and Linda C. Gugin write that the chief justice's law clerks did the actual opinion writing, although they reviewed instructions before beginning and had their work product reviewed by the chief justice.[332] In my interviews as well, former Vinson clerks confirmed that they prepared original opinion drafts. The law clerk who had prepared the cert. memorandum in the case assigned to the chief justice would be given the responsibility of drafting the opinion, a draft that Vinson relied on in preparing the final draft.[333]

After the Saturday conference, Vinson met with his clerks, read orders to the clerk of the Court, and then discussed the Saturday conference. A former clerk remarked that these meetings were more than simply rehashing the justices' votes, and that Vinson's summary of the conference discussions aided the clerks' subsequent preparation of the opinions. Remarks former clerk Howard Trienens (OT 1951):

> [After the Saturday conferences] we would then converse on the sidelights or the legal principles or the personalities of what happened. Why did Justice Black vote this way or how come Frankfurter was over here? How much discussion was there on this case or that case? He would be very, very open and frank with us. I think we all protected his confidence . . . that was the most rewarding part of the whole experience.[334]

Trienens' co-clerk during OT 1951, Newton Minow, explained that it was the strategy involved in Vinson's opinion assignment that held his attention. "[H]e would tell us who he was thinking of assigning to a particular opinion and why. . . . He went into that kind of a calculation or analysis of how he could assign cases in a way to keep a majority if he was on the majority."[335] While the clerk assigned to draft a particular opinion would meet with Vinson regarding the form and substantive content of the draft, Vinson clerks believed that they had a "broader scope in preparing their opinions" than clerks in other chambers. In short, Vinson gave his law clerks a "fair amount of leeway" in opinion drafting.[336] Recalls another clerk in an off-the-record interview:

> [Vinson] would outline for us the major issues in the case and the reasons for the Court's decision, explaining what points he wanted emphasized in the opinion. Then he left it for us to prepare the first draft of an opinion for his review . . . he reviewed our drafts thoroughly, often sending them back for further revisions until they said what he wanted to say. We had no illusions that we were influencing his opinions in any material way, although we did take some pride in the craftsmanship we tried to put into each opinion we drafted.

In the opinion of former Black law clerk John P. Frank, the result of Vinson's heavy reliance on his law clerks may be found in the opinions they helped draft:

> Perhaps the most striking personality quality of Vinson's opinions is their odd lack of personality. . . . Chief Justice Vinson had three law clerks, an administrative assistant, and a little staff of secretaries and messengers. This gave him an opportunity to be somewhat more of a supervisor than an immediate participant in the detail work of his office. Yet judicial personality is largely a matter of details: the Holmes epigram, the Black way with facts, the Frankfurter vocabulary, the Brandeis footnote, the Stone pragmatism cropping up in unexpected places.[337]

Frank writes that not only did Chief Justice Vinson's opinions lack a distinctive voice, but they also suffered from "an unevenness of quality . . . some of his good opinions being excellent and some of the others being a far cry from it, sometimes in prose and frequently in legal detail."[338] One suspects that the "unevenness" was the result of a combination of the yearly rotation of law clerks and Vinson's reliance on the law clerk drafts.

While Vinson's former clerks speak appreciatively of the lengths to which the chief justice kept his law clerks fully abreast of the voting and in-fighting of the Court's conferences,[339] as well as the chief justice's willingness to discuss circulating opinions and pending cases, this was likely a necessity given Vinson's substantial delegation of job duties to his clerks. In fact, Vinson even met with his law clerks to map out opinion assignments.[340] While it is not clear whether the law clerks had any hand in the assignment process, they were talking about the assignment decisions with Vinson.

Given the wide range of duties delegated to the Vinson clerks, the question of law clerk influence—direct or indirect, deliberate or accidental—

begins to become most relevant. As noted earlier, clerks are unlikely to exert influence over the judicial decision-making process when their responsibilities are limited. A justice who uses his law clerks to edit his opinions and perform rudimentary legal research does not create an environment in which a clerk can influence either a justice's vote or the justice's legal analysis in an opinion. Empires do not fall and fortunes are not lost when a law clerk recommends that a justice remove a semicolon or correct a cite. When, however, a justice relies on a law clerk's analysis of a cert. petition (as to whether there is a split among the circuits, for example) or the clerk's drafting of a majority opinion, a clerk can exert influence.

At a minimum, Chief Justice Vinson created the environment in which the potential for influence existed. While other justices asked their law clerks to review cert. petitions and prepare cert. memoranda, there is no evidence that Vinson himself reviewed the original records and briefs as closely as a Hugo Black or a Wiley Rutledge. Moreover, on- and off-the-record interviews demonstrate that Vinson gave his law clerks free rein in drafting judicial opinions. Granted, the clerks had to retain the conference majority and loosely adopt the reasoning of said majority when drafting an opinion. Yet it was often the clerks, not the chief justice, who initially decided which jurisprudential path to select in moving from point A to point B.[341] Moreover, there were occasions when the law clerks directly influenced Vinson's decision in a pending case. Former law clerk Howard Trienens recounts an instance during his clerkship when an opinion "wouldn't write" as directed by Vinson, and the law clerks convinced the justice to vote in the opposite direction.[342]

Vinson's best-known law clerk is Byron White, who returned to the Supreme Court as a Supreme Court justice in 1962. White, already a public figure due to his professional football career, clerked for Vinson during OT 1946. In May 1946, White interviewed with Justices Burton and Douglas but did not receive employment offers. After Chief Justice Stone's death on April 22, 1946, and Fred Vinson's subsequent appointment, Justice Douglas wrote the new chief justice and recommended that he hire White:

> You have probably read of him [in] the sports section of the newspapers. He was an All-American football player whose nickname was Whizzer White. He played professional football. He was in the service for a couple of years. He has led his class at Yale Law School for three years. Members of the faculty tell me he is the most outstanding man they have had in a long time. As a matter of fact, he probably will have an all-time scholastic record at Yale Law School. He is a delightful person, of great charm and poise.[343]

White received the clerkship offer, joining Karl Price (the senior clerk) and Francis A. Allen for OT 1946.

According to White biographer Dennis Hutchinson, at first White's celebrity made his co-clerks question whether he truly merited a clerkship position. Hutchinson quotes former co-clerk Francis A. Allen, who commented: "It is hard to overstate how famous he was. That bred skepticism, although I could tell in five minutes of conversation that he was extraordinarily bright. I could not at the time tell how well educated he was, but he quickly disabused anyone who underestimated his native ability."[344]

Vinson did not become close with his law clerks. Hutchinson writes that the chief justice "was a demanding taskmaster who expected six-day weeks and saw no reason to bestow the warm, avuncular attention on his staff that made Black, Frankfurter, and Jackson so popular with their clerks."[345] Former law clerk Karl Price (OT 1946) remarked that the chief justice "was not what I would call real chummy. He did not spend long hours socializing with the law clerks. . . . He was a very dignified man, and a man that you didn't get to be casual or extremely informal with." While the law clerks might have the occasional chat with the chief justice about sporting events, Price adds: "I don't really ever recall having a sustained discussion with him of anything except the business we were working on."[346] In short, the personal side of Vinson's clerkship model differed dramatically from the ones crafted by Black or Frankfurter.

Only two new justices joined the Vinson Court: Tom C. Clark and Sherman Minton. I was not able to uncover much information regarding how Justice Clark hired his law clerks,[347] although some court observers have concluded that the sons of Clark's friends and political allies filled the ranks of his law clerks. Interviews were not necessary for a clerkship offer, and two former law clerks report that their law school deans (University of Texas Law School and Yale Law School) recommended their names to Clark.[348] Justice Clark's chambers were supervised by secretary Alice O'Donnell, herself a 1954 graduate of George Washington University Law School and Justice Clark's secretary from his days at the Department of Justice.[349] Former law clerk Ernest Rubenstein remembers "Miss Alice" (as she was called by Justice Clark) as "a delight," a woman who was "intensely loyal to the Justice, and unfailingly warm, helpful, kind and sweet-tempered."[350]

Byron White was not the only NFL veteran to clerk on the Supreme Court. One of Justice Clark's law clerks was Raymond Brown (OT 1962), who played quarterback for the old Baltimore Colts for three seasons before attending law school. During the 1960 season, Brown completed six of fourteen pass attempts for sixty-five yards and one touchdown. Unfortunately for Brown's career aspirations, the starting quarterback for the Baltimore Colts throughout his career was Johnny Unitas. Brown attended law school at the University of Mississippi, serving as associate editor of the *Mississippi Law Journal* and earning his law degree in 1962.

Former law clerks Frederick Rowe (OT 1952), Ernest Rubenstein and Ellis H. McKay (OT 1953), Robert W. Hamilton (OT 1955), Larry E. Temple

(OT 1959), and Charles D. Reed (OT 1965) state that Justice Clark routinely required his law clerks to prepare cert. memoranda. "We wrote cert. memos on every case unless we knew the justice had to disqualify himself because he had contact with the case while AG [attorney general]," writes Rubenstein, adding that the law clerks used a contact person at the Justice Department to determine whether Clark had previous involvement with the case. Reed writes that Justice Clark gave his law clerks "great discretion" in preparing the memoranda: "Our job was to *assist* the justice and give him the information, facts, views, etc. we thought would be most helpful. He shaped the process by giving us feedback, asking further questions, and treating us very collegially."[351]

Justice Clark prepared the first draft of opinions in cases that interested him or fell within an area of his expertise. His law clerks reviewed the draft opinions, checked cites, and "offered comments on both style and substance."[352] If the case did not interest Clark, then his clerks prepared the first draft:

> [O]verall clerks were permitted to do first drafts. Generally, the only instructions were the outcome. We were told how votes went at conference. Sometimes he would give "deeper" instructions or rationale, etc. In one case that I drafted [*Graham v. John Deere*, 383 U.S. 1 (1966)], Clark told the bar that it was my draft; in that case, a patent case, he allowed me great license.[353]

The degree of law clerk involvement in opinion writing appears to have varied over the years, perhaps due the number of cases that interested Clark. Rowe (OT 1952) and Rubenstein (OT 1953) write that the law clerks drafted almost all the opinions, McKay (OT 1953) states that the clerks "often" prepared the first drafts, and Temple recalls that during OT 1959 the clerks "did not routinely prepare first drafts of opinions. The Justice did that." Temple adds: "We frequently would prepare a draft of some specific point Justice Clark wanted included in the opinion."

Finally, Clark "rarely" asked his clerks to prepare bench memoranda. "Clark was a very hardworking justice who would read and digest trial briefs pretty much on his own. Occasionally he would have one of us ... do some ancillary preparation of specific issues."[354] Former law clerk Robert W. Hamilton provides a similar account, recalling that occasionally Justice Clark would ask the clerks to research a point of law in a case scheduled for oral argument.[355] There is no evidence that Justice Clark felt that his clerkship model needed special rules designed to monitor his law clerks. Clark did not have his clerks review their work before it was submitted to the justice,[356] and there was no staff hierarchy among the clerks. Nor did Justice Clark impose intrachamber rules regarding clerk confidentiality. "In the culture at that time (1953–1954), it was understood that total confidentiality was the rule. It was taken for granted."[357] With the arrival of Chief Justice Earl Warren, confidentiality rules would no longer be taken for granted.

While Justice Clark's former law clerks uniformly remember him fondly, they do not recount stories of familiarity and closeness. "Clark was neither a father figure nor a mentor," writes an anonymous clerk, but he "treated us as mature, competent men, entitled to respect based on our own demonstrated achievements." The same clerk explains that Justice Clark's "native personality, his life outside the Court and the stage of his tenure combined in a way that he did not really feel a need, nor did he have an evident desire, to actively tutor or mentor his clerks." Almost all the former clerks credit the relaxed and congenial nature of the Clark chambers to secretary Alice O'Donnell, explaining that she served as the intermediary between the clerks and Justice Clark. In short, while Justice Clark did not follow the Frankfurter model of making surrogate children out of his law clerks, neither did Clark engage in the intellectual jousting of the Frankfurter chambers. "Justice Clark never sought to dominate his law clerks intellectually," writes former law clerk Frederick M. Rowe, "but engaged them in a joint enterprise as a public service to dispose of cases fairly and expeditiously in working with the Court as an institution."[358] Perhaps former law clerk Ernest Rubenstein best summarizes the Clark law clerks' recollections of their former employer: "Justice Clark was a soft spoken, unfailingly courteous, kind, thoughtful human being . . . and unfailingly correct employer."[359]

Our last justice is Sherman "Shay" Minton, a former U.S. senator and federal appellate court judge who was nominated by President Truman to replace Wiley Rutledge after his sudden death. Justice Minton served approximately seven years on the Supreme Court, and his unremarkable tenure as a Supreme Court justice and small pool of former law clerks results in limited data regarding his clerkship practices.

Minton's clerks reviewed all cert. petitions, prepared cert. memoranda,[360] and *sometimes* prepared the first draft of opinions. Minton's clerks rarely prepared bench memoranda.[361] Although Minton gave his law clerks substantial responsibility, he did not adopt staffing practices designed to monitor and limit his law clerks. According to former law clerks Rowe, Wallace, and Butler, there was no hierarchy of "senior" and "junior" law clerk, the two clerks did not review each other's work, and there were no formal rules regarding law clerk confidentiality.[362]

Minton did not craft precise instructions regarding the review of cert. petitions. David Atkinson writes that the justice "seldom gave any formal instructions to his clerks as to how petitions for certiorari, jurisdictional statements, or applications *in forma pauperis* should be handled."[363] Former law clerk Raymond Gray recalls that the cert. memoranda included both basic information regarding the appeal and the law clerk's recommended disposition, but added, "I doubt that he ever paid any attention to my recommendations."[364]

As for opinion writing, Atkinson concludes:

> His standard procedure was to first reread the briefs on the merits. Occasionally, he would ask a clerk to research a particular point. Sometimes he would do the first draft of the opinion himself and then ask the clerks for comments. On other occasions he would ask the clerks to prepare the first draft after he had told them his view of the case. Justice Minton did not usually solicit advice on the merits of the case itself. He would go through an analysis of a case with a clerk before he asked him to write a draft. The clerk had an opportunity at that time to ask questions about the analysis but he did not feel free to question the basic decision on the merits.[365]

When Minton himself prepared the first draft, the law clerks performed the traditional tasks of cite checking and proofreading. The clerks, however, felt obligated to closely examine the Justice's recitation of the case facts—as explained by a former Minton law clerk: "Often in the initial drafts . . . he would state the facts not as the record had revealed them but as would best support the decision. He had to be closely watched on such misstatements of fact . . . [and] expected his law clerks to force him to hew to the record."[366]

From his former clerks' comments, one gets the impression that Justice Minton was less reliant on his clerks in terms of substantive responsibilities. The law clerks are split on whether their cert. memoranda influenced Minton, and none of the law clerks interviewed by Atkinson undercut the conclusion by one former clerk that "Justice Minton was a strong-minded man who was not easily influenced by anyone except himself insofar as the decision of cases was concerned." While apparently one former clerk was successful in convincing Justice Minton to change his vote in a pending case, the only arena in which the clerks held the possibility of influence was acting as sounding boards or debating partners for the justice. Atkinson writes that Minton "used his clerks as reflectors against which he tested the strength of his arguments," adding that the justice "delighted in engaging his clerks in violent argumentation and was not displeased if he succeeded in out-shouting and out-swearing them."[367]

There is no evidence that Minton enjoyed (or even tried to foster) a tight bond with his law clerks. Former clerk Harry Wallace (OT 1952) writes that Minton "did not try to be a mentor," but adds, "nor was he a stern taskmaster. I don't remember any criticisms [from the justice] ever. There was very little interchange with the Justice at all—what there was was always pleasant."[368] Wallace did not recall socializing outside of chambers with Justice Minton, and the Minton law clerks neither held annual reunions nor played an official role in the justice's funeral. The law clerks did hold a retirement party for Justice Minton at the Mayflower Hotel in October of 1956, however, bestowing a gold watch and leather-bound editions of his judicial opinions upon the surprised justice.[369]

Conclusion

By the 1940s, the stenographic clerk was no more. The Supreme Court's caseload had approximately tripled since Attorney General Garland's original recommendation that Congress authorize the hiring of stenographic clerks, and
the clerkship institution evolved to the point where two bright young men
from the nation's finest law schools assisted each justice (save Douglas) in reviewing cert. petitions, conducting legal research, and honing judicial opinions. While Justice Brandeis may have fretted that the growing numbers of
law clerks and their expanded duties undercut the public's impression that the
justices were the only members of the national government that still did their
own work, there is no evidence—with the exception of Chief Justice Vinson
and Justice Murphy—that the reins had grown slack in the justices' hands. True,
more justices had delegated the initial review of cert. petitions to their law
clerks. Yet the available evidence shows that these justices still spent hour after
hour reviewing the cert. memoranda and combing through the original appeals papers. To assist comparison of the different justices, law clerks' main job
duties during the early- to mid-twentieth century are displayed in Table 4.1.

Because most justices had delegated only limited duties, the possibility that
law clerks would "frolic" or "defect" was improbable and the consequences

TABLE 4.1. Main Job Duties of Law Clerk as Legal Assistant

	Cert. Memos	Bench Memos	Opinion Editing	Opinion Writing
Black	Yes	No	Yes	Infrequently
Burton	Yes	Yes	Yes	No
Butler	Yes	Unknown	Yes	No
Byrnes	Unknown	Unknown	Unknown	Unknown
Cardozo	Yes	Yes	Yes	No
Clark	Yes	Infrequently	Yes	Yes
Douglas	Yes	No	No	No
Frankfurter	Infrequently	Infrequently	Yes	Yes
CJ Hughes	Yes	Unknown	Unknown	No
Jackson	Yes	No	Yes	Infrequently
Minton	Yes	Infrequently	Yes	Yes
Murphy	Yes	Unknown	Yes	Yes
Reed	Yes	Infrequently	Yes	Infrequently
Roberts	Unknown	Unknown	Unknown	Unknown
Rutledge	Yes	Yes	Yes	No
CJ Stone	Yes	No	Yes	No
Taft	Yes	No	Yes	No
CJ Vinson	Yes	Yes	Yes	Yes

of such defection minimal. Therefore, the justices did not put into place measures designed to monitor clerks and minimize the likelihood of defection. With the dawn of the Warren Court, the institutional rules of the game were about to change.

CHAPTER 5

The Law Clerk as Law Firm Associate

"I would have the Courtier devote all his thought and
strength of spirit to loving and almost adoring the prince he
serves above all else, devoting his every desire and habit and
manner to pleasing him."
—Baldassare Castiglione, *The Book of the Courtier*

WHILE IN THE 1920S THROUGH THE 1940S the law clerk acted as a legal
assistant, the 1950s and 1960s witnessed the transformation of the law clerk
into an attorney involved in all aspects of chamber work. Some have labeled
this new breed of law clerk as the "junior justices," but a more accurate label
may be "law firm associate," in that the law clerk assumed the same responsibilities that an associate would in a small but very prestigious law firm.
Former Marshall law clerk Mark V. Tushnet writes that by the late 1960s the
relationship between law clerk and justice had evolved:

The Justices had become accustomed to working within the Court as if they
ran, as Justice Powell put it, nine small law firms, with one senior partner and several junior associates, the law clerks. Senior partners in law firms draft little of their
office's work and the analogy holds for the Supreme Court as well. If the chambers
are thought of as law firms and the Justice as senior partner, we must immediately
think about the different ways lawyers organize their offices. The possibilities range
from the senior partner who micromanages the office work to the senior partner
who sets the office's direction and motivates his or her subordinates to produce the
very best work the office can.[1]

At either extreme, the associate is a full-blown attorney. Unlike the law clerk
as legal assistant, the law clerk as associate is relied on to master complex
areas of the law, counsel the senior partner as to the best method of resolving
tricky legal issues, and draft complex legal documents, namely, judicial opinions. Stenography is no longer a necessary skill. While those justices who
predated the Warren Court would maintain the model of law clerk as legal
assistant, all subsequent justices adopted the law clerk as associate model.

The Warren Court, 1953 to 1969

In 1953, President Dwight Eisenhower nominated former California governor Earl Warren to succeed the late Fred Vinson as chief justice of the U.S.
Supreme Court. At the time Eisenhower believed that he was nominating a
conservative to the bench. Warren was Thomas Dewey's running mate in the
1948 presidential election, and in 1952 Warren battled Eisenhower for the
Republican party's presidential nomination. Despite Warren's Republican
credentials, Eisenhower's assumption about Warren's Supreme Court voting
behavior proved to be utterly mistaken. By the time Earl Warren retired in
1969, he had supervised the virtual rewriting of the Bill of Rights. Warren
would also play an important but less heralded role in the evolution of the
clerkship institution.

Once appointed to the Supreme Court, Earl Warren learned that a state
governor commanded a larger staff than a U.S. Supreme Court chief justice:
"In Washington, Warren discovered, the chief justice's staff consisted of a
single secretary, three law clerks, and two aging messengers—one of whom
died within six months. The young messenger, past seventy, spent his afternoon dozing in an unused conference room; he retired the next year."[2]

As with previous justices who took office upon the sudden death of
a predecessor, Chief Justice Warren inherited Vinson's office staff: secretary
Margaret McHugh and law clerks William Oliver, Richard Flynn, and Earl
Pollock. Biographer Ed Cray writes that Warren decided to use Vinson's law
clerks out of a sense of fairness and expediency. "Replacing them at this late
date would be unfair to them and the families they had moved to Washington; it would also take time, which he did not have."[3] Warren expanded
the office staff when he hired former California secretary Margaret Bryan.
While Margaret McHugh supervised all matters related to the chief justice's
official work, Ms. Bryan was responsible for the chief justice's personal correspondence and related matters.[4]

According to biographer Bernard Schwartz, Justice Frankfurter influenced Chief Justice Warren's law clerk selection practices during Warren's
first years of the Court. As evidence of Frankfurter's influence, Schwartz
cites the large number of Harvard Law School graduates in Warren's initial
batch of law clerks. Schwartz writes, that "after the relationship between the
Chief and Frankfurter cooled, Warren set up his own system of selecting
clerks."[5] The historical record, however, only weakly supports this conten-
tion. As noted above, Warren inherited his first three law clerks from Vinson. Of the next ten clerks hired by Warren, only three—Gerald Gunther,[6]
Samuel Stern, Martin Richman—attended Harvard Law School. Hence, if
it existed at all, Felix Frankfurter's beachhead in the Warren chambers was
modest and temporary. In subsequent terms Warren would seldom turn to

Harvard Law School for his clerks. Warren did not want to select "little Frankfurters" who "might pose some security problems in his chambers, since they might talk to their old professors, and it would ultimately get back to Frankfurter himself."[7]

The first version of the Warren selection model relied on the recommendations of a handful of trusted law school professors, while a second version called upon former Warren law clerks Murray H. Bring and William H. Dempsey (both clerks from OT 1959) to screen applications and make recommendations to Warren.[8] At some point, Chief Justice Warren created a separate selection committee that looked only to California law schools to fill one of the three clerkship positions. Former Boalt Hall professor Adrian Kragen (who served as deputy attorney general when Warren was California Attorney General) spent ten years as a one-man selection committee.

Kragen stated that he made a yearly pilgrimage to Washington, D.C., to meet with Warren and discuss the type of law clerk the chief justice wanted. Kragen commented that Warren generally stated that he "didn't want too conservative of a person."[9] The chief justice's preferences are reflected in an October 24, 1957, letter from Kragen to Chief Justice Warren, in which Kragen discusses the political philosophy of clerkship candidate Arthur O. Armstrong, Jr.:

> I felt from discussions with him that his basic philosophy as to the law might be quite conservative and, therefore, I spent some time with him yesterday discussing this question. He suggested that he try to express his attitude in that regard and I am enclosing a copy of his memorandum to me. I feel that he is the type of young man who would never let his personal attitude or thoughts to any extent influence the work which he would do as a lawyer or, in the case of the court, as a law clerk. I believe that he would do an exceptional job as a clerk for you.[10]

I do not know whether Chief Justice Warren extended a clerkship offer, but Armstrong did not serve as a Warren law clerk. Being politically conservative, however, was not always a death knell to a candidate's chances if the candidate was able to put aside personal issues and look dispassionately at the legal issues.

In the early years of Chief Justice Warren's tenure on the bench, he did not consider female applicants.[11] This apparently changed in December of 1959. In a letter to the chief justice, Kragen asks permission to interview a female law student. He writes: "I know, of course, that you have no personal prejudice in the use [of] women clerks, but thought that it might be that the character of the entire group working as law clerks might be such as to make it impossible or impractical to fit in a woman." A handwritten note on the top of Kragen's letter reads: "Wire him it is okay."[12] Regardless of the change in Warren's hiring practices, the chief justice never hired a female law clerk.

After meeting with Warren, Kragen traveled to four California law schools—University of California–Berkeley, University of California–Los Angeles, Stanford, and University of Southern California—and interviewed one or two candidates at each school. Kragen also met with law professors to gather additional information on the candidates' "attitudes." While Kragen recalls that law review membership was one determining factor, lower court clerkship experience was not—one element of clerkship selection practices that changed with Warren Burger. Kragen subsequently returned to Washington, D.C., and made his recommendation to Warren. Kragen stated that the chief justice "always" accepted his recommendation.[13]

Finally, during the 1960s several justices considered a qualification unique to the time: whether the clerks would be drafted into the armed services. For example, a memorandum written to Chief Justice Warren by an unknown law clerk summarizes the top clerkship applicants for OT 1967. The memo discusses law review membership, law school and undergraduate grades, letters of recommendation, and draft status. The final rankings of the applicants are based, in part, on their draft eligibility.[14]

Warren established a hierarchy among his office staff, in which one clerk was designated the "chief" clerk. Former law clerk Richman writes that the chief clerk "was nominally responsible for output of the office, but basically each clerk took responsibility for [his or her] own output."[15] Former law clerk Michael Smith (OT 1965) recalls that the only unique duties he was assigned as chief law clerk was organizing monthly meetings of the Supreme Court law clerks.[16]

This author spoke with two former Warren law clerks—Dallin H. Oaks (OT 1957) and Jesse H. Choper (OT 1960)—about the clerkship experience.[17] Oaks kept a diary during his tenure with the chief justice, which provides a fascinating look into Warren's chambers. Additionally, I interviewed former Reed law clerk Earl Dudley, Jr. (OT 1967), whom Justice Reed "loaned" to Chief Justice Warren upon retirement,[18] and I corresponded with former Warren law clerks Martin F. Richman (OT 1956), Ralph Moore (OT 1959), Michael E. Smith (OT 1965), and Paul J. Meyer (OT 1967). Although technically a Reed law clerk, Dudley's job duties with Warren did not differ from the chief justice's full-time, "official" law clerks.[19]

In a July 1957 diary entry, new law clerk Dallin Oaks records that he spent time training with one of Warren's outgoing clerks. He summarizes the meeting as follows:

> The law clerk's job before the Court sits, and to a lesser extent after the Court is in session, is to prepare memoranda on the petitions for certiorari. . . . The Chief never examines these, relying entirely on the clerk's memoranda. . . . The memo ends with a recommendation (Grant, Deny, Disqualify, Reverse, etc.). As near as can be determined the Chief relies very heavily on these recommendations.

The *in forma pauperis* . . . are handled exclusively in the Chief's Office. . . . The memo prepared on these go to the whole Court, though only the Chief's copy carries the recommendation. About 3% of these, selected by the Chief's clerks as meritorious, are circulated to the whole court . . . Writing the IFP memos is touchy, as you must "write for the nine," and any information irrelevant for some may be crucial for others. The IFP memos are usually very short, most do little more than say generally what the petitioner complains of and, for the Chief, why he has no claim. Unlike in the cert. memos, no effort is made to set out the facts so that the Justice can judge for himself. *The law clerk makes the decision.*[20]

The outgoing clerk's summary of the chief justice's reliance on his law clerks in the review of the cert. petitions is rather extraordinary. Until now, no other former law clerk has provided any evidence that a justice was so detached from the decision-making process. The law clerks wielded influence not only in the presentation of facts and the issues, but also in their recommendations. Unlike other justices, the law clerks' recommended disposition reflected the clerks' attitudes, not Warren's. In a September 21, 1957, meeting, Chief Justice Warren himself stressed that the clerk memoranda should reflect their opinions, not what they anticipated his to be. "Our memos to him should be independent—our own views," writes Oaks. "He doesn't want 'yes men.' He welcomes any criticism."[21]

As for the preparing of opinion drafts, the outgoing clerk stated: "The Chief is not a good writer. His first drafts are commonly very bad. Happily, however, he is quite willing to accept criticism or, indeed, to have his clerks reject the thing in toto. As a result, the preparation of his opinions is left in great measure to his clerks." Regardless of the intellectual firepower and academic credentials of the law clerks, it is still jarring to see a young attorney so blithely summarizing the chief justice's legal skills.

During OT 1960, 1965, and 1967, law clerks prepared the first draft of every opinion.[22] The law clerk who prepared the bench memorandum in a specific case also drafted the opinion (if the majority opinion was assigned to the chief justice). Before beginning the opinion, the law clerk met with the chief justice and received his marching orders. In many instances, these orders were minimal. Choper remarks that a significant amount of the opinion writing was given to the law clerks "with very little instruction."[23] At least during OT 1967, Warren reviewed the draft with his law clerk. Dudley recalled an "excruciating process" in which the chief justice read the clerk's draft out loud, stopping whenever he had a question or comment. The clerk would then take the draft, make the revisions suggested by Warren, and return the draft to the chief justice for a second review.[24]

The dearth of specific directions permitted the law clerk to wield influence over the content, but not the ultimate holding, in a specific opinion. Oaks stated that law clerks had "zero influence on where the chief justice wanted to go, [but] significant influence on how it was expressed."[25] Cray recounts one instance: "In a case dealing with technicalities in the tax code, the chief simply told clerk Henry Steinman, 'This is the result. Write it up.'"[26] While Warren carefully reviewed how his law clerks expressed the reasoning in his opinions, he often deferred to his clerk's work product, and in many instances opinions were printed without major revisions.[27]

The third major responsibility for Warren's clerks: reviewing the voluminous court files and preparing bench memoranda. These reports were prepared in all cases set for oral argument, and they tended to be much more detailed than the cert. memoranda.[28] While former clerk Earl Dudley does not recall Warren asking the clerks to suggest questions for oral argument, the clerks did include a summary of the facts and the parties' main arguments as well as a recommended disposition of the appeal.[29]

Warren's rules on chamber confidentiality reflect the evolution of the clerkship institution toward minimizing clerk defection and misbehavior. Former Reed law clerk Julian Burke comments: "[Earl Warren] had some very unusual rules that governed his chambers . . . like, after every session . . . with his clerks . . . he would decide whether or not his clerks could repeat or discuss whatever they had discussed . . . and, if so, what part of it they could discuss with other clerks or with other justices."[30] These rules were a reflection of Warren's position that "they were *his* clerks, not the Court's, and that what went on in his chambers was not to be revealed outside, not even to the other justices or their clerks.[31] Schwartz writes that Warren's general policy of confidentiality stemmed, in part, from his belief that Justice Frankfurter was trying to "subvert" Warren's clerks.[32] Of course, this was not a new phenomenon—former law clerks from different chambers have reported (usually with amusement) the lectures and lobbying of the former Harvard Law School professor.

In a September 21, 1957, diary entry, Oaks records the lecture regarding law clerk confidentiality that Warren gave his clerks (Oaks, Jon Newman, and Donald Cahan):

[The law clerks] are to take orders from and be subject to persuasion or pressure from no one save him. Be sensitive from other clerks to influence him. OK to discuss matters freely with other clerks, but distinguish that from propagandizing by them or us. Improper to correspond with another Justice. OK to "drop in" on their request but use great care on such visits. Law clerk should feel responsible for good name of his justice both at present and for all time. Don't discuss Warren's views on unpublished matters with other clerks. If we have ideas for court or other justices route them thru Warren.

The confidentiality rules established by Chief Justice Warren had the effect of isolating his law clerks from direct and indirect pressures from other justices and their law clerks. In effect, these rules minimized their chances of being influenced by outside sources and being diverted from the main task at hand—implementing Earl Warren's policy goals. Such barriers against outside influences were required in light of the enormous responsibilities shouldered by the Warren law clerks.[33]

Moreover, the available evidence indicates that Earl Warren was the first chief justice to meet with the law clerks from all nine chambers and discuss their duty of confidentiality (this became an annual ritual for Chief Justice Rehnquist). Several former, non-Warren law clerks recall the chief justice giving such talks during the 1950s and 1960s. For example, former Frankfurter law clerk John French (OT 1960) writes about the duty of confidentiality: "The rule was, you do not discuss the Court's business with others. The chief justice gave a clear presentation on this at a meeting of all clerks at the beginning of term."[34]

Like many justices of the 1950s and 1960s, Warren was a "genial father figure" who "continued to take a paternal interest in his current clerks, and their families."[35] Warren watched football games with his clerks, relaxed with them over drinks, got to know their families, and reunited with them at the annual law clerk dinners at the National Lawyers Club. While Warren may have viewed the clerks as his trusted aides[36] he did not indulge their occasional shenanigans.[37] The bonds between the chief justice and his clerks extended to Warren's death. When Warren lay in state at the Supreme Court, his law clerks stood by his casket as an honor guard.[38]

During Warren's tenure on the Supreme Court, two clerkship models existed. The model followed by the majority of the justices in the early 1950s involved the law clerks reviewing cert. petitions, preparing cert. memoranda, editing draft opinions, doing legal research, and informally chatting with their justice about pending cases. This is the "law clerk as legal assistant" model. The majority of the Supreme Court justices (Black, Burton, Douglas, Reed) almost always prepared the first draft of majority, concurring, and dissenting opinions, and no justice—save Harold Burton—had his law clerks routinely prepare bench memoranda. The sole justice who maintained complete control over the reviewing of cert. petitions was Felix Frankfurter.

The majority of the aforementioned justices took a hands-off approach to the selection of law clerks. In many instances, clerks were selected by a handful of trusted law school professors. The professors often had carte blanche in selecting the clerks, and no ideological vetting of the applicants occurred.

Upon his arrival at the Supreme Court, Earl Warren adopted a clerkship model in which law clerks continued the traditional role of writing cert. memoranda but assumed two new duties: preparing bench memoranda and drafting opinions. As we will see, every new addition to the Warren Court adopted a variation of this new clerkship model. Justices William J. Brennan, Jr., Abe Fortas, Arthur Goldberg, John Marshall Harlan II, Thurgood

Marshall, Potter Stewart, and Byron White routinely assigned their law clerks responsibility for drafting opinions (Charles Evans Whittaker's practices as to opinion writing are unclear, although he spoke disparagingly of the idea of clerks writing judicial opinions) and—save Harlan and perhaps Stewart—preparing bench memoranda. With the exception of Justice Brennan, all the new Warren Court justices had their law clerks prepare cert. memoranda.

The new Warren Court justices also deviated from the traditional clerkship selection practices. No longer would law professors be given sole discretion to select law clerks. We begin to see the rise of the law clerk selection committee, in which former law clerks subjected applicants to a formal screening process—a process that often contained an ideological litmus test.

There is no evidence that any of the earlier justices (Black, Douglas, Burton, Clark, Frankfurter, or Reed) altered their existing practices and adopted the new clerkship model, namely, the clerk as law firm associate. Given the fact that the justices who served on the Warren Court (both new additions and veterans) were subject to the same rising caseload pressures, workload considerations alone cannot explain the adoption of a new clerkship model. I believe that the answer instead lies with Chief Justice Earl Warren's leadership. Before Warren's elevation to the center seat, a strong norm existed as to the relationship between justice and law clerk. To paraphrase Louis Brandeis, the justices did their own work. With Earl Warren, doing one's own work was redefined—justices were still the ultimate decision makers, but they no longer did the tedious legwork of reviewing briefs, gathering information, and drafting opinions. That role was reserved for the law clerk. All new appointees to the Warren Court adopted the chief justice's belief that it was appropriate to delegate these duties to the clerks, thus creating a new norm.[39]

The argument that chief justices of the Supreme Court can reshape institutional practices has been previously tested by social scientists in the area of dissent rates. Walker, Epstein, and Dixon concluded that Chief Justice Harlan Fiske Stone bore "much [but not all] of the responsibility for changing the operational norms of the Court from institutional unity to permitting free expression of individual views," due to Stone's personal belief that "good law was the product of the class of individually expressed positions."[40] Additionally, Caldeira and Zorn have used more advanced statistical methodology to conclude that changes in a chief justice's leadership are partially responsible for variations in the consensual norms that restrain and shape justices' behavior.[41]

One last point: what of Chief Justice Fred Vinson and the impact of his leadership style on changing norms? The evidence is more problematic, given Vinson's shorter tenure on the Supreme Court, the fewer number of new appointees, and his general inability to lead the individual members of the

Supreme Court. As chief justice, Fred Vinson adopted a set of new expectations regarding what law clerks can (and should) do—prepare cert. and bench memoranda and draft opinions. The historical evidence, however, simply doesn't demonstrate whether Justices Clark and Minton—the only justices appointed during Vinson's term—responded to Vinson's creation of a new norm. While Justice Clark did have his law clerks prepare cert. memoranda, they "rarely" prepared bench memoranda. Moreover, the evidence regarding Clark's opinion-writing practices is ambiguous. As for Sherman Minton, the evidence is simply incomplete. While it is safe to conclude that Minton's law clerks did prepare cert. memoranda and did not prepare bench memoranda, it is unclear what role the clerks played in the opinion-writing process.

With the sudden death of Robert H. Jackson in 1954, President Eisenhower had a second opportunity to select a new member of the Supreme Court. His choice was John Marshall Harlan II, a Second Circuit Court of Appeals judge and the grandson of former U.S. Supreme Court justice John Marshall Harlan. Upon Harlan's confirmation in March of 1955, E. Barrett Prettyman, Jr. (a former Jackson law clerk who subsequently worked for Justice Frankfurter during Harlan's confirmation hearings) worked for the remainder of OT 1954 as Harlan's law clerk. Prettyman was joined by William T. Lifland, Harlan's Court of Appeals law clerk. Prettyman watched Harlan invest a substantial amount of time in selecting his OT 1955 clerks (Wayne G. Barnett and Leonard M. Leiman, both from Harvard Law School) and states that, unlike Justice Jackson, "Harlan was more interested in [the] IQ of clerks and academic skills than personality." Prettyman does not believe that Harlan was interested in applicants' political ideology. "He wanted brilliant people, and he would take care of the rest."[42]

Justice Harlan's clerkship model evolved during his first years on the Court. Former law clerk Norbert A. Schlei (OT 1956) writes:

> When I began my clerkship, Justice Harlan had just completed his first full Term on the Court. He had not yet worked out fully what his relationship with his clerks should be and what functions they should perform. In a matter that arose at the beginning of the Term and required an opinion, he drafted it himself, asking my co-worker, Paul Bator, and me to make comments, and this led me to believe he would draft all of his own opinions. Later in the Term, however, when the number of required opinions increased, the Justice asked us for drafts.[43]

Information about the later operations of Harlan's chambers comes from three former law clerks—Michael M. Maney (OT 1964), William T. Lake (OT 1969), and Thomas Krattenmaker (OT 1970). All three men provide almost identical descriptions of their job duties: Harlan's clerks prepared cert. memoranda, rarely wrote bench memoranda, prepared opinion drafts, and edited/cite checked final opinion drafts. The cert. memoranda contained much of the same information requested by other justices, with one wrinkle—Justice Harlan also asked his clerks for an "identification of the legal issues with specific reference to the positions the Justice had taken in the past."[44]

I have hypothesized that the clerkship institution is shaped by both micro- and macro-level forces, the latter being forces beyond the justice's control. In John Harlan's case, these pressures included the aging process—specifically, failing eyesight. Former law clerk Thomas B. Stoel, Jr. (OT 1967 and 1968) writes:

> The Justice's near blindness made him especially dependent on his law clerks, and when he was in Chambers, he spent virtually all his time with one or more of us. Like the other clerks, I would preview with him the docket for the Court's weekly conference, go over cases prior to oral argument, read to him from previous opinions that were relevant to current cases, and talk with him about the pros and cons of decisions . . . After drafting an opinion, I would read the scrawled changes and comments he laboriously entered on the draft and sit with him while he explained the additional modifications.[45]

Due to Harlan's poor vision, as well as a flurry of obscenity cases before the Court, more than one poor law clerk was asked to read these offending materials to the justice—including *The Housewife's Handbook on Selective Promiscuity* and *Fanny Hill*. The question that froze former law clerk Charles R. Nesson into indecision: "Could I sit there and read pornography to a Supreme Court Justice who had impressed me as the most dignified, genteel man I had ever met?"[46] Another law clerk attended the showing of a pornographic movie with Justice Harlan and six other justices, sitting next to the justice and "narrating the actions on the screen."[47]

Repeatedly, Harlan's former law clerks use three words—"patrician," "courtly," and "kind" to describe the justice. Former law clerk Norman Dorsen writes that Justice Harlan "treated all people, whatever their station, with consummate politeness and consideration. An unusual aspect of his civility was that, to the best of my recollection, in our entire year together he never personally criticized another Justice or anyone else."[48] Harlan demonstrated a kindness and solicitude toward his clerks—demonstrated in both small and large acts—that was recalled with great feeling decades later.[49] Former law clerk Nathan Lewin, a practicing Orthodox Jew, writes that Justice Harlan permitted Lewin to come into the office on Sunday (rather than the customary Saturday) and made sure that his young law clerk left the office on Friday afternoons before sundown,[50] while Bert W. Rein recounts a snowy afternoon when Justice Harlan insisted that his Court driver take Rein home to his Prince George's County residence (and his new wife) before the driver took Harlan home.[51] For former clerk Charles L. Fabrikant, Harlan's generosity was manifested in late night visits to the justice's home for rambling conversations and a glass of Rebel Yell bourbon.[52]

The spouses and children of Justice Harlan's law clerks also grew close to the justice. Harlan joined the clerks' families for dinner, attended their weddings, and entertained their children in his chambers. Former law clerk Paul Brest (OT 1968) tells the story of Justice Harlan inviting his three-year-old daughter Hilary to tea in the justice's chambers. "After having tea . . . we went into the courtroom. The Justice placed Hilary in the Chief Justice's seat and then stood at the lectern making an oral argument to her. Whether from direct recollection or from its frequent retelling, this experience remains vivid for Hilary—now a lawyer—thirty years later."[53]

The loyalty felt by Harlan's law clerks is best demonstrated by the bedside visits that many made to the dying justice in 1971. During these visits, former and current law clerks kept vigil over their former employer and eased his discomfort by sneaking in Lark cigarettes and Rebel Yell bourbon to the justice. Former law clerk Henry R. Sailer (OT 1958) describes entering the hospital room at George Washington University Hospital and finding the justice "almost mute and comatose from pain." Sailer writes: "After kissing him and stroking his forehead, I left only to burst into tears outside the door."[54] Rein tells of a story of another hospital visit when the dying Harlan, upon hearing that Rein was a new father: "Without hesitation, but with an enormous effort . . . raised himself on one elbow and reached out to shake my hand and congratulate me. I can still see his frail arm emerging from the hospital sheet. I realize now that he had to do this because he always did the right thing."[55]

It was during one of these hospital visits that Justice Harlan demonstrated what many law clerks referred to as his "grace." After telling then law clerk Martin Minsker (OT 1970) that he was delaying his retirement, Harlan explained that he did not want to detract from Hugo Black's similar announcement. "In further explanation, he said something that struck me at the time as remarkable, in light of his fundamental jurisprudential differences with Justice Black: 'You see, Marty, Hugo is truly a great man.'"[56] Justice Harlan died on December 29, 1971.

The next addition to the Warren Court was William J. Brennan, Jr. The son of Irish immigrants, Brennan attended Harvard Law School and sat on the New Jersey Supreme Court before being selected by President Eisenhower to replace the retiring Sherman Minton. Brennan would faithfully serve as the chief justice's right-hand man during the Warren Revolution.

Seventh Circuit Court of Appeals judge and former Brennan law clerk Richard A. Posner describes the Supreme Court in the early years of the Brennan judgeship:

> The world of the Supreme Court was different then, and from a clerk's perspective better. Justices had two clerks rather than four, and most clerks came directly from law school rather than from a clerkship with a judge of a lower court. . . . The

Court had no computers, there was no cert. pool, and law clerks had no secretarial assistance; my fellow clerk . . . and I typed our cert. memos and opinion drafts ourselves. Despite the fewness of the clerks and the absence of what have come to seem indispensable support facilities, the atmosphere was calm and the pace relaxed.[57]

Former law clerk Richard S. Arnold (OT 1960) agrees with the description of the rather sleepy state of the clerkship institution. "No one told us how to do the job. . . . there was nothing like an orientation program, a law clerks' manual, or similar formal indoctrination."[58] For Arnold and his co-clerk, Dan Rezneck, the only training they received was some casual "pointers" from an outgoing Brennan clerk.

According to Arnold, in the early 1960s Justice Brennan's law clerks were selected by Harvard Law School professor Paul Freund. "Justice Brennan's confidence in Professor Freund was so great that the task of choosing law clerks was delegated entirely to him. If you were picked, Mr. Freund called you into his office and asked you if you wanted the job. This occurred without warning and without any gathering of resumes, references, transcripts, or the like."[59]

Former law clerk Robert O'Neil (OT 1962) observes, however, that Freund used different selection criteria in picking the two Brennan law clerks: while the first clerk was selected based on his credentials, the second clerk was usually a Harvard Law School student who had worked as a research assistant for Freund.[60] In the case of the OT 1962 law clerks, O'Neil added that Richard Posner was tapped to fill the first slot and O'Neil the second.

In later years, Brennan began to look to other law schools for clerks. Some former clerks suggest that Brennan's decision was motivated by personal, rather than professional reasons—including tensions with faculty members, anger over Harvard Law School awarding Justice Harlan an honorary degree, and Harvard Law School denying admission to one of the justice's children—but O'Neil asserts that Brennan simply wanted to diversify his selection practices to include, at a minimum, the Third Circuit.

There is no direct evidence that Justice Brennan requested law clerks who shared his ideological preferences. Nevertheless, O'Neil believes that ideology placed some role in the selection process. O'Neil notes that—with the sole exception of one former clerk—the Brennan law clerks shared similar political views with the justice. In fact, of the 45 (out of 107) former Brennan law clerks who answered the party affiliation question on my survey, 40 stated that that at the time of their clerkship they more closely associated with the Democratic party.

Moreover, Justice Brennan was sensitive to the political repercussions of his selection practices. The most notorious law clerk hiring and firing of the modern Court involved both O'Neil and Brennan. As a law professor at the University of California–Berkeley, O'Neil recommended that Justice Brennan select law student Michael E. Tigar for a clerkship position. Tigar had been involved in political protests and had been a member of several radical political groups as an undergraduate student at UC-Berkeley—facts that O'Neil believed shouldn't disqualify him for consideration. Justice Brennan subsequently hired Tigar, but later fired the young man after his past political activities were publicly criticized and Chief Justice Warren and Associate Justice Fortas purportedly pressured Brennan to terminate him—*and* after Tigar and his young family had driven across the country to begin the clerkship.[61]

Surprisingly, the Tigar episode is not the only example of personal biases that shaped Brennan's (and other justices') clerk hiring practices. UCLA law professor Alison Grey Anderson was first in her class at the University of California–Berkeley but was told by a member of the Brennan clerkship committee that no faculty member would "waste" a clerkship selection on her. Anderson subsequently accepted a clerkship position with Fourth Circuit Court of Appeals judge Simon Sobeloff, and she later applied and interviewed with Justices Harlan and Stewart. Although eminently qualified, Anderson was not offered a clerkship position by either justice. Anderson writes: "I was told later by Stewart's clerk that Stewart was very tempted by the idea of hiring a woman clerk and being seen as 'daring' or 'progressive' but he couldn't quite bring himself to do it."[62]

With the possibility of a Supreme Court clerkship apparently over, Anderson took an associate's position with the prestigious Washington, D.C., law firm of Covington & Burling. In approximately 1970, a member of Justice Brennan's clerkship committee contacted Anderson and asked if she would be interested in clerking for the justice. "I was told that no one in that year's third year class seemed very distinguished and so they wanted to nominate me for the clerkship." After taking time to consider the inquiry, Anderson contacted the selection committee and expressed her interest. "They then informed Justice Brennan and shortly thereafter told me . . . that Brennan had said he could not take a woman clerk."[63] Understandably, Anderson was "outraged." She later wrote Justice Brennan a letter, expressing her anger at the justice's gender-based selection practices. Anderson did not receive a response. "I didn't expect him to, what could he say after all?"[64]

On one occasion, Justice Brennan publicly discussed some of his law clerks' job duties. Regarding the review of cert. petitions, he wrote:

> I try not to delegate any of the screening function to my law clerks and to do the complete task myself. I make exceptions during the summer recess when their initial screening of petitions is invaluable training for next term's new law clerks. And I also must make some few exceptions during the term on occasion when opinion work must take precedence. When law clerks do screening, they must prepare a

memorandum of not more than a page or two in each case, noting whether the case is properly before the Court, what federal issues are presented, how they were decided by the courts below, and summarizing the petitions of the parties pro and con the grant of the writ.[65]

The former clerks with whom I spoke generally confirmed Brennan's description of the cert. writing duties in his office,[66] with some minor variation across the terms. For example, former law clerk William Maledon (OT 1972) recalled that during his clerkship the Brennan law clerks reviewed all "paid" cert. petitions, but that the justice himself reviewed the IFP petitions.[67] At least during the 1980s, the Brennan clerks did not draft bench memoranda.[68]

As for opinion writing, the evidence suggests that Brennan's practices varied over the years. O'Neil recalls that at the beginning of OT 1962, both he and Richard Posner were assigned the task of preparing draft opinions. After the opinions were prepared, Justice Brennan took them home to review. The next morning, Brennan—feigning anger—announced that the law clerks had done such a fine job that he couldn't find anything to change in the opinions. O'Neil believes that the clerks succeeded because they were able to "mimic" Brennan's style or voice, and the two men continued to prepare opinion drafts throughout the term.[69]

O'Neil's experiences in opinion writing were not shared by all Brennan law clerks. O'Neil recalls at least one former Brennan law clerk lamenting the fact that he did not get to draft any opinions during his clerkship, while a former clerk from the early 1980s claimed that the law clerks prepared all majority, concurring, and dissenting opinion drafts. Maledon estimated that during his clerkship (OT 1972) the law clerks drafted approximately 75 percent of the opinions.[70] One fact, however, remained constant—when the law clerks prepared opinion drafts, they first received detailed oral or written instructions from the justice.

I asked O'Neil whether Brennan's law clerks wielded any influence over the justice's decision making. He replied that law clerks did have some influence, but an influence that involved exposing the justice to salient facts in the record rather than an influence that changed the justice's mind once all the facts were before him. This definition of influence is echoed by many former law clerks. Yes, on the rare occasion a law clerk might actually change the justice's position by exposing faulty logic or the misapplication of a doctrinal test; more commonly, law clerks wielded influence by educating the justice as to the complete record before the Court.

Justice Brennan is one of the last modern-day Supreme Court justices who shared a strong personal bond not only with his law clerks but also with their families. Former Brennan clerks warmly recall sharing morning coffee with the justice, casual lunches in chambers, and notes from the justice (often years after their clerkship) on special family occasions. For at least one former law clerk, the morning coffees were "a Justice Brennan institution" that served an important purpose:

> For one thing, they gave us quality time with the justice at which we could raise issues arising in our work so that we were not popping in . . . to interrupt him during the rest of the day. The "coffees" also provided a way for Justice Brennan to convey his way of thinking about legal issues generally, and those before the Court specifically, to aid us in working with him on opinions and memoranda. At the same time, the "coffees" provided a way for the Justice to hear our views about the Court, the Court's cases, and the ideas we had honed in the academy while keeping his counsel.[71]

Arguably, coffee time served yet another function—to tighten the bonds of loyalty between law clerk and justice, to monitor law clerk activity, and to minimize the potential for law clerk "shirking."

President Eisenhower's mixed record of appointing Supreme Court justices was perpetuated with the 1957 appointment of Charles Evans Whittaker. Nominated to replace the retiring Stanley Reed, Whittaker had previously served as both a federal district court and court of appeals judge. While Whittaker seemed to have both the professional and political credentials to guarantee Eisenhower a solid conservative on the Supreme Court, Whittaker's history of continuing, untreated depression undermined any effectiveness he might have enjoyed on the bench.

In recent years a number of authors have shed new light on Justice Whittaker's difficulties while on the Supreme Court.[72] David Atkinson writes that Whittaker suffered from depression throughout his life, and he was plagued with insecurity and recurrent depression throughout his time on the Court—no doubt intensified by a divided Court that often looked to Whittaker as a deciding vote. According to Atkinson: "[Whittaker] had been on the Supreme Court only a few months when Justice Burton made an ominous observation in his diary: 'Justice Whittaker has been on the edge of a nervous breakdown but hopes to finish the term and then recuperate.'"

In fact, it was a deep depression that ultimately triggered the justice's resignation. In March of 1962, Justice Whittaker was hospitalized at the Walter Reed Army Hospital. Doctors struggled to find the appropriate medicine to treat him, and his condition worsened. "The justice's condition was more severe than the general public could have known: he became suicidal."[73]

Justice Whittaker's medical condition is relevant to our examination of the clerkship institution because a case has been made that the illness shaped his relationship with, and utilization of, his clerks. Atkinson writes:

> Unease with some colleagues and indecision about the cases have been the usual explanations for what happened, but these were problems he contended with from the very beginning of his service. . . . More likely . . . the depression that forced him to

resign was precipitated by three factors: first, *his inability to delegate more to his law clerks made it difficult for him to accommodate the sheer volume of work on the Supreme Court.*[74]

Justice Whittaker's failure to delegate to subordinates was also fueled by his general suspicion of their abilities.

> Whittaker had small regard for the talents of his law clerks: "They are bright but immature and inexperienced. They stay only one year generally and sometimes two but when they leave [they] have just gotten enough savvy to be of any real help to you. So you are really running a training school." He saw them as having the same relation to his work that an undergraduate teenage assistant might have to the research of a mature distinguished professor.[75]

Whittaker's disdain for delegating duties to his assistants stretched back to his days in private practice. Biographer Richard L. Miller writes that as a successful Kansas City attorney Whittaker insisted that he, not his secretary, calculate the proper postage rates for outgoing mail. As a federal district court judge, Whittaker "insisted on absolute control of his chambers" and "normally limited his highly trained assistants to routine trivia."[76] The pattern persisted when he was elevated to the Eighth Circuit Court of Appeals.

Miller suggests that upon elevation to the Supreme Court, Whittaker redoubled his efforts at self-reliance:

> He once read that Supreme Court opinions were produced by law clerks rather than the justices, and the accusation had an untoward impact; he was determined that history's record would find that opinions attributed to him were his own work. His Supreme Court brethren routinely had law clerks prepare rough drafts of opinions, but Whittaker seldom allowed his clerks to do so and never adopted the few drafts he permitted. Clerks found their literary efforts unwelcome.[77]

In short, Whittaker created needless workload pressure for himself.[78] He often reminded his law clerks that "everything you write is to be etched in marble and takes great care," and Atkinson quotes a former law clerk as observing that "what [Whittaker] agonized over was writing opinions. . . . Writing opinions was more of a chore for him than it need be or must be for someone who must write."[79]

Justice Whittaker's first law clerk was Manley O. Hudson, a Harvard Law School graduate whom the justice inherited from the departing Justice Reed. Whittaker's subsequent law clerks would be selected from a number of midwestern schools, such as the Universities of Chicago, Kansas, Michigan, Minnesota, Missouri, and Notre Dame. I have been unable to uncover any information as to Justice Whittaker's selection criteria,[80] and a former law clerk states that Whittaker never used any variation of a selection committee.

According to former law clerks Manley O. Hudson (OT 1956) and Alan Kohn (OT 1957), Justice Whittaker had his law clerks prepare cert. memoranda.[81] Kohn recalls that the memos were typically three to five pages long (lengthier than the norm), and contained a brief synopsis of case facts, the issues present to the Court, a discussion of said issues, and a recommended disposition. Another Whittaker clerk adds that the law clerks met with Whittaker and discussed the memoranda before conference. Whittaker required his law clerks to prepare bench memoranda in every case set for oral argument, reports that averaged ten to fifteen pages in length.[82] After oral argument but before conference, the law clerks would again meet with the justice to discuss pending cases. A former law clerk stated: "However, we would not have heard every argument, so we were somewhat disadvantaged in terms of the input we could provide."

As for opinion writing, the law clerks contributed little. If they were given the opportunity to prepare the first draft of an opinion, their work product seldom pleased Justice Whittaker. Biographer Craig Alan Smith quotes former law clerk Heywood Davis (OT 1958) as stating: "Bill Canby and I thought we drafted some good opinions . . . Whittaker accepted parts of them. Words like 'an' and 'the.' In fairness, though, he had difficulty delegating responsibility; he did not want to accept our 'prose' on how a case ought to be decided."[83]

Kohn was more circumspect. He declined to state whether law clerks prepared the first draft of opinions, commenting instead that during his clerkship "the Whittaker law clerks generally did not do first drafts of opinions." Kohn added, however, that the law clerks "provided whatever assistance was requested by the Justice."[84] Hudson did not prepare any opinion drafts for Justice Whittaker but believes that this was a function of Whittaker's arrival at the end of OT 1956.

When the law clerks attempted to offer further help, their assistance, at best, was simply declined. Author Craig Alan Smith recounts an instance during OT 1957, when clerks Kohn and Kenneth Dam decided to approach Justice Whittaker about a mediocre draft that the justice had prepared. Smith writes that when Kohn broached the subject, "Whittaker became so angry that he picked up the opinion and threw it at his clerk, screaming, 'If you can do better, you take a crack at it.'"[85] Kohn redrafted the opinion, and the next day it was accepted by Whittaker without comment.

Not surprisingly, Whittaker was not close with his law clerks. Smith writes: "Because of his disdain for his clerks' assistance, Whittaker remained aloof with them, maintaining a professional detachment that precluded social intercourse."[86] Whittaker's distant demeanor unnerved some of his clerks, and one law clerk recalled that he would not meet with Justice Whittaker "without a mental rehearsal of points to be covered."[87] Whittaker law clerks have never held any clerkship reunions.

President Eisenhower's last nominee to the Supreme Court was Potter Stewart. A former federal appeals court judge on the Sixth Circuit, the forty-three-year-old Stewart was one of the youngest justices to serve on the modern Supreme Court.[88] Unfortunately, little printed information exists regarding Stewart's Supreme Court career. No full-length biography has been published, and only a few former law clerks have written the now-standard tribute article.[89]

I interviewed two former Stewart law clerks—Terrance Sandalow (OT 1958) and Andrew Hurwitz (OT 1973). Sandalow was originally selected to clerk for Justice Burton. After Burton's retirement and Stewart's subsequent confirmation, the new justice asked Sandalow to remain as his law clerk. Sandalow never interviewed with Stewart. In later years, however, Sandalow did recommend law clerks to Justice Stewart. When asked if Justice Stewart used an ideological litmus test in selecting law clerks, Sandalow replied that "Stewart was indifferent to the law clerks' ideology."[90] Upon reflection, former clerk Hurwitz believes that Stewart interviewed law clerks solely to determine whether the justice and the applicant were personally, not politically, compatible.[91]

Interestingly, Stewart was one of the few Supreme Court justices to modify his clerkship model while on the Court. While law clerks routinely prepared cert. memoranda throughout Stewart's tenure on the High Court, Sandalow commented that Justice Stewart originally decided that he would not have his law clerk prepare opinion drafts because he did not want to be constrained by another individual's writing. "I believe he thought, rightly in my view, that the opinions would not be truly his if someone else wrote the initial draft, and beyond that that the opinions would not reflect his personal writing style."[92]

Justice Stewart followed this model throughout OT 1958, and former clerk Sandalow recalled drafting only one minor dissenting opinion.[93] Sandalow states, however, that Stewart abandoned this practice in the 1960s. Sandalow did not know why Stewart changed this practice, but former clerk Andrew Hurwitz confirms that by the early 1970s the law clerks were preparing first drafts of all majority, concurring, and dissenting opinions.[94]

Neither Sandalow nor Hurwitz recall preparing bench memoranda.[95] The justice instead relied on conversations with his law clerks to gear up for oral argument. Moreover, there is no evidence that Stewart had formal rules regarding a law clerk's duty of confidentiality. Sandalow remarked:

> I don't recall that Justice Stewart ever raised the issue with us. I'm certain he assumed that we would maintain absolute secrecy about pending cases and would do the same regarding internal discussions of the justices even after decisions were handed down. I have a vague recollection that Chief Justice Warren did meet with all the clerks shortly after we arrived and stressed our obligation of confidentiality.[96]

Given the law clerks' more limited duties during OT 1958, perhaps Justice

Stewart felt that formal confidentiality rules were not necessary. Nevertheless, it is still remarkable that a modern Supreme Court justice would rely on his law clerks to determine the bounds of their ethical duty to maintain chamber confidences. Stewart was not unique in this omission. Until Chief Justice Warren began lecturing the Court's clerks on confidentiality, most justices never discussed the topic with their clerks—it was assumed that the clerks understood their duty.

In his first years on the Supreme Court, Justice Stewart decided that one law clerk would serve for a one-year term and the second clerk for a two-year term. Sandalow explained that "Stewart always had at least 2 clerks and at least in the early year[s] thought it would be good to have them for two years so that he would always have one experienced clerk."[97] Stewart subsequently dropped his practice of keeping one law clerk for two years; a former clerk guessed that the increasing number of applicants with prior clerkship experience placated the justice.

Unfortunately, I have not unearthed information describing the personal relationship between Justice Stewart and his clerks. In part, my failure is due to an unusually high number of former Stewart law clerks who declined my repeated interview requests. I suspect, however, that the Stewart clerkship simply lacked the distinctive flavor of a Black, Douglas, Frankfurter, or Harlan clerkship.

On April 16, 1962, former Vinson law clerk Byron White returned to the Supreme Court as President John F. Kennedy's first appointment to the High Court. A former football star, Rhodes scholar, deputy attorney general, and Kennedy family confidant, Justice White would carve out a reputation as an intensely private, gruff man whose decisions defied categorization as liberal or conservative. White's approach to his law clerks could be summarized in one word: competition.

White biographer and former law clerk Dennis J. Hutchinson writes that White's selection practices changed over time. Initially, Justice White tended to select the very top law school students (editor-in-chief of the law review, top class ranking) from a handful of elite law schools. White subjected the candidates to substantive interviews, meetings that "emphasized substance and resembled class recitation in law school."[98] After a decade on the Supreme Court, White began to search for a different type of clerk:

By the mid-1970s, White had begun to look for other qualities. He told Rex Lee at that time, *Look, there are a hundred people a year who could do the job adequately. I might as well have someone who's interesting, and that doesn't mean the ones that the fancy law professors recommend.* Interviews evolved into free-form discussions about family, personal interests, and unusual experiences. One clerk was convinced that he was hired because he had been a coal miner during the summers while in college, another because he had been a high school administrator for several years before attending law school. Rex Lee points out that White posed as an antisentimentalist but hired children of friends and relatives of political allies.[99]

Former law clerk Robert V. Percival (OT 1979) writes that Justice White tried to hire law clerks from schools that had not been traditional sources for clerks.[100] In fact, White did select his law clerks from a wide range of law schools—including Brigham Young University (one clerk), SUNY-Buffalo (one clerk), Tulane University (one clerk), and the Universities of Colorado (two clerks), Denver (two clerks), Georgia (one clerk), Iowa (one clerk), Kansas (one clerk), Minnesota (one clerk), Mississippi (one clerk), Missouri (one clerk), and New Mexico (one clerk).

Justice White remarked that he selected law clerks who satisfied two criteria: that they "would be fun to have around and could get along with me."[101] As with previous justices who took the bench during the term, White "inherited, for all practical purposes, Justice Whittaker's files, his secretary, and his law clerk, Larry Gunnels."[102] White's staff was rounded out with a second law clerk, Yale Law School graduate Richard H. Stern.

From the start, White's law clerks assisted in the opinion-writing process—as did White himself when clerking for Chief Justice Vinson. By the 1980s, the law clerks followed a simple set of instructions: "*Write a page a day for no more than twelve days. Do not create or apply any tests—simply resolve the case on the basis of precedent. Cite no law review articles.*"[103] Even opinion writing became a competition between law clerk and justice. Former law clerk Kevin Worthen writes:

> Sometimes the Justice would not even wait for the clerk's draft to arrive on his desk. Many clerks have had the experience of working furiously to finish a draft opinion within the ten-day deadline imposed by the Justice, only to find the Justice in their office on day nine with a set of papers in his large hands and the "suggestion" that "we work with this [his own version] as a draft" on his lips.[104]

By all accounts, Justice White did not give his clerks case-specific guidelines for drafting opinions. Worthen writes that, in response to a law clerk's stream of questions about an opinion assignment, White curtly replied: "If I had wanted someone to write down my thoughts, I would have hired a scrivener."[105] White's retort is supporting evidence for former law clerk Stephen R. McAllister's (OT 1989 and 1990) observation that Justice White was a "demanding" employer who "did not suffer fools . . . He sometimes humored the clerks by discussing pending cases at some length with us, but I always had the impression that, with his almost three decades of experience on the Court, in many ways he really could have operated without any law clerks at all."[106]

The other main job duties of White's law clerks were reviewing cert. petitions, preparing cert. memoranda,[107] and drafting bench memoranda.[108] After Justice White joined the cert. pool, his law clerks were responsible for drafting their share of cert. memoranda as well as reviewing the cert. pool memos of other chambers and indicating whether they agreed with the analysis.[109] Former White law clerk Kathryn Webb Bradley (OT 1989) remarked that during her clerkship some of the more politically conservative law clerks would occasionally mischaracterize facts in the cert. pool memoranda, thus requiring White's law clerks to redo the memos.[110] Additionally, the clerks were responsible for drafting dissents from the denial of certiorari.[111]

In the opinion of one former law clerk, the clerks' most important role was helping the justice consider all relevant aspects of a legal issue. Explains Worthen: "For Justice White, the judicial decision-making process was a two-step process: first, make sure the problem had been fully considered, and, second, decide. The primary role of the clerks was to assist with the consideration, not the decision. The Justice did the deciding on his own." At least for Worthen, this role was "the most gratifying aspect of their clerkship. To be able to engage in free-flowing debate on important legal issues . . . was an unforgettable and, for many White clerks, a never-again-to-be-paralleled experience."[112]

Worthen's description of the role of law clerk as sounding board provides the best example of how a law clerk/agent truly helps influence the decision-making process. It is improbable to conclude that law clerks systematically influence how their justices vote, either in deciding cases or granting cert. petitions. While the history of the clerkship institution is sprinkled with examples of law clerks who changed a justice's vote, such examples are the exception and not the rule. If influence exists, it is found in the process of analyzing highly complex factual records and legal claims and pulling out a dispositive fact or compelling legal argument that would not have been otherwise considered by the justice.

Through humor, Justice White consistently reminded his clerks that he, not the clerks, was the constitutionally appointed decision maker. Recounts former law clerk Kevin Worthen: "One former clerk recalls that he once wrote 'we have previously held' when referring to a previous Supreme Court decision in a memorandum to the Justice. Justice White's response to the memo characteristically reminded the clerk of the nature of the relationship: 'I didn't know you were on the Court then, Bill.'"[113] Worthen adds that Justice White used another expression to remind the law clerks of their place, namely, that "the clerks were 'rarely in doubt and often in error' while the Justices 'were often in doubt and rarely in error.'"

To the OT 1979 law clerks, White assigned one additional, unique responsibility: reading *The Brethren*.

White told his clerks for the 1979 Term that he would not read the book, but he assigned them each to read a portion so that he could be told if there were specific examples of vote trading or irrational behavior that were recounted. After the assignment was completed, White said no more to his staff about "the book," and for several years he left an impression of unrequited rage with all those who touched on the issue with him. He was also the old Naval Intelligence officer again, trying to determine quietly which of his own former clerks had spoken to the authors; there was no retaliation planned or executed, only private complaint.[114]

Yet, *The Brethren* had a real impact on White's approach to the clerkship institution. Hutchinson writes that thereafter White was not as open with his staff and stopped participating in a Court tradition, namely, the once-per-term lunch with all the law clerks.[115] Hutchinson observes: "Although many developed frequent contacts with White over time, the relationships did not tend to be close. A former law clerk once asked White how well he knew his clerks: *Know them? Not at all. I never see them with their families, never see them off guard, never see them under stress. I can't say I really know them.*"[116] Former clerk Bradley agrees with Hutchinson's assessment that *The Brethren* widened the gap between justice and law clerk. Bradley believes that White blamed some of his former clerks for participating, and after the book's publication White "clammed up" and distanced himself from his clerks.[117]

Competition was the consistent thread of nonjudicial activities of justice and law clerk. Law clerks played basketball with Justice White, often falling victim to the justice's aggressive style of play. At the 2002 memorial proceedings held at the Supreme Court, former White law clerk David M. Ebel recounted the following story:

> In one of the now legendary basketball games in the highest court in the land, Justice White's massive hand inadvertently smashed the glasses off of one of the clerks and broke them. After the game, the Justice called one of his prior clerks from the previous year and said, "Hey, I've got a new clerk here who has a problem with his glasses. Where did you used to get your fixed?" When the new clerk took his broken glasses to the recommended optician, the only sympathy he got from the optician was, "You work for that man White? He is an animal. You have to get contacts."[118]

The law clerks also engaged in putting competitions in which White's chambers served as three-room putting green.

Even a simple handshake was a subtle test of wills. Former law clerk Stephen R. McAllister (OT 1989) recalls arriving at the Supreme Court to interview with White and receiving the following warning from a security guard: "Watch out for his handshake, he will crush your hand." Adds McAllister, "Sure enough, when I met Justice White, he gave me his characteristic grin and proceeded to slowly but surely mash every bone in my hand, despite being almost three times my age."[119] Worthen is quick to point out, however, that Justice White did not use athletic competition to remind his law clerks of his superior physical prowess. Like Hugo Black's reading assignments or Felix Frankfurter's morning quizzes about the news of the day, in White's eyes "competition was a way of bringing out the best in those who competed. If that did not happen, the competition ended."[120]

Justice White and his clerks did socialize outside of his chambers, however, with trips to professional football, basketball, and baseball games, Thanksgiving dinner at the Whites' home, visits to the National Arboretum, and meals in the Supreme Court cafeteria—"where if we were lucky the Justice would treat us to Klondike Bars."[121] If anybody helped solidify ties between White and his clerks, it was the justice's wife. "Marion White took a propriety interest in her husband's law clerks—recording marriages and births, encouraging the unmarried to settle down, and offering advice on the proper balance between career and family."[122]

Perhaps Stephen McAllister offers the best assessment of Justice White's relationship with his clerks, describing White as a "fair, but sometimes demanding" boss who "did not suffer fools, and he expected work to be done in a timely and efficient fashion." A private man, Justice White simply did not become close to his law clerks in the same fashion that Felix Frankfurter or Hugo Black did. Concludes McAllister: "with his almost three decades of experience on the Court, in many ways he really could have operated without any law clerks at all."[123]

President Kennedy's last nominee to the Supreme Court was Arthur J. Goldberg, who in 1962 replaced the ailing Felix Frankfurter. Goldberg served less than three years before accepting President Lyndon Johnson's nomination to be the U.S. ambassador to the United Nations. During his brief time on the Court, Goldberg employed only eight law clerks: former Frankfurter law clerks Peter Edelman and David Filvaroff, Alan Dershowitz, Lee McTurnan, Stephen Breyer (the fourth former law clerk to return to the High Court as a Supreme Court justice), Stephen Goldstein, John Griffiths, and Daniel P. Levitt. Griffiths and Levitt worked for Justice Goldberg only during the summer of 1965 and were subsequently hired by Justice Abe Fortas, President Johnson's nominee to replace the departing Goldberg.

There is a dearth of information about the clerkship hiring and utilization practices of Justice Goldberg. There are only a handful of Goldberg law clerks from whom interviews may be sought, and the majority of them have declined interview requests. Justice Goldberg originally created a clerkship committee composed of Newton Minow, Abram Chayes, Adam Yarmolinsky, and Abner Mikva. All former law clerks, the committee members arguably represented the greatest concentration of legal talent ever assembled for the sole purpose of selecting interns—at the time, Newton Minow was busy running the Federal Communications Commission, Abram Chayes was State Department legal counsel, and Adam Yarmolinsky was a special assistant to the Defense Secretary. In private practice at the time, Abner Mikva would later serve in the U.S. House of Representatives, as a federal appellate court judge, and as White House counsel to President Bill Clinton.

It is unclear whether Justice Goldberg completely relied on his committee's selection decisions. In a 1962 letter to Minow, the justice writes: "Upon reflection, I do not believe any useful purpose would be served by my arranging personally the selectees. The Committee has done so on my behalf and I trust its judgment."[124] Despite Goldberg's announcement that he would not take an active role in the selection process, former law clerk Alan M. Dershowitz (OT 1963) interviewed with Justice Goldberg prior to receiving a job offer. Dershowitz writes:

> When I went for my interview with him, he simply tossed a petition for a writ of certiorari . . . across the desk and asked me to read it quickly. When I finished perusing the ten-page document, he asked for my "considered judgment" about whether it should be granted or denied and why. A heated discussion ensued and, to my amazement, he offered me the job on the spot.[125]

In subsequent terms, the selection committee appears to have been headed by former Frankfurter and Goldberg law clerks David Filvaroff and Peter Edelman.[126]

Stephen Breyer penned a short article titled "Clerking for Justice Goldberg" but provided few details about the nuts and bolts of his clerkship experience. Breyer writes that Goldberg's law clerks witnessed the justice's "strong and imaginative legal mind at work" and learned from him "a highly practical view of the Constitution," but he doesn't tell us whether these lessons were learned while checking cites or drafting opinions.[127] The only substantive information that I have gathered about Goldberg's clerkship practices comes from former Frankfurter and Goldberg law clerk, Peter Edelman. He writes that Justice Goldberg required his law clerks to prepare cert. memoranda, which included a case summary and a recommended disposition. Edelman does not recall writing bench memoranda. As for whether the law clerks prepared draft opinions, Edelman simply states: "Justice Goldberg put his imprint on opinions from start to finish. He articulated the theory he wanted developed, dictated the basic framework of opinions, and went over every draft line by line, inserting language at each stage."[128]

Both Breyer and Edelman write that Justice Goldberg and his law clerks shared tight personal bonds. Breyer states that the justice "followed our lives and those of our families with interest; he called us with help and advice. . . . his clerks quickly and permanently became convinced that there were no limits on the respect in which we held the Justice nor upon the devotion for him that we shall continue to feel."[129] Edelman writes that the justice was "extremely close to both current and former law clerks," adding that "anybody who ever worked for or with him was part of his extended family."[130]

President Lyndon Johnson appointed two justices to the Supreme Court during the 1960s: Abe Fortas and Thurgood Marshall. The two men would have dramatically different careers on the Court. Thurgood Marshall served as the champion of personal freedoms and individual equality for over two decades, retiring in 1991. Fortas resigned in disgrace in less than four years, and only in the last years of his life was the former justice able to rehabilitate his shattered reputation.

Few details are available regarding Justice Fortas' methods of selecting law clerks.[131] He agreed to hire Goldberg's law clerks on the condition that they would clerk for two years, and the new justice didn't seem to care that the two young men—Daniel Levitt and John Griffiths—differed from each other in terms of their political ideology.[132] The only evidence that I have uncovered regarding Justice Fortas and his selection practices involves an unfortunate incident that—like Justice Brennan's encounters with law clerk candidates Mike Tigar and Alison Grey Anderson—places the justice in a less-than-flattering light. Former Thurgood Marshall law clerk Thomas Grey (brother of Alison Grey Anderson) writes that Justice Fortas and D.C. Court of Appeals chief judge David Bazelon reached an agreement in which Judge Bazelon would hire a Yale Law School graduate each year, who would first clerk for Bazelon and then for Fortas. The clerks were to be selected by Yale Law School professors Joseph Goldstein and Abraham Goldstein.[133]

In approximately 1967, Yale Law School student Thomas Grey was selected by Professors Goldstein and Goldstein to clerk for Judge Bazelon and Justice Fortas. Grey writes that "I must have mentioned at the interview [with the professors] that I was a grand mal epileptic, though the disorder was controlled by medication." The information about Grey's medical condition somehow reached Justice Fortas, who informed the selection committee that he did not want to hire an epileptic. "[I]t was some time later that I was told . . . that when Justice Fortas heard about the epilepsy, he decided he didn't want to deal with it. Apparently he had grown up with an aunt who frequently had seizures around the house, and the memory filled him with horror."[134]

Yale Law School classmate William Iverson replaced Grey as the Bazelon/Fortas law clerk. Ironically, it was Grey, not Iverson, who made it to the Supreme Court. While Grey subsequently clerked for D.C. Court of Appeals Judge J. Skelly Wright and Justice Thurgood Marshall, Iverson completed the Bazelon clerkship but was left in the lurch when Justice Fortas abruptly resigned.

If Justice Whittaker's use of his law clerks was molded by mental illness and his distrust of delegation, and Justice Harlan's by his blindness, then one might hypothesize that Justice Fortas' clerkship utilization practices were shaped by the outside pressures imposed on Fortas. Once on the Supreme

Court, Fortas continued his role as informal adviser and confidant to Lyndon Johnson. "Depending on the occasion, Fortas served as political adviser, speechwriter, crisis manager, administration headhunter, legal expert, war counselor, or just plain cheerleader."[135] Moreover, in subsequent terms Fortas' energies were devoted to Senate hearings and behind-the-scenes maneuvering related to his nomination to replace Chief Justice Warren as well as damage control regarding his financial relationship with businessman Louis Wolfson and the Wolfson Family Foundation.[136] Given the sheer number of outside distractions, one would hypothesize that Fortas could not help but depend heavily on his law clerks.

In fact, there is no evidence to support this hypothesis. I interviewed former law clerk Daniel Levitt (OT 1965 and 1966) and corresponded with former clerks John Griffiths (OT 1965 and 1966), H. David Rosenbloom (OT 1967), and Walter Slocombe (OT 1968). All four former clerks report that they reviewed cert. petitions and drafted cert. memoranda and prepared opinion drafts. Slocombe writes: "Most opinions were first drafted by one of us. The Justice would tell us the result and basic line of analysis. Sometimes (especially on dissents [and] concurrences, but also on opinions) he did the first draft. He always reviewed our drafts carefully. He was an excellent editor."[137]

Rosenbloom flatly rejected the suggestion that Fortas' extrajudicial commitments forced him to delegate unusual responsibility to his law clerks. "Fortas believed that in most matters he knew far more about the law than the clerks. He was probably right on many subjects. Those subjects that bored him . . . he left to the clerks."[138] Griffiths also rejected my hypothesis, namely, that excessive outside obligations forced Fortas to lean on his clerks. "[Fortas] was a very good and fast lawyer (especially in his own estimation)," writes Griffiths, "and if I may be immodest, we were damned good clerks."[139]

Biographer Laura Kalman suggests that Fortas' lack of a coherent judicial philosophy shaped the function of the law clerks in opinion drafting. Kalman observes "Fortas's approach to a case instead reflected the opportunistic outlook of a good lawyer. . . . Griffith suggested that Fortas regarded [legal principles] as 'a necessary form of packaging that had to provide for things he wanted to do.'"[140] Therefore, law clerks "decorated" opinions:

> Griffiths remembered giving a draft of a particular memorandum to Fortas. After telling his clerk that the draft was unsatisfactory, Fortas "took it off and wrote it himself with the very strong emphasis on the factual part." On his return, Fortas threw the memorandum on Griffiths's desk. "Decorate it," he ordered. The "decorations" consisted of legal cases that would justify a decision Fortas had already reached. . . . Observers have commented that Fortas's opinions contained more than the requisite number of legal citations. But they were there to a large extent because his clerks insisted upon them.[141]

Some clerkship duties changed over time. Initially, Justice Fortas had his law clerks prepare memoranda arguing against conference votes in which Fortas was in the minority. The memoranda were circulated to the other justices, but Fortas discontinued the practice after irritating his peers. While the law clerks during OT 1965 prepared bench memoranda in all cases, Justice Fortas abandoned this practice by OT 1967.[142]

Given Justice Fortas' ongoing role as the consummate Washington insider, it is not surprising that his law clerks had nonjudicial duties as well. Daniel Levitt recalled making written recommendations on how Justice Fortas might diffuse the public backlash to the Warren Commission's report (Levitt's suggestions included releasing the Kennedy autopsy photographs). Moreover, at the end of the week Levitt would drive Fortas to the White House, where Fortas helped President Johnson select bombing targets.[143] During the scandal over the Wolfson Foundation, Fortas assigned a law clerk the task of researching the applicable criminal law and preparing a report on whether his nonjudicial behavior was legally punishable.[144]

Contradictory evidence exists regarding the personal relationship between Justice Fortas and his clerks. Griffiths writes that Fortas was "distant" with his clerks, and biographer Bruce Allen Murphy quotes former Warren law clerk Benno Schmidt:

> [Fortas'] law clerks absolutely despised him. They said the most awful things about him, which really surprised me since most clerks tend to revere their justice. They said that he was not a man of principle on a principled court, what with the finished jurisprudential philosophies of men like Black, Douglas, and Harlan . . . In time, the clerks came to see Fortas as totally unprincipled, and intellectually dishonest.[145]

Yet in remarks delivered at a memorial proceeding before the Supreme Court, Daniel Levitt offered a moving tribute to the former justice. Observing that "anyone who came into contact with Abe Fortas was greatly touched by him," Levitt spoke of the "kind, even tender personality" that Fortas occasionally displayed toward his clerks and their families.[146]

The final addition to the Warren Court was Thurgood Marshall, whose work as a civil rights attorney, federal appeals court judge, and solicitor general preceded his appointment as the first African American justice to the U.S. Supreme Court. Of all the former justices who served on the modern Supreme Court, Marshall's clerkship practices are the most difficult to determine accurately. His former clerks have built a formidable wall of silence around the late justice, with the unintended consequence that the most sensational allegations about the Marshall law clerks—namely, that they were running his chambers and influencing his decision making while the justice watched television—either go unanswered or are flatly denied without sufficient elaboration.

The explanation for the defensiveness of the Marshall law clerks lies with the publication of *The Brethren*, which alternately described the justice as lazy, bored, tired, defeated, or intellectually outmatched. "Some of the clerks in other chambers came to the conclusion that Marshall was unfit to sit on the Court. He was not willing to do his homework, not willing to prepare for his cases, not of the intellectual caliber of Douglas, White, Stewart or Brennan."[147] Arguably most stinging, however, was the implication that some of Justice Marshall's own law clerks found their employer's antics tiresome and disheartening (and had expressed the same to authors Woodward and Armstrong):

> Often Marshall would corner one of his clerks after lunch and spend hours in the special chair they reserved for him in their office. By the time he had worn out his own clerks' patience, clerks from other chambers might have wandered in for a new round of the endless storytelling. But they could always leave. His own clerks had nowhere to go. At one point, his clerks tried piling books on Marshall's chair to discourage him from settling in for the afternoon. . . . Finally, the clerks took to hiding in his second-floor office.[148]

Far more galling for Justice Marshall must have been details about the interchamber dynamic between the justice and his law clerks regarding work duties—again, information that could only have come (directly or indirectly) from Marshall clerks. Not only were the law clerks allegedly shouldering the lion's share of work in the chambers, but the clerks themselves also were capable of insubordination; the authors reported that during the summer of 1974, a Marshall law clerk, consumed with antiwar sentiments and anger at "Marshall's timidity and inattention," refused to write an opinion overruling a previous order filed by Justice Douglas in *Schlesigner v. Holtzman*.[149] If true, this is the only example that I have found of a clerk/agent directly refusing a justice/principal's work assignment.

Marshall biographer Juan Williams writes that Marshall was furious about his portrayal in *The Brethren*, and that his clerks and wife "grew even more fierce in guarding his reputation."[150] In fact, the book had an impact on how Marshall ran his chambers. Writes former law clerk Kenneth Simons (OT 1981): "The Justice was emphatic that we should not discuss any of the Court's work with anyone outside the building . . . In part, I believe that his stringent stance was due to his unhappiness at the (unjustly) unflattering portrayal of him in the book."[151]

In regards to this project, my highest rejection rates for interviews with clerks of a *former* Supreme Court justice came from the Marshall clerks. When they did agree to speak with me, the scope of the interview was often limited and their responses off-the-record. Former Marshall law clerks Kenneth Simmons and Bruce A. Green (OT 1982) were the only clerks who provided on-the-record responses to my written survey questions. Finally, I am a bit leery of secondary materials written by former Marshall law clerks; the articles and tributes by the clerks are questionable data sources because I suspect that the authors might be overcompensating for the aforementioned attacks upon Marshall's reputation.[152] In short, any conclusions drawn about Marshall's clerkship practices are tentative.

For a portion of his time on the Supreme Court, Justice Marshall relied on a selection committee composed of former law clerks to screen clerkship applications, interview candidates, and select clerks.[153] A former clerk who experienced the screening process recalled that the committee was very protective of Justice Marshall and sought clerks who would be loyal and personally compatible with the justice. The same clerk believes that Justice Marshall never interviewed applicants screened by the search committee.

Marshall clerks prepared all cert. and bench memoranda as well as opinion drafts in all cases.[154] There is no evidence suggesting that this clerkship model changed during Marshall's lengthy tenure on the Supreme Court. The cert. petitions tended to be short (usually one page in length). Former clerk Kenneth Simons writes that the law clerks "were careful to examine petitions from criminal defendants and the indigent especially closely." At least during the early 1980s, Justice Marshall was not a member of the cert. pool. As for bench memorandum, Simons reports that the clerks prepared memoranda for all cases scheduled for oral argument. "The memos contained our detailed analysis of the legal issues, and our recommendation of how the Justice should vote, and why."[155]

Marshall gave limited instructions to his clerks regarding opinion writing, and his law clerks used an intrachambers editing process whereby one law clerk wrote the opinion, a second (and sometimes third) clerk served as editor, and then the three clerks reviewed the edited draft and made additional changes before submitting the draft opinion to the justice.[156] Former law clerk Glen Darbyshire (OT 1986) writes about Marshall:

> Perhaps more than any other justice, he gave his law clerks creative freedom in drafting opinions. He would define the central focus and rationale and then allow the clerks to organize the arguments consistent with his prior opinions. Nonetheless, his review of draft opinions could be exacting. He edited with a thick blue pencil that could, with a single stroke, obliterate pretentious or ineffective wording. . . . His law clerks, before submitting drafts to him, followed a detailed procedure for reviewing and editing them for substantive or grammatical errors—all in a determined effort to avoid the blue pencil.[157]

Darbyshire's article is unique among materials written by former Marshall law clerks in that he not only discusses the clerk's substantive job duties, but he also concedes that Marshall's clerks had more latitude than their peers.[158]

Almost all articles written by the former law clerks focus on the justice's larger-than-life personality, his affectionate relationship with his young assistants (nicknamed "knuckleheads"), and his jurisprudence.[159] Humor undeni-ably formed the bond between justice and law clerk, but it was humor often deployed to tweak an unsuspecting law clerk or deflate the solemnity of a moment. Writes former law clerk Scott Brewer (OT 1990): "On the day he announced his retirement, he called us into his office to tell us of his deci-sion. When he saw how upset we all were, he barked out, in his own consol-ing way, 'When I saw this group of clerks, I shoulda quit the first week!' "[160] The law clerks themselves felt free to use humor in their correspondence with the justice. In an October 13, 1972, letter to Marshall, former law clerk Thomas C. Grey writes: "I hear that you come to the bench with a cane this year. Please don't give way to the temptation to use it on the clerks, but maybe once in a while in conference."[161]

Assuming that an aging and disengaged Justice Marshall did delegate enormous responsibility to his law clerks, there is no evidence establishing that he created elaborate monitoring and sanctioning mechanisms. While former law clerk Kenneth Simons states Marshall asked his clerks to review each others' draft opinions, he adds that there was no hierarchical arrange-ment among the clerks. The lack of data regarding such rules results from the general dearth of information regarding the justice's clerkship practices. Alternatively, if Justice Marshall was as detached and bored as claimed by Woodward and Armstrong, then a case could be made that he wouldn't have cared about law clerk defections and misadventures.

As was becoming the norm in the new clerkship model, Justice Mar-shall enjoyed a warm, but not close, relationship with the majority of his law clerks. Each term, Justice and Mrs. Marshall would invite the current clerks over for dinner, and the law clerks themselves "venerated" the justice. *The Brethren* was right on one account—storytelling was part of the Mar-shall clerkship experience. Former law clerk Bruce Green recalls that Justice Marshall was a "spellbinding speaker,"[162] and occasionally Marshall would share stories of his youth and days as a civil rights leader with his clerks.

The Burger Court, 1969 to 1986

On June 23, 1969, Warren Burger was sworn in as the fifteenth chief justice of the U.S. Supreme Court. A former D.C. Court of Appeals judge, the stately, silver-haired Burger represented the first of many judicial selections through which President Richard M. Nixon attempted to roll back what he and members of his administration considered the liberal excesses of the Warren Court. While Burger would not erase the constitutional changes crafted under Earl Warren, by his retirement in 1986 the Burger Court had, at the very least, halted the advances in areas such as the protections afforded criminal defendants and individual privacy rights.

In approximately 1972, Chief Justice Burger created a law clerk screening committee composed of former law clerks. The committee's informal name was "The Chief Justice's Law Clerk Screening Committee," because the committee did not pick law clerks but merely screened applications and created a list of finalists from which Burger chose his law clerks.[163] For the first five years, the screening committee consisted of five former Burger law clerks; two more former clerks were added in later years. Former committee member Charles Hobbs states that Chief Justice Burger did not give the committee specific, binding instructions or selection criteria. The chief justice told the committee that "he was interested in diversity of law schools; that is, he did not want all of his clerks to be from Harvard and Yale." Hobbs states that the committee achieved the chief justice's goal of academic diversity; of the 56 clerks selected by Burger from the committee's list of finalists, 26 different law schools were represented.

Hobbs writes that Chief Justice Burger did not request, and the committee did not weigh, an applicant's personal political ideology when screening applications.

As everyone knows, the Chief normally tended to be on the conservative side of issues, but was not entirely predictable in this respect. He never told us "don't send me any liberals." We occasionally sent him some [on the finalists list], and he occasionally selected one of them. . . . The committee never ruled out any strong candidate who seemed to be "liberal," provided there was evidence that the candidate was not an extremist, that (s)he had capacity to see both sides of a question, and that his/her apparent ideology would not interfere with doing the Chief's work faithfully.[164]

Prior clerkship experience was the factor that the chief justice explicitly asked the committee to consider. While the lack of a lower court clerkship did not automatically disqualify a candidate, Chief Justice Burger emphasized its value. Writes Hobbs: "He believed that it was an important factor that would enable the new clerk to hit the ground running at the Supreme Court. Of the about 56 clerks selected by the Chief that passed through our committee, virtually all had been law clerks on lower courts."

In the two decades before Chief Justice Burger's appointment to the Supreme Court, it was not the norm that Supreme Court law clerks must first clerk for a federal appellate or trial court judge. In the 1940s and 1950s, less than half of all law clerks had prior clerkship experience. We find a dramatic increase in the 1970s—from 1970 to 1978, over 90 percent of those clerks for whom data was available had held lower court clerkships. One explanation for this change: Chief Justice Burger established a new norm on the Supreme Court that was quickly adopted by the other justices.

There were other obvious qualifications that the screening committee looked for in a candidate, although the criteria were not mandated by Chief Justice Burger. Law review membership, law school grades, letters of recommendation, and personal compatibility were deemed relevant by the committee. Each member of the selection committee would personally interview the top candidates. While Hobbs did not know the interview structure used by the other committee members, he used the following approach:

> I would call in (or go to meet) anywhere from 10 to 15 of the leading candidates in my pile of applications, and spend about 3 hours talking with each of them, to get a feel for their intellectual horsepower, ability to manipulate and articulate complex issues, ability to work smoothly with other clerks, ability to perform capably under deadlines, and general poise, decency and integrity.[165]

A candidate's intellectual prowess was tested at the end of the interview, when Hobbs engaged the young man or woman in a discussion of a recent Supreme Court case. One of Hobbs' favorite cases for this intellectual give-and-take was *Fullilove v. Klutznick* [448 U.S. 448 (1980)], a complicated opinion in which a sharply divided Supreme Court held that a minority set-aside program in the Public Works Employment Act of 1977 did not violate the Equal Protection Clause. Although the chief justice reserved the task of selecting law clerks from the screening committee's finalist list, on average he did not interview the finalists before making his selections.

During his time on the Supreme Court, Chief Justice Burger employed four full-time law clerks. Additionally, he employed both a "special" administrative assistant and an administrative assistant. The special AA's job duties overlapped with those of the law clerks, and they would review draft opinions and discuss opinion assignments with the chief justice. Armstrong and Woodward write that the special AA "exercised the Chief's authority on matters of format, paper flow, red tape, appearance, security and bureaucratic procedure."[166] If this description is accurate, then the special AA position is an example of a modification to the clerkship model designed to minimize mistakes (intended and unintended) by the clerk/agent. Chief Justice Burger's special AAs included current federal appellate court judges J. Michael Luttig, Robert Mayer, and Kenneth Ripple.

The chief justice's law clerks prepared cert. and bench memoranda. When Burger joined the cert. pool, his law clerks reviewed all pool memos and made handwritten recommendations on the cert. pool memoranda for the chief justice.[167] Bench memoranda usually contained a summary of the factual and procedural backgrounds of the appeal, the issue or issues presented to the Court, an analysis of the parties' arguments, and a recommended disposition. Recalls former clerk Christopher J. Wright (OT 1981): "[W]e were required to say how we thought the case should be decided. I think that was to prevent 'on the one hand, on the other hand' discussions from getting 'out of hand.'"[168]

Additionally, Burger asked his clerks to supply significant questions for oral argument. The bench memoranda were sufficiently detailed that the law clerk preparing the draft opinion used them as a jumping-off point.

Chief Justice Burger's law clerks routinely prepared majority opinions. Before beginning the writing process, they had "a detailed discussion with the Chief Justice regarding the case, the discussion at the Conference, the views of the Justices in the majority, and the Chief Justice's analysis."[169] Additionally, Burger sometimes provided his clerks with a written outline or synopsis of the opinion with his intended holding and reasoning.[170] After the law clerk prepared the opinion draft, the other clerks and the special administrative assistant reviewed the opinion before it was submitted to Burger. Finally, Burger and the law clerk together worked through the draft opinion.

As with other justices, Burger's law clerks felt free to politely disagree with him on issues before the Court. Former law clerk John Edward Sexton (OT 1980) writes that in his very first bench memorandum he took a position contrary to one advocated by the chief justice in a prior term's dissent from denial of cert. Sexton met with Chief Justice Burger to discuss the bench memorandum. "Three hours and many arguments later, he asked: 'Any more to say?' And, when I said, 'No,' he announced: 'Well, I'm where I started, but now I'm ready for conference.'" Sexton recounts the story as evidence that Burger "never asked his clerks to toe a party line; he welcomed disagreement; and he invariably considered patiently each argument of even the most inexperienced advocate."[171] Yet the tale is indicative of another fact—based on conversations with former Burger law clerks, I believe that Burger was less likely than other justices to be swayed by even the most persuasive arguments of his clerks.

While Chief Justice Warren spoke informally with his law clerks about the duty of confidentiality owed to his chambers, Chief Justice Burger issued a formal memorandum regarding confidentiality. According to Woodward and Armstrong, the memorandum read in part:

> [C]onfidentiality is not limited to the minimum and obvious aspect of preserving the security of all information *within* the Court. Equally important is the private nature of everything that transpires in the Chambers of the Justice, including what he says, what he thinks, whom he sees and what his thinking may be on a particular issue or case.

> Any matters of a confidential nature which tend to place the Chief Justice in an unfavorable light should not be revealed to other Law Clerks.

> The Chief's clerks are not to reveal which opinions they are personally working on . . . The Chief Justice has a strict rule that suggestions are to be accepted from other offices *only* after another Justice has first considered the matter and then communicated directly and formally to the Chief Justice.

[The Chief Justice] does not want his views on a case—or those of his law clerk(s)—made known *outside* his Chambers until his final position is reached.[172]

Woodward and Armstrong claim that Burger's law clerks from OT 1969 were dismayed with the memorandum—not only because it prevented them from joining in the "fun" of discussing pending cases and negotiating changes with clerks in other chambers, but also because the instructions "reflected [Burger's] deep insecurity over control and a fear that somehow the clerks would try to manipulate him."[173]

Woodward and Armstrong do not discuss whether the aforementioned confidentiality requirements were effective throughout Chief Justice Burger's time on the Court, and in fact there is evidence that future Burger law clerks were not bound by these dictates. Stephen Walters clerked for Chief Justice Burger during OT 1974, only five years after the issuance of the above memorandum. Walters states:

> My memory . . . is that the chief had no formal confidentiality policy. He had an appropriate concern that information regarding pending cases not become public, so he instructed his clerks to be discreet in their conversations with other law clerks. In particular, we were cautioned about discussing cases in areas that were accessible to the public . . . We also considered our conversations with the Chief to be confidential; he was, after all our "client" and we took that relationship seriously. On the other hand, we had many discussions of pending cases with clerks from other chambers in the Clerks' dining room, on the basketball court on the top floor of the Court building . . . and in secure areas of the Court. . . . We certainly discussed our own views of the cases in those discussions and it was no secret which one of us was working on a particular case.[174]

Walters adds that Armstrong and Woodward's "portrayal of the Chief as a paranoid control freak is a complete fabrication."

Walter's statement that the Burger clerks were not under a confidential "gag order" is echoed by subsequent law clerks. Former clerk Bruce P. Brown (OT 1985) stated that there were no formal restrictions on what Burger's clerks could discuss with other clerks, and former clerk Judith McMorrow (OT 1981) commented that the chief justice did not care if his clerks talked with other clerks about Court business.[175] Finally, former Burger special administrative assistants Robert Mayer and Jan Horbaly do not recall any unusual confidentiality rules.[176]

What is clear, however, is that Chief Justice Burger considered the dissemination of confidential information to the general public and to the press as a problem that cut across all chambers. In the summer of 1973, the chief justice asked Associate Justices William Rehnquist and Potter Stewart to examine the problems of "leaks" on the Court. Justices Rehnquist and Stewart carefully researched the problem, talking to law clerks from the different chambers, Supreme Court Reporter of Decisions Henry Putzel, Jr., Burger

Administrative Assistance Mark Cannon, Supreme Court Information Officer Bert Whittington, and former U.S. Solicitor General and Harvard Law School dean Erwin Griswold. After reviewing recent leaks and suggesting procedures that the individual chambers could follow in safeguarding confidential information, Justices Rehnquist and Stewart stressed the unique problems raised by law clerks:

> [E]xcept only for those of us who are members of the Court, the law clerks have the most constant and extensive access to Conference deliberations, draft circulations, and the like, of any employees of the Court. For both of these reasons, we think it would be desirable that a group discussion be had with all new law clerks some time just before the beginning of the Term . . . Because of the close relationship between an individual Justice and his law clerks, we think that the session should be attended by every member of the Court who wishes to do so, and that the general outline of the proposed discussion regarding confidentiality be reviewed in advance by all of us.[177]

It is interesting to note that as chief justice, William Rehnquist would build upon these earlier efforts at stopping leaks and institute a formal law clerk code of conduct.

On average, Burger's law clerks enjoyed a cordial, but not overly familiar, relationship with the chief justice—notwithstanding Armstrong and Woodward's claim that his law clerks considered him insecure and paranoid. Sexton writes that Burger viewed himself as a teacher and spent Saturday afternoons talking for hours with his law clerks over bowls of his homemade soup. Moreover, Sexton states that the chief justice took a personal interest in the lives of both his law clerks and their families. Over the years, Burger provided the clerks' families with personal tours of the Supreme Court, bounced babies on his knee, and offered advice and support when spouses or children fell ill.[178] With the exception of confidentiality rules and the emphasis on previous appellate clerkship experience, Warren Burger did not modify the clerkship model that was formally adopted by Earl Warren and followed by every new addition to the Warren Court.

There were two justices who joined the Burger Court but did not serve throughout the tenure of the Rehnquist Court: Harry Blackmun and Lewis Powell. Blackmun was the second Nixon appointee elevated to the Supreme Court, but he was not Nixon's first choice to replace the fallen Abe Fortas. Nixon originally nominated in quick succession U.S. Court of Appeals judges Clement F. Haynsworth, Jr., and G. Harrold Carswell and watched as a hostile U.S. Senate rejected both candidates.[179] Blackmun used the failed nominations as a method of maintaining humility while on the Supreme Court. Writes former Blackmun secretary Wanda S. Martinson, the justice "often referred to himself as 'Old Number Three' . . . and said it served to keep him in his place."[180] Blackmun took the Supreme Court bench on June 9, 1970.

Unlike some justices from earlier courts, Blackmun received and considered unsolicited clerkship applications. "So far as I am concerned, anyone interested is free to apply directly," wrote Blackmun in response to an inquiry regarding his clerkship hiring practices. "I confess that I prefer to have clerks who have had a year's experience as a clerk with a federal appellate judge or with a judge of the highest state court. This, I believe, is helpful preparation for a clerkship here."[181] Blackmun concluded by noting that the selection of a new law clerk was "an excruciating process" in that "nearly every applicant is highly qualified."

Blackmun interviewed clerk finalists, referring to a stock set of written questions that he used every year: family background (*how many brothers and sisters, state of parents' health*), work ethic (*could the applicant work long hours*), vices (*smoker or nonsmoker*), marital status, law school courses taken, and the Supreme Court's rule against concurrent law practice.[182] In later years, during the interview Blackmun would rise from his desk, walk over to his dictionary stand, and ask a candidate if he or she would have trouble working for the author of *Roe v. Wade*.[183] This would be the closest that Blackmun came to asking questions involving the candidate's personal political ideology. Writes former law clerk Randall Bezanson (OT 1972): "I am confident that there was no ideological litmus test when I applied . . . I think the Justice looked for bright people who he would enjoy working with, whose discretion he could trust, and who would respect the fact that he was the Justice."[184]

During the visit to the Blackmun chambers, the candidates also met with Blackmun's secretaries and current law clerks. These meetings were designed to determine whether the individual would be personally compatible with the justice and his staff—an important consideration, given the long hours that the Blackmun clerks spent at the Court. At the end of the interview, Justice Blackmun did not extend a job offer. He would say, "I want you to go home and think about whether this job is right for you."[185] If, after reflection, the candidate was still interested in the clerkship, then he or she was instructed to call the justice's chambers.

Blackmun law clerks were assigned the now-traditional duties of preparing bench memoranda, reviewing cert. petitions and preparing cert. memoranda, and drafting opinions. The *scale* of the job assignments, however, made the Blackmun clerkship unique. The clerks prepared lengthy, highly detailed bench memoranda in all pending cases.[186] The memoranda included an "extensive" summary and discussion of arguments contained in any amicus briefs.[187]

In a July 1978 memorandum, Justice Blackmun described how the clerks should approach the bench memo.

This, of course, is an in-depth study of the briefs on the merits. I like these to begin with the title and other informational material set forth in the flimsy [cert. pool memo]. The pertinent facts should be recounted. The issues should be stated. This should be followed by the argument for each side. If one feels that any portion of the argument is weak, he should say so. The purpose of the bench memo is to relieve me of a time-consuming pre-argument review of the briefs. I shall go over the briefs, but if the bench memo is well done, it will almost stand in place of the briefs. If a decided case is pivital [*sic*], I like its citation and the division of the Court (with the names of the Justices concerned) and two or three lines of holding. This gives me some initial concept of the case and enables me to go direct to it for further study.[188]

Former law clerk Pamela Karlan (OT 1985) stated that the shortest bench memorandum she prepared was a scant 18 pages in length, while the longest was 45 pages. Karlan suggests that 30–40 pages was the average length of a Blackmun bench memo. Not surprisingly, Blackmun's law clerks worked long hours. Former law clerk Lynn Blais estimated that at the midpoint of her clerkship, she and her clerks logged eighteen-hour days during the work week—slacking off to a twelve-hour day on Saturday and a mere six hours on Sunday.[189]

Justice Blackmun was a member of the cert. pool, and his law clerks prepared their proportional share of cert. memoranda. Additionally, Blackmun's law clerks reviewed all cert. pool memoranda written in other chambers as well as the applicable petition and response. If the law clerks disagreed with a cert. pool memorandum, then they prepared their own memo for the justice's review.[190] Justice Blackmun, like Hugo Black, did not rely solely on the cert. memoranda—he personally reviewed every cert. petition.[191]

After conference, Justice Blackmun met with his law clerks, went over his detailed conference notes regarding what each justice said about specific cases and their individual votes, and then assigned opinions to draft. According to Karlan, Justice Blackmun divided up the initial drafting between himself and the law clerks. Blackmun tended to assign himself draft opinions in cases involving issues that interested him, such as tax cases.[192] The type of draft prepared by the law clerks, however, was determined by the importance of the case. Writes former law clerk Bezanson:

> A few first drafts bore close resemblance to the final drafts. These tended to be the cases in which the outcome and the required reasoning were clear, and the opinions were fairly straightforward and brief. On bigger cases, especially where the Court was divided, we would often do a draft of part of the opinion or a memo about how the logic of the opinions might proceed.[193]

The Blackmun clerks often were asked to review each other's work product before the drafts were subjected to Justice Blackmun's exacting scrutiny. "He would review the opinion and the underlying research independently, [and] often make changes, both substantive and stylistic."[194]

Finally, Blackmun required his clerks to review opinions circulated by other chambers. "It is of assistance to me if [the clerk who prepared the

bench memorandum] prepares a one or two page comment about the opinion and his general reaction to it. Should I or should I not join it? If not,
why not?" There was one job duty that Blackmun did not share with his law
clerks—reading his voluminous hate mail. Writes Meserve: "Each day the
Justice receives a volume of mail attacking him for his decisions on abortion
matters. He does not share that mail with his clerks. But, he reads it all."[195]
Occasionally, Justice Blackmun asked his clerks to assist in the preparation of
a speech or in preparation for attending a circuit conference.

In later years, the Blackmun law clerks generated a written, in-chambers
procedural guide, containing directions for substantive job duties (such as the
proper way to prepare a bench memorandum) as well as tips on the justice's
expectations of his law clerks (communicate in writing and be punctual
in work assignments). Former Blackmun secretary Wanda Martinson states
that the guide was not created at Justice Blackmun's request, although he
was aware of it. She does not believe that he ever read the guide, which was
handed down and amended by subsequent generations of law clerks.[196]

It is undeniable that the Blackmun law clerks worked long hours and
generated a virtual blizzard of memoranda and opinion drafts for the justice
to review. Yet Justice Blackmun's extensive demands on his clerks, made apparent with the opening of his personal papers, caused legal historian David
Garrow to conclude that Justice Blackmun "ceded to his law clerks much
greater control over his official work than did any of the other 15 justices
from the last half-century whose papers are publicly available."[197] Calling
the justice's clerkship practices "indefensible," Garrow concluded that the
Blackmun papers served as a "powerful and poignant warning to present and
future justices that the failure to closely supervise young clerks can damage
the court's reputation and undermine its authority."

Garrow's interpretation and condemnation of Justice Blackmun's clerkship practices drew furious responses from a number of former clerks, including William McDaniel, Jr. (OT 1978), David Ogden (OT 1982), and
Edward Lazarus (OT 1988). If a common theme emerges in the comments
of the former clerks, it is that Garrow's analysis of the Blackmun papers
and his clerkship practices fails to account for the fact that while the clerks
communicated with Justice Blackmun in writing, their work product was
shaped by repeated conversations with, and precise verbal instructions from,
the justice. Writes McDaniel:

> Mr. Garrow reads the clerks' memoranda and drafts as though they were the whole
> story. But they are not the whole story, and, in so doing, Mr. Garrow misses the truth
> of the matter: that the clerks in those writings were responding to what the justice
> had said and following his direction, not telling him what to do. Mr. Garrow presents
> half the evidence, then draws erroneous conclusions accordingly, like the fellow who
> mistook "lightning bug" for "lightning" and ran around spreading storm warnings.[198]

Based on my own limited review of the Blackmun papers, combined with interviews of former clerks, I do not find Garrow's characterization of the Blackmun clerkship model to be convincing.

One of the unique aspects of the Blackmun clerkship was the breakfast ritual.[199] Every morning Justice Blackmun and his law clerks walked down to the Supreme Court cafeteria for breakfast (in some terms Blackmun would have pancakes, in others, fried or scrambled eggs, coffee, juice, toast (raisin or rye), and conversation—not only with the members of the Blackmun chambers but also with their families and friends. "The breakfast conversations covered the waterfront, from talking about cases, draft opinions from other chambers, and the like, to talking about lawyers and oral arguments, politics . . . and of course baseball and our children and families."[200] On Saturdays, the law clerks joined the justice for lunch.

Blackmun's clerkship model is unique only in its increased reliance on his law clerks for a highly detailed flow of information. In keeping with this reliance, I hypothesized that a justice would create additional rules or practices designed to ensure the accuracy of the information. While Justice Blackmun himself reviewed the written record before the Court (not relying merely on the law clerks' summary of the record itself), there is no evidence that Blackmun's clerks monitored each other's work product. The daily breakfasts with his law clerks were another technique through which the justice discussed relevant cases with all four law clerks. These conversations may have helped Justice Blackmun determine whether incomplete or inaccurate information was being provided through the cert. memoranda, bench memoranda, and opinion drafts.

The Blackmun law clerks and staff socialized outside of chambers with Justice and Mrs. Blackmun. Every term Mrs. Blackmun took the law clerks on a tour of the White House and the FBI building, while in the spring the justice and his staff visited the tidal basin to see the cherry blossoms. During the winter holidays, Justice and Mrs. Blackmun had the chamber staff and spouses over for a dinner prepared by Mrs. Blackmun. Despite (or because of) the long hours and high expectations, the law clerks grew close to Justice Blackmun. In a letter written at the end of her employment with the justice, former law clerk Michelle Alexander wrote:

> I regret being the first [clerk] to say good-bye. I have enjoyed this year tremendously. Working for you truly has been one of the most rewarding experiences of my life. I feel particularly honored to be among your very last clerks. Your retirement represents to me the end of an era on this Court, an era in which a steady candle burned for the less privileged in our society. I fear that in your absence the flame may dim or even disappear for a while, but not forever.[201]

In another farewell letter, former Vicki Been writes: "Your concern for the people behind the cases, your attention to detail and insistence on perfection in all that you do, and your humility and integrity, are truly remarkable. You are a model for the type of lawyer and person I would like to be."[202] Finally, Justice Blackmun's file contain a staggering number of cards, pictures, and letters from current and former law clerks. One of the more amusing cards is a February 1985 Valentine's Day note to Justice Blackmun from his current clerks, which reads: "Respondents are red, petitioners are blue. We're very lucky to have a Justice like you."

The law clerks played a visible role during Justice Blackmun's funeral. The former Blackmun law clerks and select Court staff served as an honor guard when the justice lay in state in the Supreme Court, and former clerks William McDaniel, Pamela Karlan, and Harold Koh spoke at the funeral service. "By being with him, we learned about ourselves," Karlan told the assembled mourners. "He appealed, in the words of his hero Abraham Lincoln, to the better angels of our individual natures."[203]

President Nixon's final two appointments to the Supreme Court were announced on October 21, 1971: Lewis F. Powell, Jr., and William Rehnquist. While Rehnquist would face a difficult confirmation hearing, Powell serenely sailed through the confirmation process. The former president of the American Bar Association and a senior partner at a prestigious Virginia law firm, Lewis Powell was reluctant to leave his legal practice and don the robes of a Supreme Court justice. Despite Powell's hesitancy, once on the Supreme Court he poured his energies into the role and played an important role as a "swing vote" on the Burger and Rehnquist Courts.

According to former Powell law clerk (OT 1973) and biographer John J. Jeffries, Jr., the move from the South's wealthiest and most prestigious law firm to the "slightly antiquated" Supreme Court facilities was a bit jarring for a man used to an abundance of support staff and junior associates. Powell himself commented:

> I have an office suite of only three rooms. I have one secretary, who serves as a file clerk, receptionist, as well as a highly confidential personal secretary. . . . My three law clerks are crowded into a single small room, each doing his own typing in the absence of secretarial help. . . . There is no permanent legal staff available on the Court; no experienced lawyers to call on; and no one to do protracted and scholarly research—beyond the basic legal research—under the direction of a Justice. In short, each Justice is on his own, with resources—both physical and in personnel—far less adequate than those of a partner in a well-organized law firm.[204]

At the time of his appointment, Justice Powell's original office staff was composed of Sally Smith, his former legal secretary at Hunton & Williams, Larry Hammond and Peter Parnell (the final law clerks hired by Justice Black),[205] new law clerk J. Harvie Wilkinson III, and Hugo Black's former messenger.

Upon his arrival at the Supreme Court, Powell was remarkably candid with his law clerks regarding what the justice viewed as his limitations as a justice and the impact that these limitations would have on the law clerks. Referring to himself as a "rookie justice, who will continue to need more help and education than others," and noting the rising workload pressures facing the entire Court, Powell observed: "Obviously, I will never acquire the background, knowledge and skills of some of the other Justices. This means more work for me and—unfortunately for you—a heavier load for my law clerks."[206] While Justice Powell's comments may have been colored by a touch of false modesty, his memorandum is still striking in its unblinking assessment of its author's abilities.

Motivated by his professed limitations, Powell immediately began pushing for a larger staff. In a November 8, 1972, letter to Warren Burger, Powell writes:

> What would you think of including in the budget a request for funds for a *fourth* law clerk for me and for any other Justice who may desire one? I do not have the background in constitutional and criminal law which enables me to function without a great deal of reading and research. There is simply not enough time for me to do this on my own . . . Accordingly, I keep my three clerks heavily committed. What I would really like to try out is having four clerks, with each to serve two-year terms on a staggered basis . . . If one always had two experienced clerks, the new incoming ones could come directly from law school without being required to serve a year at the Circuit Court level.[207]

While Chief Justice Burger initially expressed pessimism regarding Powell's proposal, by the mid-1970s all associate justices were authorized to hire a second secretary and fourth law clerk. Powell was pleased with the addition of the fourth clerk, writing the chief justice that he "felt better briefed and better supported, especially by additional research on argued cases."[208] As the justices took on a fourth law clerk, their individual chambers were expanded from three to four rooms to accommodate the increase in judicial staff. Powell also led the Supreme Court into the computer age, having the first office staff to use word processors.[209]

Former Powell law clerk J. Harvie Wilkinson III (OT 1972 and 1973) writes that the small, cramped working environment positively impacted the relationship between justice and law clerk:

> The small size and staff of each Justice's chambers is one of the Supreme Court's most distinctive features. It gave to Justice Powell's chambers, as I believe it did to others, a sense of unity and compactness, the feeling of being harnessed together that was necessary to accomplish the arduous job of research and analysis a Supreme Court case frequently requires. It made possible a collective pride in the quality of legal work produced by the chambers as well as a rivalry among individual chambers even as they worked in the larger sense together. It encouraged within our own chambers frank and often heated debate on many a legal issue that would have become diffused and less vital in a more formal setting or among larger numbers.[210]

In the language of P-A theory, the understaffed, tight chambers bind the clerk/agents more tightly to the justice/principal.

Wilkinson's perception of a "small" judicial staff must be placed within the proper historical context. He quotes Louis Brandeis' now-familiar observation that the Supreme Court retained its political legitimacy because "it did its own work," but Brandeis made this observation when the justice worked at home and employed a single law clerk and a messenger. By the 1970s, the number of law clerks and secretaries hired by the associate justices had tripled in size. Wilkinson writes that it is "the small chamber size that allows a Justice to concentrate directly on the Court's cases, free of administrative obligations to set lines of supervision and responsibility among a large staff,"[211] but staff hierarchy and confidentiality rules were slowly becoming important institutional considerations in the 1960s and 1970s.

In fact, in later years Powell was not entirely free of administrative considerations. Every term the justice selected one "senior" law clerk who had limited administrative supervision over the other clerks—including the division of the cert. pool memoranda. Moreover, Powell paid close attention to individual case assignments within his chambers, oversaw the creation of the law clerk office manual and a legal form file, and monitored the transition between the outgoing and incoming set of law clerks.

Wilkinson writes that "Justice Powell often said that the selection of his clerks was among the most important decisions he made during a term."[212] As for selection criteria, Powell states "I prefer candidates who have attended strong colleges and law school, with good records at both, with experience as an officer of a quality law review, and with service preferably with a strong circuit court judge."[213] Powell adds that "I consider the human qualities of personality, character and congeniality to be quite as important as first rate scholarship." Wilkinson further explains what Powell sought in a law clerk:

> He obviously wanted a clerk with a sense of integrity and trustworthiness as to the confidences of Court, as well as a sense of personal loyalty, not as a yes man, but as someone who would go the extra mile in a pinch. He sought clerks of unselfish talent; he often referred to our chambers as "our team" and saw its product as the result of hard collective effort. He had no set views, however, on the personal politics of a prospective clerk and, in fact, never expected his clerks to agree with each vote he cast or opinion he wrote. He preferred that his clerks be of different persuasions and stir "crosswinds," as he once put it, through his office.[214]

John C. Jeffries, Jr., writes that the justice "did care about Law Review experience, and indeed much preferred candidates who had been on Managing Board. I don't recall [the justice] being especially concerned with class rank, but I doubt he ever had a clerk who wasn't near the top."[215] Jeffries agrees that Justice Powell did not use a political litmus test. "He wanted to make sure that his clerks could work comfortably with him," states Jeffries.

"That meant that he rather distrusted evidence of strong ideological commitment in any direction."[216]

As with other justices, Powell had a slight preference for applicants from his region of birth and his former law school.[217] Finding law clerks with southern roots sometimes proved difficult for Justice Powell, a fact that he noted with some humor. Writing to his current law clerks about his selection practices, Powell wryly observed: "I have tried, not always successfully, to follow Justice Black's practice of having one law clerk with Southern connections. [J. Peter Byrne] is my 'southerner' this Term, as he spent five years at *The* University. I try not to mention that he is a product of the Bronx."[218] As for how Justice Powell located such clerks, the justice eschewed selection committees and personally screened clerkship applications. Often Justice Powell asked his current clerks to review applications and prepare a tentative list of which applicants should be granted interviews. Current clerks also met applicants during their visit to the Powell chambers.

From the start, Justice Powell required his law clerks to review cert. petitions and prepare memoranda.[219] Wilkinson refers to the cert. review process as a "baptism by fire" for a new clerk, estimating that he prepared between twenty and thirty cert. memoranda per week and "had typed Justice Powell over one thousand pages of cert. notes" in the first five months of his clerkship.[220] It was Justice Powell who suggested that the justices combine their law clerks' talents and energies and create a cert. pool, and in subsequent terms the Powell clerks prepared their proportionate shares of pool memoranda. For those pool memos prepared by non-Powell clerks, the justice asked his clerks to review the memoranda and add their own written comments.

Besides drafting cert. memoranda, the clerks also prepared bench memos. In some terms the clerks prepared the bench memos through the year, while in other terms the memo assignments were more limited. Explains a former clerk: "Over the summer, we did bench memos on a couple of cases per clerk, but we stopped doing them once the Term began." As for the format of the memoranda, Justice Powell "wanted the arguments summarized and evaluated, including those by respectable amici, and questions raised."

Finally, Powell's law clerks prepared opinion drafts. Writes Jeffries:

Powell's long experience in working with junior lawyers was now turned to his clerks. He did not simply take a clerk's draft and edit it into a final opinion. Rather, there was a sort of written dialogue between clerk and Justice. Typically, the clerk would write a first draft, to which Powell would respond with a memorandum proposing changes great and small. . . . The clerk would produce a revised draft, to which Powell would respond with another memorandum, and so on. If all went well, the memoranda got shorter as the opinion moved through successive drafts. Powell did not expect his clerks to follow blindly each instruction. A clerk told to add a certain paragraph to a draft opinion might do so, or make some other change to take account of the point, or suggest why the addition should not be made. Of course, some response was required. If Powell was not satisfied, he would return to the point in [the] next memorandum. By this method, Powell kept several clerks busy on opinions that he in an important sense "wrote," even when he never put pen to paper.[221]

Preexisting rules regarding the style of opinion writing were crafted by Powell to guide his clerks. While Powell claimed that "I am certain that you law review editors write far better than I ever will," he added that "I feel some responsibility for preserving a semblance of consistent style, as well as for the substantive views." These rules included a dislike for split infinitives; the sparing use of commas, personal pronouns, adjectives, and adverbs; and a preference for simple sentence structure.[222]

Once an opinion draft was pronounced completed, Justice Powell assigned a second law clerk the task of "perform[ing] a substantive review, including studying all authorities cited and, often, going back to first principles on the reasoning of the opinion itself."[223] This was a modification to the standard clerkship model, which had the effect of catching clerk errors and refining the product. The second law clerk's review, defined by a former clerk as "a rigorous edit," often led to further revisions by the justice and the first law clerk, followed by a review by the justice and all clerks of the opinion draft.

Former Powell law clerk Anne M. Coughlin (OT 1985) writes that Justice Powell had high expectations for his law clerks and their opinion drafts. "Justice Powell cared deeply about the quality of the writing, for he was acutely aware of the work, for good and for ill, that words perform in our lives." For Powell and his law clerks, opinion writing should produce a streamlined product devoid of footnotes, legalese, and repetitive phrases. Because of the justice's high expectations, his law clerks often agonized before turning in their draft opinions. "We shuddered at the thought of his eyes falling on a typo, and you cannot imagine the horror of having him view an infelicitous word, a mangled phrase, or a garbled argument."[224]

Powell appreciated the effort that his law clerks placed on achieving perfection. In a 1973 memorandum to law clerks Larry Hammond and William C. Kelly, Jr., Powell thanks the two young men for spending a sleepless night editing an important opinion. While Powell lauded his clerks for their "fidelity to duty" and "physical and intellectual stamina," he warned them not to repeat their performance: "I do indeed appreciate your doing this, but hope it will not set a precedent for the future. If the word gets around that Powell clerks put in 24 hour days here at the Court, I am afraid my recruiting program will collapse. Moreover, and more importantly, I don't want to be cited by Cindy and Frances in divorce actions."[225]

As we might expect with a clerkship model that placed substantial responsibility in the hands of law clerk/agents, Justice Powell paid careful attention to the issue of law clerk confidentiality. Warning his law clerks that "[s]ome elements of the media . . . are persistent, resourceful and sometimes devious in attempting to obtain information as to the outcome of a case," Powell reminded his staff that confidentiality rules applied not only to the outside world but also to the other chambers. "I hardly need add that no Justice would like for his clerks to quote him to personnel from other Chambers, except where the views of the Justice have been circulated or are generally known."[226] Additionally, in later years Powell would caution his clerks about the pitfalls of debating pending cases with clerks from other chambers. "While sharing views on pending cases may be constructive, it is prudent not to become clerk 'politicians' who try to lobby the clerks of other Chambers."

While Powell conceded that "[h]ard and fast rules [regarding confidentiality] are difficult to formulate and in many situations would be inappropriate," he added that "[g]ood judgment, discretion, and loyalty usually provide the requisite guidance."[227] Powell suggested in a subsequent memorandum that his law clerks respond to any press inquiry by stating that they were "[n]ot authorized to talk, either on or off the record, about Justice Powell or the Court to any representative of the press."[228]

Powell's former law clerks lovingly describe the former justice as a kind southern gentleman who expected much from his law clerks and gave his friendship (and occasionally his Washington Redskins season tickets) in return. "The Justice told us from the beginning that he and Mrs. Powell regard[ed] us as their own sons and daughters," writes former Powell clerk David Westin. "Over the course of our time in the Powell chambers we indeed became part of the professional 'Powell family' with all of the rights and responsibilities that entailed."[229] One of Powell's first law clerks, current Fourth Circuit Court of Appeals judge J. Harvie Wilkinson III, was so moved by the clerkship experience that he wrote Justice Powell on the first day of his honeymoon trip, commenting that "I never felt that I was just a Supreme Court clerk—I always saw myself as a Powell clerk—and that meant serving a man whose standards of quality were far higher than the ordinary, who was doing what was right for the country."

As for Justice Powell, the men and women who passed through his chambers were an invaluable part of his time on the Court. Reflecting back on his first decade on the Supreme Court in a letter written to former law clerk John Jeffries, Jr., Powell writes:

An especially gratifying aspect of serving here has been the personal and professional association with law clerks—especially mine. The clerks do not make the decisions but they contribute more to the quality of opinions than is generally recognized. For me, the personal relationship and yes—inspiration—of working closely with the "brightest and best" from the great law schools, has illuminated this decade for me in a very special way.[230]

A select handful of former law clerks remained confidants of Justice Powell, receiving over the years a steady stream of letters from the justice on a variety of topics—ranging from judicial business to U.S. foreign policy. The former clerks provided Justice Powell with a needed outlet for his private thoughts and political observations. "Apart from family, there are few people with whom I can talk politics," wrote Justice Powell in a 1980 letter to former law clerk J. Harvie Wilkinson III.[231] In short, Powell tacitly acknowledges one benefit of the clerkship institution that was first recognized by Justice Holmes, to wit, that trusted current and past clerks could provide a momentary escape from the "splendid isolation" of the Marble Palace.

The transformation in the clerkship institution begun in the Warren Court continued in the Burger Court. Law clerks routinely prepared cert. and bench memoranda. Moreover, what was unspeakable and unthinkable thirty years prior became the norm: law clerks prepared opinion drafts in almost all cases. A summary of the duties performed by law clerks in the role of firm associate is presented in Table 5.1.

The Rehnquist Court, 1986 to 2004

Any study that involves collecting data on Supreme Court law clerks faces one formidable hurdle: the duty of confidentiality owed by the clerk to his or her justice. As their justices leave the bench, law clerks tend to become

TABLE 5.1.   Main Job Duties of Law Clerk as Law Firm Associate

	Cert. Memos	Bench Memos	Opinion Editing	Opinion Writing
Blackmun	Yes	Yes	Yes	Yes
Brennan	Infrequently	No	Yes	Yes
Burger	Yes	Yes	Yes	Yes
Fortas	Yes	Infrequently	Yes	Yes
Goldberg	Yes	Unknown	Yes	Unknown
Harlan II	Yes	Infrequently	Yes	Yes
Marshall	Yes	Yes	Yes	Yes
Powell	Yes	Yes	Yes	Yes
Stewart	Yes	No	Yes	Yes
Warren	Yes	Yes	Yes	Yes
White	Yes	Yes	Yes	Yes
Whittaker	Yes	Yes	Yes	Unknown

more willing to discuss the details of their clerkship. For the majority of former clerks whose justices currently sit on the Supreme Court, however, their commitment to confidentiality is steadfast. If anything, the former law clerks of sitting justices have become more, not less, tight-lipped since the 1998 publication of Lazarus' *Closed Chambers*—not only due to a sense of duty but also because of a fear of retribution by the justices.

Given these current conditions, it is very difficult to find former law clerks willing to talk candidly about their clerkship experiences. Many former clerks have so broadly defined the scope of the duty of confidentiality that they refuse to answer even the most innocuous questions, such as "does Justice O'Connor still conduct an aerobics class" and "do the law clerks still have lunch during the term with justices from different chambers?" Even when the rare individuals who will candidly discuss their clerkship are found, the data gathered are limited—at best, the clerks can only speak authoritatively about an individual justice's rules and practices during a specific term. While multiple interviews with a wide range of former law clerks is desirable before drawing conclusions about a justice's employment practices, such data is almost impossible to collect.

As discussed earlier, this author originally wrote all nine members of the Rehnquist Court and requested interviews regarding their law clerk employment practices. The first letter requested a personal interview, but if a rejection letter was received, a second letter was sent that asked if the justice would consider answering written interview questions. Of the ten justices contacted (I also wrote retired justice Byron White), only Justice Stevens agreed to an on-the-record interview, while Justice Scalia consented to an off-the-record conversation. Basic informational requests were also denied by the current Court. Chief Justice Rehnquist declined to make available a copy of the *Law Clerk Code of Conduct*, and the Public Information Office refused to provide any information regarding how the Supreme Court conducts background checks of its law clerk applicants—including when the practice was formalized and what federal agency or agencies perform the check.

Accordingly, any conclusions drawn about the Rehnquist Court justices are tentative. Given this disclaimer, one can safely conclude that no other set of sitting Supreme Court justices have delegated as much responsibility to their law clerks as those on the Rehnquist Court. All justices relied on their law clerks to review cert. petitions and prepare cert. memoranda, and eight of the nine justices—save John Paul Stevens—joined the "cert. pool."[232] All justices except Justice Stevens routinely assigned their clerks the task of preparing the first draft of opinions, and the majority of the justices depended on bench memoranda to prepare them for oral argument. There is no evidence to suggest that any of these practices have changed during the first term of the Roberts Court.

Before turning to the specific clerkship practices of the individual justices, it is instructive to consider briefly the Rehnquist Court's workload. During OT 1995, the justices disposed of eighty-seven cases by signed opinion and a scant three cases by per curiam opinion. The last time the Supreme Court disposed of fewer cases by signed opinion was 1955.[233] The number of new cases filed with the Supreme Court, however, has continued to rise; while in 1968 the number was 3,271, it climbed to 4,413 in 1985 and 7,852 in 2000. Nevertheless, with the creation of word processors, electronic databases, and the cert. pool, as well as the increased number of law clerks, it is legitimate to ask if the workload pressures on the Rehnquist Supreme Court justices were significantly higher than for those members of the Stone, Vinson, and Warren Courts.

Let's consider two points in time—1945 and 1995. In 1945, the Supreme Court saw the filing of 1,316 new cases and disposed of 170 cases by signed opinion. The individual justices did so with a small staff (typically, one secretary and one law clerk), either dictating their opinions or writing them out in longhand. Legal research was conducted by opening up a book, not a laptop computer. In 1995, 6,597 cases were filed with the Supreme Court and only 87 were disposed of by signed opinion. The individual justices were now authorized to hire four law clerks and two secretaries, opinions were typed and edited on computers, communications between justice and law clerk took place via e-mail, and legal research was conducted on electronic databases such as Westlaw.

Assuming for the sake of argument that workload pressures are roughly comparable for these two eras, why didn't any Rehnquist Court justices (other than Stevens) adopt clerkship models that deviated from the norm established by Chief Justice Earl Warren? I again submit that the answer lies in the role played by consensual norms. In short, the justices have grown comfortable with the standard institutional practice of delegating the preparation of draft opinions as well as cert. and bench memoranda to their clerks. Letting one's clerks draft opinions no longer draws the scorn of one's fellow justices. Moreover, the illusion that the justices "do their own work" has been dashed, and the public has—with only an occasional murmur of protest—accepted these new institutional norms. Therefore, the justices have no incentive to take on the more challenging task of drafting their own opinions; it is undeniably easier to edit the work product of your trusted young subordinate than to put pen to a blank sheet of paper.

Nevertheless, there was some variation in the clerkship practices of the Rehnquist Court justices. In his 2001 book on the Supreme Court, Chief Justice Rehnquist provided a detailed account of his law clerk employment practices. Rehnquist wrote that his clerks prepared the first draft of majority (and presumably, although it is unclear) and dissenting opinions.[234] Anticipating protest from the reader, Rehnquist explained that "the law clerk is not simply turned loose on an important legal question to draft an opinion embodying the reasoning and the result favored by the clerk."[235] Instead, Rehnquist characterized the assignment as a "highly structured task" in which the chief justice would meet with his clerk and provide "a summary of the conference discussion, a description of the result reached by the majority in that discussion, and my views as to how a written opinion can best be prepared embodying that reasoning."[236] Rehnquist imposed the further constraint of a ten-day to two-week deadline for drafting opinions, recognizing that his young charges—all products of elite law reviews—might otherwise take a month writing a scholarly treatise.

It is easy in October, when the work of the Court is just starting up for the term, to imagine that there is an infinite amount of time in which to explore every nuance of a question and to perfect the style of every paragraph of the opinion. But, as I learned long ago, and as the clerks soon find out, there is not an infinite amount of time. . . . It is far more useful for me to get something in fairly rough form in two weeks than to receive after four or five weeks a highly polished draft that I feel obligated nonetheless to substantially revise.[237]

Former Rehnquist law clerks echo the chief justice's description of the opinion-writing process as a "highly structured task": "This is a guy you didn't get anything by," stated former law clerk Dean C. Colsen (OT 1980). "The chief would say: 'Here's the way I want it outlined. Here's the way I want it written.' And then he'd edit heavily."[238]

After reviewing the draft opinion as well as lower court opinions and the parties' briefs, Rehnquist commenced editing the draft. Often the editing process involved not substantive changes, but reshaping the work product so it more resembled a judicial opinion than a law review article. "Clerks also have been exposed to so much 'legal writing' on law reviews and elsewhere that their prose tends to stress accuracy at the expense of brevity and clarity."[239]

The degree of editing is partially a function of law clerk experience. "The drafts I get during the first part of the term from the clerks require more revision and editing than the ones later in the term, after the clerks are more accustomed to my review and my approach to writing."[240] Presumably the law clerk has become more competent and proficient during the term as well. After Rehnquist completed the edits, the second draft was given back to the clerk for additional polishing and revisions.

Rehnquist conceded that his law clerks had "considerable responsibility" in drafting opinions but appeared satisfied that bounded responsibility did not equal unfettered discretion. Even in those circumstances in which the clerk discovered that Rehnquist's original orders must be modified (for example, if the clerk believed that the legal analysis of the conference majority did not hold up to more careful analysis), it was Rehnquist himself who determined whether the law clerk was correct and, if so, the chief justice worked with the clerk to address the problem.[241]

Chief Justice Rehnquist was a member of the "cert. pool" and thus depended on both his own law clerks and those from other chambers to perform an initial evaluation of the cert. petitions. In explaining the origins of this institutional practice, Rehnquist wrote:

> During the first term in which I served on the Court, there was no "cert. pool," and each chambers did all of its own certiorari work as well as its other work. I could not help but notice that my clerks were frequently pressed for time, scrambling between having memos describing the certiorari petitions ready when they should be, and drafts or revisions of Court opinions or dissents ready when they should have been.[242]

In summarizing the problems inherent in the old system, Rehnquist does not mention the concerns of a younger Rehnquist, namely, that the political biases of liberal law clerks are "unconsciously" reflected in the cert. memoranda. It appears, however, from the institutional rules adopted by the chief justice that he remained concerned about clerk competency—if not bias—in reviewing cert. petitions. Rehnquist required his law clerks to review all cert. memoranda prepared by other chambers, "and, if necessary, go back to the petition and response in order to make a recommendation to me as to whether the petition should be granted or denied."[243] Rehnquist later wrote that he received "the *annotated* certiorari memos from his law clerks," suggesting that the clerks performed additional legal research as well as a review of the parties' filings and briefs.[244] This involved duplication of work, since the cert. pool memoranda already included a recommendation on whether the petition should be granted or denied.[245]

Once Rehnquist's law clerks reviewed all cert. pool memoranda, Rehnquist himself read through the reports. Although there may have been times when he would personally review the pleadings and briefs filed by the parties, it appears that the chief justice depended heavily on his law clerks' analysis. "As soon as I am confident that my new law clerks are reliable, *I take their word and that of the pool memo writer* as to the underlying facts and contentions of the parties in the various petitions, and with a large majority of the petitions it is not necessary to go any further than the pool memo."[246]

It is difficult to determine the degree of discretion that was given to Rehnquist's clerks in the preparation of their own cert. pool memoranda and their review of the memoranda prepared by other law clerks. Certainly many of the cert. petitions filed with the Supreme Court are so frivolous that reasonable minds could not differ on their fate—the "dead list" and automatic denial. It is equally certain that some cert. petitions present novel legal issues over which reasonable minds could differ, both on jurisprudential and ideological grounds. For these latter petitions, might "taking the word" of a law clerk have injected undue influence into the decision-making process?

Unlike many current justices, Rehnquist did not have his law clerks prepare formal bench memoranda. Instead, Rehnquist and the law clerk assigned to the specific case individually read the lower court opinions, the parties' briefs, and relevant Supreme Court cases. After reviewing these materials, Rehnquist would informally meet with his law clerk and they discussed the case—"sometimes walking around the neighborhood of the Court building, sometimes sitting in my chambers."[247] After these discussions, Rehnquist occasionally asked the clerk to research a legal issue that the briefs did not thoroughly address and to prepare a formal memorandum. Rehnquist did not state whether his other clerks formally or informally contributed to the case discussion.[248]

Unlike most modern justices, Chief Justice Rehnquist selected three, not four, law clerks each term (Justice Stevens follows a similar practice). Some have suggested that there was a nonjudicial explanation for Rehnquist's limited number of clerks—it permitted him to have the right number of players for games of doubles tennis. During the term, clerks also joined the chief justice for walks around the Court building, charades at his home, NCAA tournament basketball pools, and sing-alongs at holiday parties.

The only other Rehnquist Court justices for whom I have gathered solid information on their clerkship practices are Justices John Paul Stevens, Sandra Day O'Connor, and Ruth Bader Ginsburg. Again, I will assume that these practices remain unchanged despite the selection of a new chief justice. Appointed by President Gerald Ford, Northwestern Law School graduate Justice John Paul Stevens is the senior associate justice on the Court. Stevens is the only sitting Supreme Court justice who has not fully adopted the rules and norms of the modern clerkship model. As noted earlier, Stevens clerked for Justice Wiley Rutledge during OT 1947. Arguably, it was this clerkship—and the prevailing Court norms of the 1940s—that helped shape Justice Stevens' conception of the proper roles of justice and clerk.

Like Justice Rutledge, Stevens always prepares the first draft of an opinion. When asked why he does not delegate this duty, Stevens initially replied that "I'm the one hired to do the job." When pressed to explain further, Stevens stated that the process of becoming educated about the factual and legal issues involved in a case does not end at oral argument—Stevens continues to learn about the case as he drafts his opinions, honing his interpretation of the applicable legal theories and even reevaluating his ultimate position on a case. Writing the first draft has a practical benefit—the draft is typically much shorter than a law clerk's draft, and the justice is less likely to showboat with long cites and flowery language.[249]

Former Stevens law clerk Deborah Pearlstein further elaborates on Stevens' position on opinion writing. "He believes that without forcing himself through the exercise—most importantly, reading large parts of the record and summarizing the facts of the case—it would be too easy to avoid engaging fully."[250] By immersing himself in the factual records and the parties' briefs as he writes the opinion, Stevens is able to satisfy himself that the outcome he has supported is correct.

After Stevens writes the first draft, he gives it to the clerk assigned to the case and tells him or her "to make it an opinion." Specifically, Stevens wants the law clerk to polish the language, check the grammar, review the legal analysis, and make sure that Stevens has not omitted any meritorious arguments made by the parties.[251] While the original draft is the product of Stevens' efforts alone, the clerks do not feel constrained in their review and editing of the draft—keeping in mind, however, that the ultimate goal was to "further the opinion."[252]

Since Stevens is not a member of the cert. pool, his law clerks spend a great deal of time reviewing and summarizing cert. petitions. Like the other justices, Stevens has his clerks prepare cert. memoranda that both educate Stevens as to the issues involved and suggest a recommended disposition. If the Stevens law clerks conclude that the petition was utterly lacking in merit, however, they do not prepare a cert. memoranda.[253] Stevens states that he listens to his law clerks' recommendations, and the clerks often persuade him on how to vote.

Stevens' clerks do not prepare bench memoranda—another aspect of his "older" clerkship model—but are involved in preparing Justice Stevens for oral argument. Pearlstein writes:

> Once we had picked [cases], we threw ourselves into the details, reading the stacks of papers submitted by the parties, the opinions of the lower courts in the case, and any relevant law or scholarship that might help our Justice decide which side should win the case and why. All this in preparation for a conference with Justice Stevens in which we'd talk through the issues, and, in the end, advise the Justice—with his quarter-century on the high court and years as a lawyer before that—what we thought he should do.[254]

Pearlstein takes great pains to explain that these conferences were not formal, scheduled meetings but instead bull sessions that occurred at odd times both before and after oral argument.

Since Justice Stevens thoroughly reviews the parties' briefs, the law clerks are not called upon to familiarize him with the basic facts or legal issues of a case. Instead, Justice Stevens and his clerks engage in what might be best described as a Socratic dialogue, a joint inquiry toward the "right" outcome. These meetings permit the free exchange of ideas and arguments.

Comments Pearlstein: "I can imagine few bosses so interested in the views of their employees, so prepared to engage in free-flowing debate, and so enthusiastic to be proven wrong."[255]

Appointed by President Ronald Reagan in 1981, Sandra Day O'Connor became the first woman to sit on the U.S. Supreme Court. An Arizona native, O'Connor graduated third in her class from Stanford Law School and worked as a local prosecutor, state legislator, and state appellate court judge in her home state of Arizona. After two decades on the High Court, many Court observers consider O'Connor to be an important "swing vote" on controversial issues such as abortion rights.

In a 1989 interview, Justice O'Connor stated that she personally scans the law clerk applications, looking at "the courses they have taken, their grades, the honors achieved" until approximately 50 files remain.[256] Sometimes her current law clerks perform the initial screening of applications. Justice O'Connor then reviews the applications that survived the screening process, selecting a few candidates for personal interviews.[257]

As for O'Connor's selection criteria, she states:

One thing I do look for is the person who has the ability to remain unruffled and get along . . . Maturity, stability, and congeniality are important to me because we work long hours and every weekend and holidays, other than Christmas Day and New Year's Day. It is a very intense year and because of the intensity and pressure of all the deadlines that have to be met, we really don't have time around here to solve many personal problems. We need to concentrate on the work.[258]

Supreme Court reporter Tony Mauro writes that Justice Sandra Day O'Connor "usually comes up with a gender-balanced foursome. She also looks for some representation from a law school in her native West."[259] Mauro adds that additional selection criteria include "at least one clerk with musical talent—for the court's Christmas party—and another who could join her in tennis."

Justice O'Connor states that a law clerk's ideological beliefs are relevant to her selection process only if an applicant's views interfere with his or her ability to perform as a law clerk. "I am the one who has to make the decisions around here, so I am not concerned or interested in the individual's particular philosophy," O'Connor states. "However, I don't want to hire someone who has a particular ax to grind in terms of legal structure." O'Connor adds that what she seeks are "people who can be objective."[260]

Justice O'Connor has stated that the most important task performed by her law clerks is the review of cert. petitions.[261] At least during OT 1981, O'Connor did not ask her law clerks to review cert. pool memoranda written by other chambers.[262] Justice O'Connor requires her law clerks not only to prepare lengthy written bench memoranda but also to give oral presentations on the individual cases to the justice and the other law clerks.[263] Rosen writes that these meetings "are more formal, like a senator's receiving briefings from her staff" and less like the "freewheeling debates" held by Justices Antonin Scalia and Clarence Thomas with their law clerks.[264] Information contained in the bench memoranda includes a case summary, analysis of the briefs, a personal recommendation as to case disposition, and suggested questions for oral argument.[265]

Justice O'Connor routinely assigns her law clerks the task of preparing opinion drafts. Former clerk Simon Steel writes that during OT 1995 "Justice [O'Connor] assigned opinions to individual clerks to draft, usually by who did the bench memo; usually clerks did 1st draft; Justice always instructed result and outline[d] reasoning—sometimes more, sometimes less detailed."[266] Other clerks claim that O'Connor provides "extraordinarily detailed instructions" regarding the writing process.[267] These instructions included a ban on footnotes, since the justice believes that her opinions are more readable without footnotes. Moreover, all four law clerks review circulating draft opinions and provide written comments.[268]

Based on the limited information regarding Justice O'Connor and her law clerks, I believe that she shares a warm but not overly familiar bond with the young men and women who work in her chambers. Former law clerk Gary Francione (OT 1982) has commented that the justice was not "the easiest person to work for, because she is extraordinarily demanding,"[269] and the demands placed on the O'Connor clerks result in long hours at the office. Yet genuine affection exists. During the term, O'Connor clerks joined their justice for her aerobics and yoga classes, trips to the National Arboretum, and horseback riding in Rock Creek Park. Justice O'Connor prepares home-cooked dishes during Saturday work sessions, and every Halloween she brings in a pumpkin for her chambers staff. The justice and her clerks also enjoy regular reunions.

In 1993, Ruth Bader Ginsburg became the second woman to wear the black robes of a Supreme Court justice. Since arriving at the Court, she has formulated a substantial number of formal rules regarding the clerkship institution. Justice Ginsburg's clerks follow a law clerk manual that was adapted from older manuals prepared by Justices Clarence Thomas and Byron White.[270] The manual is divided by topics and includes information on the preparation of cert. and bench memoranda as well as Justice Ginsburg's expectations regarding opinion writing. Additionally, the manual includes a section on state and federal court jurisdiction and the justice's own rules about language to be used in opinion writing.[271]

Justice Ginsburg is a member of the cert. pool, but she also requires her law clerks to review and evaluate memoranda prepared by other chambers.[272] A former law clerk anonymously explains that the review occurs because (1) some clerks' efforts at preparing pool memoranda were mediocre, and (2) some law clerks were driven by a particular political agenda. The former clerk adds that the latter type of law clerks quickly developed a reputation,[273] and their cert. memoranda (identified by their initials) were subjected to more exacting scrutiny by the different chambers.

In the majority of cases set for oral argument, Justice Ginsburg requires her clerks to prepare written bench memoranda. The purpose of the bench memoranda is to highlight the salient issues and provide a framework for resolving the appeal. The memoranda include a summary of the dispositive legal issues, suggested questions for oral argument, and a recommended disposition.[274] They also include what Justices Ginsburg calls a "guided tour of the briefs," namely, "which [briefs] to read, which to skip, which to skim, and highlights of arguments on both sides."[275] Justice Ginsburg reviews the bench memoranda before reading the parties' briefs, in part so she does not have to review the briefs more than once. She writes down questions as she reviews the bench memoranda, which require the law clerk to provide follow-up responses.[276]

After receiving her opinion assignments, Justice Ginsburg meets with her clerks. In most instances she requires them to prepare the initial opinion draft, although there are exceptions to this rule. If a law clerk is assigned to write the first draft, he or she typically receives extensive instructions from Justice Ginsburg as well as a written outline to follow.[277] Once the law clerk completes the first draft, it is reviewed by the other law clerks so that the justice receives the benefit of her staff's best collective effort. When an opinion draft emerges from the justice's office, it is typically extensively rewritten. The opinion draft then goes through additional rounds of editing between the justice and her clerks.

As for the personal bond between Ginsburg and her clerks, the justice is reportedly a stickler for in-chambers celebrations of all clerk and staff birthdays. In some terms, she will sponsor trips to a local opera house or Gilbert and Sullivan productions, and at least once during the term the law clerks join her for a home-cooked meal, courtesy of husband Martin Ginsburg. Former law clerk Margo Schlanger (OT 1993 and 1994) recalls an outing with the Ginsburgs and several former, married Ginsburg law clerks in which dinner ended with fortune cookies containing Eskimo love poems—courtesy of Justice Ginsburg.

Information regarding the other justices' hiring and employment practices is spottier. It appears that the remaining justices have adopted a clerkship model similar to that of former chief justice Rehnquist, although the other justices—save Justice Antonin Scalia—impose the additional requirement of preparing bench memoranda. Justice Scalia has his law clerks prepare the first draft of majority, concurring, and dissenting opinions. It is unclear how much guidance is provided to the clerk assigned the draft opinion. After the draft is completed, it is circulated to the other Scalia law clerks for review. Only after the other clerks complete their review is the draft forwarded to Justice Scalia.

Former clerks anonymously write that Scalia is a member of the cert. pool but that clerks do not evaluate the memoranda written by other chambers. Like many of the current chambers, the Scalia law clerks follow an in-chambers procedural manual.

While information on the internal functioning of Justice Clarence Thomas' chambers is limited, biographer Andrew Peyton Thomas writes that Justice Thomas depends on feeder court judges Larry Silberman and J. Michael Luttig for a steady stream of law clerks, primarily graduates of Harvard, Yale, and the University of Chicago. Justice Thomas employs four law clerks, one of whom is designated the chief clerk and given the responsibility of supervising the work product of the other clerks. As for law clerk selection, Justice Thomas asks his current law clerks to first meet with the applicants for what a former law clerk described as a "very rigorous interview to make sure you understand where [Thomas] stands on the issues" before the justice himself interviews the applicants. In biographer Thomas' eyes, Justice Thomas thereby "smartly delegated the unpleasantness of ideological vetting to subordinates."[278]

As for the type of law clerks he hires, author Ken Foskett writes that Justice Thomas selects law clerks who are at the top of their law school class, are "good, clean" writers, and have "personality, who aren't afraid to express themselves and mix it up with him."[279] Foskett adds that there are limits, however, to the clerk diversity. "Thomas only hires clerks who share his conservative philosophy." Justice Thomas himself has stated that "I'm not going to hire clerks who have profound disagreements with me . . . That is a waste of my time. Someone said that is like trying to train a pig. It's a waste of your time, and it aggravates the pig."[280]

Justice Thomas is a member of the cert. pool, and he requires his law clerks to prepare bench memoranda for all cases scheduled for oral argument. After the bench memoranda are completed, Thomas meets with all four clerks for a "clerk conference" during which they discuss the memoranda. The discussion topics include not only basic information about the case and the legal issues at stake, but also suggestions on how the justice should vote on the cases before the Court. Author Andrew Peyton Thomas claims that these conferences "were the most uninhibited and wide-ranging on the Court."[281] After the clerk conferences, the law clerks prepare drafts of all opinions assigned to the justice.

Biographer Thomas' summary of the law clerks' duties is confirmed by a former Thomas law clerk. According to the clerk, Justice Thomas required his law clerks to prepare bench memoranda. These reports summarized the lower court's holding, the parties' arguments on appeal, and an analysis as to the merits of the appeal. Justice Thomas also had his law clerks prepare the first draft of majority opinions. He would first meet with the clerk, summarize the conference vote, and provide guidance on other aspects of the opinion. After the clerk prepared the opinion draft, it was reviewed by the other clerks before being sent to the justice. The former clerk stated that during OT 1992, the justice did not have a formal hierarchical structure in which junior clerks reported to a senior clerk, but that the law clerk for retired Chief Justice Warren Burger served as a "part-time" Thomas clerk and "officially ranked below" the full-time Thomas clerks. This part-time clerk worked on cert. pool memoranda and "spillover work" on pending cases.[282]

The creation of the "chief clerk" position with administrative responsibilities is, in part, a function of the increasing number of law clerks and the attendant need for efficiency. Moreover, another modification to the clerkship institution—the creation of the "clerk conference"—undoubtedly permits Justice Thomas "to tap the collective intelligence of the crew of young lawyers at his disposal."[283] Both institutional changes, however, arguably serve a different function—the imposition of a hierarchical structure combined with review of bench memoranda by all law clerks permits the monitoring of law clerk behavior and the threat of intrachamber exposure of clerk mischief. The practice of having all law clerks review the work product of a single clerk extends beyond the bench memoranda; Justice Thomas also requires all four law clerks to review draft opinions and be in agreement with the opinion before forwarding it to the justice for his review.[284]

Biographer Thomas claims that "[n]o other justice could boast of greater loyalty from his clerks,"[285] and Justice Thomas himself has publicly stated that his clerks "are like family."[286] Ken Foskett provides multiple examples of the kindnesses Thomas extends to his clerk family, from worrying about the bald tires on a clerk's car to offering emotional support to the ailing wife of a former clerk. At the start of each term, Thomas requires his law clerks to watch the movie version of Ayn Rand's *The Fountainhead*. "'The justice makes you watch it, and then you have to groan, and say how bad it is.' Said [former law clerk Helgi] Walker. 'Then he laughs. But there is a message in all of that, and the message is: Do not let other people change what you think is right.'"[287]

The available evidence (which is very limited) indicates that Justice Anthony Kennedy forwards the names of a select number of applicants to a screening committee composed of former law clerks (past members have included federal appeals court judge Alex Kozinski) and son Gregory Kennedy. The committee interviews the candidates and forwards the names of finalists to Justice Kennedy, who himself meets with the applicants. During the interview, Justice Kennedy will ask the applicant to identify and discuss a recent Supreme Court case that the applicant believes was wrongly decided.

It is frankly unclear whether Justice Kennedy uses an ideological litmus test in picking law clerks. A former Kennedy law clerk firmly believes that ideology is irrelevant to the selection process, anonymously commenting: "one thing that is clear is that there is no ideological screen . . . Kennedy routinely has liberal law clerks—much to the consternation of his former, conservative clerks." Yet former Kennedy law clerk Miguel Estrada faced a flurry of questions during his own judicial confirmation hearings as to whether he, as a member of the Kennedy screening committee, rejected candidates because of their liberal leanings.

Former law clerk Ward Farnsworth (OT 1995) writes that Kennedy's law clerks prepared bench memoranda, cert. pool memoranda, and the first draft of opinions. A former clerk anonymously adds that the bench memoranda prepared by the Kennedy clerks varied from those written in other chambers. "They are not a comprehensive analysis of the case . . . [they] would be short overviews of the case, ideally two pages in length and single spaced."[288] Justice Kennedy does not want long bench memoranda, and he simply stops reading the memos after the second or third page. In some years, the law clerks recorded their bench memoranda onto audiotapes, and Justice Kennedy listened to the tapes while driving to work.

Regarding opinion writing, a former clerk writes that Justice Kennedy "did not give a lot of instructions before the law clerk started the draft. It wasn't that he had no views on the case—he just preferred to work off of a written draft." Former clerk Ward Farnsworth adds that Justice Kennedy's instructions did include the following: "He would explain the basic thrust of the analysis and arguments he wanted to use; it would be obvious anyway from long prior discussions of the case with him." At times the law clerks work off a written opinion outline or even paragraphs of "key language" prepared by the justice. When the law clerks did prepare opinion drafts, they would first circulate them to their fellow Kennedy clerks for review and comment.[289] The drafts were then "heavily edited" by Justice Kennedy.

I have not been able to construct an accurate picture of the role of the Kennedy clerks in regards to the cert. pool. While Justice Kennedy's law clerks drafted their share of cert. pool memoranda, it remains unclear whether they examined cert. pool memoranda written by other chambers. One former clerk anonymously states that it was "very seldom" that the Kennedy clerks reviewed cert. pool memos.[290] Yet a second clerk anonymously observes that they routinely reviewed cert. pool memoranda, decided whether they agreed with the analysis, and annotated the front of the memorandum itself with handwritten comments. The second law clerk added that this review was necessary because occasionally law clerks' cert.

memoranda were agenda-driven. "I can remember one case in which I thought that a liberal clerk from a liberal chambers was making an effort to get the case denied . . . I thought that the pool memo was dishonest."

As for the question of law clerk influence, Justice Kennedy himself has stated that his clerks "served a function akin to one performed in England by the opposing parties' barristers, who often have 'discursive' exchanges with the judges in informal oral arguments."[291] A former law clerk anonymously explains that "Justice Kennedy's method of deciding cases was by way of discussion," adding that the justice "wanted to know what we thought of an issue." For this former Kennedy clerk, the relevant question to ask regarding the influence debate was "whether the justice was exercising his own judgment based on the information given to him by his law clerks." In short, the former clerk believes that it is entirely appropriate for justices to seek advice and feedback from their law clerks. "You are paid to help the justice do his or her job. Influence becomes pernicious when the law clerk is making the decisions."

Hardly any details regarding the selection and utilization of law clerks by Justices Stephen Breyer and David Souter are available. No Breyer law clerks responded to my interview requests, and the only written account of the justice's work habits is found in the flurry of clerkship articles appearing in *USA Today.* According to Supreme Court reporter Tony Mauro, Justice Breyer "reputedly tears apart most of a clerk's first draft."[292] As for Justice Souter, former law clerks Alison M. Tucher (OT 1993) and Ernest A. Young (OT 1995) state that they prepared both bench memoranda and cert. pool memoranda.[293] Young added that he did prepare opinion drafts as well, but Tucher did not comment. Both clerks declined to provide any further details about their job duties.

It is too early to determine what clerkship model Chief Justice John G. Roberts, Jr., has adopted. To date, all that is publicly known is that the new chief justice retained both of Rehnquist's incoming law clerks as well as his two appeals court clerks. Roberts declined an interview request that I made immediately upon his confirmation by the Senate. Regardless of whether Justice Roberts' ideological preferences were shaped by his clerkship with William Rehnquist, I believe that his clerkship practices will be. My prediction is that Chief Justice Roberts will follow the "law firm associate" model, requiring his law clerks to prepare bench memoranda and opinion drafts. I also predict that Roberts will join the cert. pool, thus marking another justice who has moved away from Louis Brandeis' belief that "deciding to decide" without law clerk input is a critical judicial function.

Finally, the Rehnquist Court modified the Burger Court's clerkship model in one significant way—the promulgation of formal ethical canons regarding the law clerk duties of confidentiality and responsibility. Political scientist David M. O'Brien writes that in 1987 Supreme Court law clerks received the first version of the *Code of Conduct for Supreme Court Clerks*, which was revised on March 3, 1989, and reissued with the slightly different title of the *Code of Conduct for Law Clerks of the Supreme Court of the United States*.[294] No copies of the code are publicly available, and as mentioned above, Chief Justice Rehnquist declined to provide this author with a copy. Nevertheless, a copy was found in the Thurgood Marshall Papers at the Library of Congress.

The *Code of Conduct* is divided into six canons. These canons dictate that the law clerk owes both the individual justice and the Court "complete confidentiality, accuracy, and loyalty."[295] In short, the law clerk is an agent of the justice. Both the law clerk and the justice hold positions of "public trust," and both are "held to the very highest standards of conduct."[296] Accordingly, a law clerk "should be dignified, courteous, and fair to all persons with whom the law clerk deals in the law clerk's official capacity," including both "the general public as well as the legal profession."[297]

While the duty of loyalty does not prevent a law clerk from engaging in an "exchange of ideas" with his or her justice, the clerk "must be aware of the respect due the Justice" and "should carry out to the fullest and to the best of his or her ability the Justice's instructions."[298] Finally, the "exchange of ideas" must occur within an environment of complete trust and confidentiality. In short, the law clerk must remember that "[t]he relationship between Justice and law clerk is essentially a confidential one." A clerk cannot divulge "any confidential information received in the course of the law clerk's duties.... Even discussions with law clerks from other chambers should be circumspect."[299]

The *Code of Conduct* applies from the start of the clerkship and is intended to survive after the clerkship is completed. Law clerks are required to sign the code. If a law clerk violates the Code, the range of punishments includes termination. Finally, the Code of Conduct establishes only the minimal ethical duties owed by the clerk to the justice. "The standards of this Code shall not affect or preclude other more stringent standards required by law, by Court order, or by direction of the appointing Justice."[300]

Note what the *Code of Conduct* does not say—it does not exempt present or former law clerks from their duties of confidentiality, loyalty, and discretion if the law clerks feel betrayed by the justices or the Court. Nevertheless, this is the rationale given for an extraordinary breach of confidentiality by several law clerks from OT 2000. The October 2004 edition of *Vanity Fair* magazine featured an article titled "The Path to Florida," a breezy but interesting take on the events surrounding the 2000 presidential election.[301] A portion of the article focuses on the internal operations of the Supreme Court leading up to the issuance of the *Bush v. Gore* opinion, information courtesy of former Supreme Court law clerks. Clearly much of what the former clerks divulged violates the ethical canons articulated in the *Code of Conduct*, a fact acknowledged by at least one of the law clerks who talked to *Vanity Fair* reporters. "We feel that something illegitimate was done with the Court's power, and such an extraordinary situation justifies breaking an obligation we'd otherwise honor."[302] Such a rationale, however, arguably makes the *Code of Conduct* meaningless. An agent cannot unilaterally redefine the terms of the fiduciary duty owed to the principal.

Conclusion

At no other time in the history of the Supreme Court have law clerks been given as many substantive responsibilities as were assigned to the Rehnquist Court clerks. Today's law clerk routinely edits, drafts, and revises judicial opinions (save Justice Stevens' law clerks); reviews, analyzes, and summarizes cert. petitions; and prepares bench memoranda. Moreover, the creation of the cert. pool means that the justices (again, save Justice Stevens) depend on law clerks selected and trained by other justices to review cert. pool memoranda and generate recommendations regarding the thousands of appeals filed each year with the High Court. Combined with the other duties given to the Rehnquist Court law clerks (such as reviewing death penalty stays, writing speeches, and assisting their justices with circuit duties), the modern law clerk has become an integral part of the Supreme Court—a fact that is unlikely to change during the administration of Chief Justice Roberts.

CHAPTER 6

Courtiers of the Marble Palace

"Now, you have asked me to write my opinion as to what
form of Courtiership most benefits a gentleman living at the
court of princes . . . in short, what manner of man he must
be who deserves the name of the perfect Courtier, without
defect of any kind."
                    —Baldassare Castiglione, *The Book of the Courtier*

FOR THE LAST FIFTY YEARS, a debate has waxed and waned about the
degree of influence exercised by Supreme Court law clerks, both over their
individual justices and, more critically, Supreme Court decision making.
Both Court insiders and Court observers have joined the battle, fiercely
arguing whether rising caseloads and aging jurists have led to the delegation
of Article III authority to inexperienced, overconfident young legal stars.
The American public loves a good conspiracy story, and tales of deception,
manipulation, and the wielding of power among a secretive group hidden
away in the Marble Palace have fired the imagination.

The changes in the clerkship institution—namely, the rules and norms
that constitute the clerkship institution as well as the conditions necessary for the exercise of influence. To affect judicial decision
making, law clerks must have more than simply the opportunity to exercise
discretionary authority to determine the winners and losers. They must also
possess preferences or goals that differ from those of their justices; if law
clerks and justices share the same policy preferences or ideological positions,
then any influence over decision making is not troubling because the clerks
are pursuing the same policy goals as the justices. Finally, even if the law
clerk has the ability and the interest to implement his or her own goals, the
clerk must circumvent a justice who has the institutional tools to limit and
defeat such behavior. The necessary conditions for the exercise of influence
by law clerks have rarely, if ever, existed on the Supreme Court.

The changes in the clerkship institution—namely, the rules and norms
shaping the hiring and utilization practices of the justice—are best explained

through the application of P-A theory. Such a theoretical framework suggests that as a justice delegates more critical, substantive responsibilities to his or her clerks, the probability of divergent clerk/justice interests increases and the risks associated with clerk "shirking" loom large. Now the justice is forced to devote significant resources to (1) reducing the likelihood that the justice and law clerk have different preferences, (2) monitoring the law clerks' job duties, and (3) increasing benefits/penalties associated with the incentive/sanctioning structure.

In other words, both the justice and his or her clerks are rational actors who seek to achieve a combination of different goals through the clerkship institution. While this is hardly a novel suggestion, the literature discussing whether law clerks influence judicial decision making fails to recognize that both parties to the contractual relationship are rational actors. The justices have the incentive and the institutional tools to circumvent law clerk shirking. Tools that they do, in fact, use.

The hypotheses generated from P-A theory are supported by the historical evolution of the clerkship institution. In the late nineteenth and early twentieth centuries, the majority of law clerks were stenographers and personal assistants. The probability of law clerk shirking was low, and the consequences typically insignificant. Poor stenographic skills might produce embarrassing spelling and grammatical errors in judicial opinions, but justices were certainly not concerned that law clerks had the tools to pursue their own personal political agendas.

The only type of significant defection costs revolved around the clerks' access to information. Law clerks were not positioned to influence judicial decision making; they were Court insiders who possessed advanced knowledge as to the timing and content of upcoming decisions. Joseph McKenna's longtime law clerk Ashton Fox Embry allegedly took advantage of such access, and he was accused of passing along word of upcoming Supreme Court holdings to co-conspirators speculating on the stock market.[1] Embry's alleged breach of the duty of confidentiality to his justice and the High Court was an isolated incident, and the justices did not formally amend the clerkship institution to prevent further breaches of duty. Of the clerks I interviewed who clerked from the 1930s through 1950s, none reported being bound by formal confidentiality rules.

Moreover, the law clerk as stenographer did not serve for a single term of court (with the exception of the Gray, Holmes, and Brandeis clerks), as is the modern norm. Many clerks worked years for the same justice, and occasionally moved from one justice to another.[2] As suggested by former Powell law clerk J. Harvie Wilkinson III, the limited, one-year clerkship norm is an institutional rule with the consequence of preventing law clerks from fully mastering the job and consolidating power. If a law clerk is simply taking dictation, maintaining files, and answering the justice's mail, there is no concern about influence. The justice wants his clerk to master the job. Hence, no need for "term limits." The fact that Justices Gray, Holmes, and Brandeis were the only justices who regularly rotated their law clerks during this time period—and who delegated substantive legal responsibilities to their clerks—supports Wilkinson's insight into the rationale behind the one-year clerkship.[3]

During the 1930s through the early 1950s, justices delegated more substantive duties to their law clerks. Asking clerks to review cert. petitions and draft memoranda summarizing appeals became the standard practice in all but the Brandeis and Frankfurter chambers. Many justices did not require their clerks to prepare bench memoranda. The justices themselves—with the exception of Chief Justice Fred Vinson and Associate Justice Frank Murphy—routinely prepared opinion drafts, depending on their clerks to play the role of editor and cite checker. Law clerks were not decision makers. They were legal assistants charged with providing their justices with the information and case law relevant to the justices' decision-making process.

The justices did not impose formal confidentiality rules on their law clerks, did not create office procedures in which the clerks verified the accuracy of the other's work, and often gave trusted law school professors carte blanche to select their clerks. The justices seldom supplied these professors with selection criteria, and the law clerks I interviewed soundly rejected the suggestion that their personal political ideology was a relevant consideration. While the justices relied on their law clerks to accurately perform legal research and to summarize cert. memoranda, conference discussion and opinion circulation were sufficient institutional checks. If any law clerks did place their own interests or goals before the justice's, the one-year clerkship tenure proved to be another check. Finally, the smaller number of law clerks (one clerk from 1919 to the late 1940s; two clerks in the 1940s and 1950s) provided the opportunity for a justice and his clerk(s) to forge intense personal bonds during the term. Law clerks became the surrogate sons, confidants, and trusted advisers for such justices as Hugo Black and Felix Frankfurter, while other clerks—although not achieving the status of an adopted family member—were fiercely loyal to their employers. These bonds of friendship and loyalty further served to minimize clerk shirking.

Chief Justice Earl Warren's time on the Supreme Court is often referred to as the "Warren Revolution" in light of the sweeping changes made by the High Court in the area of civil liberties and rights. The Warren Court also oversaw a revolution in how law clerks were selected and used on the Supreme Court. While older justices such as Black, Douglas, and Frankfurter maintained the "legal assistant" clerkship model, every justice appointed after

Earl Warren—save John Paul Stevens—has employed a "law firm associate" clerkship model. As the amount of information flowing past the law clerk rises, the level of "benign" influence wielded by the clerk also increases. Justices may hold the decision-making authority as to the case outcome or appeal status, but they exercise that authority based on information (facts of the case, relevant precedent, and so on) supplied by their clerks.

Another unique aspect of this new clerkship model is that law clerks draft opinions. Still, there is no evidence that any justices have abdicated their authority to make decisions regarding the winners and losers of a case. Justices, not law clerks, vote. Some justices, however, have vested their law clerks with substantial authority to decide how to reach the preferred outcome. A litigant can be declared a winner based on narrow jurisdictional grounds or through a complex doctrinal test, and in many instances it is the law clerk who selects the jurisprudential path.

P-A theory suggests that the "law firm associate" clerkship model would include new rules and norms regarding the selection, monitoring, and sanctioning of law clerks. The available evidence supports this hypothesis. Justices no longer blindly relied on law school professors to select their law clerks. Either they use law clerk selection committees staffed by trusted former clerks and provided with selection criteria, or they screen the applicants themselves. When Warren Burger became chief justice in 1969, he created a screening committee that placed emphasis on finding law clerks with prior clerking experience. Burger stated that he wanted such clerks because of their experience in the lower federal courts, but social scientists Corey Ditslear and Larry Baum provide an alternative explanation—justices use specific feeder court judges as a proxy measure of the law clerks' political ideology.

Based on an exhaustive study of law clerks from 1975 to 1998, Ditslear and Baum find a strong relationship between justice and feeder court judge ideology—a relationship that has grown even stronger in the 1990s. They write: "If choosing clerks is like 'selecting mates in a foxhole,' as Justice Thomas has said, today's justices feel more comfortable with mates who have been certified as faithful agents by ideological comrades in the courts of appeals."[4] The Court followed Burger's lead, and within ten years the number of law clerks on the Supreme Court who had previously clerked in the federal appeals court doubled. Whether modern justices adopted Burger's practice because of ideological or administrative reasons, appellate court training is now an informal prerequisite for a Supreme Court clerkship.

The justices also depend on other proxy measures. For example, applicants' membership in such law school organizations as the Federalist Society, the Environmental Law Society, the Legal Aid Society, or the ACLU can be a strong signal as to their political and judicial ideology. Such information is contained in an applicant's résumé. While data on law clerk ideology is limited, analysis suggests that the justices have successfully filled their chambers with "ideological comrades."

As clerks gain more and more access to information and are privy to conference debates and feuds, the possibility increases that law clerks might "leak" confidential information to other chambers or to Court outsiders. Hence, the clerkship model has been amended—both by individual justices regarding the duty of confidentiality imposed upon their personal law clerks as well as by the chief justice regarding all law clerks. Both Chief Justices Warren and Burger imposed general confidentiality rules upon all clerks, and in 1987 the Supreme Court promulgated an ethical code of conduct for its clerks. Under the code, the duties owed by the law clerk/agent to the justice/principal are clearly spelled out. In sum, a clerk must be respectful and loyal to both his or her justice and the Court. The clerk must perform his or her duties with exacting accuracy and unwavering professionalism, aware at all times that confidentiality, discretion and dignity are the hallmark of the devoted law clerk.[5]

Moreover, some justices have created intrachamber rules that result in law clerks monitoring law clerks. In these chambers, clerks are required to have their fellow clerks check opinion drafts, and in many instances all clerks join their justice to discuss circulating opinions or upcoming oral argument. Not only does the justice get the benefit of the collective wisdom of his or her clerks, but the clerks also act as a check on each other—both in terms of a free exchange of ideas and regarding materials prepared by the clerks. Moreover, some justices (such as Chief Justice Burger) have created an office hierarchy in which one clerk (a "senior" clerk or "special administrative assistant") reviews the work product of all other clerks before it is presented to the justice. All these institutional modifications ensure accuracy of the information flowing to the justice, but the amended rules also serve as monitoring devices.

Finally, the creation of the cert. pool has produced another important monitoring device. Intended as a means to reduce law clerk workload, the cert. pool has heightened the scrutiny that each cert. petition receives. In the 1940s and 1950s, usually the author of the cert. memorandum and his justice reviewed the memo. Today, each cert. pool memoranda (in a "cert. worthy" appeal) can be potentially read and analyzed by the law clerks of eight chambers and by eight justices. The majority of the justices have their law clerks review cert. pool memoranda prepared by other chambers, perform additional research, and annotate the cert. pool memo with their own recommendations. The practical effect—intentional deception or sloppy analysis is quickly discovered.

Arguably, the only aspect of the modern clerkship model that might encourage law clerk shirking is the weakening bonds of loyalty between law clerk and justice. As the number of law clerks has increased from one to four, it is inevitable that the justice cannot be as close with his or her clerks. Laws clerks may still play tennis, attend the opera, or sing Christmas carols with their justices, but there is no evidence to suggest that former clerks of the present justices generally consider themselves to be surrogate sons and daughters. As the bonds of loyalty weaken, the personal costs (or sanctions) of disloyalty also lessen.

The practical effect of the evolution of the clerkship institution is that law clerks do not wield an inordinate amount of influence. While the substantive job duties delegated to law clerks have expanded, the ideological distance between clerks and their justices has diminished—thus minimizing the likelihood that divergent goals of the clerk and justice would result in law clerk shirking or defection. Moreover, traditional monitoring devices—the weekly conferences and the circulation of opinions—have been supplemented by intrachamber review of work product by multiple law clerks. Clerks arguably wield some influence in how judicial opinions are drafted and which doctrinal tests are used, but even the cleverest law clerk must still hold together a majority of the justices.

At the same time, a public spotlight has been shone on the Supreme Court's hiring practices. Demands for diversity have been met with modest changes, but the demands will continue. If the justices begin to move toward more untraditional clerkship candidates and larger staffs—looking to a broader range of academic and ethnic backgrounds—I hypothesize that they will have to employ additional selection practices to guarantee ideological compatibility between justice and law clerk. Former clerks anonymously whisper that some current Supreme Court justices and their current roster of law clerks quiz applicants on their judicial and political philosophy; such practices may become more widespread. Furthermore, faced with more diverse, less ideologically compatible law clerks, the justices may contemplate more stringent monitoring and sanctioning devices.

Law clerks will remain courtiers to the princes and princesses who occupy the Marble Palace. Almost 500 years ago, Baldassare Castiglione penned *The Book of the Courtier*, which discussed the characteristics of the perfect courtier. Adopting the voices of a number of different characters, Castiglione wrote that a courtier must be "a man of honor and integrity," a "cautious and reserved" servant of noble birth who should never be "vile or disorderly in his way of life" nor "get the mistaken notion that he knows something he does not know."[6] A man educated in the arts and in letters, the courtier must shun the spotlight and devote his energies to service.

This does not mean that the courtier is a mindless flatterer, without an original thought in his head. "[T]he aim of the perfect Courtier . . . is so to win for himself . . . the favor and mind of the prince whom he serves that he may be able to tell him, and always will tell him, the truth about everything he needs to know, without fear or risk of displeasing him."[7] In short, "to bring or help one's prince toward what is right and to frighten him away from what is wrong are the true fruits of Courtiership."[8] Courtiers may give advice and counsel to their princes, but they should never doubt the ultimate decision maker. Stripping away the more flowery expressions from Castiglione's prose, he has described the ideal law clerk as defined by the Supreme Court's *Code of Conduct*.

Of course, there will remain law clerks who become intoxicated by the trappings and powers of their noble court. Over the last 125 years, courtiers have fallen prey to the temptations of Supreme Court life, engaging in "foolish presumption,"[9] affectation, and boasting, but they were quickly checked by a web of institutional norms and rules. There is no evidence, moreover, that these courtiers struggled to overcome or amend these rules in pursuit of their flights of fancy, for the punishment is exile from the court to which they so eagerly sought entry—a price too great to pay for the illusion of wielding power.

What is certain is that a Supreme Court clerkship will remain a highly contested prize. Law clerks will continue to be granted unprecedented levels of responsibility. Law firms will continue to vie for former clerks. A Supreme Court clerkship will remain a necessary credential for an elite law school professorship or a high-level position in the Department of Justice. And we will remain fascinated by the life of these young courtiers, with their dazzling résumés and their access to the corridors of the Marble Palace.

What is less certain, however, is whether the clerkship experience will retain its uniqueness. As workload pressures increase, office staffs expand, and the clerkship institution becomes more formalized and rule-bound, it is inevitable that clerkships will become more bland and less memorable. Just as the modern Supreme Court opinion is devoid of "the Holmes epigram, the Black way with facts, the Frankfurter vocabulary, the Brandeis footnote, the Stone pragmatism,"[10] I suspect the modern Supreme Court clerkship will lack animated discussions about democracy in ancient Greek city-states, paper cups filled with Rebel Yell bourbon, rambling tales of young hearts touched by the fire of war, and tears at a dying mentor's bedside. While courtiers will remain at the Marble Palace, I believe that the bonds of affection and intimacy between courtiers and princes will continue to slowly wither away.

Reference Matter

Appendices

Appendix 1
Author's Personal Interviews with Former Law Clerks

Sam Bagenstos	(Ginsburg—OT 1997)
Vicki L. Been	(Blackmun—OT 1984)
Bennett Boskey	(Reed—OT 1940; Stone OT 1941)
Kathryn Lovill Bradley	(White—OT 1990)
Bruce P. Brown	(Burger—OT 1985)
Carol S. Bruch	(Douglas—OT 1972)
Jesse H. Choper	(Warren—OT 1960)
William T. Coleman, Jr.	(Frankfurter—OT 1948)
Earl C. Dudley, Jr.	(Reed and Warren—OT 1967)
Brett Dunkelman	(Rehnquist— OT 1981)
Lawrence Ebb	(Vinson—OT 1947)
Wilbur Friedman	(Stone—OT 1930)
Warner W. Gardner	(Stone—OT 1934)
S. Elizabeth Gibson	(White—OT 1977)
C. David Ginsburg	(Douglas—OT 1938)
Eugene Gressman	(Murphy—OT 1943–1948)
Larry Hammond	(Black and Powell—OT 1971)
Louis Henkin	(Frankfurter—OT 1946)
Roderick Hills	(Reed—OT 1955)
Truman Hobbs	(Black—OT 1948)
A. E. Dick Howard	(Black—OT 1962)
Manley O. Hudson	(Reed and Whittaker—OT 1956)
Dennis J. Hutchinson	(White—OT 1975)
William Joslin	(Black—OT 1947)
Pamela Karlan	(Blackmun—OT 1985)
Andrew Kaufman	(Frankfurter—OT 1955–1956)
Alan Kohn	(Whittaker—OT 1957)

Louis Lusky	(Stone—OT 1937)
William J. Maledon	(Brennan—OT 1972)
Judith McMorrow	(Burger—OT 1981)
Daniel Meador	(Black—OT 1954)
Abner Mikva	(Minton—OT 1951)
Dallin H. Oaks	(Warren—OT 1957)
Louis Oberdorfer	(Black—OT 1946)
Robert O'Neil	(Brennan—OT 1962)
Daniel Ortiz	(Powell—OT 1984)
Carter G. Phillips	(Burger—OT 1978)
Richard A. Posner	(Brennan—OT 1962)
E. Barrett Prettyman, Jr.	(Jackson, Frankfurter, and Harlan— OT 1953–1954)
Charles A. Reich	(Black—OT 1953)
George Rutherglen	(Douglas and Stevens—OT 1975)
Terry Sandalow	(Stewart—OT 1958)
John T. Sapienza	(Reed—OT 1937)
Robert A. Schapiro	(Stevens—OT 1991)
Margo Schlanger	(Ginsburg—OT 1993)
Arthur R. Seder	(Vinson—OT 1948)
Alexandra Shapiro	(Ginsburg—OT 1993)
John Paul Stevens	(Rutledge—OT 1947)
Stephen Susman	(Black—OT 1966)
Kent Syverud	(O'Connor—OT 1984)
Howard J. Trienens	(Vinson—OT 1951)
Robert Von Mehren	(Reed—OT 1947)
Harry Wellington	(Frankfurter—OT 1955)
Harris K. Weston	(Burton—OT 1946)

Appendix 2
Author's Correspondence and Interviews with Non-Clerks

Alison Grey Anderson
Hugo Black, Jr.
Charles Hobbs
Adrian Kragen
Wanda Martinson
Josephine Black Pesaresi
Antonin Scalia
Virginia Morsey Wheeler Talley

Appendix 3
Author's Correspondence with Former Law Clerks

Below is the list of former law clerks with whom I corresponded (either by letter or by written survey) regarding their clerkship duties. This list does not include law clerks who were mailed the original survey with questions limited to their personal and professional backgrounds.

Lynn Blais	(Blackmun—OT 1990)
Charles Blanchard	(O'Connor—OT 1986)
Jeffrey Blatiner	(Stewart—OT 1982)
David R. Boyd	(Powell—OT 1974)
Kevin R. Boyle	(Rehnquist—OT 1999)
James O. Browning	(Powell—OT 1982)
James J. Brudney	(Blackmun—OT 1980)
Samuel C. Butler	(Minton—OT 1954)
David Campbell	(Rehnquist—OT 1981)
Paul W. Cane, Jr.	(Powell—OT 1980)
Jim Chen	(Thomas—OT 1992)
David M. Clark	(Black—OT 1957)
Richard Conway	(Minton—OT 1953)
Jerome A. Cooper	(Black—OT 1937)
Gordon B. Davidson	(Reed—OT 1954)
Walter E. Dellinger	(Black—OT 1968)
Jan Ginter Deutsch	(Stewart—OT 1962)
Paul M. Dodyk	(Stewart—OT 1963)
Peter B. Edelman	(Goldberg—OT 1962)
Clifton S. Elgarten	(Brennan—OT 1981)
Richard Fallon	(Powell—OT 1981)
Ward Farnsworth	(Kennedy—OT 1995)
John Fee	(Scalia—OT 1996)
William Fletcher	(Brennan—OT 1976)
George T. Frampton	(Blackmun—OT 1971)
John D. French	(Frankfurter—OT 1960)
Richard W. Garnett IV	(Rehnquist—OT 1996)
Raymond Gray	(Minton—OT 1951)
Bruce A. Green	(Marshall—OT 1982)
John Griffiths	(Goldberg and Fortas—OT 1965)
Carl S. Hawkins	(Vinson—OT 1952)
Irving J. Helman	(Frankfurter—OT 1947)
Luther Hill, Jr.	(Black—OT 1950)
Roderick Hills	(Reed—OT 1955)
W. William Hodes	(Ginsburg—OT 1996)
Frank S. Holleman III	(Blackmun—OT 1981)

Andrew Hurtwitz	(Stewart—OT 1973)
Jerold H. Israel	(Stewart—OT 1959)
Edward W. Keane	(Brennan—OT 1957)
Michael Klausner	(Brennan—OT 1983)
Thomas Krattenmaker	(Harlan—OT 1970)
Peter Kreindler	(Douglas—OT 1972)
William T. Lake	(Harlan—OT 1969)
Albert G. Lauber	(Blackmun—OT 1978)
Daniel P. Levitt	(Goldberg and Fortas—OT 1965)
Charles Luce	(Black—OT 1943)
Dennis G. Lyons	(Brennan—OT 1958)
Gregory P. Magarian	(Stevens—OT 1994)
Michael M. Maney	(Harlan—OT 1964)
Ellis H. McKay	(Clark—OT 1953)
Paul J. Meyer	(Warren—OT 1967)
Ralph Moore	(Warren—OT 1959)
C. Roger Nelson	(Stone—OT 1941)
John E. Nolan	(Clark—OT 1956)
Michele Odorizzi	(Stevens—OT 1979)
J. Paul Oetken	(Blackmun—OT 1993)
Thomas O'Neill	(Burton—OT 1954)
Earl E. Pollock	(Vinson—OT 1953)
Charles D. Reed	(Clark—OT 1965)
Steven A. Reiss	(Brennan—OT 1977)
Martin F. Richman	(Warren—OT 1956)
William D. Rogers	(Reed—OT 1952)
H. David Rosenbloom	(Fortas—OT 1967)
Frederick Rowe	(Clark—OT 1952)
Ernest Rubenstein	(Clark—OT 1953)
Carl Schneider	(Burton—OT 1957)
Mark D. Schneider	(Blackmun—OT 1984)
Marvin Schwartz	(Burton—OT 1950)
Andrew Siegel	(Stevens—OT 2000)
Kenneth Simons	(Marshall—OT 1981)
Walter B. Slocombe	(Fortas—OT 1968)
Michael Smith	(Warren—OT 1965)
Simon A. Steel	(O'Connor—OT 1995)
Samuel A. Stern	(Warren—OT 1955)
David O. Stewart	(Powell—OT 1979)
Michael Sturley	(Powell—OT 1982)
Larry Temple	(Clark—OT 1959)
Alison M. Tucher	(Souter—OT 1993)
E. Lawrence Vincent	(Kennedy—OT 1987)

James L. Volling	(Burger—OT 1980)
Harry Wallace	(Minton—OT 1952)
Stephen Walters	(Burger—OT 1974)
Harold A. Ward III	(Black—OT 1955)
Jack M. Weiss	(Burger—OT 1972)
G. Edward White	(Warren—OT 1971)
Diane P. Wood	(Blackmun—OT 1976)
Kevin Worthen	(White—OT 1983)
Christopher J. Wright	(Burger—OT 1981)
Ernest A. Young	(Souter—OT 1995)
Michael K. Young	(Rehnquist—OT 1977)

Appendix 4
Law Clerks of the U.S. Supreme Court, 1882 to 2004

Hugo Black

Kenneth Bass
Robert T. Basseches
Guido Calabresi
David M. Clark
Jerome A. Cooper
Margaret Corcoran
C. Sam Daniels
Sidney M. Davis
Walter E. Dellinger
Chris J. Dixie
Allison Dunham
Floyd F. Fenney
John P. Frank
George Clemon
  Freeman, Jr.
Robert A. Girard
David Haber
Lawrence Hammond
John M. Harmon
Luther L. Hill, Jr.
Truman Hobbs
A. E. Dick Howard
Huey Howerton
Maxwell Isenbergh
Nicholas Johnson
William Joslin

John G. Kester
Marx Leva
Clay C. Long
Charles Luce
Robert B. McKaw
John K. McNulty
Daniel J. Meador
Drayton Nabers, Jr.
James L. North
Louis F. Oberdorfer
Covert Parnell
J. Vernon Patrick
Joseph Price
Charles A. Reich
Neal P. Rutledge
George L. Saunders
Stephen Schulhofer
Robert W. Spearman
Gustave Speth
James Stewart
Stephen Susman
George M. Treister
David J. Vann
John W. Vardaman
Lawrence Wallace
Harold A. Ward III
Frank N. Wozencraft

Harry A. Blackmun

Michelle Alexander
Ann Alpers
Vikram D. Amar
Richard Bartlett
Vicki L. Been
Randall Bezanson
Lynn E. Blais
William Block
Richard Blumenthal
Beth S. Brinkmann
James J. Brudney
Emily Buss
Sarah H. Cleveland
Daniel Coenen
Sherry F. Colb
Michael Conley
Charlotte Crane
Stephanie Dangel
John P. Dean
Ellen E. Deason
Laura A. Dickinson
William S. Dodge
Donald F. Donovan
Anne P. Dupre
Anna L. Durand
Daniel B. Edelman

Keith P. Ellison
Danny Ertel
James Fanto
Chai R. Feldblum
Edward B. Foley
George T. Frampton
David A. Gates
Robert E. Gooding, Jr.
Robert A. Green
Penda D. Hair
Beth R. Heifetz
Frank S. Holleman
M. Ann Hubbard
Clare Huntington
Alan Jenkins
Ann M. Kappler
Pamela S. Karlan
Kevin M. Kearney
Mary "Kit" Kinports
Geoffrey Klineberg
James J. Knicely
Harold H. Koh
Michael LaFond
Susan G. Lahne
Albert G. Lauber
Edward P. Lazarus
Alan S. Madans
Deborah Malamud
Martha A. Matthews
William McDaniel
Scott R. McIntosh
Molly McUsic
Thomas W. Merrill
Richard Meserve
Jeffrey Meyer
Alan C. Michaels
Ralph I. Miller
Karen N. Moore
Helane L. Morrison
Luther T. Munford
Donna M. Murasky
William J. Murphy
J. Paul Oetken

David W. Ogden
David C. Patterson
Mark C. Rahdert
John Townsend Rich
Robert I. Richter
Charles Rothfeld
Andrew Schapiro
Mark D. Schneider
Paul H. Schwartz
Benjamin S. Sharp
David A. Sklansky
Malcolm Stewart
Cory Streisinger
Michael Sundermeyer
Bruce C. Swartz
Elizabeth G. Taylor
David E. Van Zandt
Cecilia D. Wang
Andrea Ward
Ruth Glushien
   Wedgwood
Richard Willard
Michael J. Wishnie
Diane P. Wood
James W. Ziglar

Samuel Blatchford

William Dennis

Joseph P. Bradley

Eldwin Raphael Hayden
Charles Wood

Louis Brandeis

Dean Acheson
Thomas H. Austern
William Claytor
Warren Stilson Ege
Adrian S. Fisher
Paul A. Freund
Henry J. Friendly
Irving B. Goldsmith

Henry M. Hart, Jr.
Willard Hurst
James M. Landis
Calvert Magruder
Samuel Henry Maslon
William McCurdy
Robert Page
William Rice
David J. Riesman
Harry Shulman
William Sutherland

William J. Brennan, Jr.

Richard Arnold
Stephen Barnett
Stuart Baskin
Hugh Baxter
Loftus E. Becker
Marsha Berzon
James R. Bird
Timothy Bishop
Richard Bronstein
Peter J. Busch
Evan H. Caminker
Mark S. Campisano
David W. Carpenter
James E. Castello
Steven L. Chanenson
Michael Chertoff
Richard Cooper
Richard Cotton
Charles Curtis
Marie R. Deveney
Clifton S. Elgarten
Einer Elhauge
Mark H. Epstein
James A. Feldman
Stanley Fickle
William Finley
Peter M. Fishbein
Raymond Fisher
Owen M. Fiss
William Fletcher

Stephen Friedman
Jay M. Fujitani
Merrick Garland
Julius Genachowski
Stephen Goldberg
Gerald Goldman
Stephen Goodman
Francis Gregory
Joseph R. Guerra
Mark E. Haddad
Daniel M. Harris
Dean M. Hashimoto
Lisa Heinzerling
Paul R. Hoeber
Thomas M. Jorde
Lawrence A. Kasten
Jerold Kayden
Edward W. Keane
Edward J. Kelly
Jeffrey Kindler
Michael Klausner
Larry B. Kramer
Steven G. Krone
Edward R. Leahy
Jeffrey Leeds
Carmen D. Legato
Bruce R. Lerner
Rory K. Little
Frederick C. Lowinger
Jordan A. Luke
Gerard Lynch
Dennis G. Lyons
William J. Maledon
Regina Maloney
Jonathan Massey
Michael McConnell
Frank I. Michelman
Mary Mikva
Nory Miller
Robert B. Miller
Michael C. Moran
Jeffrey Nagin
Daniel J. O'Hern

Robert M. O'Neil
Joseph Onek
Lawrence B. Pedowitz
F. Whitten Peters
Elliot Polebaum
Richard Posner
S. Paul Posner
Robert C. Post
Eric P. Rakowski
Milton C. Regan
Steven A. Reiss
W. Taylor Reveley
Daniel A. Rezneck
Richard S. Rhodes
Michael Rips
Gerald Rosberg
Jeffrey Rosen
Joshua Rosenkranz
Michael Rubin
John F. Savarese
John H. Schapiro
Roy A. Schotland
Virginia A. Seitz
Robert B. Shanks
Barry S. Simon
Abraham Sofaer
Geoffrey R. Stone
Peter L. Strauss
Clyde A. Szuch
Charles S. Treat
Donald B. Verrilli
Paul F. Washington
Robert M. Weinberg
John M. West
Frederick Woocher

David J. Brewer

Henry M. Clapp
Frederick J. Haig
Harry A. Jetmore

Stephen G. Breyer

Priya R. Aiyar
Yochai Benkler
Henk J. Brands
Christina D. Burnett
Vince Chhabria
Linda T. Coberly
James P. Dowden
Aimee A. Feinberg
Erin H. Glenn
John M. Golden
Risa Goluboff
Caitlin Halligan
Rachel A. Harmon
Robert N. Hochman
Mirah Horowitz
Marc E. Isserles
Ketanji B. Jackson
Neal K. Katyal
Julie E. Katzman
Michael Leiter
Robin A. Lenhardt
Stacey M. Leyton
Jennifer S. Martinez
Deanne E. Maynard
Arela M. Migdal
Jonathan T. Molot
Charles C. Moore
Jennifer G. Newstead
Maritza U. Okata
Aaron M. Panner
Alexander A. Reinert
Russell K. Robinson
Theodore Ruger
Kevin K. Russell
Lisa B. Schultz
Pratik A. Shah
Carolyn E. Shapiro
Anne K. Small
Danielle Spinelli
Colin S. Stretch
Jacob J. Sullivan

Alexandra M. Walsh
Davis J. Wang
Timothy S. Wu

Henry B. Brown

Frederick E. Chaplin
Albert B. Hall
Charles F. Wilson

Warren E. Burger

John C. Ale
James R. Atwood
John E. Barry
David O. Bickart
Lee C. Bollinger
David G. Boutte
Ashby Boyle
Bruce P. Brown
Stephen Burbank
Ray W. Campbell
Paul G. Cassell
John M. Coleman
Karl S. Coplan
Daniel R. Coquillette
Richard Diamond
Gregory Dovell
Rochelle C. Dreyfuss
William Drinkwater
W. Neil Eggleston
William Elmore
Robert Fabrikant
Arthur F. Fergenson
Chesney Floyd
Daniel H. Foote
Richard Friedman
James E. Gauch
Eric A. Grant
Thomas B. Green
David G. Hanes
John M. Harmon
Mark B. Helm
James D. Holzhauer

Rebecca Hurley
James D. Hutchinson
Stewart Jay
Von G. Keetch
Timothy Kelly
William Kelly
John H. Korns
Candace Kovacic-
    Fleischer
Alex Kozinski
Robinson B. Lacy
Michael Lazerwitz
Charles Lettow
Douglas Levene
Peter M. Lieb
Wallace Lightsey
J. Michael Luttig
Brian J. Martin
Judith A. McMorrow
George M. Moriarty
Matthew M. Neumeier
Paul J. Ondrasik
Henry L. Parr, Jr.
Carter G. Phillips
Douglas Poe
Walter F. Pratt
Harry Rissetto
Bruce E. Rosenblum
Robert A. Rosenfeld
Peter L. Rossiter
Gene C. Schaerr
John E. Sexton
Paul L. Shechtman
Richard Skillman
Kenneth Starr
Monte Stewart
Karl M. Tilleman
James L. Volling
Michael Wahoske
Christopher G. Walsh, Jr.
Stephen Walters
Jack M. Weiss
Christopher Wright

Joseph C. Zengerle
Michael Zimmerman

Harold Burton

R. Markham Ball
Norman W. Colquhoun
Roger C. Cramton
P. J. DiQuinzio
John Douglas
Timothy Dyk
H. Bruce Griswold
Charles Hileman
Goncer M. Krestal
James A. Lake
John M. Leahy
Harvey Levin
W. Howard Mann
William Matteson
Alan J. Moscov
Thomas N. O'Neill
Stewart Pollack
James Ryan
Terrance Sandalow
Carl W. Schneider
Marvin Schwartz
Ray Simmons
Preble Stolz
Ray Troubh
David E. Wagoner
Harris K. Weston

Pierce Butler

Irving Clark
John F. Cotter
Morris D. Darrell
William Dyke
Luther E. Jones
Richard Sullivan

James F. Byrnes

James E. Doyle

Benjamin Cardozo

Ambrose Doskow
Joseph M. Paley
Joseph L. Rauh
Percy Hickling Russell
Christopher Sargent
Melvin H. Siegel
Alan M. Strook

Tom C. Clark

C. Taylor Ashworth
Raymond Brown
Thomas D. Corrigan
John J. Crown
Carl L. Estes II
Martin J. Flynn
Lee A. Freeman, Jr.
Theodore Garrett
Robert P. Gorman
Marshall Groce
Robert W. Hamilton
William M. Hannay
Harry L. Hobson
Thomas D. Hughes
Vester T. Hughes
Stafford Hutchinson
William Jones
John Kaplan
James E. Knox
Malachy Mahon
John T. Marten
Burke W. Mathes, Jr.
Michael Maupin
James L. McHugh
Ellis H. McKay
J. Larry Nichols
John E. Nolan
Charles Phillips
James H. Pipkin
William Powell
Thomas W. Reavley
Charles D. Reed

Stuart P. Ross
Frederick Rowe
Ernest Rubenstein
Larry E. Temple
Stuart W. Thayer
T. Lawrence Tolan
Max O. Truitt
Donald F. Turner
Charles Walker
Bernard Weisberg
Percy D. Williams
Thomas C. Wray

John H. Clarke

S. Edward Widdifield

William R. Day

Joseph G. Bachman
Rufus Day
Luther Day
John A. Lombard

William O. Douglas

William Alsup
Charles Ares
Thomas C. Armitage
Alan K. Austin
Richard Benka
Eugene A. Beyer
Dennis C. Brown
Carol S. Bruch
John Burnett
James C. Campbell
Jared G. Carter
Walter B. Chaffe
Warren M. Christopher
Michael Clutter
William Cohen
Donald Colvin
Vern A. Countryman
James F. Crafts
Robert L. Deitz

Stephen Duke
Ira M. Ellman
Jerome B. Falk
C. David Ginsburg
Harvey Grossman
Dennis J. Hutchinson
Bernard Jacob
Richard Jacobson
Donald E. Kelley
Snyder "Jed" King
Thomas J. Klitgaard
Peter Kreindler
Hans Linde
Lucile Lomen
Janet Meik
Lewis B. Merrifield III
Charles Miller
William A. Norris
Monty J. Podva
Lucas A. Powe
Kenneth Reed
William Reppy
Charles Rickershauser
George Rutherglen
Evan L. Schwab
Carl J. Seneker
Donald G. Simpson
Marshall Small
Stanley Soderland
Stanley Sparrowe
Alan B. Sternstein
Gary J. Torre
Peter K. Westen
J. Roger Wollenberg
Jay K. Wright

Stephen Field

George O'Doherty
George B. Edwards
Sherwood Gorham
Irwin B. Linton
E. D. York

Abe Fortas

Martha F. Alschuler
John Griffiths
Daniel P. Levitt
H. David Rosenbloom
Walter B. Slocombe
Peter L. Zimroth

Felix Frankfurter

Anthony G. Amsterdam
Paul Bender
Alexander Bickel
Hugh Calkins
Abram J. Chayes
William T. Coleman, Jr.
David P. Currie
Jesse W. Doolittle
Weaver W. Dunnan
Phillip Elman
David B. Filvaroff
Adrian S. Fisher
Fred N. Fishman
John D. French
Richard Goodwin
Philip L. Graham
Irving J. Helman
Louis Henkin
Matthew Herold
Roland S. Homet
Howard I. Kalodner
Andrew Kaufman
Philip Kurland
Harry K. Mansfield
John H. Mansfield
Daniel K. Mayers
Vincent McKusick
Edward F. Prichard, Jr.
Elliot L. Richardson
Albert J. Rosenthal
Albert M. Sacks
Frank E. A. Sander
Richard Sherwood

Stanley Silverberg
Donald J. Trautman
James Vorenberg
Harry A. Wellington
Morton M. Winston

Melville Fuller

Colley W. Bell
Stephen A. Day
Thomas H. Fitnam
James S. Harlan
C.M. Lark
Clarence Melville York

Ruth Bader Ginsburg

Ginger D. Andrews
Samuel E. Bagenstos
Hugh W. Baxter
Lisa C. Beattie
Paul S. Berman
Eric O. Bravin
Laura W. Brill
David C. Codell
Alexandria Edsall
Heather Elliott
David L. Franklin
Abbe R. Gluck
Robert M. Gordon
Toby J. Heytens
W. William Hodes
Aziz Z. Huq
Anne M. Joseph
Alisa B. Klein
Katherine H. Ku
Daniel B. Levin
Goodwin H. Liu
Linda C. Lye
Mary E. Magill
Gillian E. Metzger
Trevor H. Morrison
David O'Neil
John B. Owen
Joseph Palmore

Elizabeth G. Porter
David G. Post
Richard A. Primus
Aaron J. Saiger
William D. Savitt
David Schizer
Margo J. Schlanger
Alexandra Shapiro
Rochelle L. Shoretz
Neil S. Siegel
Maria C. Simon
Karl R. Thompson
David B. Toscano
Dorothy H. Tran
Amanda L. Tyler
Deirdre D. Von Dornum
Michael L. Wang
Paul J. Watford
Jay D. Wexler

Arthur J. Goldberg

Stephen Breyer
Alan M. Dershowitz
Peter Edelman
David B. Filvaroff
Stephen Goldstein
John Griffiths
Daniel P. Levitt
Lee Bowe McTurnan

Horace Gray

Charles L. Barlow
Edward Twisleton Cabot
William Dunbar
Roland Gray
Gordon T. Hughes
Francis Richard Jones
Moses D. Kimball
Langdon Parker Marvin
James M. Newell
John Gorham Palfrey
Robert Romans

Thomas A. Russell
William Schofield
Jeremiah Smith
Ezra R. Thayer
Henry Eldridge Warner
Joseph Warren
Samuel Williston

John M. Harlan I

Perry Allen
Julius T. Baldwin
Henry M. Clapp
Benjamin W. Hanna
Edwin P. Hanna
John May Harlan
John Maynard Harlan
William Harr
John E. Hoover
Blewitt Lee
William Lewis
Edgar R. Rombauer

John M. Harlan II

Bruce A. Ackerman
Wayne G. Barnett
Paul M. Bator
James R. Bieke
Michael Boudin
Paul Brest
Newton Centre
Louis R. Cohen
Norman Dorsen
Jay A. Erens
Charles L. Fabrikant
Charles Fried
Marvin L. Gray
Robert K. Greenawalt
Philip B. Heymann
Richard J. Hiegel
Thomas G. Krattenmaker
William T. Lake
Leonard M. Leiman

Howard Lesnick
Nathan Lewin
William Lifland
Charles Lister
Michael M. Maney
Martin D. Minsker
Robert H. Mnookin
Charles R. Nesson
Matthew Nimetz
E. Barrett Prettyman, Jr.
Bert W. Rein
John B. Rhinelander
Henry P. Sailer
Norbert A. Schlei
David L. Shapiro
Stephen Shulman
Allen R. Snyder
Henry J. Steiner
Thomas B. Stoel, Jr.
Lloyd L. Weinreb

Oliver Wendell Holmes, Jr.

Chauncey Belknap
Robert M. Benjamin
Francis Biddle
Harvey Hollister Bundy
Stanley Clarke
Laurence Curtis
Charles Denby
Augustin Derby
Erland Frederick Fish
Shelton Hale
George Leslie Harrison
Alger Hiss
Donald Hiss
Mark De Wolfe Howe
Day Kimball
Lloyd Harold Landau
Walter B. Leach
John E. Lockwood
Vaughn Miller
Stanley Morrison

James Mount Nicely
Irving Sands Olds
Charles K. Poe
H. Chapman Rose
James H. Rowe
Howard J. Stockton
Arthur E. Sutherland
Robert W. Wales

Charles Evans Hughes

Richard Hogue
John E. Hoover
Francis Kirkham
Edwin McElwain
Maurice M. Moore
Reynolds Robertson

Howell E. Jackson

Frederick E. Chapin

Robert H. Jackson

Howard G. Buschman
Alan Y. Cole
John F. Costelloe
Donald Cronson
John F. Cushman
Murray Gartner
James M. Marsh
Phil C. Neal
Cornelius G. Niebank
E. Barrett Prettyman, Jr.
William H. Rehnquist

Anthony Kennedy

Bertrand-Marc Allen
David L. Anderson
Andrew C. Baak
John R. Beck
James F. Bennett
Bradford A. Berenson
Ashutosh Bhagwat
Stephanos Bibas

Rachel L. Brand
William A. Burck
Paul T. Cappuccio
Adam H. Charnes
Daniel C. Chung
Elizabeth Collery
Nancy L. Combs
Jacqueline G. Cooper
Richard Cordray
Susan M. Davies
Edward C. Dawson
Grant M. Dixton
Michael Dorf
Miles F. Ehrlich
John P. Elwood
Steven A. Engel
Miguel A. Estrada
Ward Farnsworth
Gary S. Feinerman
Frank A. Ferrell
Nathan A. Forrester
Brett C. Gerry
Jack L. Goldsmith
Lisa Grow
Jeanne M. Hauch
Kathryn R. Haun
Michael J. Hirshland
Thomas G. Hungar
Brett M. Kavanaugh
Peter D. Keisler
Orin S. Kerr
Raymond Kethledge
Stephen Kinnaird
Kelly M. Klaus
Chi T. Steve Kwok
Matthew H. Lembke
Renee B. Lettow
Harry P. Litman
David Litt
Gregory Maggs
Brian R. Matsui
Daniel Meron
Kevin J. Miller

Michael Mollerus
Howard C. Neilson, Jr.
John C. Neiman, Jr.
Stephen M. Nickelsburg
Christopher Pace
Eugene M. Paige
Edward S. Pallesen
R. Hewitt Pate
Nicholas Q. Rosenkranz
John C. Rozendaal
Michael E. Scoville
Michael Y. Scudder, Jr.
John Shaffer
Matthew C. Stevenson
Harry P. Susman
Igor V. Timofeyev
E. Larry Vincent
Anthony J. Vlatas
Michael F. Williams
Alexander Willscher
Christopher S. Yoo
Cheryl K. Zemelman

Joseph Lamar

John E. Hoover
S. Edward Widdifield

Lucius Q. C. Lamar

Harvey M. Friend

Horace H. Lurton

Harvey D. Jacob

Thurgood Marshall

Janet Cooper Alexander
Kevin T. Baine
David A. Barrett
Sondra E. Berchin
Susan L. Bloch
Scott Brewer
Rebecca Brown
William Bryson

Bernard J. Carl
Stephen Carter
Sheryll Cashin
Richard Clary
Debra L. W. Cohn
Glen M. Darbyshire
Michael Davis
Gregory Diskant
Michael P. Doss
Steven M. Dunne
Paul A. Engelmayer
Ira M. Feinberg
William Fisher
Phillip Frickey
Elizabeth Garrett
Gay Gellhorn
Roger J. George
Paul D. Gewirtz
Douglas Ginsburg
Stephen Glover
Bruce A. Green
Ronald J. Greene
Thomas C. Grey
Rosemary Herbert
Virginia Whitner
   Hoptman
Howell Jackson
Vicki C. Jackson
Elena Kagan
Dan M. Kahan
Walter A. Kamiat
Allen M. Katz
Randall Kennedy
Harry P. Litman
Peter V. Lockwood
Paul G. Mahoney
J. Nicholas McGrath
Robert D. McLean
David D. Meyer
Martha L. Minow
Paul Mogin
Eben Moglen
Crystal Nix

David G. Norrell
Adebayo Ogunlesi
Richard H. Pildes
Gregory Priest
Radhika Rao
Margaret Raymond
Richard Revesz
Deborah Rhode
Daniel Richman
Miles N. Ruthberg
Stephen Saltzburg
Lewis D. Sargentich
Edwin G. Schallert
Jonathan Schwartz
Daniel Segal
Louis M. Seidman
Nicole K. Seligman
David M. Silberman
Ellen S. Silberman
John A. Siliciano
Kenneth Simons
Phillip Spector
Carol S. Steiker
Jordan M. Steiker
Stuart C. Stock
Cass R. Sunstein
Margaret Tahyar
Allan B. Taylor
Steven M. Tennis
Lawrence Tu
Mark V. Tushnet
Barbara Underwood
Michael Vatis
Jonathan T. Weinberg
Robert N. Weiner
David B. Wilkins
Karen H. Williams
Gary D. Wilson

Stanley Matthews

Everett York

Joseph McKenna

Robert F. Cogswell
Ashton F. Embry
James Cecil Hooe

James C. McReynolds

T. Ellis Allison
Carlyle Baer
Andrew P. Federline
John T. Fowler
Norman B. Frost
Harold L. George
Chester Gray
John Knox
Ward E. Lattin
Maurice Mahoney
Blaine Mallan
Tench T. Marye
John T. McHale
Milton S. Musser
Raymond Radcliffe
Leroy E. Reed
J. Allan Sherier
S. Milton Simpson

Samuel F. Miller

Noble E. Dawson
E. D. York

Sherman Minton

William Bachelder
Samuel C. Butler
Robert H. Cole
Richard Conway
Laurence Fordham
Raymond Gray
Charles Kelso
Gerald Levenberg
Thomas M. Lofton
J. Keith Mann
Abner J. Mikva

Richard S. Rhodes
Lawrence Taylor
Harry L. Wallace
James R. Wimmer

William Moody

John A. Kratz
Sheldon Eaton Wardwell
Charles Wilson

Frank Murphy

John J. Adams
John R. Dykema
Eugene Gressman
Edwin E. Huddleson
John H. Pickering
William Schrenk
J. R. Swenson
T. L. Tolan, Jr.

Sandra Day O'Connor

Katherine L. Adams
Matthew Adler
Gail B. Agrawal
Iman Anabtawi
W. Scott Bales
Stuart A. Banner
Joel C. Beauvais
Sharon L. Beckman
Rebecca Beynon
Rick A. Bierschbaach
Charles Blanchard
Caroline Brown
Daniel J. Bussel
Janet R. Carter
Brian G. Cartwright
Steven T. Catlett
Christopher Cerf
Susan A. Creighton
Viet D. Dinh
Susan A. Dunn
E. Vaughn Dunnigan

John P. Dwyer
Elizabeth L. Earle
David G. Ellen
Theano D. Evangelis
Tali F. Farhadian
Ivan K. Fong
James Forman
Gary L. Francione
Carolyn Frantz
Michelle Friedland
Sean W. Gallagher
Jeremy Gaston
Stephen Gilles
Sandra S. Glover
Joan I. Greco
Lisa K. Griffin
Sean C. Grimsley
Leslie A. Hakala
Marci A. Hamilton
Oona A. Hathaway
Linda R. Helyar
Emily J. Henn
Brian M. Hoffstadt
Peter W. Huber
Sandra C. Ikuta
RonNell A. Jones
Traci L. Jones
Bradley W. Joondeph
Adalbert Jordan
Kevin M. Kelly
Amy F. Kett
Joshua Klein
Richard Klingler
David C. Kravitz
Jeffrey A. Lamken
Noah A. Levine
Denise P. Lindberg
Nelson Lund
Anup Malani
Daniel M. Mandil
Jennifer M. Mason
Tamarra D. Matthews
Andrew G. McBridge

Ruth V. McGregor
Deborah Jones Merritt
Glen D. Nager
William J. Nardini
Justin A. Nelson
Allyson P. Newton
Julie Rose O'Sullivan
Stanley J. Panikowski
Mark A. Perry
Cristina M. Rodriquez
Victoria Radd Rollins
Gretchen C. Rubin
Sambhav N. Sankar
Austin Schlick
Stewart J. Schwab
Michael A. Scodro
John K. Setear
Julia B. Shelton
Patricia L. Small
M. Kathleen Smalley
Mark S. Snyderman
Srikanth Srinivasan
Simon A. Steel
Matthew Stowe
Silvija Strikis
Jame E. Stromseth
Kent D. Syverud
Richard Taranto
Jane F. Vehko
Eugene Volokh
Barbara Woodhouse
Shirley D. Woodward

Rufus W. Peckham

Jesse C. Ball
Leland Blodget Duer
John E. Hoover
S. Edward Widdifield

Mahlon Pitney

William Dike
Horatio Stonier

Lewis F. Powell, Jr.

James D. Alt
Charles C. Ames
Eric G. Anderson
Tyler A. Baker
Mary E. Becker
James J. Benjamin, Jr.
A. Lee Bentley III
James B. Boisture
David R. Boyd
Nancy J. Bregstein
James O. Browning
John J. Buckley
J. Peter Byrne
Paul W. Cane, Jr.
Ronald G. Carr
David A. Charny
Carter C. Chinnis
Julia P. Clark
Eugene J. Comey
Robert D. Comfort
Robert M. Couch
Anne M. Coughlin
Samuel Estreicher
Richard Fallon
George C. Freeman
Lawrence Hammond
Mark D. Harris
Cammie Robinson
   Hauptfuhrer
Leslie Gielow Jacobs
John J. Jeffries, Jr.
J. Phillip Jordan
William Kelly
Daniel R. Kistler
Joel I. Klein
Andrew D. Leipold
David F. Levi
Annmarie Levins
Michael Levy
Robert A. Long, Jr.
Ronald J. Mann

David A. Martin
Gregory May
Deanne E. Maynard
Richard Morgan
Michael Mosman
Joseph E. Neuhaus
Mark E. Newell
Daniel R. Ortiz
Jack B. Owens
Gregory Palm
R. Hewitt Pate
Mary E. Richey
Jonathan Sallet
Carl R. Schenker
Lynda G. Simpson
Paul M. Smith
Paul B. Stephan
David O. Stewart
William Stuntz
Michael Sturley
Jeffrey Sutton
Robert W. Werner
David L. Westin
Christine B. Whitman
John S. Wiley, Jr.
J. Harvie Wilkinson III
Rebecca Womeldorf

Stanley Reed

F. Aley Allan
Mac Asbill, Jr.
Russell Baker
Robert M. Ball
Joseph Barbash
David M. Becker
Luther E. Birdzell
Theodore Boehm
Bennett Boskey
Julian Burke
John D. Calhoun
George C. Cochran
Gordon B. Davidson
Earl C. Dudley, Jr.

John D. Fassett
Harold B. Finn III
Hamilton P. Fox III
Phillip Graham
C. Boyden Gray
Lewis C. Green
David G. Hanes
Roderick Hills
Manley O. Hudson, Jr.
Byron E. Kabot
William Koontz
Joel A. Kozol
Carl D. Lawson
Harold Leventhal
Christopher Lipsett
John H. Maclay
Bayless Manning
George B. Mickum
Stewart Pollack
Robert E. Randall
William D. Rogers
Arthur I. Rosett
John T. Sapienza
David Schwartz
Jerry Siegel
John B. Spitzer
Richard Urowsky
Robert Von Mehren
Emanuel Weiss
Adam Yarmolinsky
Edwin M. Zimmerman

William H. Rehnquist

Audrey Anderson
James R. Asperger
Donald B. Ayer
Rosemarie Blasé
Jeffrey Bleich
Ronald L. Blunt
Gary B. Born
Christopher Bowers
Kevin R. Boyle
Craig M. Bradley

Leah O. Brannon
Bruce Braun
Lindley Brenza
C. Michael Buxton
David G. Campbell
Eric R. Claeys
Steven M. Colloton
Dean C. Colson
Charles J. Cooper
Gregg Costa
Mariana L. Cox
Rafael E. Cruz
Leon F. DeJulius
Andrew R. DeVooght
Heidi C. Doerhof
James A. Downs
Brett L. Dunkelman
Michael Q. Eagan
William Eggeling
Courtney Elwood
John C. Englander
Shawn F. Fagan
H. Bartow Farr III
Parker C. Folse
Richard W. Garnett IV
Gregory C. Garre
Courtney C. Gilligan
Robert J. Giuffra, Jr.
Randall Guynn
Robert T. Haar
David H. Hoffman
Joseph L. Hoffman
Gordon Horiss
Robert K. Hur
Thomas H. Jackson
William S. Jacobs
David B. Jaffe
Jay T. Jorgensen
Sarah O. Newland
   Jorgensen
William F. Jung
Michael Kellogg
John P. Kelsh

Robert B. Knauss
Scott Knudson
Mark R. Kravitz
David G. Leitch
William Lindsay
Laura E. Little
Maureen Mahoney
Jody A. Manier
Matthew T. Martens
Kerri L. Martin
John M. Mason
Barry P. McDonald
W. Thomas McGough
Brett H. McGurk
Richard C. Miller
Brian M. Morris
Hugh G. Moulton
John M. Nannes
Jeffrey L. Oldham
John E. O'Neill
Frederic Paff
Richard Pepperman II
Celestine J. Richards
Neil M. Richards
Julius N. Richardson
John G. Roberts, Jr.
James E. Ryan
Stephen M. Sargent
Melissa Saunders
Robert G. Schaffer
Eric Scheuermann
Monica Wahl Shaffer
Ryan A. Shores
Allen R. Snyder
Luke A. Sobota
Mark T. Stancil
James A. Strain
Jocelyn E. Strauber
Aaron M. Streett
William L. Taylor
Ronald J. Tenpas
Barton H. Thompson
Alan B. Vickery

James K. Vines
Michael B. Wallace
Robert W. Wild
Michael Young
Paul J. Zidlicky

Owen J. Roberts

William Loney
Albert J. Schneider

Wiley B. Rutledge

Victor Brudney
W. Howard Mann
Louis H. Pollak
Harry L. Shniderman
John Paul Stevens
Stanley Temko
Philip W. Tone
Richard Wolfson

Edward T. Sanford

William Loney

Antonin Scalia

Wendy E. Ackerman
Alex M. Azar II
James Ballenger
Amy Coney Barrett
Kathleen S. Beecher
Anthoney Bellia, Jr.
Richard D. Bernstein
Brian D. Boyle
Richard Bress
Steven G. Calabresi
Paul T. Cappuccio
Bradford Clark
Paul D. Clement
Daniel Collins
John F. Duffy
Charles S. Duggan
Shay Dvoretzky
John E. Fee

Louis E. Feldman
Mark R. Filip
D. Cameron Findlay
Brian Fitzpatrick
Emmet T. Flood
Noel J. Francisco
Curtis E. Gannon
Griffith Green
Jordan B. Hansell
Benjamin L. Hatch
Bruce L. Hay
Christopher S. Hemphill
Kevin B. Huff
William M. Jay
Christine M. Jolls
Joel D. Kaplan
Joseph D. Kearney
Susan Kearns
Tara S. Kole
Robert K. Kry
Christopher Landau
Joan Larsen
Gary Lawson
Lester L. Lessig
Lee S. Lieberman
Ara Lovitt
John F. Manning
Kevin P. Martin
Roy McLeese
Alan J. Meese
Stephen A. Miller
Jonathan F. Mitchell
Edward Morrison
Brian J. Murray
Kristin Linsley Myles
David E. Nahmias
Andrew J. Nussbaum
Aaron Van Oort
John C. O'Quinn
John R. Phillips
Julian W. Poon
Howard M. Radzely
Michael Ramsey

Patrick Schiltz
Rachel Selinfreund
Gil Senfeld
Kannon K. Shanmugam
Howard Shelanski
Glen E. Summers
Robert H. Tiller
Theodore Ullycot
C. Adrian Vermeule
Kevin C. Walsh
Henry Weissmann
M. Edward Whelan
Jeffrey Wintner
Eric B. Wolff
Mary Beth Young

George Shiras

Eldwin Raphael Hayden

David H. Souter

William D. Araiza
Kenneth A. Bamberger
Michael S. Barr
Stuart M. Benjamin
Henk J. Brands
Robert F. Brauneis
Catherine M. A. Carroll
Jonathan Cederbaum
Thomas B. Colby
Nestor M. Davidson
Steven M. Dunne
Meir Feder
Noah Feldman
Mark C. Fleming
Jesse M. Furman
Julius Genachowski
Heather K. Gerken
David T. Goldberg
Craig T. Goldblatt
Kent H. Greenfield
Benjamin Gruenstein
Daniel H. Halberstam
Deborah L. Hamilton

Matthew S. Hellman
Derek Ho
William M. Hohengarten
Riyaz Kanji
Ellen D. Katz
Jay L. Koh
Thomas H. Lee
Gerald F. Leonard
Sarah L. Levine
Benjamin L. Liebman
Ann M. Lipton
Jeremy Maltby
Julian D. Mortenson
Mark L. Movesian
Kevin C. Newsom
Jonathan E. Nuechterlein
Mary-Rose Papandrea
Gregory G. Rapawy
Samuel J. Rascoff
Kermit Roosevelt III
Monica W. Rothbaum
Peter J. Rubin
Paul Salamanca
Catherine Sharkey
Timothy Simeone
Peter Spiro
Max I. Stier
Jeannie C. Suk
John Sullivan
Alison M. Tucher
Rebecca L. Tushnet
Christine B. Van Aken
Molly S.
   Van Houweling
Daniel S. Volchok
Matthew C. Waxman
Ernest A. Young

John Paul Stevens

Diane M. Amann
Mellisa B. Arbus
Stewart A. Baker
Sharon Baldwin

Preeta D. Bansal
David J. Barron
Francis Blake
Elizabeth A. Cavanagh
David W. DeBruin
Jeffrey C. Dobbins
Sean H. Donahue
Christopher Eisgruber
Susan R. Estrich
Daniel A. Farber
Jeffrey L. Fisher
David S. Friedman
Ian H. Gershengorn
Roberto J. Gonzalez
Michael J. Gottlieb
Abner S. Greene
Pamela A. Harris
Melissa R. Hart
Kathleen R. Hartnett
Marina Hsieh
Gregory Huffaker
Peter D. Isakoff
Olatunde Johnson
Richard B. Kapnick
David V. Kirby
Daniel M. Klerman
Leondra R. Kruger
Gilbert Kujovich
Carol F. Lee
Ronald D. Lee
Jeffrey Lehman
Amanda C. Leiter
Margaret H. Lemos
Jonathan E. Levitsky
James S. Liebman
Lewis J. Liman
Gregory P. Magarian
Nancy S. Marder
Lawrence Marshall
Allison A. Marston
Stephen J. Marzen
James E. McCollum
Troy A. McKenzie

Christopher J. Meade
Benjamin C. Mizer
Kathleen Moriarty
Randolph Moss
John E. Muench
Eileen M. Mullen
Alison J. Nathan
Michele Odorizzi
Eric P. Olson
Charles Paul
Deborah N. Pearlstein
Eduardo Penalver
Daniel J. Powell
Stephen R. Reily
Matthew Roberts
Teresa W. Roseborough
Lawrence Rosenthal
George Rutherglen
Adam M. Samaha
John R. Schaibley III
Robert A. Schapiro
Andrew M. Siegel
Craig D. Singer
Edward N. Siskel
Clifford M. Sloan
Jeffrey Tone
Constant Trela
Matthew Verschelden
Anne M. Voigts
Joshua P. Waldman
Kathryn A. Watts
Sonja R. West
Amy J. Wildermuth
Douglas Winthrop
Corinne B. Yates
Peter M. Yu

Potter Stewart

Eric B. Amstutz
Leonard Becker
James R. Bieke
Jeffrey Blattner
Ellen Borgerson

E. Edward Bruce
William Davey
Evan A. Davis
Frederick T. Davis
Jan Ginter Deutsch
Paul M. Dodyk
John L. Evans
Daniel R. Fischel
James N. Gardner
David Geronemus
Elliot F. Gerson
Saul B. Goodman
Ronald M. Gould
Henry T. Greely
Howard W. Gutman
Barbara Hauser
Benjamin Heineman
Curtis A. Hessler
David D. Hiller
C. Stephen Howard
Robert E. Hudec
Andrew D. Hurwitz
Jerold H. Israel
William H. Jeffress, Jr.
Thomas E. Kauper
Duncan M. Kennedy
Virginia Kerr
John G. Koeltl
Gilbert Kujovich
Robert S. Litt
Rory K. Little
Daniel J. Meltzer
Judith A. Miller
Alan R. Novak
Alan K. Palmer
Richard D. Parker
W. Carey Parker
Michael Patterson
Dennis M. Perluss
Terrence Perris
Mark F. Pomerantz
Monroe E. Price
Thomas D. Rowe

Terrance Sandalow
Carl E. Schneider
David M. Schulte
Jay M. Spears
Robert Stack
Ronald A. Stern
Richard Stewart
Laurence Tribe
Steven M. Umin
Silas J. Wasserstrom
Robert Weisberg

Harlan Fiske Stone

Bennett Boskey
Roger Cogswell
Alexis C. Coudert
Francis Downey
Edward L. Friedman
Wilbur Friedman
Warner Gardner
Walter F. Gellhorn
Milton Handler
Thomas Harris
Adrian C. Leiby
Harold Leventhal
Louis Lusky
Alfred McCormack
Alvin B. Merrill
James L. Morrison
C. Roger Nelson
Eugene Nickerson
Herbert Prashker
Herbert Wechsler
Howard C. Westwood

George Sutherland

John W. Cragun
Alan E. Gray
S. Edward Widdifield

William Howard Taft

John J. Byrne

William Crosskey
John E. Parsons
Reynolds Robertson
T. Hayden Smith
Leighton Surbeck
Charles Williams

Clarence Thomas

Matthew B. Berry
Steven G. Bradbury
Jimmy C. Chen
Jonathan F. Cohn
Gregory S. Coleman
Kathryn Comerford
Richard M. Corn
Steven T. Cottreau
Brendan P. Cullen
Victoria Dorfman
John C. Eastman
Allison H. Eid
John A. Eisenberg
Laurie A. Gallancy
Nicole Garnett
Dan Himmelfarb
Laura A. Ingraham
Erik S. Jaffe
Eric J. Kadel, Jr.
Greg Katsas
Jennifer L. Koester
Christopher Landau
Thomas R. Lee
Arthur S. Long
Gregory Maggs
Sigal P. Mandelker
C. Kevin Marshall
Stephen McAllister
Diane L. McGimsey
Eric D. Miller
Adam K. Mortara
Caleb E. Nelson
Eric C. Nelson
Carl J. Nichols
Patrick L. O'Daniel

Michael E. O'Neill
Martha M. Pacold
Patrick F. Philbin
Saikrishna B. Prakash
Craig S. Primis
Neomi J. Rao
Peter B. Rutledge
Margaret A. Ryan
Ann M. Scarlett
Arnon Siegel
Kristen L. Silverberg
Hannah C. Smith
Stephen F. Smith
Wendy E. Stone
David R. Stras
Emin Toro
Helgard C. Walker
Jeffrey B. Wall
Sanford I. Weisburst
Henry C. Whittaker
John F. Wood
John C. Yoo

Willis Van Devanter

Frederick H. Barclay
George Howland Chase
M.D. Kiefer
J. Arthur Mattson
John T. McHale
Richard E. Repath
James W. Yokum

Fred M. Vinson

Francis A. Allen
Melford Cleveland
Lawrence Ebb
David E. Feller
Richard Flynn
Isaac Groner
Carl S. Hawkins
Newton Minow
William Oliver
James C. Paul

Earl E. Pollock
Karl R. Price
Murray L. Schwartz
Arthur R. Seder
John A. Thompson
Howard J. Trienens
Daniel Walker
Byron R. White

Earl Warren

William Allen
Joseph W. Bartlett
Francis Beytagh
Scott H. Bice
Theodore Boehm
Murry H. Bring
Tyrone Brown
Donald M. Cahen
Jesse H. Choper
Jerome A. Cohen
William Dempsey
Timothy Dyk
Peter D. Ehrenhaft
Theodore Eisenberg
John Hart Ely
Dennis M. Flannery
Richard Flynn
Marc A. Franklin
James C. Gaither
Robert G. Gooch
James M. Graham
Gerald Gunther
James T. Hale
Ira M. Heyman
James K. Hoenig
Robert J. Hoerner
Phillip Johnson
John Keker
Conrad Kranwinkle
Robert T. Lasky
Peter W. Low
Paul J. Meyer
Graham B. Moody

Ralph J. Moore
Jon O. Newman
John D. Niles
Dallin H. Oaks
William Oliver
Earl E. Pollock
Curtis R. Reitz
Martin F. Richman
Benno C. Schmidt
Larry G. Simon
Michael Smith
Henry J. Steinman
Samuel A. Stern
Edward L. Strohbehn
Peter R. Taft
G. Edward White
Charles Wilson
Kenneth Ziffren

Byron White

Lee A. Albert
Ellen P. Aprill
Rhesa H. Barksdale
Robert B. Barnett
Bernard Bell
Robert B. Bell
Ronald L. Blanc
Albert J. Boro, Jr.
Curtis A. Bradley
Kathryn Lovill Bradley
Kingsley Browne
Jonathan Bunge
David W. Burcham
Lisa D. Burget
David J. Burman
J. Brett Busby
Thomas J. Campbell
Raymond Clevenger
Charles Cole
Dale S. Collinson
Richard Cordray
R. George Crawford
Richard Danzig

Patricia Dean
Stuart F. Delery
Samuel J. Dimon
Christopher Drahozal
William D'Zurilla
David M. Ebel
Charles Eskridge III
Martin S. Flaherty
John L. Flynn
David C. Frederick
S. Elizabeth Gibson
W. John Glancy
Jeffrey Glekel
Dean M. Gloster
John C. P. Goldberg
Neil Gorsuch
Donald L. Gunnels
Michael Herz
Stephen Higginson
Richard L. Hoffman
Dennis J. Hutchinson
Allan P. Ides
Leon E. Irish
Paul W. Kahn
Peter J. Kalis
David E. Kendall
Ronald A. Klain
Gilbert Kujovich
Rex E. Lee
Lance Liebman
Robert W. Loewen
James B. Loken
Robert Malley
James T. Malysiak
Stephen McAllister
Barbara McDowell
Thomas B. Metzloff
David D. Meyer
Geoffrey P. Miller
Laura A. Miller
Randall C. Nelson
Scott L. Nelson
William L. Nelson

John W. Nields, Jr.
Pierce H. O'Donnell
Robert V. Percival
Andrea L. Peterson
Benjamin A. Powell
Kate S. Pressman
Jeffrey F. Pryce
Cara W. Robertson
Allan A. Ryan
Gary L. Sasso
Richard Sayler
James E. Scarboro
Andrew G. Schultz
Hal S. Scott
Larry L. Simms
Stuart H. Singer
Benna R. Solomon
E. Philip Soper
Nicolas Spaeth
John W. Spiegel
Mary Gay Sprague
Richard Stern
Palma J. Strand
Jospeh T. Thai
Jonathan Varat
David Victor
Susan A. Weber
Philip J. Weiser
Richard I. Werder, Jr.
Richard A. Westfall
Natalie Wexler
Paul R. Q. Wolfson
Kevin Worthen

Edward D. White

John J. Byrne
William Cullen Dennis
William Pope
James T. Ruiggold
Bertram Shipman
Leonard Zeisler

Charles E. Whittaker

James N. Adler
William C. Canby, Jr.
Kenneth Dam
Heywood H. Davis

James M. Edwards
D. Lawrence Gunnels
Manley O. Hudson
Alan Kohn
Jerome B. Libin
Patrick F. McCartan

Notes

NOTES TO CHAPTER I

1. Tony Mauro, "Big Bucks Used to Woo High Court Clerks," *Fulton County Daily Report*, June 24, 2004.

2. Tom McCann, "Clerks See Life on the Inside of the U.S. Supreme Court," *Chicago Lawyer*, Sept. 1, 2003.

3. "The Bright Young Men Behind the Bench," *U.S. News & World Report*, July 12, 1957.

4. "New Clerks Begin High Court Tasks," *New York Times* (Oct. 14, 1958).

5. William H. Rehnquist, "Who Writes Decisions of the Supreme Court?" *U.S. News & World Report*, Dec. 13, 1957.

6. Alexander M. Bickel, "The Court: An Indictment Analyzed," *New York Times*, sec. 6 (Apr. 27, 1958).

7. Forty-nine clerks from OT 1950 to 1956 responded to my surveys. Of the 42 respondents who provided their political party affiliation at the time of their clerkship, 10 identified themselves as Republicans, 31 as Democrats, and 1 as an Independent.

8. William D. Rogers, "Do Law Clerks Wield Power in Supreme Court Cases?" *U.S. News & World Report*, Feb. 21, 1958.

9. William H. Rehnquist, "Another View: Clerks Might 'Influence' Some Actions," *U.S. News & World Report*, Feb. 21, 1958.

10. In his 2001 book on the Supreme Court, Chief Justice Rehnquist was silent as to the concerns voiced by private attorney Rehnquist, mentioning neither clerk influence nor the ideological views of former and current law clerks. Rehnquist did write, however, that his law clerks reviewed cert. petitions—an activity troubling to the younger Rehnquist. William H. Rehnquist, *The Supreme Court* (New York: Knopf, 2001).

11. The entire text of Stennis' speech is contained in "Investigate Supreme Court's 'Law Clerk' System?" *U.S. News & World Report*, May 16, 1958.

12. In 1973, Congressman John R. Rarick made a similar suggestion when he introduced H.R. 1627: "A Bill to provide that the appointment of law clerks to Justices of the Supreme Court shall be confirmed by the Senate and the House of Representatives to the Committee on the Judiciary."

13. John W. Dean, *The Rehnquist Choice:The Untold Story of the Nixon Appointment that Redefined the Supreme Court* (New York: Simon & Schuster, 2001).

14. "Supreme Court: Memo from Rehnquist," *Newsweek*, Dec. 13, 1971.

15. Dean, *Rehnquist Choice*, 275.

16. Ibid., 276 (citing *Congressional Record—Senate*, Dec. 8, 1971, 45440).

17. Dean, *Rehnquist Choice*, 277.

18. John P. MacKenzie, "Controversy Deepens Over Rehnquist Memo," *Washington Post*, sec. A (Dec. 10, 1971). See also Joseph L. Rauh, Jr., "Historical Perspectives: An Unabashed Liberal Looks at a Half-Century of the Supreme Court," *North Carolina Law Review* 69, no. 1 (Nov. 1990): 213–49; Laura K. Ray, "A Law Clerk and His Justice: What William Rehnquist Did Not Learn from Robert Jackson," *Indiana Law Review* 29 (1996): 535–92; Mark Tushnet, "What Really Happened in *Brown v. Board of Education*," *Columbia Law Review* 91, no. 8 (Dec. 1991): 1867–930.

19. Dean writes that the controversial memo was also debated in the Senate during Rehnquist's confirmation hearings for the chief justice position. Dean, *Rehnquist Choice*, 278–84.

20. Bob Woodward and Scott Armstrong, *The Brethren: Inside the Supreme Court* (New York: Simon & Schuster, 1979).

21. Woodward and Armstrong, *Brethren*, 241.

22. Ibid., 196–97, 258, 429.

23. Margaret Truman, *Murder in the Supreme Court* (New York: Arbor House, 1982), 38.

24. Brad Meltzer, *The Tenth Justice* (New York: Morrow, 1997); Paul Levine, *9 Scorpions* (New York: Pocket Books, 1998); David Baldacci, *The Simple Truth* (New York: Warner Books, 1998).

25. Meltzer, *Tenth Justice*, 4.

26. The law clerk's foray into the realm of popular culture has not stopped at the written word. In 2001 and 2002, two television shows premiered that offered dramatic stories about the inner workings of the Supreme Court. In "First Monday," James Garner and Joe Mantegna starred as Supreme Court Justices who must battle each other, their consciences, and their mettlesome (if well-intentioned) law clerks as they decide critical issues of constitutional law; in "The Court," Sally Field starred as Kate Nolan, a former state governor propelled to the Supreme Court after the sudden death of a female justice. Like her peers on "First Monday," the newly minted Justice Nolan must battle fellow justices (Pat Hingle, Diahann Carroll), her conscience, and her mettlesome (if well-intentioned) law clerks as she decides critical issues of constitutional law. Sadly, neither of these groundbreaking dramas survived the television season.

27. Edward Lazarus, *Closed Chambers: The First Eyewitness Account of the Epic Struggles Inside the Supreme Court* (New York: Random House, 1998).

28. Ibid., 267–68, 269, 270.

29. On the other hand, most legal scholars believe that the review of cert. petitions, not opinion writing, is the one area where the potential for real influence by law clerks exists.

30. Lazarus, *Closed Chambers*, 270.

31. Ibid., 274.

32. See, for example, Sally J. Kenney, "Puppeteers or Agents? What Lazarus' *Closed Chambers* Adds to Our Understanding of Law Clerks at the U.S. Supreme Court,"

Law and Social Inquiry 25, no. 1 (Winter 2000): 185–222; Alex Kozinski, "Conduct Unbecoming," *Yale Law Journal* 108 (Jan. 1999): 835–78. Some court observers were less critical of Lazarus' alleged breach of confidentiality. See David J. Garrow, "The Lowest Form of Animal Life? Supreme Court Clerks and Supreme Court History," *Cornell Law Review* 84, no. 3 (Mar. 1999): 855–94.

　33. Examples include: John H. Pickering, Eugene Gressman, and T. L. Tolan, Jr., "Mr. Justice Murphy—A Note of Appreciation," *Michigan Law Review* 48, no. 6 (Apr. 1950): 742–44; Charles Nesson, "Mr. Justice Harlan," *Harvard Law Review* 85, no. 1 (Nov. 1971): 390–91; Bennett Boskey, "Justice Reed and His Family of Law Clerks," *Kentucky Law Journal* 69, no. 4 (1980–81): 869–76; Stephen Breyer, "Clerking for Justice Goldberg," *Journal of Supreme Court History* (1990): 4–7; Robert O'Neil, "Clerking for Justice Brennan," *Journal of Supreme Court History* (1991): 3–5; Susan Low Bloch, "The Privilege of Clerking for Thurgood Marshall," *Journal of Supreme Court History* (1992): 23–25; Sherry F. Colb, "Breakfast with Justice Blackmun," *North Dakota Law Review* 71 (1995): 13–14; Kenneth W. Starr, "The Man from Minnesota: A Remembrance from Things Past," *Texas Law Review* 74, no. 2 (Dec. 1995): 223–24; Richard H. Fallon, "In Memoriam: In Remembrance of Justice Lewis F. Powell, Jr.," *Columbia Law Review* 99, no. 3 (Apr. 1999): 544–46.

　34. Douglass C. North, *Institutions, Institutional Change and Economic Performance* (New York: Cambridge University Press, 1990): 3.

　35. Ibid., 5.

　36. Ibid., 41.

　37. Terry Moe, "The New Economics of Organization," *American Journal of Political Science* 28 (1984): 756.

　38. Corey Ditslear and Lawrence Baum, "Selection of Law Clerks and Polarization in the U.S. Supreme Court," *The Journal of Politics* 63 (Aug. 2001): 869–85; Sally J. Kenney, "Beyond Principals and Agents: Seeing Courts as Organizations by Comparing Referendaires at the European Court of Justice and Law Clerks at the U.S. Supreme Court," *Comparative Political Studies* 33 (June 2000): 593–625.

　39. Moe, *New Economics*, 754–56.

　40. Ibid., 755.

　41. David E. M. Sappington, "Incentives in Principal-Agent Relationships," *Journal of Economic Perspectives* (Spring, 1991): 45.

　42. Moe, *New Economics*, 757.

　43. Ditslear and Baum write that "the selection of law clerks is an important mechanism with which to obtain the desired behavior from subordinates," suggesting that Supreme Court justices used lower court judges to maximize the likelihood of selecting like-minded clerks. Ditslear and Baum, "Selection of Law Clerks," 870.

　44. Richard Posner, *The Federal Courts: Crisis and Reform* (Cambridge, Mass.: Harvard University Press, 1985).

NOTES TO CHAPTER 2

　1. Law reviews and legal periodicals often feature general "tribute" or "testimonial" articles written by former clerks. Unfortunately, these materials tend to be long on lofty rhetoric about the individual author's justice and his place in the annals of history and short on data regarding the actual clerkship. *The Journal of Supreme Court History* proved to be one of the best periodical sources for information regarding former

clerks. As for oral histories, the University of Kentucky interviewed a large number of former law clerks for the Stanley Reed and Fred Vinson Oral History Projects.

2. In an April 26, 1943, letter to Chief Justice Harlan Fiske Stone, Justice Douglas discussed his law clerk selection problems in light of WWII. Douglas requested permission to employ a law clerk prior to the candidate's September 1943 graduation from Yale Law School. The clerk would be protected from the draft due to an unspecified disability. The law clerk was likely Eugene A. Beyer. William O. Douglas Papers, Box 1118, Manuscript Division, Library of Congress.

3. Douglas to Vern Countryman, January 10, 1944, Douglas Papers.

4. Interestingly, Justice Black evidenced his willingness to hire a female law clerk as early as 1950. Responding to a letter from a female application, Black wrote: "I should have no objection whatever to appointing a woman clerk provided she met the qualifications desired." Black to Sarah Livingston Davis, October 17, 1950, Hugo L. Black Papers, Box 442, Manuscript Division, Library of Congress.

5. I have found only a few examples of children following a parent into the law clerk corps. Other parent-child combinations include Robert O'Neil (for Justice Brennan) and son David O'Neil (for Justice Ginsburg), Victor Brudney (for Justice Rutledge) and son James Brudney (for Justice Blackmun), Newton Minow (for Chief Justice Vinson) and daughter Martha L. Minow (for Justice Marshall), Walter Gellhorn (for Justice Stone) and daughter Gay Gellhorn (for Justice Marshall), Abner Mikva (for Justice Minton) and Mary Mikva (for Justice Brennan), Mark Tushnet (for Justice Marshall) and Rebecca Tushnet (for Justice Souter).

6. Hugo L. Black and Elizabeth Black, *Mr. Justice and Mrs. Black: The Memoirs of Hugo L. Black and Elizabeth Black* (New York: Random House, 1986): 168.

7. Stephen Susman, interview with author.

8. David McKean, *Tommy the Cork: Washington's Ultimate Insider from Roosevelt to Reagan* (South Royalton, Vt.: Steerforth Press, 2004): 296–97.

9. Martha A. Field (formerly Alschuler) presently serves as a professor at Harvard Law School.

10. A graduate of Radcliffe College and Georgetown University Law Center, Underwood clerked for Judge David L. Bazelon before working for Justice Marshall.

11. Mark R. Brown, "Gender Discrimination in the Supreme Court's Clerkship Selection Process," *Oregon Law Review* 75, no. 2 (Summer 1996): 359–88.

12. "Supreme Court Justice to Have a Negro Clerk," *New York Times* (Apr. 27, 1948); "Frankfurter's Negro Clerk to be First in Court History," *Washington Post* (Apr. 27, 1948). Coleman also applied for a clerkship with Justice Hugo Black. In his application, Coleman writes: "Despite my training due to the fact that I am a negro I have encountered considerable difficulty in getting a suitable position. Your efforts and expressions in your judicial utterances led me to inquire if you would consider me for the position as your legal clerk." Coleman to Black, June 20, 1946, Black Papers. In his reply, Black congratulated Coleman on his "excellent" record but stated that the law clerk for the coming term "was selected some months ago." Black to Coleman, June 24, 1946. After his clerkship, Coleman worked on the NAACP's Legal Defense Fund with Thurgood Marshall and later served as the secretary of transportation in the Ford administration. He was awarded the Presidential Medal of Freedom in 1995.

13. Tyrone Brown did not apply for a Supreme Court clerkship. A Cornell Law School professor submitted his name to Chief Justice Earl Warren, and Brown subsequently interviewed with Warren's selection committee. As for whether race played a role in his selection, Brown commented: "I would be very surprised if it weren't the case that Chief Justice Warren had said that it would be nice to have a qualified negro law school graduate on the Court," said Brown, "but I don't have any indication that Warren 'put out a net' for qualified black students." Brown downplays the significance of his selection, believing it is more significant that the son of "a common laborer" and a graduate of Cornell Law School was selected to clerk on the High Court. (Tyrone Brown, interview with author.) Brown subsequently served as the director of Black Entertainment Television and as commissioner of the Federal Communications Commission.

14. Tony Mauro, "Only 1 New High Court Clerk Is a Minority," *USA Today* (Sept. 10, 1998). The first article by Mauro on law clerk diversity had appeared six months earlier: Tony Mauro, "Corps of Clerks Lacking in Diversity," *USA Today* (Mar. 13, 1998).

15. This was not the first time attention had been focused on the Supreme Court's hiring practices. In a 1979 editorial discussing the number of minority law clerks, the *Washington Post* questioned whether the justices truly comprehended "phrases like employment discrimination and equal opportunity." "Some Deliberate Speed," *Washington Post*, sec. A (June 12, 1979).

16. Examples include: Robert M. Agostisi and Brian P. Corrigan, "Do as We Say or Do as We Do: How the Supreme Court Law Clerk Controversy Reveals a Lack of Accountability at the High Court," *Hofstra Labor & Employment Law Journal* 18 (Spring 2001): 625–58; Randall Kennedy, "The Clerkship Question and the Court," *American Lawyer* (Apr. 1999): 114–15; Trevor W. Coleman, "Supreme Bias," *Emerge* (July-Aug. 1999): 59–61; Laura Gatland, "A Clerkship for White Males Only," *Student Lawyer* (Oct. 1999): 34–39; William Raspberry, "Clerks and Color," *Washington Post*, sec. C (Dec. 13, 1998).

17. Michael A. Fletcher, "As Term Opens, Lack of Diversity Is Decried," *Washington Post*, sec. A (Oct. 6, 1998).

18. Joan Biskupic, "In Testimony, Justices Defend Court's Hiring Practices," *Washington Post*, sec. A (Mar. 11, 1999); Joan Biskupic, "Two Justices Defend Lack of Minority Court Clerks," *Washington Post*, sec. A (Mar. 16, 2000). At the March 1999 hearing before a House Appropriations subcommittee, Justice Clarence Thomas commented that while the justices wanted to hire more minority clerks, "At this level you just can't take chances." Biskupic, "In Testimony," 1999.

19. Tony Mauro, "Rehnquist: Diversity a Grad Pool Function," *USA Today*, sec. A (Dec. 8, 1998).

20. American Bar Association.

21. The Thomas M. Cooley Law School has gone beyond rhetoric in the attack against educational elitism, publishing the "profiles of the brightest and best law graduates from all around the nation." *The National Law School Deans' List* (Arlington: National Jurist Publishing, 1999): iii. For OT 1998, Justice John Paul Stevens hired the first known law clerk with a physical handicap—Adam Samaha, who has generalized dystonia (a neurological disorder).

22. Justice Horace Gray hired 19 law clerks, all of whom attended Harvard Law

School. While the first law clerk of Oliver Wendell Holmes, Jr., attended George Washington University, his subsequent 29 law clerks were all Harvard Law School graduates. Felix Frankfurter plucked 36 of his 38 law clerks from the ranks of Harvard Law School, turning to the University of Chicago and the University of Pennsylvania for one clerk each.

23. Harris K. Weston, interview with author.

24. Justice Alex Keith of the Minnesota supreme court is the only state court judge to have had a law clerk employed on the Rehnquist Court. In prior decades, the following state supreme court justices sent clerks on to the High Court: California supreme court justices Phillip Gibson, Thomas Lawson, Stanley Mosk, Edward Panelli, Ray Peters, Roger Traynor, and Matthew Trobiner; Colorado supreme court justice Luis Lowera; Illinois supreme court justices Walter Schaefer and Seymour Simon; Massachusetts supreme judicial court justices Robert Braucher and Benjamin Kaplan; Mississippi supreme court justice Harry Walker; New Jersey supreme court justice Sidney Schreiber; and Pennsylvania supreme court justice Sam Roberts.

25. Tony Mauro, "Clerks Taking Detours on Road to High Court," *Legal Times* (Oct. 21, 2002).

NOTES TO CHAPTER 3

1. Bernard Schwartz, *A History of the Supreme Court* (New York: Oxford University Press, 1993): 33.

2. Kermit L. Hall, ed., *The Oxford Companion to the Supreme Court of the United States* (New York: Oxford University Press, 1992): 100, 101.

3. Ibid., 159.

4. Carl B. Swisher, *History of the Supreme Court of the United States: The Taney Period, 1836–1864*, vol. 5 (New York: Macmillan, 1974): 296.

5. Ibid., 293, 294.

6. Hall, *Oxford Companion*, 727, 818.

7. Swisher, *History of the Supreme Court*, 294.

8. Chester A. Newland, "Personal Assistants to Supreme Court Justices: The Law Clerks," *Oregon Law Review* 40, no. 4 (June 1961): 300.

9. *Congressional Globe*, 31st Congress, 1st session (1850): 197.

10. Ibid. Cartter served in the House of Representatives for two terms before returning to his home state of Ohio to practice law. He served as the chief justice of the District of Columbia Supreme Court from 1863 to 1887. History does not record whether, as a jurist, Cartter depended on any support staff or other types of "thinking machines."

11. *Congressional Globe*, 197.

12. Ibid. (emphasis added). Twenty years later, Strong served as an associate justice on the U.S. Supreme Court, from 1870 to 1880.

13. Swisher, *History of the Supreme Court*, 289.

14. 44 Stat. 433 (1867).

15. Felix Frankfurter and James M. Landis, *The Business of the Supreme Court: A Study in the Federal Judicial System* (New York: Macmillan, 1927): 61.

16. Ibid., 60.

17. Willard L. King, *Melville Weston Fuller: Chief Justice of the United States* (New York: Macmillan, 1950): 148.

18. Loren Beth describes the chambers as follows: "The courtroom had columns of native Potomac marble, gray, painted walls, and mahogany furnishings with red draperies and carpeting." Loren B. Beth, *John Marshall Harlan: The Last Whig Justice* (Lexington: University of Kentucky Press, 1992): 142.

19. Alexander M. Bickel, *The Judiciary and Responsible Government, 1910–21*, vol. 9 (New York: Macmillan, 1984): 81.

20. Frankfurter and Landis, *Business of the Supreme Court*, 70.

21. Ibid., 88.

22. Samuel Miller, "Judicial Reforms," *The United States Jurist* 2 (Jan. 1872): 3.

23. Morrison R. Waite, "Remarks of Chief Justice Waite," *The Albany Law Journal* 36 (1887): 318.

24. Stephen J. Field, "The Centenary of the Supreme Court of the United States," *American Law Review* 24 (May-June 1890): 363–65.

25. *Annual Report of the Attorney General of the United States for the Year 1885* (Washington, D.C.: Government Printing Office, 1885): 43.

26. For an interesting discussion of the role of stenographers in early twentieth century America, see "Stenographer's Mighty Influence in Our Legal and Political Life," *Washington Post*, sec. E (Sept. 20, 1908).

27. A. H. Garland, *Experience in the Supreme Court of the United States With Some Reflections and Suggestions as to That Tribunal* (Washington, D.C.: John Byrne & Co., 1898): 36-37. Garland does not indicate whether he intended that men possessing both legal and stenographic skills would be hired by the justices.

28. 24 Stat. 254 (1886).

29. Stephen Robert Mitchell, "Mr. Justice Horace Gray" (Ph.D. diss. University of Wisconsin, 1961): 100.

30. Ibid. Shorter biographical essays include: John Malcolm Smith, "Mr. Justice Horace Gray of the United States Supreme Court," *South Dakota Law Review* 6, no. 2 (Fall 1961), 221–47; Elbridge B. Davis and Harold A. Davis, "Mr. Justice Horace Gray: Some Aspects of His Judicial Career," *American Bar Association Journal* 41 (May 1955): 421–71; *Proceedings of the Bar and of the Supreme Judicial Court of Massachusetts in Memory of Horace Gray* (Jan. 17, 1903); Samuel Williston, "Horace Gray," ed., William Draper Lewis, *Great American Lawyers: A History of the Legal Profession in America* (Philadelphia: J. C. Vinson, 1909).

31. Samuel Williston, *Life and Law: An Autobiography* (Boston: Little, Brown, 1940): 92.

32. *Proceedings of the Bar and of the Supreme Judicial Court of Massachusetts*, 12, 50.

33. Ibid., 30.

34. Williston, "Horace Gray," 141.

35. Francis C. Lowell, "Horace Gray," *Proceedings of the American Academy of Arts and Sciences* 39 (Boston: American Academy of Arts and Sciences, 1904): 628.

36. Williston, "Horace Gray," 150, 151, 156.

37. Davis and Davis, "Some Aspects of His Judicial Career," 11.

38. George F. Hoar, "Mr. Justice Horace Gray," *Massachusetts Historical Society Proceedings* (Boston: Massachusetts Historical Society, 1904): 21.

39. Williston, "Horace Gray," 157.

40. Williston, *Life and Law*, 87. Gray fought in the Civil War before beginning a

successful career as a Harvard Law School professor. He was the author of *The Nature and the Sources of the Law* (New York: Macmillan, 1921).

41. Oakley and Thompson, *Law Clerks and the Judicial Process*, 11. Williston writes that Gray wrote 1,367 opinions in his seventeen years on the Massachusetts court, 852 of which were penned while he was chief justice—yet another reason why a young assistant may have proved necessary. Williston, "Horace Gray," 153.

42. Ibid., 157.

43. Melvin I. Urofsky and David W. Levy, eds., *The Letters of Louis D. Brandeis, Volume 1 (1870–1907): Urban Reformer* (Albany: State University of New York Press, 1971): 38.

44. Lowell, "Horace Gray," 631.

45. Ibid., 630.

46. Justices Samuel Blatchford, Joseph McKenna, Samuel Miller, George Shiras, Jr., Edward Douglass White, and William B. Woods, did not preserve their personal papers. Justices Stephen Field, Horace Gray, Howell E. Jackson, Lucius Lamar, Horace Lurton, Stanley Matthews, and Rufus Peckham, left behind minor holdings.

47. There are no records regarding any clerks appointed by Chief Justice Waite or Associate Justices Day, Lamar, Lurton, Matthews, McKenna, Miller, Moody, Peckham, Shiras, White, or Woods. Supreme Court records do not list Justice Howell Jackson as hiring an assistant, but newspaper accounts of his funeral identify a Frederick E. Chapin as his private secretary. "Funeral of Justice Jackson: Chief Justice Fuller and Justice Brewer Go to Attend," *New York Times* (Aug. 10, 1895). Chapin was an attorney and counselor for the Japanese embassy, but it isn't clear whether he was a lawyer at the time of his appointment to the Jackson chambers. "Rites for Frederick E. Chapin," *Washington Post* (Mar. 22, 1923); "Mrs. Mary Chapin Burial Set Today," *Washington Post* (Nov. 30, 1937).

48. Williston, *Life and Law*, 101.

49. "May Lose His Place: A Department Clerk Charged with Lese Majeste," *Washington Post* (Nov. 28, 1899).

50. *1890 City of Washington, D.C., Directory*.

51. "Clerk Dawson Discharged," *Washington Post* (Nov. 29, 1899).

52. The January 14, 1905, and May 23, 1905, issues of the *Washington Post* both praised Linton for his "splendid work" as a church choir director.

53. Justice Harlan was not the last Supreme Court justice to hire family members as judicial assistants. Associate Justice William Rufus Day hired all three of his sons—Luther (1903), Stephen (1906), and Rufus (1907)—as law clerks. It is unclear whether sons Luther and Rufus were attorneys at the time of their clerkships, although subsequently both sons practiced law in the Cleveland law firm of Jones, Day, Cockley & Reavis. Joseph E. McLean, *William Rufus Day: Supreme Court Justice from Ohio* (Baltimore: Johns Hopkins University Press, 1946): 64. By the mid-twentieth century, federal anti-nepotism legislation ended the practice of the justices hiring their own sons and daughters, or the children of other justices, as law clerks.

54. The 1920 Federal Census lists Fredrick J. Haig as an appointment clerk at a federal bank.

55. The *D.C. Directory* lists Noble E. Dawson as a stenographer with the business of Dawson, Son & Company.

56. Supreme Court records state that Clarence M. York began working for Chief Justice Fuller in 1889, but the *Washington Post* reports that in October 1889 a C. M. Lark was appointed as Fuller's private secretary. "Chief Justice Fuller's Secretary," *Washington Post* (Oct. 19, 1889). Thus I have concluded from later news accounts that York started in 1890. I have been unable to find any additional information on Mr. Lark.

57. Like his two companions, Barnes would die at a relatively young age. He passed away at age forty-one after serving for several years as the District of Columbia postmaster. "Barnes Is Chosen: President Appoints Him as City Postmaster," *Washington Post* (Apr. 1, 1906); "Barnes Funeral Tomorrow," *Washington Post* (Oct. 22, 1909).

58. "Were Boys Together: Three Washington Secretaries Who Have Been Lifelong Intimates," *Washington Post* (June 11, 1905): F1.

59. "Fall Causes Death: Clarence M. York Found Dead Under Hospital Window," *Washington Post* (June 21, 1906); "Clarence M. York Killed: Secretary of Chief Justice Fuller Falls from Hospital Window," *New York Times* (June 21, 1906).

60. "Fall Causes Death."

61. "Lieut. Crawford May Be Suicide," *Washington Post* (Nov. 23, 1907); "No Clew to Crawford," *Washington Post* (Nov. 25, 1907); "Crawford Is Not Dead: Naval Officer Believed to Be Near Washington," *Washington Post* (Nov. 30, 1907); "Dewey Relieves Crawford: Action of Admiral Is Regarded as Significant," *Washington Post* (Dec. 3, 1907); "Crawford Is Dead," *Washington Post* (Jan. 16, 1908); "Bury Crawford Today," *Washington Post* (Jan. 17, 1908).

62. "Crawford's Friends Won: All of Class of Four Young Men Gained Distinction Here," *Washington Post* (Nov. 26, 1907).

63. William Rufus Day to Melville Fuller, June 28, 1906, Melville Fuller Papers, William R. Day Correspondence File, Manuscript Division, Library of Congress.

64. Stephen Day to Fuller, October 8, 1907, Fuller Papers, Correspondence File, "D" Miscellany.

65. The "Legal Record" sections of the *Washington Post* issues of October 20, 1914, and August 10, 1915, list Bell as an attorney of record.

66. "Stephen J. Field Dead: Served Longest of All the Federal Supreme Court Justices," *New York Times* (Apr. 10, 1899).

67. Despite these long periods of service, there is no mention of either assistant in Justice Brown's memoirs. Given Brown's near-blindness toward the end of his judicial career, one would assume that he leaned heavily on his clerks in reviewing pleadings and briefs as well as in preparing opinions.

68. "Resigns to Practice Law: Charles F. Wilson Retires as Private Secretary to Secretary Knox," *Washington Post* (Nov. 15, 1911).

69. "Harlan May Retire: Supreme Court Justice Likely to Leave Bench Soon," *Washington Post* (Mar. 26, 1908).

70. Williston, "Horace Gray," 158, 159.

71. Williston, *Life and Law*, 92.

72. Ibid., 93.

73. *Massachusetts Historical Society Proceedings*, 36, 38.

74. Williston, *Life and Law*, 92.

75. Williston, "Horace Gray," 159 (emphasis added).

76. Williston, *Life and Law*, 92.

77. Ferd. Houck to Waite, November 9, 1874; Chas. H. Regiea to Waite, November 20, 1874, Morrison R. Waite Papers, Manuscript Division, Library of Congress.

78. The 1880 Federal Census, however, lists Raphael Hayden's birthday as 1864, meaning he would have been twenty-four years old when Chief Justice Waite left the Court and forty years old in 1904.

79. Edgar R. Rombauer, Jr., "Secretary to Justice Harlan: The Early Days," *The Supreme Court Historical Society Quarterly* 24, no. 1 (2003): 6–7.

80. Ibid., 16.

81. Newland, "Personal Assistants," 311.

82. Ibid., 312.

83. Bickel, *Judiciary and Responsible Government*, 82.

84. Carl Brent Swisher, *Stephen J. Field: Craftsman of the Law* (Hamden, Conn.: Archon Books, 1963).

85. *In Memoriam: Joseph Bradley* (Philadelphia: Allen, Lane & Scott, 1892): 18.

86. Michael J. Brodhead, *David J. Brewer: The Life of a Supreme Court Justice, 1837–1910* (Carbondale: Southern Illinois University Press, 1994).

87. George Shiras III, *Justice George Shiras, Jr. of Pittsburgh: Associate Justice of the United States Supreme Court, 1892–1903* (Pittsburgh: University of Pittsburgh Press): 122.

88. I. Scott Messinger writes that Holmes referred to his young charges as "legal secretaries" rather than the original title of "stenographic clerk" or the latter title "law clerk." Messinger observes that this title "was a reflection of Holmes's view that the primary function of a judicial assistant was not to dispense advice on legal matters or to help draft opinions. . . . Nor was it simply to take dictation. . . . Rather, it was to serve as the Justice's confidant and to minister to his needs in a wide variety of private and professional matters." I. Scott Messinger, "The Judge as Mentor: Oliver Wendell Holmes, Jr., and His Law Clerks," *Yale Journal of Law & The Humanities* 11, no. 1 (Winter 1999): 124.

89. Francis Biddle, *Mr. Justice Holmes* (New York: Scribner's (1942): 10.

90. Ibid., 12.

91. John Monagan writes that Ezra Thayer, dean of the Harvard Law School and former law clerk of Horace Gray, also provided some limited input regarding law clerks. Besides selecting law clerks for Justice Holmes, Frankfurter helped select law clerks for Justices Brandeis and Cardozo. John S. Monagan, *The Grand Panjandrum: The Mellow Years of Justice Holmes* (Landham, Md.: University Press of America, 1988).

92. Frankfurter's influence over the selection of law clerks extended beyond Justice Holmes. Former McReynolds law clerk John Knox, a Harvard-educated law clerk who was not handpicked by Frankfurter to clerk on the Supreme Court, quotes Justice Brandeis as commenting: "There isn't one chance in a thousand for any graduate of the Harvard Law School to come to the Court these days without Professor Frankfurter's approval." Dennis J. Hutchinson and David J. Garrow, eds., *The Forgotten Memoir of John Knox: A Year in the Life of a Supreme Court Law Clerk in FDR's Washington* (Chicago: University of Chicago Press, 2002): 56.

93. Monagan, *Grand Panjandrum*, 115.

94. Robert M. Mennel and Christine L. Compston, eds., *Holmes and Frankfurter: Their Correspondence, 1912–1934* (Hanover, N.H.: University Press of New England, 1996): 178.

95. Monagan, *Grand Panjandrum*, 120–21.

96. Holmes Papers.

97. Former secretary Thomas Corcoran observed that Holmes composed his opinions while standing "because he said it was conducive to brevity." Katie Louchhiem, ed., *The Making of the New Deal: The Insiders Speak* (Cambridge, Mass.: Harvard University Press, 1983): 24.

98. Ibid., 27.

99. Augustin Derby, "Recollections of Mr. Justice Holmes," *New York University Law Quarterly Review* 12 (Mar. 1935): 346.

100. Ibid., 349.

101. Holmes did not enjoy reviewing the cert. petitions, referring to them as the "bloody certs." Monagan, *Grand Panjandrum*, 114.

102. Charles Denby, "An Extraordinary Man" and Robert Wales, "Some Aspects of Life with Mr. Justice Holmes in the 90th Year" (Holmes Symposium: Personal Remembrances of Mr. Justice Holmes by His Former Law Clerks: A Retrospective Note) *University of Florida Law Review* 27 (1976): 392–98. Contained in the Holmes Papers is a "Memorandum for the Secretary," written in a precise, neat hand by secretary James M. Nicely (OT 1923). Besides summarizing the same duties mentioned above, Nicely instructs the secretary as to when he should arrive in the morning ("nine thirty will be a suitable hour"), to maintain a sharp eye on the justice's four bank accounts, and to timely file the income tax returns. Nicely concludes the memo as follows: "It will be quite the happiest year you've had and I wish you all success in it." Oliver Wendell Holmes, Jr., Papers, Harvard Law School.

103. Holmes biographer G. Edward White concludes that there is "no evidence that he ever asked a secretary to draft even the smallest part of an opinion for him." G. Edward White, *Justice Oliver Wendell Holmes: Law and the Inner Self* (New York: Oxford University Press, 1993).

104. Hiss, *Reflections*, 34.

105. Denby, "An Extraordinary Man."

106. Charles Denby to Augustin Derby, July 11, 1935, Holmes Papers.

107. Wales, "Some Aspects of Life with Mr. Justice Holmes," 395–96.

108. Denby, "An Extraordinary Man," 393.

109. Wales, "Some Aspects of Life with Mr. Justice Holmes," 396. See also, Monica Lynne Niznik, "Thomas G. Corcoran: The Public Service of Franklin Roosevelt's 'Tommy the Cork.'" (Ph.D. diss., University of Notre Dame, 1981): 18. "As secretary, Corcoran's official duties include reviewing petitions of 'certiorari' and condensing each petition to one page."

110. White, *Law and the Inner Self*, 313.

111. Hiss, *Reflections*, 34.

112. Derby, "Recollections," 349.

113. Denby, "An Extraordinary Man," 393.

114. Monagan, *Grand Panjandrum*, 116.

115. Ibid., 177–18.

116. "The Reminiscences of Harvey H. Bundy," Holmes Papers. Bundy later served as assistant secretary of state for Economic and Financial Affairs from 1931 to 1933 and as special assistant to Secretary of War Henry L. Stimson. As Stimson's assistant, Bundy served as liaison between Stimson and General Leslie Groves, director of the Manhattan Project.

117. Hiss, *Reflections*, 36–37.

118. 1933 Diary of Mark De Wolfe Howe, Harvard Law School.

119. "Justice Holmes Succumbs to Pneumonia at Age of 93," *New York Times* (Mar. 6, 1935); "Taps for Holmes Will Sound Today," *New York Times* (Mar. 8, 1935).

120. The *D.C. Directory* lists James C. Hooe as a stenographer, but Hooe appears have been more than a "mere" secretary. The *Washington Post* December 10, 1904, issue states that Hooe held a leadership position in the New York Republican Club, and the November 18, 1910, issue lists him on the board of directors of the Commercial National Bank. He died in December 1910 of tuberculosis. His obituary states that Hooe, a "well known business man," once served as private secretary to William Randolph Hearst's mother and married the daughter of a Congressman. Justice McKenna and five U.S. senators attended Hooe's funeral. "Funeral of James C. Hooe," *Washington Post* (Jan. 1, 1911); "James Cecil Hooe Is Dead," *Washington Post* (Dec. 29, 1910).

121. "Dead Law Student Honored," *Washington Post* (Jan. 4, 1895).

122. John B. Owens, "The Clerk, the Thief, His Life as a Baker: Ashton Embry and the Supreme Court Leak Scandal of 1919," *Northwestern University Law Review* 95, no. 1 (2000): 271–308.

123. Ibid., 305.

124. David J. Danelski and Joseph S. Tulchin, eds., *The Autobiographical Notes of Charles Evans Hughes* (Cambridge, Mass.: Harvard University Press, 1973): 163.

125. Educated at Harvard Law School, in 1929 Dennis became the president of his undergraduate alma mater, Earlham College in Richmond, Indiana. "William C. Dennis Named President of Alma Mater," *Washington Post* (June 5, 1929).

126. Bertram F. Shipman was a native of Leon, Iowa, who graduated from Columbia Law School in 1912. From 1914 to 1918, he served as a law clerk to Chief Justice White. "Bertram Shipman, a Lawyer Here, 78," *New York Times* (Nov. 23, 1963).

127. Danelski and Tulchin, *Autobiographical Notes*, 163 (emphasis added).

128. Maurice M. Moore graduated from George Washington Law School in 1913, while working for Hughes, and then spent an additional year with the justice. A native of Grand Rapids, Michigan, Moore served in the U.S. Navy Flying Corps during World War I and subsequently practiced law in the Minneapolis law firm of Moore, White & Burd.

129. The obituary of another Washington attorney, John E. Hoover, states that Hoover clerked for Justices Harlan, Pitney, Peckham, and Lamar over an eight-year period and that he later worked for Chief Justice Charles Evans Hughes. "J. E. Hoover Rites to Be Here Today," *Washington Post* (May 4, 1954). Supreme Court records list Hoover as a clerk for only Harlan, Peckham, and Lamar, however, so there is some confusion whether Hoover or Widdifield holds the record for clerking for the most justices. J. E. Hoover is likely the same John E. Hoover who later worked for the Department of Justice and was a cousin of J. Edgar Hoover.

130. Widdifield to Black, August 12, 1937, Hugo L. Black Papers, Box 442, Manuscript Division, Library of Congress.

131. "Former Aide of Supreme Court Dies," *Washington Post*, sec. B (Oct. 2, 1960).

132. Danelski and Tulchin, Autobiographical Notes, 163.

133. Melvin L. Urofsky and David W. Levy, eds., *The Letters of Louis D. Brandeis*, vol. 5 (Albany: State University of New York Press, 1975): 268.

134. Ibid., 509.

135. Ibid. Brandeis did not have the ironclad rule against married law clerks.

136. Ibid., 320.

137. William Sutherland, Louis Brandeis' second law clerk, also served for two years. His first law clerk was Calvert Magruder, who would later serve as a federal appeals court judge. In a March 25, 1920, letter to Thomas Nelson Perkins, Brandeis writes: "[Magruder] has a good legal mind and good working habits—and is a right-minded Southern gentleman. He is not of extraordinary ability or brilliant or of unusual scholarship, but he has stability." Ibid., 454.

138. Even after the construction of the Supreme Court building, Brandeis and his law clerks continued to work at home. Justice and Mrs. Brandeis later moved to a second apartment building on California Street in Washington. Paul A. Freund, "Justice Brandeis: A Law Clerk's Remembrance," *American Jewish History* 68 (1978): 7–18.

139. Dean Acheson, *Morning and Noon* (Boston: Houghton Mifflin Company, 1965): 57–58. In 1920, Congress authorized the justices to employ both a law clerk and a stenographic assistant. Unlike many of the other justices, Brandeis did not hire either a secretary or a second law clerk. "Why Brandeis dispensed with secretarial aid was never explained, but I surmise that he was loath to share the confidences of the office more widely than the absolute minimum. That, and perhaps his general avoidance of belongings." Freund, "A Law Clerk's Remembrance," 9.

140. Acheson, *Morning and Noon*, 58. Acheson is mistaken in lumping together the Holmes and Brandeis clerkship models; while Justice Brandeis may have sought the "constant refreshment and challenge" of a recent law school graduate, Justice Holmes wanted a refreshed audience, not an audience that challenged him.

141. Ibid., 80.

142. James Landis served as commissioner of the Federal Trade Commission, chairman of the Security and Exchange Commission, dean of Harvard Law School, and White House counsel to President John F. Kennedy. Landis suffered a dramatic reversal in his personal and professional fortunes in later years, culminating in a conviction for tax evasion and his accidental drowning.

143. James M. Landis, "Mr. Justice Brandeis: A Law Clerk's View," *American Jewish Historical Society* (1957): 468.

144. Acheson, *Morning and Noon*, 96–97. See also, Freund, "A Law Clerk's Remembrance," 10: "Never in my experience did Brandeis invite the law clerk's view concerning how a case should be decided—that was distinctly the judge's responsibility—but the law clerk's ideas about the structure and content of the opinion were highly welcome."

145. Acheson, *Morning and Noon*, 80–81.

146. Ibid., 80. Freund writes that "On occasion some sentences in the law clerk's memoranda would find their way into the opinion; more often they suffered the fate of the Justice's own first drafts—radical revision, transposition, strengthening and polishing." Freund, "A Law Clerk's Remembrance," 10.

147. Paul A. Freund, "Mr. Justice Brandeis: A Centennial Memoir," *Harvard Law Review* 70, no. 5 (Mar. 1957): 776.

148. Acheson, *Morning and Noon*, 81.

149. Landis, "A Law Clerk's View," 468.

150. Freund, "A Centennial Memoir," 776.

151. Acheson, *Morning and Noon*, 82.

152. Landis, "A Law Clerk's View," 468. Landis describes a research project that required that he review every page of sixty-odd years of Senate journals. Ibid., 471.

153. Acheson, *Morning and Noon*, 49.

154. Ibid. Assisting at the Brandeis' teas appears to be a duty of all the justice's law clerks. Landis writes that he assisted at both teas and dinners, and his duties included making sure "both that the guests were served and that the Justice should not be cornered too long by anyone of them." Landis, "A Law Clerk's View," 470. For the evening functions, Landis also was responsible for guaranteeing that the Brandeis' guests left at 10:00 P.M.—any failure in this duty would result in an "accusing" stare from Mrs. Brandeis.

155. Acheson, *Morning and Noon*, 62, 63.

156. Urofsky and Levy, *Letters of Louis D. Brandeis*, 510.

157. Ibid., 359.

158. Ibid., 359, 360.

159. Ibid., 404.

160. Ibid., 98.

161. Ibid., 358.

162. "Reed Secretary to McReynolds," *Washington Post* (Oct. 24, 1914).

163. Reed died in 1919 during a flu epidemic. His widow, Helana D. Reed, was a graduate of Washington College of Law and later became an assistant U.S. attorney. "Washington Woman Named an Assistant U.S. Attorney," *Washington Post*, sec. B (Mar. 17, 1943).

164. "S. Milton Simpson, Lawyer Here, Dies," *Washington Post*, sec. B (May 30, 1965).

165. "T. E. Allison, Retired U.S. Attorney," *Washington Post*, sec. C (Oct. 31, 1974); "N. B. Frost Chosen Director of Bank," *Washington Post* (Apr. 19, 1930). In 1917, McReynolds hired a recent graduate of the University of Virginia School of Law—Newman Blaine Mallan. Other McReynolds clerks who likely were attorneys include Andrew P. Federline (OT 1921), Carlyle Baer (OT 1921), Tench T. Marye (OT 1921), and Ward Elgin Lattin (OT 1934). OT 1922 clerk James T. Fowler, Jr., was a graduate of Georgetown University Law Center, and OT 1935 clerk J. Allan Sherier was a graduate of George Washington University Law School.

166. Hutchinson and Garrow, *Forgotten Memoir*, xv, xvi, xviii.

167. Ibid., 10. In order to get the job, Knox lied about his ability to take dictation.

168. Ibid., 10, 110 fn 10.

169. Ibid., 11.

170. Ibid., 12, 13.

171. Ibid., 35, 36–37. Despite their warnings, Knox did arrange a meeting with Justices Brandeis and Cardozo. One can only imagine Brandeis' curiosity when a McReynolds law clerk asked to make a social call at his apartment!

172. Ibid., 17.

173. *P. J. Carlin Construction Co., et al. v. Heaney, et al.*, 299 U.S. 41 (1936).

174. Hutchinson and Garrow, *Forgotten Memoir*, 132, 134, 136.

175. In fact, Jacob combined his secretarial duties with a busy law school schedule. During the 1910 school year he served as class secretary, and in his second and

third year of studies he was a yearbook editor, member of the Morris Law Club, chancellor of the student group "The Tredecium," and founder of the *Georgetown Law Journal*. For his efforts, Jacob was voted both "Most Popular Man in Class" and "Man Who Has Done the Most for the Class." Information provided by Georgetown University Law Center, Office of the Registrar.

176. "Off for Lurton Home: Family Leaves Atlantic City with Justice's Body," *Washington Post* (July 14, 1914); "Lurton's Wishes Granted," *Washington Post* (Aug. 23, 1914).

177. Hoyt Landon Warner, *The Life of Mr. Justice Clarke: A Testament to the Power of Liberal Dissent in America* (Cleveland: Western Reserve University Press, 1950): 76 (citing interview with former clerk S. Edward Widdifield).

178. On September 26, 1922, Justice Clarke gave a talk to the Cleveland Bar Association on the subject of "Methods of Work of the United States Supreme Court Judges." He mentioned neither law clerks in general nor his own law clerks.

179. Repath to Van Devanter, November 14 and 22, 1916, and January 31, 1917, Willis Van Devanter Papers, General Correspondence File, Manuscript Division, Library of Congress.

180. Edw. F. Henderson to Van Devanter, April 18, 1929, Van Devanter Papers, Files G–L.

181. Mattson to Van Devanter, July 25, 1929, Van Devanter Papers, Files M–S.

182. Mattson to Van Devanter, June 21, 1929, ibid.

183. "W. R. Stansbury, 71, 45 Years Supreme Court Officer, Dies," *Washington Post* (June 6, 1927).

184. "United States Supreme Court," *New York Times* (Feb. 21, 1928).

NOTES TO CHAPTER 4

1. 41 Stat. 209 (July 19, 1919).

2. Chester A. Newland, "Personal Assistants to Supreme Court Justices: The Law Clerks," *Oregon Law Review* 40, no. 4 (June 1961): 303. See 41 Stat. 686–87 (May 29, 1920).

3. Newland, "Personal Assistants," 303.

4. See, generally, the websites of National Association of Legal Assistants (www.nationalparalegal.org) and National Federation of Paralegal Associations (www.paralegals.org).

5. C. Dickerman Williams, "The 1924 Term: Recollections of Chief Justice Taft's Law Clerk," *Supreme Court Historical Society Yearbook* (1989): 40–51. Charles Dickerman Williams was the editor-in-chief of the Yale Law Review and graduated magna cum laude from Yale Law School. After clerking for Chief Justice Taft, Williams served as an assistant U.S. attorney and a partner in the New York law firm of Maclay & Williams.

6. John J. Byrne to Taft, July 6, 1921, William Howard Taft Papers, Reel 229, Manuscript Division, Library of Congress.

7. "Liquor Prosecution to Be Decentralized: Stone Appoints Regional Prosecutor for New England," *Washington Post* (July 30, 1924).

8. Taft to Thomas Swan, May 30, 1924, Taft Papers, Reel 265.

9. Taft to Thomas Swan, May 17, 1924, Taft Papers, Reel 264.

10. Thomas Swan to Taft, May 21, 1924, Taft Papers, Reel 265.

11. Swan to Taft, May 24, 1924, Reel 265.

12. Taft to Swan, May 26, 1924, Reel 265.

13. Taft to Swan, May 31, 1924, Reel 265.

14. Williams, "Recollections," 40. Taft provided a similar description of a clerk's responsibilities: "I have a law clerk who goes over the records and briefs. He makes a statement for me of what is in each, and then with that statement before me I read the briefs and make such references to the records as seem necessary. But I always read the briefs so as to know what the claim on both sides is, and then I read the opinions of the courts below so I become familiar with the case and know what the issues are. When these petitions for review come before us we know what the cases are about, and whether they present questions we should pass upon." Allen E. Ragan, *Chief Justice Taft* (Columbus: Ohio State Archaeological and Historical Society, 1939): 112.

15. Williams, "Recollections," 41.

16. Taft to Williams, August 20, 1924, Taft Papers, Reel 267.

17. Williams to Taft, September 5, 1924, Taft Papers, Reel 267.

18. Taft to Williams, September 9, 1924, Taft Papers, Reel 267.

19. Ragan, *Chief Justice Taft*, 112.

20. "Secretary to Prof Taft," *Washington Post* (Feb. 11, 1913).

21. "Taft Secretary Acquainted Here," *Sandusky Star Journal* (July 23, 1921).

22. "The Greatest of Globe Trotters for Humanity," *Wichita Daily Times* (July 17, 1921). An autographed picture that Taft gave Mischler bore the following inscription: "To my dear friend and indispensable co-worker, Wendell W. Mischler, a model in accuracy, foresight, intelligence, and loyalty, without whose aid I could not do half the work I do." *The Marion Star*, "Ohioan Served Two Chief Justices" (June 6, 1941).

23. Charles P. Taft, "My Father the Chief Justice," *Supreme Court Historical Society Yearbook* (1977). Charles Taft does not elaborate on how Mischler assisted the chief justice.

24. Williams, "Recollections," 43.

25. Ibid., 48.

26. Williams' successor was Thomas Hayden Smith, a Phi Beta Kappa graduate of Yale University who Dean Swan described as "a tall, good looking chap, very quiet in manner and emulates the honored President of the United States [Calvin Coolidge] in not wasting words" (Swan to Taft, February 17, 1925, Taft Papers, Reel 271). Smith was succeeded by William Winslow Crosskey, who the Yale Law School faculty considered "having the best mind of any man in the School" (Swan to Taft, December 4, 1925, Taft Papers, Reel 278). Taft selected Leighton Surbeck rather than Herbert Brownell, Jr. (both men recommended by Dean Swan) as his OT 1927 clerk. Brownell would later serve as the chair of the Republican National Committee and as attorney general in the Eisenhower administration.

27. Urofsky and Levy, *Letters of Louis D. Brandeis*, 403.

28. Taft Papers, Reel 303.

29. Parsons to Taft, July 3, 1929, Taft Papers, Reel 312.

30. Taft to Parsons, July 9, 1928, Taft Papers, Reel 312.

31. To date, I have not unearthed any historical data regarding the hiring and utilization practices of Justice Sutherland. Justice Edward Sanford employed William R. Loney for seven years. After Sanford's death, Loney tried unsuccessfully to get a permanent position with Justice Roberts. Newland, "Personal Assistants," 303.

32. It is commonly believed that all of Stone's law clerks came from Columbia University Law School—which is not surprising, given his prior position as the law school's dean. Alfred McCormack, "A Law Clerk's Recollections," *Columbia Law Review* 46, no. 5 (Sept. 1946): 710–18. While the majority of Stone's law clerks did come from Columbia, three clerks—Roger Cogswell, Bennett Boskey, and Milton Handler—graduated from Harvard Law School.

33. William O. Douglas biographer Bruce Allen Murphy writes that Douglas was a Columbia Law student at the time of Stone's nomination, and Douglas was sure he would be chosen to be Stone's first clerk. When McCormack was selected, Douglas was devastated. Bruce Allen Murphy, *Wild Bill: The Legend and Life of William O. Douglas* (New York: Random House, 2003): 51.

34. Warner W. Gardner, "Harlan Fiske Stone: The View from Below," *The Supreme Court Historical Society Quarterly* 22 (2001): 10.

35. Wilbur Friedman, interview with author.

36. Lauson H. Stone, "My Father the Chief Justice," *Supreme Court Historical Society Yearbook* (1978): 15.

37. Louis Lusky, interview with author.

38. With a few exceptions, since the 1940s justices have routinely selected new clerks on a yearly basis. Although the justice/principal suffers from the loss of experienced clerks at the end of the term, from the risk of hiring a new, unknown agent/clerk, and from the cost of training that agent, arguably the limited tenure prevents agents from consolidating power and pursuing their own goals.

39. Lusky, interview. Stone biographer Alpheus Mason writes: "Since 1925 [Stone's law clerks] had been selected by him annually from a group nominated by Dean Young B. Smith and Professor Noel T. Dowling of the Columbia Law School." Alpheus Thomas Mason, *Harlan Fiske Stone: Pillar of the Law* (New York: Viking Press, 1956): 646.

40. Warner W. Gardner, interview with author.

41. Friedman, interview. Lauson H. Stone writes that his father always depended on the dean of Columbia Law School to select a law clerk. Stone, "My Father the Chief Justice," 14.

42. Lusky, interview.

43. Alpheus Thomas Mason, *Harlan Fiske Stone: Pillar of the Law* (New York: The Viking Press, 1956): 646.

44. Ibid.

45. Milton C. Handler, "Clerking for Justice Harlan Fiske Stone," *Journal of Supreme Court History* (1995): 113.

46. Friedman, interview.

47. Gardner and Lusky, interviews.

48. Bennett Boskey, interview with author.

49. Friedman, interview.

50. "Memorandum by Howard C. Westwood," October 30, 1947, Personal Papers of Harlan Fiske Stone, Box 48, Manuscript Division, Library of Congress.

51. Gardner, Lusky, and Bennett, interviews.

52. Gardner and Boskey, interviews.

53. Gardner, "The View from Below," 8.

54. Handler, "Clerking for Justice Harlan Fiske Stone," 115.

55. Ibid., 116.
56. Gardner, "The View from Below," 8.
57. *Alaska Packers Assn. v. Industrial Accident Comm'n*, 294 U.S. 532 (1935).
58. Handler, "Clerking for Justice Harlan Fiske Stone," 114.
59. Stone Papers, Box 48, Library of Congress.
60. Mason, *Pillar of the Law*, 214.
61. Handler, "Clerking for Justice Harlan Fiske Stone," 114.
62. Mason, *Pillar of the Law*, 215.
63. Gardner, interview.
64. "Westwood Memorandum," Stone Papers, Box 48.
65. Mason, *Pillar of the Law*, 216.
66. McCormack, "Law Clerk's Recollections," 717.
67. Handler, "Clerking for Justice Harlan Fiske Stone," 121.
68. Friedman, interview.
69. Donnelly to Black, August 27, 1937, Black Papers, Box 442.
70. "William D. Donnelly, Former D.C. Lawyer," *Washington Post*, sec. C (Mar. 12, 1975).
71. Hutchinson and Garrow, *Forgotten Memoir*, xxi. Yale Law School did not begin placing significant numbers of its graduates on the Supreme Court until the 1950s.
72. David J. Danelski and Joseph S. Tulchin, eds., *The Autobiographical Notes of Charles Evans Hughes* (Cambridge, Mass.: Harvard University Press, 1973): 323.
73. Edwin McElwain, "The Business of the Supreme Court as Conducted by Chief Justice Hughes," *Harvard Law Review* 63, no. 1 (Nov. 1949): 12.
74. Ibid., 15–16.
75. Ibid., 18, 19.
76. "In writing his own opinions, the Chief . . . re-examined his combined set of notes plus any memoranda he might have made on points emphasized in the conference. Then he outlined the points he would cover in his opinion and the order in which he would deal with them. His writing began only after this pattern had taken definite shape in his mind and he had thought out precisely what he wished to say. A first draft was then scratched out in longhand with little regard for paraphrasing or any refinements." Merlo Pusey, *Charles Evans Hughes*, vol. 2 (New York: Macmillan, 1951): 679.
77. Ibid., 667.
78. Executive Order 7,751 (Nov. 23, 1937): "Roosevelt Waives 70-Year Act, Holds Hughes Aid [*sic*] on Job," *Washington Post* (Nov. 24, 1937).
79. Felix Frankfurter Papers, Reel 9, Harvard Law School. Shupienis was a lawyer and a member of the District of Columbia Bar.
80. "William Loney Dead; Formed 1st Boys Club," *Washington Post*, sec. B (Dec. 11, 1956).
81. "2 Men Conclude 74 Years as Official Reporters for House," *Washington Post*, sec. A (Oct. 24, 1965).
82. Andrew L. Kaufman, *Cardozo* (Cambridge, Mass.: Harvard University Press, 1998): 473, 474.
83. Law clerk Alan Stroock stayed a second year because of Cardozo's first heart attack and subsequent request that Stroock remain and spare Cardozo the stress of training a new clerk. Alan Stroock, interview with Andrew L. Kaufman.

84. Kaufman, *Cardozo*, 474.

85. Stroock was selected by Yale Law School professor Charles Clark. Stroock, interview.

86. Ambrose Doskow, interview with Andrew L. Kaufman.

87. Joseph Rauh, interview with Andrew L. Kaufman.

88. Kaufman, *Cardozo*, 480.

89. Rauh, interview.

90. Ibid.

91. Ibid.

92. Kaufman, *Cardozo*, 481. Rauh recalls an instance in which he was thrilled because one sentence from his memorandum was used in Cardozo's subsequent opinion. Rauh, interview.

93. Stroock, interview.

94. Rauh, interview.

95. Joseph L. Rauh, Jr., Melvin Siegel, Ambrose Doskow, and Alan M. Stroock, "A Personal View of Justice Benjamin N. Cardozo: Recollections of Four Cardozo Law Clerks," *Cardozo Law Review* 1 (Spring 1979): 6.

96. Doskow, interview.

97. Rauh, interview.

98. Rauh et al., "A Personal View of Justice Benjamin N. Cardozo," 6.

99. Kaufman, *Cardozo*, 481.

100. Rauh et al., "A Personal View of Justice Benjamin N. Cardozo," 6 fn 1, 7, 11.

101. Doskow, interview.

102. On April 20, 1965, retired justice Stanley Reed swore in Harold Leventhal as a federal appeals court judge. "Leventhal Sworn by Justice Reed," *Washington Post*, sec. A (Apr. 21, 1965). Leventhal had previously served as general counsel to the Democratic National Committee.

103. Unlike today's Supreme Court law clerks, lower court clerkships were a rarity at this time.

104. John T. Sapienza, interview with author.

105. Ibid.

106. Roderick Hills, interview and correspondence with author.

107. Sapienza, interview.

108. The law clerks included John T. Sapienza (OT 1938), Bennett Boskey (OT 1940), David Schwartz (OT 1942), F. Aley Allan (OT 1946), Robert Von Mehren (OT 1947), Mac Asbill, Jr. (OT 1948), Joseph Barbash and Bayless Manning (OT 1949), Adam Yarmolinsky and Edwin M. Zimmerman (OT 1950), George B. Mickum III (OT 1953), Gordon B. Davidson (OT 1954), Julian Burke and Roderick M. Hills (OT 1955), and Arthur I. Rosett (OT 1959).

109. F. Aley Allan, Joseph Barbash, Bennett Boskey, Bayless Manning, George B. Mickum III, David Schwartz, Robert Von Mehren, Adam Yarmolinsky, and Edwin Zimmerman, interviews with *Stanley Forman Reed Oral History Project*, University of Kentucky.

110. Julian Burke, interview with *Stanley Forman Reed Oral History Project*, University of Kentucky (emphasis added).

111. In correspondence with this author, Hills was more specific: "We were seldom asked to draft an opinion—only once in two years [as I] was leaving did the

justice do so and left my draft mostly intact in a minor case." Former law clerk Gordon Davidson stated that the law clerks "prepared first drafts in only a very few cases. Generally Justice Reed prepared first draft and clerks reviewed it and made suggestions." Gordon B. Davidson, correspondence with author.

112. Burke, interview with Oral History Project.

113. Von Mehren, Zimmerman, Barbash, and Asbill, interviews with Oral History Project. Asbill recalls that often the clerks would request to prepare the first draft of opinions in cases that interested them. Asbill concludes that clerk and justice "sort of shared, on a very informal basis, in the . . . writing task." While Boskey states that Reed wrote more opinion drafts than his fellow justices, his clerks would prepare drafts of portions of opinions. Boskey could remember only one case in which he, the clerk, prepared the *entire* draft of a majority opinion (*Best & Co. v. Maxwell, Commissioner of Revenue for North Carolina*).

114. Von Mehren, interview with Oral History Project.

115. William D. Rogers, correspondence with author.

116. Barbash and Zimmerman, interviews with Oral History Project.

117. Newland, "Personal Assistants," 304.

118. Manning, interview with Oral History Project.

119. Boskey, interview with Oral History Project.

120. Von Mehren, interview with Oral History Project.

121. Barbash, interview with Oral History Project. At least a few of Reed's law clerks took the justice's distaste for "yes men" to heart. In describing his relationship to Justice Reed, former clerk Julian Burke commented that his coworker, Roderick Hills, was "very interested in trying to change [Reed's] mind." Burke, interview with Oral History Project.

122. Hills, interview with Oral History Project. Former clerk Asbill succinctly adds that Frankfurter would "frequently try to persuade Reed to his point of view, and if he couldn't persuade him, he'd try to persuade his law clerks and get them to persuade him."

123. Apparently Justice Frankfurter also used his law clerks for intelligence gathering. According to former Douglas law clerk Vern Countryman, during OT 1942 Frankfurter's law clerk "would come snooping around my office trying to find out what the hell Douglas was going to do on a particular case. And then I finally told Douglas, 'We've got to watch this guy.' So Douglas prepared a fake opinion, and I carefully left it on my desk, went away, and came back, and [the Frankfurter law clerk] was sitting in my office. And I know he read that goddamned opinion . . . Frankfurter must have thought for a while that he knew how Douglas was going to come out of it, and [Douglas]went to the other side." Murphy, *Wild Bill*, 204–205.

124. Schwartz, interview with Oral History Project.

125. Von Mehren, interview with Oral History Project.

126. Hills, correspondence.

127. Leonard Baker, *Brandeis and Frankfurter: A Dual Biography* (New York: Harper & Row, 1984): 415; William T. Coleman, Jr., Louis Henkin, and anonymous Frankfurter law clerk, interviews with author.

128. Andrew Kaufman, correspondence with author.

129. Frankfurter to Stanley Silverberg, March 13, 1943, Felix Frankfurter Papers, Reel 9, Harvard Law School.

130. "I think I ought to add that not only have I given you an unqualified power of appointment, but my experience with your exercise of it is such that I am quite happy to put that power into your hands. Each year the men are so good in their varying ways that I say to myself that Henry and Mary won't be able to do as well next year, but you always come up with trumps." Frankfurter to Henry M. Hart, Jr., April 14, 1952, Henry M. Hart, Jr. Papers, Box 4, Harvard Law School.

131. In fact, Frankfurter embraced qualified, diverse candidates. Kaufman remarks: "I remember how pleased [Frankfurter] was when Al Sacks appointed John Mansfield. He was happy to have a Catholic law clerk at last and said so." Kaufman, correspondence.

132. Felix Frankfurter Papers, Reel 9, Harvard Law School.

133. Ibid.

134. Katharine Graham, *Personal History* (New York: Knopf, 1997): 118. Luckily for the couple, Justice Frankfurter was "'heartily in favor' of the union." Ibid.

135. Tracy Campbell. *Short of the Glory: The Fall and Redemption of Edward F. Prichard, Jr.* (University of Kentucky Press, 1998).

136. Baker, *Brandeis and Frankfurter*, 415.

137. Kaufman took issue with my description of the relationship between Frankfurter and his law clerks being the equivalent of an athletic competition, pointing out that the justice and his law clerks were not equal competitors in regards to intellectual ability. He added, however, that Frankfurter treated his clerks as equals. Kaufman, correspondence.

138. Baker, *Brandeis and Frankfurter*, 415.

139. Michael E. Parrish, "Justice Frankfurter and the Supreme Court," in Jennifer M. Lowe, ed., *The Jewish Justices of the Supreme Court Revisited: Brandeis to Fortas* (Washington, D.C.: Supreme Court Historical Society, 1994): 67.

140. Baker, *Brandeis and Frankfurter*, 415. Kaufman notes that the opinion was *Galvan v. Press*, 347 U.S. 522 (1954).

141. Baker, *Brandeis and Frankfurter*, 416. Former Frankfurter law clerk E. Barrett Prettyman, Jr., established a record likely to remain unbroken among modern law clerks: he clerked for three Supreme Court justices. Prettyman clerked for Justice Robert H. Jackson during OT 1953 and had committed to a second term when Jackson suddenly died on October 9, 1954. Prettyman became Frankfurter's third law clerk while the confirmation of John Marshall Harlan was pending and became Harlan's law clerk in March 1955. Either during his brief clerkship with Frankfurter or shortly thereafter, Barrett Prettyman drafted a memorandum to Justice Frankfurter—at the justice's request—discussing those opinions from OT 1952, 1953, and 1954 "which you have written and which I would not have written." Regarding Frankfurter's concurring opinion in *May v. Anderson* [345 U.S. 528 (1953)], Prettyman states: "If what you said in this opinion is true, it should have been in the majority opinion. By writing this, did you really clarify the ground for decision or only muddy the water?" While a Frankfurter law clerk, Prettyman also drafted memoranda regarding circulating opinions written by other justices. E. Barrett Prettyman, Jr., Papers, Box No. 1, Special Collections, University of Virginia Law Library.

142. Harry Wellington, interview with author.

143. Andrew Kaufman, "The Justice and His Law Clerks," in Wallace Mendelson, ed., *Felix Frankfurter, the Judge* (New York: Reynal, 1964): 224.

144. Kaufman,correspondence.The notes are contained in Frankfurter's personal papers, bearing the title "To be passed on and kept up to date." Felix Frankfurter Papers.

145. In view of the limited responsibilities granted to the Frankfurter clerks, as well as the strong, personal relationship between the justice and his law clerks, I would have expected to find few rules or practices designed to prevent the agent/ clerk from violating the duty owed to the justice/principal.

146. Coleman and Henkin, interviews; Kaufman, Irving Helman (OT 1947)and John D. French (OT 1960), correspondence with author.

147. Kaufman,correspondence. Former law clerk French states that he prepared only a few bench memoranda during OT 1960. French, correspondence.

148. Helman (OT 1947) specifically states that he did not prepare bench memoranda. Helman, correspondence.

149. Henkin and Coleman, interviews.

150. Prettyman, interview. Louis Henkin recalled preparing the first draft in only one minor case, while Coleman never was called upon to draft an opinion. Henkin and Coleman, interviews. Helman stated that he prepared only first drafts of dissenting opinions. Helman, correspondence. Alternatively, former law clerk John D. French writes that during OT 1960 preparing first drafts of opinions "was a major responsibility. I did a number of first drafts of opinions. The Justice would meet with me, describe his position, and explain his reasoning. I then prepared a draft, which he reviewed, and modified it as he requested." French, correspondence. Kaufman states that he also prepared some first drafts of opinions during his two years with Justice Frankfurter. Kaufman, correspondence. There is not enough data from Frankfurter's final years on the Court to determine whether French's job duties were an aberration in the justice's clerkship model or a change, perhaps dictated by poor health.

151. Frankfurter chamber rules, Frankfurter Papers.

152. Kaufman, interview.

153. Fred Fishman Papers, Harvard Law School. Fishman was a partner at the New York law firm Kaye Scholer and served as president of the Bar Association of New York City. Albert Sacks worked briefly at the law firm of Covington & Burling, leaving private practice to teach at Harvard Law School. From 1971 to 1981, Sacks served as dean of Harvard Law School.

154. At least most were. Author Tracy Campbell recounts an astonishing story in which current law clerk Edward Prichard, Jr., dismayed over Justice Frankfurter's opinion draft in *Minersville School District v. Gobitis*, showed the draft to former law clerk Joseph L. Rauh, Jr., in hopes that Rauh would persuade Frankfurter to change his position. Campbell, *Short of the Glory*, 65–67.

155. A Virginia native, Claytor returned to his home state after his clerkship and became president of the Southern Railway.

156. Frankfurter Papers, Reel 6.

157. Ibid.

158. Frankfurter's lifelong interpretation of the clerkship meant that he had no reservations about advising at least one former law clerk about matters that later came before the Supreme Court. See Philip Elman, "The Solicitor General's Office, Justice Frankfurter and Civil Rights Litigation, 1946–1960: An Oral History," *Har-*

vard Law Review 100, no. 4 (Feb. 1987): 817–44; Norman I. Silber, *With All Deliberate Speed: The Life of Philip Elman* (Ann Arbor: University of Michigan Press, 2004).

159. Andrew L. Kaufman, "Constitutional Law and the Supreme Court: Frankfurter and Wellington," *New York Law School Law Review* 45 (2001): 141. The Prettyman papers contain copies of a few memos written by Prettyman to the justice.

160. Kaufman, *Frankfurter and Wellington*, 142.

161. Kaufman, "The Justice and His Law Clerks," 225.

162. Campbell, *Short of the Glory*, 64–65.

163. Kaufman, correspondence.

164. Kaufman, "The Justice and His Law Clerks," 225–26.

165. Fishman Papers, Harvard Law School.

166. Irving J. Helman Papers, Box 1, Harvard Law School.

167. The 1959 reunion dinner for Justice Frankfurter and his law clerks was held in the Tamerlaine Room of the Shoreham Hotel in Washington, D.C. The dinner included shrimp cocktail, cream of mushroom soup, roast beef, string beans, potatoes au gratin, a mixed green salad, and baked Alaska. Beverages included Manhattans, martinis, Scotch, and bourbon before dinner, a glass of sherry for each participant at the start of dinner, red wine served with the roast beef, Scotch and bourbon after dinner, and champagne with dessert. No wonder Frankfurter's law clerks were nicknamed "Felix's Happy Hotdogs."

168. Fishman Papers, Harvard Law School.

169. Eugene Gressman, correspondence and interview with author.

170. Sidney Fine, *Frank Murphy: The Washington Years* (Ann Arbor: University of Michigan Press, 1984): 163.

171. Gressman, interview.

172. Fine, *Frank Murphy*, 161. See also, J. Woodford Howard, Jr., *Mr. Justice Murphy: A Political Biography* (Princeton, N.J.: Princeton University Press, 1968). Justice Murphy selected his law clerks based on their ties to the University of Michigan, their writing skills, and their political beliefs. Ibid., 474.

173. Fine, *Frank Murphy*, 161.

174. Eugene Gressman, correspondence with author.

175. From 1943 to 1948, Murphy's law clerk was responsible for the first draft of all opinions, whether majority or dissenting. Gressman, interview. Regarding areas of law that did not interest Murphy, the law clerk also was charged with learning the applicable law.

176. Fine, *Frank Murphy*, 161.

177. Gressman, correspondence.

178. Fine, *Frank Murphy*, 162 (emphasis added). Another Murphy biographer is more reticent about drawing conclusions about the role of the law clerks. While J. Woodford Howard, Jr., agrees that Murphy "undoubtedly gave his aides a larger role in opinion writing and negotiations than was customary," Howard concludes: "[w]hether his reliance on clerks was excessive is difficult to answer because working methods are personal and because average practice is shrouded in mystery. . . . Consistency of writing style, as well as the protests of Murphy's clerks about the matter, suggest the reverse." Howard, *Mr. Justice Murphy*, 474.

179. Fine, *Frank Murphy*, 162.

180. Howard, *Mr. Justice Murphy*, 243 fn B.

181. Joyce Murdoch and Deb Price, *Courting Justice: Gay Men and Lesbians v. the Supreme Court* (New York: Basic Books, 2001): 19–21. Gressman utterly rejects such allegations about Justice Murphy and Kemp.

182. Howard, *Mr. Justice Murphy*, 242.

183. Fine concludes that Murphy himself was cognizant that Kemp's involvement was problematic, citing his chamber's practice of routinely destroying notes that Kemp made regarding pending cases. Fine, *Frank Murphy*, 164.

184. Gressman, correspondence.

185. Kemp was not the only Court outsider to provide Murphy with advice and assistance. Howard writes that Murphy occasionally sought the assistance of former law clerks in drafting judicial opinions. Howard, *Mr. Justice Murphy*, 459. See also, Fine, *Frank Murphy*, 164–65.

186. Gressman, interview.

187. Fine, *Frank Murphy*, 162. Longtime Murphy law clerk Eugene Gressman states that Murphy didn't always agree with Gressman's recommendations. Gressman, interview.

188. "Remembering U.S. Supreme Court Justice Frank Murphy, '14." *Law Quadrangle News* (Winter 2005): 41–44.

189. Douglas to Max Radin, May 27, 1946. Melvin I. Urofsky, ed., *The Douglas Letters: Selections from the Private Papers of Justice William O. Douglas* (Bethesda, Md.: Adler & Adler, 1987): 46.

190. William O. Douglas, *The Court Years, 1939–1975: The Autobiography of William O. Douglas* (New York: Random House, 1980): 170–71. In the 1940s and 1950s, former Douglas law clerk C. David Ginsburg also informally assisted Douglas in selecting clerks. David Ginsburg, interview with author.

191. It appears that the selection committee was given absolute power over the selection decision. In a February 18, 1947, letter to Professor Max Radin, Douglas writes: "On the selection of my law clerk, you have all the voting power. I don't even have a veto. That's the way I wish it." Urofsky, *Douglas Letters*, 48.

192. Ibid., 47.

193. Ginsburg, interview.

194. Urofsky, *Douglas Letters*, 171. In a 1940 letter to Harvard Law School student Richard M. Biddell, Douglas wrote: "I would like to be able to consider your application but I cannot for the following reason: I am taking each year a graduate of one of the law schools in the Ninth Circuit. . . . I do not feel that I should depart from my policy by taking a graduate from one of the eastern schools, no matter how well qualified the man is." Ibid., 46.

195. Douglas to Stanley Sparrowe, January 19, 1956. Urofsky, *Douglas Letters*, 50.

196. Douglas to Stanley Sparrowe, June 13, 1950. Ibid., 49.

197. Carol Bruch, correspondence and interview with author.

198. William O. Douglas Papers, Box 1118, Library of Congress.

199. The leash was kept short. "But the Justice was willing to entrust a first draft of a minor opinion to less capable hands only when he had thoroughly explained his position and had clearly marked the path to be followed. Even then, the finished product might bear less than a family resemblance to my first efforts." William Cohen, "Justice Douglas: A Law Clerk's View," *The University of Chicago Law Review* 26, no. 1 (Autumn 1958): 6–8. Former law clerk Carol Bruch believes, however, that in

the 1970s the law clerks were given more significant opportunities to prepare opinion drafts. Bruch, correspondence and interview.

200. Former law clerk William Cohen observes that during the 1950s, Douglas wrote nine books: *Of Men and Mountains* (1950), *Strange Lands and Friendly People* (1951), *North from Malaya* (1953), *An Almanac of Liberty* (1954), *Beyond the High Himalayas* (1955), *We the Judges* and *Russian Journey* (1956), and *The Right of the People* and *West of the Indus* (1958).

201. George Rutherglen, Ginsburg, and Bruch, interviews with author; David Ginsburg, "Reflections of Justice Douglas' First Law Clerk," *Harvard Law Review* 93, no. 7 (1980): 1403–15.

202. Ibid., 1405. Former law clerk William A. Reppy, Jr., recounts an occasion during his OT 1967 clerkship when he prepared a note to Douglas, suggesting a minor change to *Whitehill v. Elkins* [389 U.S. 54 (1967)]. "He reacted to my suggested addition to his opinion by giving me a serious dressing down. Only persons nominated by the President and confirmed by the Senate were to be writing Supreme Court opinions. I had been impertinent. . . . I retired to the clerk's office believing that I had been fired." The suggested change, however, was incorporated into footnote no. 2 of the majority opinion. William A. Reppy, Jr., "Remembrances of William O. Douglas on the 50th Anniversary of His Appointment to the Supreme Court," *Journal of Supreme Court History* (1990): 120–21. This vignette suggests that Douglas would still entertain substantive suggestions by his clerks, but only if the clerks first faced the justice's wrath by actually making the suggestion in the face of chamber norms that dictated otherwise.

203. Stanley E. Sparrowe, "W.O.D. and Me," *Remembrances of William O. Douglas by His Friends and Associates*, special anniversary booklet (1989): 60.

204. Cohen, *Justice Douglas*, 8.

205. Murphy, *Wild Bill*, 410.

206. Ibid., 201.

207. Ibid., 408, 411.

208. George Rutherglen, "A Recollection of OT, 1975," *Remembrances of William O. Douglas by His Friends and Associates*, special anniversary booklet (1989): 54. Former law clerk Carol Bruch describes Douglas as an individual "who dealt with people on a terror level" and who was "dreadful." She adds that Douglas was a brusque, cold person who was not above petty behavior. Bruch recounted one instance in which Douglas required a secretary to come into the office on Christmas Day to take personal dictation and a second instance in which he needlessly kept the Court's print shop open on Christmas Eve. Bruch, correspondence and interview. Even the most diplomatic of former Douglas law clerks—former Secretary of State Warren Christopher—writes that Douglas was "distant and demanding." Warren Christopher, *Chances of a Lifetime: A Memoir* (New York: Scribner's, 2001): 21.

209. Fay Aull Deusterman, "W.O.D. Remembered," *Remembrances of William O. Douglas by His Friends and Associates*, special anniversary booklet (1989): 18.

210. Lucas A. Powe, Jr., "Rainy Days—Clear Principles," *Remembrances of William O. Douglas by His Friends and Associates*, special anniversary booklet (1989): 47.

211. Urofsky, *Douglas Letters*, 52.

212. Reppy, *Remembrances*.

213. Jerome B. Falk, Jr., "Recollections of O.T. 1965," *Remembrances of William O. Douglas by His Friends and Associates*, special anniversary booklet (1989): 21–22.

214. During the oral arguments for *Brown v. Board of Education*, former Douglas law clerk Charles Ares hid behind a pillar so the justice wouldn't see him. "Douglas clerks had to do this because their presence in Court during argument always seemed to pose a challenge to him. It meant that the clerk had run out of work and, since that was intolerable, a note with a research project would shortly arrive by one of the messengers." Charles E. Ares, "William O. Douglas: Remembrances of O.T. 1952," *Remembrances of William O. Douglas by His Friends and Associates*, special anniversary booklet (1989): 10. George Rutherglen refers to this pillar as "The Douglas Pillar."

215. Richard L. Jacobson, "The Shower," *Remembrances of William O. Douglas by His Friends and Associates*, special anniversary booklet (1989): 34–37.

216. Murphy, *Wild Bill*, 424–25.

217. Charles A. Miller, "Remembrances of Douglas in Mid-Term," *Remembrances of William O. Douglas by His Friends and Associates*, special anniversary booklet (1989): 45.

218. Yarmolinsky, interview with Stanley Reed Oral History Project.

219. Murphy, *Wild Bill*, 363.

220. Murphy writes: "Once, a clerk for another Justice watched in amazement as Douglas returned from the airport after putting his wife on a plane, only to proposition the wife of another clerk." Ibid., 427.

221. Ibid., 1404.

222. William Alsup, "Accurately Remembering Justice Douglas: A Reply to *Wild Bill* and Recent Critics," *The Federal Lawyer* (Nov.-Dec. 2003): 28.

223. Warren Christopher to William O. Douglas, June 18, 1970, Douglas Papers, Box 1118.

224. Daniel J. Meador, "Justice Black and His Law Clerks," *Alabama Law Review* 15, no. 1 (Fall 1962): 57.

225. Being a tennis player never hurt a candidate's chances, either. Justice Black had a tennis court in the backyard of his Alexandria home, which was the site of many doubles matches between Black, his law clerks, and invited guests.

226. Black to Burrell Ives Humphreys, August 12, 1952, Black Papers, Box 442, Library of Congress.

227. Hugo Black, Jr., *My Father: A Remembrance* (New York: Random House, 1975): 121. Of course, it helped if you also had an influential Alabama relative championing your cause. In explaining how he was selected as a Black law clerk, Luther Hill, Jr. (OT 1950) writes: "My uncle, Lister Hill, was a Senator from Alabama and gave my name to Hugo Black. It was the Senator's idea and Black picked me." Hill, correspondence with author.

228. David M. Clark, correspondence with author.

229. Larry Hammond, interview with author. Hammond's clerkship was interrupted by Black's final illness and resignation from the Supreme Court on September 17, 1971. After Black's death, Hammond and his co-clerk, Covert "Pete" Parnell, spent their free hours helping Mrs. Black write responses to sympathy cards, reading the *New York Times* "cover to cover," and playing basketball. Hammond also went with Mrs. Black to pick out an appropriate casket for the justice. Hammond recalls that the funeral director had difficulty believing that Mrs. Black really wanted a simple pine casket for the late justice. After his confirmation, Justice Lewis Powell hired the former Black law clerks.

230. Hugo Black, Jr., interview with author.

231. After his clerkship, David J. Vann briefly worked in a Birmingham, Alabama,

law firm before becoming involved in local politics. He served one term as the mayor of Birmingham.

232. Charles Reich, *The Sorcerer of Bolinas Reef* (New York: Random House, 1976): 25.

233. John P. Frank, *Inside Justice Hugo L. Black: The Letters* (Austin: Jamail Center for Legal Research, University of Texas at Austin, 2000): 23.

234. For example, in their joint memoirs Elizabeth Black writes that she assisted the justice in reviewing law clerk applications. (Black and Black, *Memoirs*, 153.) Mrs. Black writes that her recommendations were not always correct, pointing out that her recommendation of Margaret Corcoran—the second female law clerk—was a mistake. Ibid., 168.

235. Black biographer Howard Ball writes: "His clerks were chosen because he liked them as persons—and since he never interviewed clerk-applicants until he had tentatively chosen his new clerks, and since he rarely met a person he didn't like, he would offer the clerkship during his first meeting with the applicant." Ball, *Hugo L. Black: Cold Steel Warrior* (New York: Oxford University Press, 1996): 167.

236. Surprisingly, not all law students wanted to clerk on the Supreme Court. Former law clerk Truman Hobbs initially declined the opportunity to clerk for Black. After serving in World War II, Hobbs enrolled in Yale Law School at the advanced age of twenty-six. He learned through fellow Yale Law School student Hugo L. Black, Jr., that the elder Black wanted Hobbs as a law clerk—if the young man made law review. Hobbs subsequently declined law review membership, but Justice Black still wanted him. When Hobbs declined the clerkship offer—believing that he was "too old" and needed to start practicing law—Yale Law School dean Wesley A. Sturges demanded to see Hobbs and chewed him out, telling him "I don't care how old you are." Hobbs then accepted the clerkship offer. Truman Hobbs, interview with author.

237. Sturges to Black November 26, 1947, Black Papers, Box 442.

238. Hobbs, interview.

239. Meador, "Justice Black and His Law Clerks," 62 fn 5.

240. Hobbs, interview.

241. Daniel J. Meador, interview with author.

242. Black and Black, *Memoirs*, 234.

243. Black, *My Father*, 187.

244. Ibid. (emphasis added).

245. William Joslin, Hobbs, and Meador, interviews with author. Joslin recalled preparing only two to three draft opinions during his entire clerkship.

246. Meador, "Justice Black and His Law Clerks," 60. Hobbs recalled that Black would sometimes write ten drafts of an opinion before he was satisfied. Hobbs, interview. Explains John Frank: "The Justice had an everlasting interest in good, compact, and precise prose. . . . on the last draft of any opinion, we went over the text sentence by sentence, searching for more concise expression and grammatical precision." Frank, *Inside Justice Hugo L. Black*, 10–11.

247. Daniel J. Meador, *Mr. Justice Black and His Books* (Charlottesville: University Press of Virginia, 1974): 6.

248. A. E. Dick Howard, interview with author.

249. Hill, Hobbs, Joslin and Meador, interviews.

250. Clark, correspondence.

251. George Freeman, "Perspectives: Justice Hugo L. Black," *Richmond Times-Dispatch* (Dec. 12, 1971).

252. Meador, *Mr. Justice Black and His Books*, 17.

253. Black, *My Father*, 121.

254. Josephine Black Pesaresi, interview with author.

255. Meador, *Mr. Justice Black and His Books*, 13, 18, 23.

256. Black, interview. Former law clerk George C. Freeman recalls, upon discovering his mediocre tennis skills, Justice Black relieved Freeman of his Saturday obligations to review cert. petitions and sent him for tennis lessons at the Army-Navy Country Club. Freeman made up for his athletic deficiencies by playing bridge with Justice Black and teaching him the "Birmingham Hop," a popular dance step. Shelley Rolfe, "Justice Hugo Black: Two Former Law Clerks Recall One of the Court's Towering Figures," *Richmond Times-Dispatch*, sec. F (Dec. 12, 1971).

257. Ball, *Cold Steel Warrior*, 277 fn 226.

258. After his clerkship, Frank taught at both Indiana University School of Law and Yale Law School before joining the Arizona law firm of Lewis & Roca. Frank was the author of eleven books, lead counsel in *Miranda v. Arizona*, and an adviser to Anita Hill during the Clarence Thomas confirmation hearings.

259. In a 1949 letter, Frank offers his assessment of Justices Harold Burton and Tom Clark: "Burton is the most incompetent Sup. Ct. member since the 1840s . . . [and] Clark will outstrip even Burton in this regard, being totally incapable of performing any of the functions of his office and being required to delegate them completely to clerks." Frank to Black, November 12, 1949, Black Papers, Frank File, Box 460. Frank adds that Chief Justice Vinson "could not even make a pretense of handling his duties without a staff four times as large as that of Hughes," concluding that the only thing preventing the Supreme Court from collapse was the practice of "delegating much of the work to young fellows just out of law school who have no public responsibility and, however great their potentialities, are 20 years away from legal maturity." At the end of the letter, Frank asks for Black's permission to share the above observations with Frank's constitutional law class, prompting Black to defend both Clark and Burton and respond that such behavior by Frank would be "unwise." Black to Frank, November 17, 1949, Black Papers, Frank File, Box 460.

260. Black and Black, *Memoirs*, 136.

261. Newland, "Personal Assistants," 303.

262. Boskey, interview. I also corresponded with C. Roger Nelson, who clerked for Chief Justice Stone during OT 1941. Nelson's description of law clerk job duties corresponds with Boskey's. Nelson, correspondence.

263. Doyle was a native of Wisconsin and a graduate of Columbia Law School who worked at the Justice Department prior to clerking for Byrnes. After his clerkship and military service, he again worked for Byrnes when the former justice was director of War Mobilization. Doyle later returned to Wisconsin and became a federal judge after an unsuccessful run for the governor's office. His son, James Doyle, Jr., was elected governor of Wisconsin in 2003.

264. James Doyle Oral History, Wisconsin Historical Society, Tape 36, Side 1. On file in James Byrnes' personal papers at Clemson University is a June 13, 1941, letter from Philip Graham, law clerk to Felix Frankfurter during OT 1940. In it, Graham

reviews the names of several potential law clerks. Given Justice Frankfurter's afore-mentioned zeal for placing Harvard Law School graduates on the Supreme Court, it is odd that Graham's letter discusses Yale and Columbia Law School candidates.

265. James F. Byrnes Papers, Supreme Court Box 6, Clemson University.

266. James F. Byrnes, *All in One Lifetime* (New York: Harper, 1959): 139.

267. Robert H. Jackson Papers, Box 165, Manuscript Division, Library of Congress.

268. Ibid.

269. Phil C. Neal, correspondence with author.

270. William H. Rehnquist, *The Supreme Court* (New York: Knopf, 2001): 4.

271. Jackson Papers, Box 157. Cole later was a partner in the Washington, D.C., law firm of Cole & Groner and was chairman of the American Bar Association's Criminal Justice section.

272. James M. Marsh, correspondence with author.

273. James M. Marsh, "Supreme Court Justice Without a College Degree," *Philadelphia Lawyer* (1999): 63.

274. Rehnquist, *Supreme Court*, 4–5.

275. Marsh, correspondence.

276. Newland, "Personal Assistants," 304.

277. Marsh, correspondence.

278. Marsh and Neal, correspondence; Rehnquist, *Supreme Court*, 8.

279. Rehnquist, *Supreme Court*, 10.

280. Marsh, correspondence.

281. Rehnquist, *Supreme Court*, 10, 11.

282. James M. Marsh, "Affirm, If Possible: How a U.S. Supreme Court Justice's Confidence in His Clerk Turned a Tentative 5–4 Vote into an 8–1 Decision," *Philadelphia Lawyer* (1997): 62. Marsh worked on the case of *New York v. Saper* [336 U.S. 328 (1949)], in which his exhaustive legal research caused three justices—Frankfurter, Vinson, and Murphy—to switch their votes and side with Justice Jackson.

283. "Responsibility for Security and Work in the Office of Mr. Justice Jackson," Jackson Papers, Box 165.

284. Marsh and Neal, correspondence.

285. "Responsibility for Security," Jackson Papers, Box 165.

286. Ibid.

287. Ibid., Box 19.

288. Brudney graduated from the City College of New York before attending Columbia Law School.

289. John M. Ferren, *Salt of the Earth, Conscience of the Court: The Story of Justice Wiley Rutledge* (Chapel Hill: University of North Carolina Press, 2004): 227. Virginia Morsey Wheeler Talley never met Wiley Rutledge, but she believes she lost the clerkship because of Brudney's experience working in the solicitor general's office and not because of her gender. Talley expressed no regret that her clerkship offer did not extend to the U.S. Supreme Court. (Virginia Morsey Wheeler Talley, interview with author.) Talley subsequently worked for the Rural Electrification Administration, the World Bank, and the United Nations.

290. Justice John Paul Stevens, interview with author.

291. Stevens, interview. Temko had been promised a clerkship with Chief Justice

Stone but had to postpone it because of WWII. Rutledge offered the clerkship to Temko to keep the promise made by Stone.

292. Victor Brudney and Richard F. Wolfson, "Mr. Justice Rutledge—Law Clerks' Reflections," *Indiana Law Journal* 25, no. 1 (Fall 1949): 456.

293. Stevens was given the responsibility of writing the first draft of the majority opinion in *Mandeville Island Farms, Inc. v. American Crystal Sugar Co.* [344 U.S. 219 (1948)]. Laughing, he commented that the draft that he submitted and the justice's final product did not closely resemble each other. Stevens was also given the chance to prepare a concurring opinion. In this second project, the final product more closely resembled Stevens' original efforts. Stevens, interview.

294. Brudney and Wolfson, "Mr. Justice Rutledge," 457.

295. Ferren, *Salt of the Earth*, 228–29.

296. Marvin Schwartz, Thomas O'Neill, and Carl Schneider, correspondence with author.

297. O'Neill, correspondence.

298. Harris K. Weston, interview with author.

299. Terrance Sandalow, interview with author. Sandalow was hired to clerk for Justice Burton but actually clerked for Justice Potter Stewart after Burton retired in the fall of 1958. Although in the spring of 1958 Burton decided to retire, President Eisenhower asked him to delay the announcement until the fall. Thus, Burton let his two incoming law clerks show up for a job that they might not be able to keep. Burton's replacement, Potter Stewart, brought clerk Jack Evans with him and retained only one of Burton's OT 1958 law clerks, Terrance Sandalow. Burton's second law clerk, Goncer Krestal, worked several months for Chief Justice Warren until he was able to find a new job. Sandalow, interview and correspondence.

300. Schwartz, correspondence.

301. Harold H. Burton Papers, Box 70, Folder "1946 Term Law Clerk Applications," Manuscript Division, Library of Congress.

302. Mary Francis Berry, *Stability, Security and Continuity: Mr. Justice Burton and Decision-Making in the Supreme Court, 1945–1958* (Westport, Conn.: Greenwood Press, 1978): 30–31.

303. Ibid., 233.

304. Weston, interview.

305. Schwartz, correspondence. O'Neill states that during the 1954 term, Burton clerks summarized all cert. petitions and prepared bench memoranda for all cases set for oral argument. O'Neill, correspondence.

306. Schwartz, correspondence.

307. Atkinson, *Justice Harold H. Burton*, 73. He quotes a second clerk as saying: "In most cases the clerks prepared a draft opinion which was never used. The Justice's opinion was in every case 95% to 100% his own language."

308. O'Neill, correspondence.

309. David N. Atkinson, *Leaving the Bench: Supreme Court Justices at the End* (Lawrence: University of Kansas Press, 1999).

310. Ray Troubh, *Proceedings of the Bar and Officers of the Supreme Court of the United States: In Memory of Harold H. Burton* (Washington, D.C., May 24, 1965): 29.

311. Ibid., 27–28.

312. Berry, *Stability, Security and Continuity*, 231.

313. White biographer Dennis Hutchinson claims that in the mid-1940s "Yale had not developed the more structured process for supporting candidates for Supreme Court clerkships that [it] eventually obtained during, and largely thanks to, the deanship of Wesley Sturges." Dennis J. Hutchinson, *The Man Who Once Was Whizzer White: A Portrait of Justice Byron R. White* (New York: Free Press, 1998): 219.

314. Off-the-record comment by a former Vinson law clerk. Hutchinson writes that Vinson stopped selecting law clerks from Yale after Yale Law School professor Fred Rodell "published a caustic attack on Vinson's views and his management of the Court." Hutchinson, *Whizzer White*, 220. Former law clerk Karl Price recalls that Vinson generally "soured" on Yale Law School and its faculty. Price states that Vinson considered some Yale faculty members to be "a little wild-eyed," adding that Vinson "didn't think Yale Law School was the greatest place in the world." Karl Price interview, *Fred M. Vinson Oral History Project*, University of Kentucky.

315. Willard Pedrick clerked for Vinson during 1939, when the chief justice was sitting on the U.S. Court of Appeals for the District of Columbia Circuit. Pedrick remarks that Vinson, as a new judge, initially struggled with crafting the clerkship position. Vinson settled on the practice of having Pedrick prepare opinion drafts, a practice that Vinson followed when elevated to the Supreme Court. "[He] developed a system for using [a law clerk] to sort of do the spade work." Willard H. Pedrick interview, *Fred M. Vinson Oral History Project*.

316. Howard J. Trienens, interview with author.

317. Lawrence Ebb, interview with author; anonymous Vinson clerk, interview with author.

318. Anonymous Vinson clerk, interview.

319. William Oliver interview, *Fred Vinson Oral History Project*.

320. Howard J. Treinens interview, *Fred M. Vinson Oral History Project*.

321. Trienens, interview; Pollock, correspondence. See, also Hutchinson, *Whizzer White*, 201.

322. Hutchinson, *Whizzer White*, 202.

323. Ebb, interview.

324. Newland, "Personal Assistants," 304.

325. "Chief Justice Vinson and His Law Clerks," *Northwestern University Law Review* 49, no. 1 (Mar.-Apr. 1954): 26–35.

326. "Vinson and His Law Clerks," 27. Brenner and Palmer find that Chief Justice Vinson agreed with his law clerks' recommended disposition 86 percent of the time. Saul Brenner and Jan Palmer, "The Law Clerks' Recommendation and Chief Justice Vinson's Vote on Certiorari," *American Politics Quarterly* 18 (Jan. 1990): 74–75.

327. "Vinson and His Clerks," 28. The added responsibility of the IFP petitions, write the Vinson clerks, was the reason why Chief Justice Vinson had three rather than two clerks.

328. Price, interview with Oral History Project.

329. Oliver, interview with Oral History Project.

330. Hutchinson writes that "Vinson was one of two justices who did none of his own opinion writing [the other Justice being Frank Murphy]. . . . The other seven justices, as their surviving working papers richly demonstrate, did almost all of their own opinion writing, starting with handwritten drafts on long yellow legal pads and proceeding through typed drafts and printed opinions produced in

the Court's basement print shop for circulation to the other justices." Hutchinson, *Whizzer White*, 206. Former law clerk Earl Pollock writes that during OT 1953 the law clerks prepared opinion drafts in "probably all" cases. Pollock, correspondence with author. A former Vinson law clerk echoes Pollock's comments, anonymously stating that "clerks prepared original drafts routinely. . . . Vinson never prepared an opinion draft. Instead, the original draft 'as amended' became the final product."

331. "It is true that he gave his clerks a great deal of responsibility in terms of drafting opinions. But as far as the results are concerned and as far as his going over the opinions and inserting his ideas which clearly reflect the man both before they were written and after they were written. . . . The fact that he wasn't going to sit down with a blank yellow pad and start from scratch was characteristic of an administrator . . . In terms of the result, out of all of the discussion we had, he decided the cases. . . . In terms of filling in the blanks and looking up the cases, writing some of the paragraphs, I don't doubt that his clerks had more than say, Douglas' clerks did. But that's a matter of personal style and had nothing to do with the results as far as I can see." Trienens, interview with Oral History Project.

332. James E. St. Clair and Linda C. Gugin, *Chief Justice Fred M. Vinson of Kentucky: A Political Biography* (University of Kentucky Press, 2002).

333. Ebb, interview.

334. Trienens, interview with Oral History Project.

335. Newton N. Minow interview, *Fred M. Vinson Oral History Project*.

336. The leeway, however, was limited. A former clerk writes that after Vinson lost confidence in his second law clerk because of his suspected liberalism, the former clerk was given the responsibility of secretly rewriting all of his co-clerk's opinion drafts.

337. John P. Frank, "Fred Vinson and the Chief Justiceship," *The University of Chicago Law Review* 21, no. 1 (Autumn 1954): 224.

338. Ibid.

339. "Vinson and His Law Clerks," 29.

340. St. Clair and Gugin, *Political Biography*, 180.

341. Former law clerk Lawrence Ebb commented that in many cases Vinson relied on his law clerks' cert. memoranda and draft opinions. Ebb, interview.

342. Trienens, interview with Oral History Project.

343. Hutchinson, *Whizzer White*, 196–97.

344. Ibid., 199.

345. Ibid., 200.

346. Price, interview with Oral History Project.

347. Justice Clark himself jokingly referred to the claims of some attorneys that the law clerks "constitute a kind of junior court" but did not delve into how he personally used his clerks. Tom C. Clark, "Internal Operation of the United States Supreme Court," *Journal of the American Judicature Society* 43 (Aug. 1959): 48.

348. Ernest Rubenstein (OT 1953) and Larry E. Temple (OT 1959), correspondence with author.

349. "She's More Than Just a Secretary: Legal Knowledge Needed—So She Passed the Bar," *Washington Post*, sec. C (Sept. 7, 1966).

350. Rubenstein, correspondence.

351. Charles D. Reed, correspondence with author. Former law clerk John E. Nolan (OT 1956) confirms that Clark's law clerks prepared cert. memoranda.

352. Reed, correspondence. Reed adds: "In retrospect, we contributed a lot less than we thought. Clark was both experienced and talented; he was also very gracious and made his clerks feel very appreciated. Yet, there was *no* influence." Ibid.

353. Ibid. Another Clark law clerk states (off the record) that Clark's directions included only case outcome and the basis of the holding—if there was more than one possible basis.

354. Reed and Nolan, correspondence. Neither Rubenstein nor Temple prepared bench memoranda.

355. Robert W. Hamilton, correspondence with author.

356. Frederick M. Rowe, Temple, and Rubenstein, correspondence.

357. Rubenstein, correspondence.

358. Rowe, correspondence. Justice Clark became the godfather to Rowe's son, Geoffrey, and in subsequent years would take Geoffrey and his own grandson to baseball games.

359. Rubenstein, correspondence.

360. Raymond Gray and Harry Wallace (OT 1952), Richard Conway (OT 1953), and Samuel C. Butler (OT 1954), correspondence with author.

361. Butler, Conway, Rowe, and Wallace, correspondence.

362. Butler, Conway, and Wallace, correspondence.

363. David N. Atkinson, "Mr. Justice Minton and the Supreme Court, 1949–1956" (Ph.D. diss., University of Iowa, 1969): 123.

364. Raymond W. Gray, correspondence with author.

365. Atkinson, "Mr. Justice Minton," 163. While Atkinson does not state approximately how often Minton had his law clerks prepare opinion drafts, former law clerk Harry Wallace prepared only one first draft during OT 1952, former law clerk Richard Conway only prepared drafts in one majority and one dissenting opinion, and former clerk Samuel C. Butler did not prepare any opinion drafts. Butler, Conway, and Wallace, correspondence.

366. Atkinson, "Mr. Justice Minton," 162.

367. Ibid., 121, 122.

368. Wallace, correspondence.

369. "18 Former Law Clerks Fete Old Boss, Minton," *Washington Post*, sec. A (Oct. 7, 1956).

NOTES TO CHAPTER 5

1. Mark Tushnet, "Thurgood Marshall and the Brethren," *Georgetown Law Journal* 80, no. 6 (Aug. 1992): 2110–11.

2. Ed Cray, *Chief Justice: A Biography of Earl Warren* (New York: Simon & Schuster, 1997): 269.

3. Ibid. Former Brennan law clerk Robert O'Neil (OT 1962) suggests that more than simply fairness and expediency explained Warren's decision to retain the Vinson law clerks; O'Neil argues that an institutional norm has arisen in which the chief justice's law clerks are considered "institutional appointments" whose positions are secure if the chief justice dies, while the associate justices' law clerks are "personal appointments" whose positions are only as secure as the whims of the incoming associate. Robert O'Neil, interview with author. Recent history supports O'Neil's

assertion: Chief Justice John Roberts hired all three of the late Chief Justice William Rehnquist's incoming law clerks.

4. Cray, *Biography of Earl Warren*, 273.

5. Bernard Schwartz, *Super Chief* (New York: New York University Press, 1983): 70.

6. A Harvard Law School graduate and longtime Stanford Law professor, Gerald Gunther's popular textbook *Constitutional Law* has been digested and studied by decades of law school students. Gunther also wrote a well-received biography on Judge Learned Hand, who Gunther clerked for prior to his clerkship with Chief Justice Earl Warren during OT 1954.

7. Schwartz, *Super Chief*, 70–71.

8. Former Reed and Warren law clerk Earl Dudley, Jr., interviewed with William Dempsey after Dudley's application survived the original screening process. The closest Dempsey came to asking about Dudley's political ideology was the following question: "I don't care about your politics, but are you comfortable working with the Chief?" Earl Dudley, Jr., interview with author.

9. Adrian Kragen, interview with author. In an interview with Warren biographer Cray, Kragen explained that Warren "wanted a top-flight student who would be able to think for himself and who was not biased either toward the right or the left." Cray, *Biography of Earl Warren*, 298. While at the University of Chicago School of Law, former law clerk Dallin Oaks also made law clerk recommendations to Warren. Oaks stated that applicant "ideology was not a significant consideration, if a consideration at all" in Warren's selection of clerks. Dallin Oaks, interview with author.

10. Earl Warren Papers, Box 387, Folder "Law Clerks—1957," Manuscript Division, Library of Congress.

11. Chief Justice Warren's executive secretary to Arline C. Matheron, December 9, 1954, Warren Papers, Box 387, Folder "Applications—Law Clerks, 1953–1955." In response to Matheron's recommendation of a female candidate, the executive secretary writes: "It has been the practice of the Justices here at the Supreme Court to fill their law clerkships *with young men* recently graduated from law school . . . The Chief Justice has followed this policy since coming to the Court and has decided that he will continue to do so" (emphasis added).

12. Kragen to Warren, December 3, 1959, Warren Papers, Box 398, Folder "Law Clerks—Selection of." The perception remained, however, that the chief justice preferred male applicants. In a 1965 letter to Warren, Georgetown Law School professor Chester J. Antineau asks the chief justice whether he would interview Georgetown Law student Jean Frohlicher. Writes Antineau: "I understand your traditional institutional concern about feminine clerks, but this is the perfect occasion for a departure from precedent." Warren Papers, Box 390, 1966 Term, Folder "A–H."

13. As chief justice, Earl Warren employed three law clerks. Warren designated one law clerk as the "senior clerk," but there appears to be no difference between the junior and senior law clerks' duties. At most, the senior law clerk had a higher salary and his own office.

14. Warren Papers, Box 390, Law Clerk Applications (A–H).

15. Martin Richman (OT 1956), correspondence with author.

16. Michael E. Smith (OT 1965), correspondence with author.

17. Oaks sat on the Utah Supreme Court and taught at University of Chicago School of Law before becoming president of Brigham Young University from 1971 to 1980. He presently sits on the Mormon Church's "Quorum of Twelve," holding the title of church apostle. Choper is the Earl Warren Professor of Public Law at the University of California, Berkeley. He attended law school at the University of Pennsylvania. Regarding the annual selection of three students by a law school committee for submission to the justices for clerkship positions, Choper believes that individual students were directed to specific justices in an effort to maximize personal and ideological compatibility. Jesse H. Choper, interview with author.

18. In recent decades, retired justices have typically let their law clerks also work for current justices. Dudley stated that Earl Warren and Stanley Reed had an arrangement in which Reed agreed to let Warren use his law clerk whenever Reed did not require his services. Dudley believes that the arrangement was motivated by the fact that—at the time—only the chief justice's law clerks reviewed the "unpaid docket" (the *in forma pauperis* petitions) and prepared memoranda for all chambers, which required a substantial time commitment by Warren's clerks. By the time Dudley clerked, Reed was in his eighties and in failing health. Dudley estimated that during OT 1967, he did at most one day's work for the retired justice. Dudley, interview.

19. Robert O'Neil recalls that in some terms the fourth law clerk in Warren's chambers, namely, the law clerk of retired Justice Reed, was a "shadow" clerk who only worked on cert. petitions. O'Neil, interview.

20. Diary of Dallin Oaks, July, 1957 (emphasis added). Both Choper and Dudley confirm that Warren's clerks reviewed and summarized all cert. and IFP petitions. Dudley writes that Warren did not impose a page limit on the cert. memoranda, and he recalled once drafting a twelve-page cert. memo for Warren. Choper and Dudley, interviews.

21. Oaks Diary (Sept. 21, 1957).

22. The percentage of opinions drafted by the law clerks varied by term. For example, during OT 1956, Richman writes that the law clerks "[p]repared draft[s] in some cases, fleshed out [Warren's] draft in others. Some he largely wrote and we checked cites, etc." Richman, correspondence.

23. Choper, interview.

24. Dudley, interview. Cray writes: "Over time, Warren's drafts of his opinions were to grow increasingly sketchy. He took pains to write out the initial statement of facts, but the legal support for the conclusion that he proffered to his clerks grew ever more skimpy. He left it to them to fill in the arguments." Cray, *Biography of Earl Warren*, 310. Cray later writes (quoting former law clerk Jesse Choper): "Virtually impotent in deciding cases, the clerks did exert 'a lot of influence on the doctrinal rationale of the opinions' Warren signed. The Chief outlined what he wanted in the decision, 'and we'd just go to work on it. He gave us a good deal of leeway.'" Ibid., 357.

25. Oaks, interview.

26. Cray, *Biography of Earl Warren*, 357.

27. Choper, interview.

28. Richman explains that bench memos were drafted for all cases. These memoranda were "[l]onger than cert. memos, [with] summary of arguments in the briefs, and occasionally some reading of key cases cited." Richman, correspondence.

29. As with prior chief justices, Warren's law clerks also reviewed the *in forma pauperis* petitions and prepared memoranda for all nine justices. Richman, correspondence.

30. Julian Burke, interview with Stanley Reed Oral History Project.

31. Schwartz, *Super Chief*, 71. Oaks recalls the chief justice "warning against engaging in or being subjected to any lobbying or pressure with or by other Justices or their law clerks. He thinks this inappropriate and forbids it. He wants his clerks to be personal just to him!" Oaks Diary (Sept. 13, 1957).

32. Schwartz, *Super Chief*, 71.

33. What remains unclear, however, is whether Chief Justice Warren consistently gave the same set of instructions regarding chambers confidentiality to each new set of clerks. Former clerk Jesse Choper (OT 1960) recalled only one rule (don't talk to the press) and expressed surprise at the detailed speech given to Dallin Oaks and the law clerks of OT 1957. Choper, interview. Warren's lecture may have been triggered by an unusual series of events. During OT 1955, law clerks in the Warren, Harlan, and Frankfurter chambers had repeated conversations about the pending "Communist party" case [*Communist Party v. Control Board*, 351 U.S. 115 (1956)]. The clerks discussed what they perceived to be the relevant issues in the case and reached some tentative conclusions about how it should be resolved. Andrew Kaufman—then a Frankfurter law clerk—shared this news with Justice Frankfurter, who suggested that the law clerks write a memorandum on their discussions and thoughts and circulate the report to Frankfurter, Harlan, and Warren. The law clerks did so, and the memo was circulated. Upon receiving the memo, Chief Justice Warren became angry and told his law clerk involved in the project not to discuss pending cases with other law clerks. Warren's distress may have carried over into subsequent terms. Kaufman, interview.

34. French, correspondence.

35. Cray, *Biography of Earl Warren*, 488.

36. Ibid., 298.

37. Cray tells an amusing story involving former law clerks Gordon Gooch and Henry Steinman. "Once mistaken as Warren's bodyguard[s] at a baseball game, Gooch and Steinman secretly started posing as Secret Service agents guarding the chief justice. 'He'd be walking down the street, talking to whomever he was walking with, and Steinman and I would drop back, and drop back. Then we'd move out on the flanks a little bit, and whenever someone would approach, we would put our hands in our pocket like we were putting it on the butt of a pistol. People would just clear the path.'" When Warren finally figured out what his law clerks were doing he brought the game to an abrupt end. "'And we couldn't be police officers anymore,' Gooch lamented. 'He said he's never had a bodyguard in his life, and he wasn't going to start now.'" Ibid., 402.

38. "Warren Honored at Supreme Court," *Washington Post* (July 12, 1974).

39. In fact, every justice appointed to the Court since Earl Warren had basically adopted this clerkship model with one very interesting exception—John Paul Stevens. While Justice Stevens has his law clerks prepare cert. and bench memoranda, he continues to prepare the first draft of opinions. One could argue, however, that Justice Stevens' clerkship model strengthens the consensual norms argument in that it represents the consensual norms in place during Stevens' own clerkship in 1947.

If Earl Warren (and, to a lesser degree, Fred Vinson) were catalysts for the dramatic evolution in the professional relationship between law clerk and justice, then why? One might hypothesize that their prior experiences as administrators of large bureaucracies (Warren as governor of California; Vinson as head of the Office of Economic Stabilization, head of the Office of War Mobilization, and secretary of the Treasury) contributed to a dependence on their legal staffs.

40. Thomas G. Walker, Lee Epstein, and William J. Dixon, "On the Mysterious Demise of Consensual Norms in the United States Supreme Court," *Journal of Politics* 50, no. 2 (1988): 361–89.

41. Gregory A. Caldeira and Christopher J. W. Zorn, "Of Time and Consensual Norms in the Supreme Court," *American Journal of Political Science* 42, no. 3 (July 1998): 874–902.

42. Prettyman, interview.

43. Norbert A. Schlei, in Norman Dorsen and Amelia Ames Newcomb, eds., "John Marshall Harlan II, Associate Justice of the U.S. Supreme Court 1955–1971: Remembrances by His Law Clerks," *Journal of Supreme Court History* 27, no. 2 (July 2002): 146.

44. William T. Lake, correspondence with author.

45. Thomas B. Stoel in Dorsen and Newcomb, "John Marshall Harlan II," 165.

46. Charles R. Nesson in Dorsen and Newcomb, "John Marshall Harlan II," 159.

47. Bert W. Rein in Dorsen and Newcomb, "John Marshall Harlan II," 163.

48. Norman Dorsen in Dorsen and Newcomb, "John Marshall Harlan II," 147.

49. An amusing example of the justice's indulgent attitude toward his law clerks comes from former clerk Philip B. Heymann (OT 1960), who observes that the justice "seemed to spend time daily in the clerks' office picking up rubber bands that Charles Fried and I had shot at each other, a task that could have been left for the janitors or even for us." Heymann in Dorsen and Newcomb, "John Marshall Harlan II," 152.

50. Nathan Lewin in Dorsen and Newcomb, "John Marshall Harlan II," 154–55.

51. Rein in Dorsen and Newcomb, "John Marshall Harlan II," 163.

52. Charles L. Fabrikant in Dorsen and Newcomb, "John Marshall Harlan II," 167.

53. Paul Brest in Dorsen and Newcomb, "John Marshall Harlan II," 166.

54. Henry P. Sailer in Dorsen and Newcomb, "John Marshall Harlan II," 149.

55. Rein in Dorsen and Newcomb, "John Marshall Harlan II," 163–64.

56. Martin D. Minsker in Dorsen and Newcomb, "John Marshall Harlan II," 174.

57. Richard A. Posner, "William J. Brennan, Jr.," *Harvard Law Review* 104, no. 1 (Nov. 1990): 13.

58. Richard S. Arnold, "A Remembrance of Mr. Justice Brennan, OT 1960," *Journal of Supreme Court History* (1991): 5.

59. Ibid.

60. O'Neil, interview.

61. For more thorough accounts of the short clerkship of Mike Tigar, see: Michael E. Tigar, *Fighting Injustice* (Chicago: American Bar Association; Andrew Kopkind, 2002); "Brennan v. Tigar," *New Republic* (Aug. 27, 1966).

62. Alison Grey Anderson, correspondence with author.

63. Anderson, correspondence.

64. Justice Brennan hired his first female law clerk, Marsha Berzon, in 1974. Berzon now serves as a judge on the U.S. Court of Appeals for the Ninth Circuit.

65. William J. Brennan, Jr., "Justice Brennan Calls National Court of Appeals Proposal 'Fundamentally Unnecessary and Ill Advised,'" *American Bar Association Journal* 59 (Aug. 1973): 836.

66. William Maledon, interview with author. Former Brennan law clerks William Fletcher (OT 1976), Steven A. Reiss (OT 1977), Michael McConnell (OT 1980), and Bruce R. Lerner (OT 1983) write that they only reviewed cert. petitions during the summer, while former clerks Edward W. Keane (OT 1957) and Clifton Elgarten (OT 1981) stated they not did prepare any cert. petitions. Correspondence with author.

67. Former law clerk Peter L. Strauss (OT 1965) believes that Justice Brennan's clerkship model was premised on the following idea: "His attitude towards allocating the work of the office was that his clerks should not waste their time on repetitive or transitory matters he could handle on his own. Once the office had opinions to write, he took the certiorari petitions home for evening reading; there was never a bench memo to write before oral argument. Our time was to be spent on what he thought would be most valuable for us, as well as him, helping him to develop the opinions that had come his way." Peter L. Strauss, "In Memoriam: William J. Brennan, Jr.," *Columbia Law Review* 97, no. 6 (Oct. 1997): 1611.

68. Michael Klausner, correspondence.

69. O'Neil, interview. O'Neil and Posner's skill at drafting opinions earned them the rare opportunity to draft an opinion for Justice Clark, whose clerks were struggling with preparing an assigned opinion.

70. Former clerks Elgarten, Fletcher, Keane, Lerner, McConnell, and Reiss all confirmed that they worked on some first drafts during their clerkship. Fletcher writes that Brennan would provide his law clerks with "general instructions as to the result and rationale. The Justice would then review, revise, and, in some cases, entirely re-write." Fletcher, correspondence. Lerner writes that the clerks received "extensive directions" from Brennan, while McConnell recalls that Justice Brennan and his clerks "would discuss all issues exhaustively before beginning drafting." Lerner and McConnell, correspondence.

71. Marsha S. Berzon, "Remarks of Marsha S. Berzon," *Proceedings of the Bar and Officers of the Supreme Court of the United States: In Memoriam Honorable William J. Brennan, Jr.* (Washington, D.C., 1998).

72. See, generally, Craig Allen Smith, *Failing Justice: Charles Evans Whittaker on the Supreme Court* (Jefferson, N.C.: McFarland); Atkinson, *Leaving the Bench;* Richard Lawrence Miller, *Whittaker: Struggles of a Supreme Court Justice* (Westport, Conn.: Greenwood Press, 2002); Craig Allen Smith, "Charles Evans Whittaker, Associate Justice of the Supreme Court: A Thesis in History," Ph.D. diss. (University of Missouri–Kansas City, 1997). Former law clerk Alan Kohn recounts an instance in which Justice Whittaker told him that the justice viewed his appointment to the Supreme Court as tantamount to selling "'himself down the river for a pot of porridge.' He should, he said, never have left the trial court bench. . . . Just a bad day at the office, I thought at the time. But it was more than that. He was not just unhappy. He was distraught and in serious emotional distress." Alan C. Kohn, "Supreme Court Law Clerk, 1957–1958, Reminiscence," *Journal of Supreme Court History* 2 (1998): 47.

73. Atkinson, *Leaving the Bench*, 130.

74. Ibid., 219 fn 127 (emphasis added).

75. Miller, *Whittaker*, 53.

76. Ibid., 28, 38.

77. Ibid., 54. Alternatively, a former Whittaker law clerk anonymously states that while Justice Whittaker originally decided that he, the justice, would draft all opinions, during OT 1959, the quality of a dissenting opinion prepared by a Whittaker law clerk resulted in five justices changing their votes; Justice Whittaker went from writing a solo dissent to writing for a six-justice majority. Subsequently, Justice Whittaker became more comfortable having his law clerks take a crack at writing dissenting opinions.

78. Whittaker's first law clerk—Manley O. Hudson—recalls that the justice "felt like he had to read the whole record" in every case, which involved an enormous amount of documents. When Whittaker asked a fellow justice if he had managed to completely review all relevant materials in pending cases, the unnamed justice laughed and said that he hadn't.

79. Atkinson, *Leaving the Bench*, 128.

80. Former law clerk Alan Kohn's interview with the newly appointed Justice Whittaker was rudimentary. "The Justice asked me a few questions about myself and said he needed help in his new job. Then he asked me when I could start. I said tomorrow and he said that would be fine. End of interview." Kohn, "Supreme Court Law Clerk," 42.

81. Manley O. Hudson started OT 1956 clerking for Justice Stanley Reed, spent one month working for Chief Justice Earl Warren while Whittaker's nomination was pending, and then clerked for Justice Whittaker from approximately March to June 1957. Hudson does not remember any discussions with the justice regarding how Whittaker would use his clerks, adding that he "guesses" that Whittaker simply adopted Reed's clerkship practices.

82. Kohn, interview.

83. Smith, *Failing Justice*, 129.

84. Kohn, interview. Kohn also is circumspect in his article on Whittaker, simply remarking that law clerks helped "the Justice in any way he wished in the drafting of opinions." Kohn, 1998: 42.

85. Smith, *Failing Justice*, 131–32.

86. Ibid., 130.

87. Kohn, interview.

88. Terrance Sandalow, "Potter Stewart," *Harvard Law Review* 95, no. 1 (Nov. 1981): 6.

89. Sandalow, "Potter Stewart"; Ben W. Heineman, Jr., "A Balance Wheel on the Court," *Yale Law Journal* 95, no. 7 (June 1986): 1325–27; Laurence H. Tribe, "Justice Stewart: A Tale of Two Portraits," *Yale Law Journal* 95, no. 7 (June 1986): 1328–33.

90. Sandalow, interview with author. As for other aspects of selecting law clerks, Sandalow added: "After what was apparently an unfortunate experience [with a law clerk] in the late sixties, Stewart regularly asked me, when inquiring about someone I had recommended, whether he or she would understand that . . . Stewart was the justice and was responsible for making decisions." Sandalow, correspondence. At least early in his career, Stewart may have depended on Yale Law School to screen

candidates and send the finalists for interviews. Jerold H. Israel (OT 1959), correspondence with author.

91. Andrew Hurwitz, interview with author.

92. Sandalow, interview and correspondence.

93. Israel confirms that Justice Stewart initially wrote his own opinion drafts. "[W]hen I was clerking, the opinions were written by Justice Stewart, although they might incorporate parts of research memoranda prepared by the clerks." Israel, correspondence.

94. Hurwitz, interview. While Justice Stewart gave his law clerks only general instructions about the substantive content of the opinion, he did have some particular stylistic rules. For example, the first paragraph of the opinion must state why the Supreme Court granted cert. and reviewed the case on its merits. Ibid.

95. Former clerk Israel writes that the law clerks "usually" did not prepare bench memoranda. Israel, correspondence.

96. Sandalow, correspondence.

97. Ibid.

98. Hutchinson, *Whizzer White*, 471.

99. Ibid.

100. Robert V. Percival, correspondence with author.

101. Ibid., 472. Former law clerk Kevin J. Worthen (OT 1983) writes: "Much has been written, and almost as much surmised, about Justice White's incredible athletic ability and his penchant for engaging in competition with his clerks. Contrary to popular belief, the Justice did not choose his clerks based on athletic ability. . . . Still, competition was a central part of a White clerkship." Kevin J. Worthen, "Shirt-Tales: Clerking for Byron White," *Brigham Young University Law Review*, no. 2 (1994): 353. One former Warren law clerk who interviewed with White, however, disagrees that athletic ability was not part of White's selection criteria. The individual, who suffers from a physical handicap, believes that his interview with Justice White was effectively over as soon as White saw his disability. From that point, White asked only listless questions, couldn't control his large dog that roamed around the office and jumped on the applicant, and "no longer cared" about the interview.

102. Hutchinson, *Whizzer White*, 337.

103. Ibid., 419. Other law clerks recall that the deadline was ten days, not twelve. Worthen, "Shirt-Tales," 352. Former law clerk Kathryn Webb Bradley (OT 1989) added that besides his distaste for law review cites, Justice White did not like his opinions to contain lengthy historical discussions. Kathryn Webb Bradley, interview with author.

104. Worthen, "Shirt-Tales," 352.

105. Ibid., 351. Former law clerk Kathryn Webb Bradley stated that sometimes Justice White wouldn't even tell the clerks the grounds for the assigned opinion, blithely commenting that the correct legal basis would "come out in the writing." Bradley would be forced to collect intelligence from clerks in other chambers as to the grounds of the conference vote so she could prepare an opinion that would hold the majority together. Bradley, interview.

106. Stephen R. McAllister, "In Memoriam: Remembering Justice Byron R. White," *University of Kansas Law Review* 50, no. 5 (June 2002): 1080.

107. White's law clerks appear to have put more energy into the review of cert.

petitions and the attendant legal research than clerks in other chambers. "When a conflict among lower courts . . . was alleged, clerks were not allowed to rely on the parties' assertion that the conflict existed. They were not even permitted to take the word of clerks from other chambers who may have prepared the cert. memo. Clerks had to read the cases themselves and certify whether the conflict was real. And while the research and writing may not have been quite as thorough as that of a full opinion, care was demanded to make sure the facts and reasoning were in order." Worthen, "Shirt-Tales," 355.

108. At least during OT 1989, Justice White required his clerks to prepare a post-argument memoranda within twenty-four hours after oral argument, recommending how he should vote at conference. Bradley, interview.

109. Bradley, interview; Elizabeth Gibson, interview with author.

110. Bradley recalled that some conservative law clerks lobbied her to write her pool memoranda differently. Bradley stated that the justices were aware that conservative law clerks were slanting facts in the cert. memoranda and that the justices' review was sufficiently detailed to undercut the clerks' efforts at influence. Bradley, interview.

111. Worthen, "Shirt-Tales," 354–55. Drafting dissents from the denial of certiorari was a regular job assignment, at least during OT 1983. Worthen estimates that "[a]t least at the time I clerked, clerks wrote nearly as many dissents from denial as they did bench memos." Ibid., 355.

112. Worthen, "Shirt-Tales," 352.

113. Worthen, "Shirt-Tales," 350.

114. Hutchinson, *Whizzer White*, 385.

115. Ibid.

116. Ibid., 472.

117. Bradley, interview. Former law clerk Elizabeth Gibson also sensed that White was not as close with law clerks from the 1980s and 1990s, but she suggests that the increasing number of law clerks caused the change. Gibson, interview.

118. "Bar and Bench Meet to Present Memorials to the Late Byron R. White," *Supreme Court Historical Society* 23 (2002): 1 (some internal citations removed for sake of readability).

119. Stephen R. McAllister, "In Memoriam: Remembering Justice Byron R. White," *Kansas Law Review* 50 (June 2002): 1077.

120. Worthen, "Shirt-Tales," 353.

121. Christopher R. Drahozal, "In Memoriam: Remembering Justice Byron R. White," *University of Kansas Law Review* 50, no. 5 (June 2002): 1084.

122. Hutchinson, *Whizzer White*, 438–39.

123. McAllister, "Remembering Justice Byron R. White," 1080.

124. Goldberg to Minow, December 12, 1962. The Personal Papers of Arthur J. Goldberg, Supreme Court File, Miscellany—Law Clerks, Manuscript Division, Library of Congress.

125. Alan M. Dershowitz, *Chutzpah* (Boston: Little, Brown, 1991): 56.

126. Goldberg Papers, Supreme Court File, "Miscellany—Law Clerks."

127. Stephen Breyer, "Clerking for Justice Goldberg," *Journal of Supreme Court History* (1990): 4–7.

128. Peter Edelman, correspondence with author.

129. Breyer, "Clerking for Justice Goldberg," 6–7. Biographies on Goldberg do not discuss his law clerks or their substantive duties. See David L. Stebenne, *Arthur J. Goldberg: New Deal Liberal* (New York: Oxford University Press, 1996); Victor Lasky, *Arthur J. Goldberg: The Old and the New* (New Rochelle, N.J.: Arlington House, 1970).

130. Edelman, correspondence.

131. As with Justice Goldberg, Justice Fortas' short career on the Supreme Court resulted in a small pool of former law clerks from which to gather information. Fortas hired only six law clerks while on the Supreme Court.

132. Daniel Levitt, interview with author.

133. Thomas Grey, correspondence with author.

134. Ibid.

135. Bruce Allen Murphy, *Fortas: The Rise and Ruin of a Supreme Court Justice* (New York: William Morrow, 1988): 235. Former law clerk John Griffiths (OT 1965 and 1966) summarizes Fortas' outside interests succinctly: "He was practically running the [Vietnam] War at some point." John Griffiths, correspondence with author.

136. See, generally Murphy, *Fortas;* Laura Kalman, *Abe Fortas: A Biography* (New Haven, Conn.: Yale University Press, 1990).

137. Walter B. Slocombe, correspondence with author. Rosenbloom also writes that the law clerks "drafted many, but not all, opinions." H. David Rosenbloom, correspondence with author.

138. Rosenbloom, correspondence.

139. Griffiths, correspondence.

140. Kalman, *Abe Fortas*, 271.

141. Ibid., 271–72.

142. Levitt, interview. While in subsequent terms Justice Fortas occasionally asked for a formal bench memorandum, the norm evolved into oral discussions between justice and clerk. Rosenbloom and Slocombe, correspondence.

143. Levitt, interview. Levitt also recalled overhearing telephone conversations between Justice Fortas and President Johnson, during which Fortas sought to bolster Johnson's spirits. Griffiths writes that Fortas kept his law clerks and their duties apart from the justice's relationship with LBJ. "[Fortas] did have a red light on his secretary's desk and in our room, and if it was on he was on the phone with LBJ [and] we were to stay out." Griffiths, correspondence.

144. Kalman, *Abe Fortas*, 372.

145. Murphy, *Fortas*, 219. Benno Schmidt served as Chief Justice Earl Warren's law clerk during OT 1966.

146. Daniel Levitt, *Proceedings of the Bar and Officers of the Supreme Court of the United States: In Memoriam Honorable Abe Fortas* (Washington, D.C., 1982): 21.

147. Woodward and Armstrong, *The Brethren*, 197.

148. Ibid. Former Marshall law clerks, however, paint a picture of a master storyteller regaling his audience with jokes. "He had an endless supply of jokes, not all of them, I must admit, appropriate to print in the pages of a law review. And he was the greatest comic storyteller I have ever heard, or ever expect to hear." Elena Kagan, "In Memoriam: For Justice Marshall," *Texas Law Review* 71 (May 1993): 1126.

149. Woodward and Armstrong, *The Brethren*, 278.

150. Juan Williams, *Thurgood Marshall: American Revolutionary* (New York: Times Books, 1998): 370. Oddly, there is no evidence that Marshall amended his clerkship model to include formal, written confidentiality rules after the publication of *The Brethren*. Former clerk Bruce A. Green writes that during OT 1982: "The Justice had no formal rules about confidentiality that I recall. . . . It was plain to the clerks that we couldn't talk about pending cases with anyone outside the Court. It was also plain that Justice Marshall considered it important for us to maintain the confidentiality of what took place in his chambers." Bruce A. Green, correspondence with author.

151. Kenneth Simons, correspondence with author.

152. The best example of the counterattack by Marshall law clerks is former clerk Mark Tushnet's (OT 1972) article "Thurgood Marshall and the Brethren," *Georgetown Law Journal* 80, no. 6 (1992): 2109–30. The thrust of Tushnet's piece is that the picture of Justice Marshall "as a lazy Justice uninterested in the Court's work" is incorrect and "perhaps racist." Ibid., 2109. One could argue that Tushnet damns Justice Marshall with faint praise, challenging not the fact that "Marshall delegated much of his office work to his law clerks" but the myth that "Supreme Court Justices typically are more directly involved in their office's work than Marshall was." Ibid., 2129.

153. The selection committee was created some time after the early 1980s.

154. This clerkship model was explained by former clerk Bruce A. Green and in an off-the-record interview with another Marshall law clerk. Green stated: "The clerks prepared the first drafts of opinions in virtually all, but not all, cases. We did so based on the discussions with the Justice prior to the voting conference and sometimes additional discussions." Green, correspondence. Other Marshall law clerks have publicly stated that they prepared opinion drafts. Williams, *American Revolutionary*, 370; Glen M. Darbyshire, "Clerking for Justice Marshall," ed. Roger Goldman and David Gallen, *Thurgood Marshall: Justice for All* (New York: Carroll & Graf, 1992): 174–79.

155. Simons, correspondence.

156. Green, correspondence.

157. Darbyshire, "Clerking for Justice Marshall," 176.

158. The only other law clerk to concede that Justice Marshall's clerkship model involved higher-than-normal levels of delegation is former clerk Mark Tushnet. In a 1992 law review article in which Tushnet vigorously defended the justice, he concedes that "Marshall relied more heavily on his law clerks for opinion writing than did the other Justices during the early years of his tenure, but his practices were not wildly out of line with those of the other[s] on the Court." Tushnet, "Thurgood Marshall and the Brethren," 2112. Tushnet adds that while at the NAACP, Marshall developed a "working style" in which "he arrived at a judgment after examining the legal materials his highly competent subordinates presented him, and then delegated to them the job of working out the details necessary to support that judgment." Ibid.

159. Gay Gellhorn, "Justice Thurgood Marshall's Jurisprudence of Equal Protection of the Laws and the Poor," *Arizona State Law Journal* 26, no. 2 (Summer 1994): 429–60; Elana Kagan, "For Justice Marshall," *Texas Law Review* 71, no. 6 (May 1993): 1125–30; Scott Brewer, "In Memoriam: Justice Marshall's Justice Martial," *Texas Law Review* 71, no. 6 (1993): 1121–24; Jordan Steiker, "The Long Road Up from Barba-

rism: Thurgood Marshall and the Death Penalty," *Texas Law Review* 71, no. 6 (May 1993): 1131–64; Susan Low Block, "The Privilege of Clerking for Thurgood Marshall," *Journal of Supreme Court History* (1992): 23–25; Deborah L. Rhode, "A Tribute to Justice Thurgood Marshall: Letting the Law Catch Up," *Stanford Law Review* 44 (Summer 1992): 1259–65; Martha Minow, "A Tribute to Justice Marshall," *Harvard Law Review* 105 (1991): 66–76; Karen Hastie Williams, "Humanizing the Legal Process: The Legacy of Thurgood Marshall," *Harvard Blackletter Journal* 6 (Spring 1989): 90–94.

160. Brewer, "Justice Marshall's Justice Martial," 1121.

161. Thurgood Marshall Papers, Box 571, Folder 12, Manuscript Division, Library of Congress.

162. Green, correspondence.

163. Charles Hobbs, correspondence with author. Hobbs clerked for Chief Justice Burger on the D.C. Court of Appeals in 1957 to 1958 and served on the clerkship committee from 1972 to 1985.

164. Ibid.

165. Ibid.

166. Woodward and Armstrong, *The Brethren*, 352.

167. Judith McMorrow (OT 1981) and Bruce Brown (OT 1985), interviews with author; Jack M. Weiss (OT 1972), Stephen Walters (OT 1974), James L. Volling (OT 1980), and Christopher J. Wright (OT 1981), correspondence with author.

168. Wright, correspondence with author.

169. Walters, correspondence.

170. Volling, correspondence.

171. John Edward Sexton, "A Tribute to Chief Justice Warren E. Burger," *Harvard Law Review* 100, no. 5 (Mar. 1987): 979.

172. Woodward and Armstrong, *The Brethren*, 34–35. *The Brethren* relied on anonymous sources, and much of the information contained within the book has been attacked (sometimes convincingly, sometimes not) by Court insiders. I am not aware of any former law clerks who have publicly challenged, however, the book's account of the August 12, 1969, memo issued by the chief justice.

173. Ibid., 36. Given the anonymous nature of the sources, this quote must be placed within context. We simply do not know whether this view of the chief justice's motivations was shared by the majority of the clerks from OT 1969.

174. Walters, correspondence.

175. Brown and McMorrow, interviews.

176. Robert Mayer and Jan Horbaly, interviews with author.

177. "Memorandum to the Conference," William Rehnquist and Potter Stewart, June 18, 1973. Lewis F. Powell, Jr., Papers, Powell Archives, Washington and Lee University School of Law.

178. Sexton, "Tribute to Chief Justice Warren E. Burger," 981; James L. Volling, "Warren E. Burger: An Independent Pragmatist Remembered," *William Mitchell Law Review* 22, no. 1 (1996): 58; J. Michael Luttig, "In Memoriam: Warren E. Burger," *Harvard Law Review* 109, no. 1 (Nov. 1995): 1–5.

179. John Dean writes that the FBI's background check of Carswell was so superficial that it missed the fact that he was gay. Dean wryly adds: "While Richard Nixon was always looking for historical firsts, nominating a homosexual to the high court would not have been on his list." Dean, *Rehnquist Choice*, 20.

180. Wanda S. Martinson, "In Memoriam: My Twenty-Five Years with 'Old Number Three,'" *Columbia Law Review* 99, no. 6 (Oct. 1999): 1407–408.

181. Justice Blackmun to University of Illinois College of law professor George T. Frampton, May 15, 1974, Harry Blackmun Papers, Box 1568, Folder 5, Manuscript Division, Library of Congress.

182. Former law clerk Richard Meserve (OT 1976) writes of his interview: "I do not recall any questions that focused on my legal knowledge. . . . Instead, much of the interview reflected his concern that a clerk's work load might intrude unduly on my family life. The Justice knew that I had young children and he wanted to be sure that I fully considered all the disadvantages of assuming a clerkship." Richard A. Meserve, "A Tribute to Justice Harry A. Blackmun," *North Dakota Law Review* 71, no. 1 (1995): 21.

183. Vicki L. Been (OT 1984), Pamela S. Karlan (OT 1985), and Lynn Blais (OT 1990), interviews with author.

184. Randall Bezanson, correspondence with author.

185. Been and Karlan, interviews.

186. Been, Blais, and Karlan, interviews; Albert G. Lauber and Thomas W. Merrill (OT 1978) and James J. Brudney (OT 1980), correspondence with author.

187. Brudney, correspondence; J. Paul Oetken (OT 1993), correspondence with author.

188. "Clerkship Duties," Blackmun Papers, Box 1568, Folder 12.

189. Nancy Wright, "Lynn Blais Gets a Lesson in Law at Highest Court," *Rutland Herald* (Dec. 24, 1990).

190. Been, Blais, and Karlan, interviews.

191. Meserve, "Justice Harry A. Blackmun," 23.

192. Blais, interview.

193. Bezanson, correspondence.

194. Ibid.

195. Meserve, "Justice Harry A. Blackmun," 24.

196. Wanda Martinson, interview with author.

197. David J. Garrow, "The Brains Behind Blackmun," *Legal Affairs* (May-June 2005).

198. William Alden McDaniel, Jr., "Readers Respond: Justice Blackmun," *Legal Affairs* (May-June 2005).

199. Sherry F. Colb, "Breakfast with Justice Blackmun," *North Dakota Law Review* 71, no. 1 (1995): 13–15; Meserve, "A Tribute to Justice Harry A. Blackmun"; Charles Rothfeld, "One Fried Egg and Rye Toast," *Legal Times* (Mar. 8, 1999): 11.

200. Bezanson, correspondence.

201. Alexander to Blackmun, June 24, 1994, Blackmun Papers, Box 1553.

202. Been to Justice and Mrs. Blackmun, July 18, 1985, Blackmun Papers, Box 1553.

203. "Blackmun Legacy Honored; Friends Recall Man and Justice," *Washington Post*, sec. A (Mar. 10, 1999).

204. J. Harvie Wilkinson III, *Serving Justice: A Supreme Court Clerk's View* (New York: Charterhouse, 1974): 16 (quoting Lewis Powell's remarks to Fourth Circuit Judicial Conference, June 30, 1972).

205. Justice Powell did not require Hugo Black's final set of law clerks to rein-

terview with the newest justice. Powell simply met with the two young men and announced that he would "be honored" to have them as law clerks. Hammonds, interview.

206. Memorandum from Powell to law clerks, March 20, 1972. Powell Papers, Box 130B.

207. Powell Papers, Box 129, Chief Justice Correspondence Folder.

208. Powell to Warren Burger, June 24, 1974. Powell Papers, Box 129, Chief Justice Correspondence Folder.

209. John C. Jeffries, Jr., *Justice Lewis F. Powell, Jr.* (New York: Scribner's, 1994).

210. Wilkinson, *Serving Justice*, 15.

211. Ibid.

212. Ibid., 53.

213. Memorandum from Powell to law clerks, August 21, 1974. Powell Papers, Box 130B.

214. Wilkinson, *Serving Justice*, 55.

215. John C. Jeffries, Jr., correspondence with author.

216. Ibid. Former law clerk David R. Boyd (OT 1972) writes that Justice Powell "placed considerable weight on his perception of 'personality match' and he considered the views of his current clerks in selecting future clerks." David R. Boyd, correspondence with author.

217. In a memorandum to law clerk John Jeffries, Jr., Powell writes: "For obvious reasons, I would like to have a Law Clerk from Washington and Lee provided I can do so without sacrifice of the absolutely high quality which is indispensable, as I view the responsibilities of this position." Memorandum from Powell to Jeffries, June 26, 1973. Powell Papers.

218. Memorandum from Powell to law clerks, June 1, 1981. Powell Papers, Box 130B.

219. In a few years, the Powell chambers would adopt a law clerk procedure book. A collaborative, evolving document, the book covered office arrangements, the review of cert. petitions and the writing of cert. pool memoranda, the writing of "bobtail" bench memoranda, the opinion-writing process (including the need to limit citation to secondary authority, the creation of head notes, and the review of circulating opinions), Justice Powell's various duties as Fifth Circuit justice, and chamber security. Law Clerk Procedure Book no. 2, 1975–1982. Powell Papers, Box 130B.

220. Wilkinson, *Serving Justice*, 20–21.

221. Jeffries, *Justice Lewis F. Powell, Jr.*, 295.

222. Memorandum from Powell to law clerks, April 17, 1972. Powell Papers, Box 130B.

223. David L. Weston, "Justice Powell and His Law Clerks," *Supreme Court Historical Society Yearbook* (1987): 17. The use of a second law clerk to review the drafted opinion has been confirmed by other clerks and appears to have been standard practice throughout Powell's tenure on the High Court. David O. Stewart (OT 1979), Richard Fallon (OT 1981), Michael Sturley and James O. Browning (OT 1982), correspondence with author.

224. Anne M. Coughlin, "In Memoriam: Writing for Justice Powell," *Columbia Law Review* 99, no. 3 (Apr. 1999): 541.

225. Memorandum from Powell to Lawrence A. Hammond and William C. Kelly, Jr., May 29, 1973. Powell Papers, Box 130B.

226. September 1976 Briefing Notes—Law Clerks. Powell Papers.

227. Memorandum from Powell to clerks, October 11, 1983. Powell Papers, Box 130B.

228. Memorandum from Powell to staff, April 27, 1977. Powell Papers.

229. Westin, "Justice Powell and His Law Clerks," 16.

230. Powell to John Jeffries, Jr., January 2, 1982. Powell Papers, Box 129B.

231. Powell to J. Harvie Wilkinson III, September 23, 1980. Powell Papers, Box 129C.

232. Members of the cert. pool divide the cert. petitions among their law clerks. Each justice's clerks are responsible for a one-eighth share of the cert. petitions, and the memoranda are circulated among the eight chambers. Rehnquist writes that the cert. pool was created "to facilitate the consideration of the petitions for certiorari," and he credits Lewis Powell with suggesting "that all the law clerks be pooled for purposes of writing memos describing the facts and contentions in each petition for certiorari." Rehnquist, *Supreme Court*, 232–33.

233. Lee Epstein, Jeffrey Segal, Harold Spaeth, and Thomas Walker, *The Supreme Court Compendium: Data, Decisions, and Developments* (Washington, D.C.: CQ Press, 1996): Table 2–7.

234. Former Rehnquist law clerks have stated that they prepared the first drafts of both concurring and dissenting opinions.

235. Rehnquist, *Supreme Court*, 262.

236. Ibid. At least one former Rehnquist law clerk has a different characterization of these meetings. David Campbell (OT 1981) stated that he was surprised that he did not receive more detailed instructions from Rehnquist when he was assigned to draft an opinion. David Campbell, interview with author. In contrast, former law clerk Kevin Boyle (OT 1999) writes that before drafting opinions the clerks "received detailed instructions as to how the case was to be decided and the rationale for the decision. Additionally, we would receive instructions as to what the key facts and arguments should be." Kevin R. Boyle, correspondence with author.

237. Rehnquist, *Supreme Court*, 261. This tight deadline on opinion writing "astonished law clerks in other chambers." Campbell, interview.

238. Adam Liptak and Todd S. Purdum, "As Clerk for Rehnquist, Nominee Stood Out for Conservative Rigor," *New York Times*, sec. A (July 31, 2005).

239. Rehnquist, *Supreme Court*, 262.

240. Ibid., 261–62.

241. Ibid., 263.

242. Ibid., 233.

243. Ibid. During OT 1981, Rehnquist had already adopted the practice of having his law clerks review all cert. pool memoranda and write comments and a recommended disposition on the top of the document. Campbell, interview. Additionally, in some years Rehnquist would have his law clerks assign a rating to the cert. memorandum (A to D) as to the importance of the petition. Brett Dunkelman, interview with author.

244. Rehnquist, *Supreme Court*, 233, 234 (emphasis added). Former law clerk

Kevin R. Boyle (OT 1999) writes that the chief justice's clerks would review the cert. pool memoranda and "annotate the incoming pool memos for the Chief with a brief description and a recommendation, but he would read all of the pool memos himself." Boyle, correspondence with author.

245. During OT 1981, there was one occasion when then Associate Justice Rehnquist got upset over a cert. pool memorandum, believing it to be "disingenuous."

246. Rehnquist, *Supreme Court*, 233–34 (emphasis added).

247. Ibid., 239, 240; Campbell, interview. Former clerk Dunkelman joked that the length of the walk sometimes depended on the complexity of the case. Dunkelman, interview.

248. At least during OT 1999, Rehnquist had his law clerks prepare a limited number of bench memoranda "if there was a particularly technical issue in a case that was difficult to discuss orally." Boyle, interview.

249. John Paul Stevens, interview with author.

250. Deborah N. Pearlstein, "The Power to Persuade: A Year in the Life of a Supreme Court Clerk," *NCJW Journal* (Oct. 31, 2000): 12.

251. Stevens, interview.

252. Robert Schapiro, interview with author.

253. Ibid.

254. Pearlstein, *The Power to Persuade*, 13.

255. Ibid., 15.

256. "O'Connor's Agonizing Search for Law Clerks," *New York Times* (Nov. 3, 1989): B7.

257. Simon A. Steel, correspondence with author.

258. "O'Connor's Agonizing Search," B7.

259. Tony Mauro, "Corps of Clerks Lacking in Diversity," *USA Today* (Mar. 5, 1999).

260. "O'Connor's Agonizing Search."

261. Comments by Associate Justice Sandra Day O'Connor at November 13, 2000, Emory University Colloquium

262. Kent D. Syverud, interview with author.

263. Jeffrey Rosen, "A Majority of One," *New York Times Magazine* (June 3, 2001); Syverud, interview.

264. Rosen, "Majority of One," 34.

265. Charles Blanchard (OT 1986), correspondence with author.

266. Steel, correspondence.

267. Syverud, interview. Blanchard writes that these first drafts were "based on a detailed outline [prepared by the justice] of the arguments/analysis to be used." Blanchard, correspondence.

268. Blanchard, correspondence. Former law clerk Steel recalled that the clerks reviewed all bench memorandum as well. Steel, correspondence.

269. "O'Connor's Agonizing Search for Law Clerks."

270. Margo Schlanger, interview with author.

271. For example, don't use "since" in place of "because." Ibid.

272. Sam Bagenstos (OT 1997), interview with author; Schlanger, interview.

273. Bagenstos adds to the anonymous clerk's comments that although some

clerks "slanted" the facts or legal arguments in a cert. memorandum, "it struck me how transparent their efforts were." Bagenstos, interview.

274. Ibid.; Schlanger, interview.

275. W. William Hodes, correspondence with author.

276. Schlanger, interview.

277. Bagenstos, interview.

278. Andrew Peyton Thomas, *Clarence Thomas: A Biography* (San Francisco: Encounter Books, 2002): 465.

279. Ken Foskett, *Judging Thomas: The Life and Times of Clarence Thomas* (New York: Harper Collins, 2004): 279–80.

280. Michael A. Fletcher and Kevin Merida, "For 'Family' of Clerks, Thomas Weighs Politics, Loyalty, and, Sometimes, Hard-Luck History," *Washington Post*, sec. A (Oct. 11, 2004).

281. Andrew Peyton Thomas, *Clarence Thomas*, 464–65.

282. Anonymous Thomas law clerk, interview with author.

283. Thomas, *Clarence Thomas*, 465.

284. John Fee, interview with author.

285. Thomas, *Clarence Thomas*, 464.

286. Fletcher and Merida, "Thomas Weighs Politics."

287. Foskett, *Judging Thomas*, 275–76, 280.

288. Ward Farsnworth, correspondence with author; anonymous Kennedy clerk, correspondence with author.

289. Farnsworth, correspondence with author.

290. E. Lawrence Vincent (OT 1987) confirms that Kennedy law clerks had the same three basic job duties (cert. memoranda, bench memoranda, and preparing first drafts of opinions), correspondence with author.

291. Stuart Taylor, "When High Court's Away, Clerks' Work Begins," *New York Times*, sec. B (Sept. 23, 1988).

292. Tony Mauro, "Justice Given Key Role to Novice Lawyers," *USA Today*, sec. A (Mar. 13, 1998).

293. Alison M. Tucher and Ernest A. Young, correspondence with author.

294. In 1981, the Judicial Conference of the United States established a code of conduct for law clerks. The Federal Judicial Center issued the *Law Clerk Handbook*, which contains its own "Code of Conduct for Law Clerks." Alvin B. Rubin and Laura B. Bartell, *Law Clerk Handbook: A Handbook for Law Clerks to Federal Judges* (Washington, D.C.: Federal Judicial Center, 1989). See also, Anthony M. DiLeo and Alvin B. Rubin, *Law Clerk Handbook: A Handbook for Federal District and Appellate Court Law Clerks* (Washington, D.C.: Federal Judicial Center, 1977).

295. Canon 2, *Code of Conduct for Law Clerks of the Supreme Court of the United States* (Washington, D.C.: U.S. Supreme Court, 1989): 1.

296. Ibid., 2.

297. Canon 3, *Code of Conduct*, 3.

298. Canon 2, *Code of Conduct*, 2.

299. Canon 3, *Code of Conduct*, 3–4.

300. Canon 1, *Code of Conduct*, 1.

301. David Margolick, Evgenia Pertz, and Michael Shnayerson, "The Path to Florida," *Vanity Fair* (Oct. 2004): 310–20.

302. Ibid., 320.

NOTES TO CHAPTER 6

1. Owens, "The Clerk, the Thief, His Life as a Baker," 271–308.

2. "Some justices retained the same clerk for several years. Justice McKenna, for example, kept his first clerk for twelve years, until the latter's death. McKenna had only two other clerks during his remaining fifteen years. As another example, Justice Butler employed one individual, first as a 'stenographic clerk' and later as a 'law clerk,' from 1923 until the justice's death in 1939. . . . Justice Roberts employed one clerk from 1930 to 1945. . . . This law clerk's wife was also employed by Roberts as a secretary." Chester A. Newland, "Personal Assistants," 300.

3. Of course, justices have proffered other explanations. Justice Holmes claimed that the rotating clerkship let him tell the same stories to new crops of young attorneys, while Chief Justice Stone felt that new attorneys should be allowed to make their own way into the world.

4. Corey Ditslear and Lawrence Baum, "Selection of Law Clerks," 883.

5. Canons 1 to 6, *Code of Conduct.*

6. Baldassare Castiglione, *The Book of the Courtier,* trans. Charles S. Singleton (Garden City, N.Y.: Anchor Books, 1959): 67, 71, 135.

7. Ibid., 289.

8. Ibid., 290.

9. Ibid., 111.

10. Frank, "Fred Vinson and the Chief Justiceship," 224

Bibliography

Manuscript Collections

CLEMSON UNIVERSITY, CLEMSON, SOUTH CAROLINA
James F. Byrnes Papers

HARVARD LAW SCHOOL, CAMBRIDGE, MASSACHUSETTS
Fred Fishman Papers
Felix Frankfurter Papers
Henry M. Hart, Jr., Papers
Irving J. Helman Papers
Oliver Wendell Holmes, Jr., Papers
Mark De Wolfe Howe Diary

LIBRARY OF CONGRESS, WASHINGTON, D.C.
Hugo L. Black Papers
Harry Blackmun Papers
Harold Burton Papers
William O. Douglas Papers
Melville W. Fuller Papers
Arthur Goldberg Papers
Horace Gray Papers
Robert H. Jackson Papers
Thurgood Marshall Papers
William Moody Papers
Wiley Rutledge Papers
Harlan Fiske Stone Papers
George Sutherland Papers
William Howard Taft Papers
Morrison R. Waite Papers
Willis Van Devanter Papers
Earl Warren Papers

UNIVERSITY OF GEORGIA, ATHENS
Joseph Rucker Lamar Papers

UNIVERSITY OF VIRGINIA SCHOOL OF LAW, CHARLOTTESVILLE
E. Barrett Prettyman, Jr., Papers

WASHINGTON AND LEE UNIVERSITY SCHOOL OF LAW, LEXINGTON, VIRGINIA
Lewis F. Powell, Jr., Papers

Oral Histories

UNIVERSITY OF KENTUCKY, LEXINGTON
Stanley Reed Oral History Project
Fred M. Vinson Oral History Project

WISCONSIN HISTORICAL SOCIETY
James Doyle Oral History

Interviews

Sam Bagenstos, Vicki L. Been, Hugo L. Black, Jr., Bennett Boskey, Kathryn Lovill Bradley, Bruce P. Brown, Carol S. Bruch, Jesse H. Choper, William Coleman, Jr., Earl Dudley, Jr., Brett Dunkelman, Lawrence Ebb, Wilbur Friedman, Warner W. Gardner, S. Elizabeth Gibson, C. David Ginsburg, Eugene Gressman, Larry Hammond, Louis Henkin, Roderick Hills, Truman Hobbs, A. E. Dick Howard, Manley O. Hudson, Dennis J. Hutchinson, William Joslin, Pamela Karlan, Andrew Kaufman, Alan Kohn, Louis Lusky, William J. Maledon, Judith McMorrow, Daniel Meador, Abner Mikva, Dallin H. Oaks, Louis Oberdorfer, Robert O'Neil, Daniel Ortiz, Josephine Black Pesaresi, Carter G. Phillips, Richard Posner, E. Barrett Prettyman, Jr., Deborah Rhode, George Rutherglen, Terry Sandalow, John T. Sapienza, Antonin Scalia, Robert A. Schapiro, Margo Schlanger, Arthur R. Seder, Alexandra Shapiro, John Paul Stevens, Stephen Susman, Kent Syverud, Howard J. Trienens, Robert Von Mehren, Harry Wellington, and Harris K. Weston.

Books

Abraham, Henry. *The Judicial Process: An Introductory Analysis of the Courts of the United States, England and France.* (7th ed.) New York: Oxford University Press, 1998.

Acheson, Dean. *Morning and Noon.* Boston: Houghton Mifflin, 1965.

Atkinson, David N. *Leaving the Bench: Supreme Court Justices at the End.* Lawrence: University of Kansas Press, 1999.

Baker, Leonard. *Brandeis and Frankfurter: A Dual Biography.* New York: Harper & Row, 1984.

Ball, Howard. *Hugo L. Black: Cold Steel Warrior.* New York: Oxford University Press, 1996.

Baum, Lawrence. *The Supreme Court.* (5th ed.) Washington, D.C.: Congressional Quarterly, 1995.

————. *The Puzzle of Judicial Behavior.* Ann Arbor: University of Michigan Press, 1997.

Berry, Mary Frances. *Stability, Security and Continuity: Mr. Justice Burton and Decision-Making in the Supreme Court, 1945–1958.* Westport, Conn.: Greenwood Press, 1978.

Best, Bradley J. *Law Clerks, Support Personnel, and the Decline of Consensual Norms on the United States Supreme Court, 1935–1995*. New York: LFB Scholarly Publishing, 2002.

Beth, Loren B. *John Marshall Harlan: The Last Whig Justice*. Lexington: University of Kentucky Press, 1992.

Bickel, Alexander. *History of the Supreme Court of the United States: The Judiciary and Responsible Government*. Vol. 9. New York: Macmillan, 1984.

Biddle, Francis. *Mr. Justice Holmes*. New York: Scribner's, 1942.

Black, Hugo L., and Elizabeth Black. *Mr. Justice and Mrs. Black: The Memoirs of Hugo L. Black and Elizabeth Black*. New York: Random House, 1986.

Black, Hugo L., Jr. *My Father: A Remembrance*. New York: Random House, 1975.

Brigham, John. *The Cult of the Court*. Philadelphia: Temple University Press, 1987.

Brown, Henry Billings. *Memoir of Henry Billings Brown: Late Justice of the Supreme Court of the United States*. New York: Duffield, 1915.

Byrnes, James F. *All in One Lifetime*. New York: Harper & Brothers, 1958.

Campbell, Tracy. *Short of the Glory: The Fall and Redemption of Edward F. Prichard, Jr.* Lexington: University of Kentucky Press, 1998.

Castiglione, Baldassare. *The Book of the Courtier*. (Charles S. Singleton, trans.) Garden City, N.Y.: Doubleday, 1959.

Christopher, Warren. *Chances of a Lifetime: A Memoir*. New York: Scribner's, 2001.

Clayton, Cornell W., and Howard Gillman, eds. *Supreme Court Decision-Making: New Institutionalist Approaches*. Chicago: University of Chicago Press, 1999.

Code of Conduct for Law Clerks of the Supreme Court of the United States. Washington, D.C.: U.S. Supreme Court, 1989.

Coffin, Frank M. *On Appeal: Courts, Lawyering, and Judging*. New York: Norton, 1994.

Cray, Ed. *Chief Justice: A Biography of Earl Warren*. New York: Simon & Schuster, 1997.

Danelski, David J., and Joseph S. Tulchin, eds. *The Autobiographical Notes of Charles Evans Hughes*. Cambridge, Mass.: Harvard University Press, 1973.

Dean, John W. *The Rehnquist Choice: The Untold Story of the Nixon Appointment That Redefined the Supreme Court*. New York: Simon & Schuster, 2001.

DiLeo, Anthony M., and Alvin B. Rubin. *Law Clerk Handbook: A Handbook for Federal District and Appellate Court Law Clerks*. Washington, D.C.: Federal Judicial Center, 1977.

Domnarski, William. *In the Opinion of the Court*. Urbana: University of Illinois Press, 1996.

Douglas, William O. *The Court Years, 1939–1975: The Autobiography of William O. Douglas*. New York: Random House, 1980.

Epstein, Lee, Jeffrey Segal, Harold Spaeth, and Thomas Walker. *The Supreme Court Compendium: Data, Decisions, and Developments*. Washington, D.C.: CQ Press, 1996.

Ferren, John M. *Salt of the Earth, Conscience of the Court: The Story of Justice Wiley Rutledge*. Chapel Hill: University of North Carolina Press, 2004.

Fine, Sidney. 1984. *Frank Murphy: The Washington Years*. Ann Arbor: University of Michigan Press.

Foskett, Ken. *Judging Thomas: The Life and Times of Clarence Thomas*. New York: HarperCollins, 2004.

Frank, John P. *Marble Palace: The Supreme Court in American Life*. Westport, Conn.: Greenwood Press, 1958.

——.*Inside Justice Hugo L. Black: The Letters*. Austin: Jamail Center for Legal Research, University of Texas at Austin, 2000.

Frankfurter, Felix, and James M. Landis. *The Business of the Supreme Court: A Study in the Federal Judicial System*. New York: Macmillan, 1927.

Garland, A. H. *Annual Report of the Attorney General of the United States for the Year 1885*. Washington, D.C.: Government Printing Office, 1885.

Goldman, Roger, and David Gallen, eds. *Thurgood Marshall: Justice for All*. New York: Carroll & Graf, 1992.

Graham, Katharine. *Personal History*. New York: Knopf, 1997.

Hall, Kermit L., ed. *The Oxford Companion to the Supreme Court of the United States*. New York: Oxford University Press, 1992.

Hiss, Alger. *Reflections of a Life*. New York: Seaver Books, 1988.

Howard, J. Woodford, Jr. *Mr. Justice Murphy: A Political Biography*. Princeton, N.J.: Princeton University Press, 1968.

Hutchinson, Dennis J. *The Man Who Once Was Whizzer White: A Portrait of Justice Byron R. White*. New York: Free Press, 1998.

Hutchinson, Dennis J., and David J. Garrow, eds. *The Forgotten Memoir of John Knox: A Year in the Life of a Supreme Court Law Clerk in FDR's Washington*. Chicago: University of Chicago Press, 2002.

Kalman, Laura. *Abe Fortas: A Biography*. New Haven, Conn.: Yale University Press, 1990.

Kaufman, Andrew L. *Cardozo*. Cambridge, Mass.: Harvard University Press, 1998.

——.“The Justice and His Law Clerks.” In *Felix Frankfurter, the Judge*, edited by Wallace Mendelson. New York: Reynal, 1964.

King, Willard L. *Melville Weston Fuller: Chief Justice of the United States, 1888–1910*. New York: Macmillan, 1950.

Klinkhamer, Sister Marie Carolyn. *Edward Douglas White, Chief Justice of the United States*. Washington, D.C.: Catholic University of America Press, 1943.

Kronman, Anthony T. *The Lost Lawyer: Failing Ideals of the Legal Profession*. Cambridge, Mass.: Harvard University Press, 1993.

Jeffries, John C., Jr. *Justice Lewis F. Powell, Jr.* New York: Scribner's, 1994.

Lasky, Victor. *Arthur J. Goldberg: The Old and the New*. New Rochelle, N.Y.: Arlington House, 1970.

Lazarus, Edward. *Closed Chambers: The First Eyewitness Account of the Epic Struggles Inside the Supreme Court*. New York: Random House, 1998.

Louchheim, Katie, ed. *The Making of the New Deal: The Insiders Speak*. Cambridge, Mass.: Harvard University Press, 1983.

Lowell, Francis C. “Horace Gray.” In *Proceedings of the American Academy of Arts and Sciences*. Vol. 39. Boston: American Academy of Arts and Sciences, 1904.

Mason, Alpheus Thomas. *Harlan Fiske Stone: Pillar of the Law*. New York: Viking, 1956.

McKean, David. *Tommy the Cork: Washington's Ultimate Insider from Roosevelt to Reagan*. South Royalton, Vt.: Steerforth Press, 2004.

McLean, Joseph E. *William Rufus Day: Supreme Court Justice from Ohio*. Baltimore, Md.: Johns Hopkins University Press, 1946.

Meador, Daniel J. *Mr. Justice Black and His Books.* Charlottesville: University Press of Virginia, 1974.

Mennel, Robert M., and Christine L. Compston, eds. *Holmes and Frankfurter: Their Correspondence, 1912–1934.* Hanover, N.H.: University Press of New England, 1996.

Metlzer, Brad. *The Tenth Justice.* New York: Weisbach, 1997.

Miller, Richard Lawrence. *Whittaker: Struggles of a Supreme Court Justice.* Westport, Conn.: Greenwood Press, 2002.

Monagan, John S. *The Grand Panjandrum: Mellow Years of Justice Holmes.* Lanham, Md.: University Press of America, 1988.

Murdoch, Joyce, and Deb Price. *Courting Justice: Gay Men and Lesbians v. the Supreme Court.* New York: Basic Books, 2001.

Murphy, Bruce Allen. *Fortas: The Rise and Ruin of a Supreme Court Justice.* New York: Morrow, 1988.

———. *Wild Bill.* New York: Random House, 2003.

Myers, Gustavus. *History of the Supreme Court of the United States.* Chicago: Kerr, 1925.

The National Law School Deans' List. Arlington, Va.: National Jurist, 1999.

North, Douglass C. *Institutions, Institutional Change and Economic Performance.* New York: Cambridge University Press, 1990.

Oakley, John Bilyeu, and Robert S. Thompson. *Law Clerks and the Judicial Process: Perceptions of the Qualities and Functions of Law Clerks in American Courts.* Berkeley: University of California Press, 1980.

O'Brien, David M. *Storm Center: The Supreme Court in American Politics.* (5th ed.) New York: W. W. Norton, 2000.

Parrish, Michael E. "Justice Frankfurter and the Supreme Court." In *The Jewish Justices of the Supreme Court Revisited: Brandeis to Fortas,* edited by Jennifer M. Lowe. Washington, D.C.: Supreme Court Historical Society, 1994.

Posner, Richard A. *The Federal Courts: Crisis and Reform.* Cambridge, Mass.: Harvard University Press, 1985.

Pratt, Walter F., Jr. *The Supreme Court Under Edward Douglass White, 1910–1921.* Columbia: University of South Carolina Press, 1999.

Pusey, Merlo J. *Charles Evans Hughes.* New York: MacMillian, 1951.

Ragan, Allen E. *Chief Justice Taft.* Columbus: Ohio State Archaeological and Historical Society, 1938.

Rehnquist, William H. *The Supreme Court.* New York: Knopf, 2001.

Reich, Charles A. *The Sorcerer of Bolinas Reef.* New York: Random House, 1976.

Rubin, Alvin B., and Laura B. Bartell. *Law Clerk Handbook.* Washington, D.C.: Federal Judicial Center, 1989.

Schwartz, Bernard. *Super Chief.* New York: New York University Press, 1983.

———. *A History of the Supreme Court.* New York: Oxford University, 1993.

Segal, Jeffrey A., and Harold Spaeth. *The Supreme Court and the Attitudinal Model.* New York: Cambridge University Press, 1993.

Silber, Norman I. *With All Deliberate Speed: The Life of Philip Elman.* Ann Arbor: University of Michigan Press, 2004.

Smith, Craig Alan. *Failing Justice: Charles Evans Whittaker on the Supreme Court.* Jefferson, N.C.: McFarland, 2005.

St. Clair, James E., and Linda C. Gugin. *Chief Justice Fred M. Vinson of Kentucky: A Political Biography*. Lexington: University of Kentucky Press, 2002.

Stenbenne, David. *Arthur J. Goldberg: New Deal Liberal*. New York: Oxford University Press, 1996.

Swisher, Carl B. *Stephen J. Field: Craftsman of the Law*. Hamden, Conn.: Archon Books, 1963.

———. *History of the Supreme Court of the United States: The Taney Period, 1836–1864*. Vol. 5. New York: Macmillan, 1974.

Thomas, Andrew Peyton. *Clarence Thomas: A Biography*. San Francisco: Encounter Books, 2002.

Tigar, Michael E. *Fighting Injustice*. Chicago: American Bar Association, 2002.

Truman, Margaret. *Murder in the Supreme Court*. New York: Arbor House, 1982.

Urofsky, Melvin I. *The Douglas Letters: Selections from the Private Papers of Justice William O. Douglas*. Bethesda, Md.: Adler & Adler, 1987.

———. *Division and Discord: The Supreme Court Under Stone and Vinson, 1941–1953*. Columbia: University of South Carolina Press, 1997.

Urofsky, Melvin I., and David W. Levy, eds. *The Letters of Louis D. Brandeis*. Albany: State University of New York Press, 1971.

Warner, Hoyt Landon. *The Life of Mr. Justice Clarke: A Testament to the Power of Liberal Dissent in America*. Cleveland, Ohio: Western Reserve University Press, 1950.

Warren, Charles. *The Supreme Court in United States History*. Boston: Little, Brown, 1937.

White, G. Edward. *Earl Warren: A Public Life*. New York: Oxford University Press, 1982.

———. *Justice Oliver Wendell Holmes: Law and the Inner Self*. New York: Oxford University Press, 1993.

Wilkinson, J. Harvie III. *Serving Justice: A Supreme Court Clerk's View*. New York: Charterhouse, 1974.

Williams, Juan. *Thurgood Marshall: American Revolutionary*. New York: Times Books, 1998.

Williston, Samuel. "Horace Gray." In *Great American Lawyers*, edited by William Draper Lewis. Philadelphia: J.C. Vinson, 1909.

———. *Life and Law*. Boston: Little, Brown, 1940.

Woodward, Bob, and Scott Armstrong. *The Brethren: Inside the Supreme Court*. New York: Simon & Schuster, 1979.

Journals and Magazines

Acheson, Dean. "Recollections of Service with the Federal Supreme Court." *The Alabama Lawyer* 18 (1957): 355–66.

Agostisi, Robert M., and Brian P. Corrigan. "Do as We Say or Do as We Do: How the Supreme Court Law Clerk Controversy Reveals a Lack of Accountability at the High Court." *Hofstra Labor and Employment Law Journal* 18 (Spring 2001): 625–58.

Alsup, William. "Accurately Remembering Justice Douglas: A Reply to *Wild Bill* and Recent Critics." *The Federal Lawyer* (Nov.-Dec. 2003): 21–28.

Arnold, Richard S. "A Remembrance: Mr. Justice Brennan, October Term 1960." *Journal of Supreme Court History* (1991): 5–8.

Atkinson, David. "Justice Harold H. Burton and the Work of the Supreme Court." *Cleveland State Law Review* 27, no. 1 (1978): 69–83.

Baier, Paul R. "The Law Clerks: Profile of an Institution." *Vanderbilt Law Review* 26 (1973): 1125–77.

Benka, Richard W., Thomas J. Klitgaard, Marshall L. Small, William A. Reppy, Jr., and Jay K. Wright. "Remembrances of William O. Douglas on the 50th Anniversary of His Appointment to the Supreme Court." *Journal of Supreme Court History* (1990): 104–24.

Berkman, Harvey. "Remembering Powell, a Gentleman Justice; His Centrist Legacy Includes 'Bakke,' 'Bowers,' and Law Clerks Who Adored Him." *The National Law Journal* 21 (1998): A7.

Bloch, Susan Low. "The Privilege of Clerking for Thurgood Marshall." *Journal of Supreme Court History* (1992): 23–25.

Boskey, Bennett. "Justice Reed and His Family of Law Clerks." *Kentucky Law Journal* 69, no. 4 (1980–81): 869–76.

Brehm, John, and Scott Gates. "Donut Shops and Speed Traps: Evaluating Models of Supervision on Police Behavior." *American Journal of Political Science* 37 (May 1993): 555–81.

Brennan, William J., Jr. "Justice Brennan Calls National Court of Appeals Proposal 'Fundamentally Unnecessary and Ill Advised.'" *American Bar Association Journal* 59 (Aug. 1973): 835–40.

———. "The Warren Court: A Personal Remembrance." *The Supreme Court Historical Society* 15, no. 4 (1994): 5.

Brenner, Saul, and Jan Palmer. "The Law Clerks' Recommendation and Chief Justice Vinson's Vote on Certiorari." *American Politics Quarterly* 18 (Jan. 1990): 68–80.

Brewer, Scott. "In Memoriam: Justice Marshall's Justice Martial." *Texas Law Review* 71, no. 6 (May 1993): 1121–24.

Breyer, Stephen. "Clerking for Justice Goldberg." *Supreme Court Historical Society Yearbook* (1990): 4–7.

"The Bright Young Men Behind the Bench." *U.S. News & World Report* (July 12, 1957).

Brown, Mark R. "Gender Discrimination in the Supreme Court's Clerkship Selection Process." *Oregon Law Review* 75, no. 2 (Summer 1996): 359–88.

Brudney, Victor, and Richard Wolfson. "Mr. Justice Rutledge—Law Clerks' Reflections." *Indiana Law Journal* 25, no. 1 (Fall 1949): 455–61.

Caldeira, Gregory, and Christopher Zorn. "Of Time and Consensual Norms in the Supreme Court." *American Journal of Political Science* 42, no. 3 (July 1998): 874–902.

"Chief Justice Vinson and His Law Clerks." *Northwestern University Law Review* 49, no. 1 (Mar.-Apr. 1954): 26–35.

Clark, Tom C. "Internal Operation of the United States Supreme Court." *Journal of the American Judicature Society* 43 (Aug. 1959): 48.

———. "The Decisional Processes of the Supreme Court." *Cornell Law Review* 50, no. 3 (Spring 1965): 385–93.

———. "Reminiscences of an Attorney General." *Houston Law Review* 6, no. 4 (Mar. 1969): 623–29.

Cohen, William. "Justice Douglas: A Law Clerk's View." *The University of Chicago Law Review* 26, no. 1 (Autumn 1958): 6–8.

Colb, Sherry F. "Breakfast with Justice Blackmun." *North Dakota Law Review* 71, no. 1 (1995): 13–15.

Coleman, Trevor W. "Supreme Bias." *Emerge* (July-Aug. 1999): 59–61.

Coughlin, Anne M. "In Memoriam: Writing for Justice Powell." *Columbia Law Review* 99, no. 3 (Apr. 1999): 541–43.

Danelski, David J. "Lucile Lomen: The First Woman to Clerk at the Supreme Court." *Journal of Supreme Court History* 23 (1999): 43–49.

Darbyshire, Glen M. "Clerking for Justice Marshall." *American Bar Association Journal* 77 (Sept. 1991): 48.

Davis, Elbridge B., and Harold A. Davis. "Mr. Justice Gray: Some Aspects of His Judicial Career." *American Bar Association Journal* 41 (May 1955): 421–71.

Denby, Charles, and Robert Wales. "An Extraordinary Man," in "Personal Remembrances of Mr. Justice Holmes by His Former Law Clerks: A Retrospective Note." Holmes Symposium. *University of Florida Law Review* 27 (1976): 392–98.

Derby, Augustin. "Recollections of Mr. Justice Holmes." *New York University Law Quarterly Review* 12, no. 3 (1935): 345–53.

Ditslear, Corey, and Lawrence Baum. "Selection of Law Clerks and Polarization in the U.S. Supreme Court." *Journal of Politics* 63 (Aug. 2001): 869–85.

Dorsen, Norman, and Amelia Ames Newcomb, eds. "John Marshall Harlan II, Associate Justice of the U.S. Supreme Court 1955–1971: Remembrances by His Law Clerks." *Journal of Supreme Court History* 27, no. 2 (July 2002): 138–75.

Drahozal, Christopher R. "In Memoriam: Remembering Justice Byron R. White." *University of Kansas Law Review* 50, no. 5 (June 2002): 1083–85.

Dudley, Earl C., Jr. "Terry v. Ohio: The Warren Court, and the Fourth Amendment: A Law Clerk's Perspective." *St. John's Law Review* 72 (Summer-Fall 1998): 891–903.

Elman, Philip. "The Solicitor General's Office, Justice Frankfurter and Civil Rights Litigation, 1946–1960: An Oral History." *Harvard Law Review* 100, no. 4 (Feb. 1987): 817–44.

Estreicher, Samuel. "I Shall Not Look Upon His Like Again." *Legal Times* 21 (1998): 10.

Feldblum, Chai. "Former Law Clerk Recalls Blackmun's Humility." *The National Law Journal* 21 (1999): 24.

Field, Stephen J. "The Centenary of the Supreme Court of the United States." *American Law Review* 24 (May-June 1890): 351–68.

Frank, John P. "Fred Vinson and the Chief Justiceship." *University of Chicago Law Review* 21, no. 1 (Autumn 1954): 212–46.

Freund, Paul A. "Mr. Justice Brandeis: A Centennial Memoir." *Harvard Law Review* 70, no. 5 (Mar. 1957): 769–92.

———. "Historical Reminiscence—Justice Brandeis: A Law Clerk's Remembrance." *American Jewish History* 68 (1978): 7–18.

Gardner, Warner W. "Harlan Fiske Stone: The View from Below." *The Supreme Court Historical Society Quarterly* 2 (2001): 1, 8–12.

Garrow, David J. "The Lowest Form of Animal Life? Supreme Court Clerks and Supreme Court History." *Cornell Law Review* 84, no. 3 (Mar. 1999): 855–94.

Gatland, Laura. "A Clerkship for White Males Only." *Student Lawyer* (Oct. 1999): 34–39.

Gellhorn, Gay. "Justice Thurgood Marshall's Jurisprudence of Equal Protection of the Laws and the Poor." *Arizona State Law Journal* 26, no. 2 (Summer 1994): 429–60.

Ginsburg, C. David. "Reflections of Justice Douglas' First Law Clerk." *Harvard Law Review* 93, no. 7 (May 1980): 1403–406.

Graglia, F. Carolyn. "In Memoriam: His First Law Clerk's Fond Memories of a Gracious Gentleman." *Texas Law Review* 74, no. 2 (Dec. 1995): 231–36.

Haig, J. Frederick. "The Supreme Court of the United States." *Independent* 69 (Nov. 1910): 1038–39.

Handler, Milton. "Clerking for Justice Harlan Fiske Stone." *Journal of Supreme Court History* (1995): 113–22.

Hoar, George F. "Mr. Justice Horace Gray." *Massachusetts Historical Society Proceedings* (1904).

Kagan, Elena. "For Justice Marshall." *Texas Law Review* 71, no. 6 (May 1993): 1125–30.

Karlan, Pamela S. "In Memorium: Harry A. Blackmun." *Harvard Law Review* 113, no. 1 (Nov. 1999): 5–10

Kaufman, Andrew L. "Constitutional Law and the Supreme Court: Frankfurter and Wellington." *New York Law School Law Review* 45 (2001): 141–47.

Kennedy, Randall. "The Clerkship Question and the Court." *American Lawyer* (Apr. 1999): 114–15.

Kenney, Sally J. "Beyond Principals and Agents: Seeing Courts as Organizations by Comparing Referendaires at the European Court of Justice and Law Clerks at the U.S. Supreme Court." *Comparative Political Studies* 33 (June 2000): 593–25.

———. "Puppeteers or Agents? What Lazarus' Closed Chambers Adds to Our Understanding of Law Clerks at the U.S. Supreme Court." *Law and Social Inquiry* 25, no. 1 (Winter 2000): 185–22.

Kohn, Alan C. "Supreme Court Law Clerk, 1957–1958: A Reminiscence." *Journal of Supreme Court History* 2 (1998): 40–52.

Kopkind, Andrew. "Brennan v. Tigar." *New Republic* (Aug. 1966): 21–22.

Heineman, Ben W., Jr. "A Balance Wheel on the Court." *Yale Law Journal* 95, no. 7 (June 1986): 1325–28.

Landis, James M. "Mr. Justice Brandeis: A Law Clerk's View." *American Jewish Historical Society* (1957): 467–73.

Lusky, Louis. "Clerking for Harlan Fiske Stone." *The Supreme Court Historical Society Quarterly* 13, no. 1 (1992): 13–14.

Luttig, J. Michael. "In Memoriam: Warren E. Burger." *Harvard Law Review* 109, no. 1 (Nov. 1995) 1–5.

Mahoney, J. Daniel. "Law Clerks: For Better or for Worse?" *Brooklyn Law Review* 54, no. 2 (1988): 321–45.

Margolick, David, Evgenia Pertz, and Michael Shnayerson. "The Path to Florida." *Vanity Fair* (Oct. 2004): 310–20.

Marsh, James M. "Affirm, If Possible: How a U.S. Supreme Court Justice's Confidence in His Clerk Turned a Tentative 5–4 Vote into an 8–1 Decision." *Philadelphia Lawyer* (1997): 62–64.

———. "Some Personal Correspondence of Justice Jackson." *The Supreme Court Historical Society Quarterly* 18, no. 1 (1997): 19.

———."Supreme Court Justice Without a College Degree," *The Philadelphia Law-yer* (1999): 63–64.

Martinson, Wanda S. "In Memoriam: My Twenty-Five Years with 'Old Number Three.'" *Columbia Law Review* 99, no. 6 (Oct. 1999): 1405–408.

McAllister, Stephen R. "In Memoriam: Remembering Justice Byron R. White." *University of Kansas Law Review* 50, no. 5 (June 2002): 1077–83.

McCann, Tom. "Clerks See Life on the Inside of the U.S. Supreme Court." *Chicago Lawyer* (Sept. 1, 2003).

McCormack, Alfred. "A Law Clerk's Recollections." *Columbia Law Review* 46, no. 5 (Sept. 1946): 710–18.

McElwain, Edwin. "The Business of the Supreme Court as Conducted by Chief Justice Hughes." *Harvard Law Review* 63, no. 1 (Nov. 1949): 5–26.

Meador, Daniel J. "Justice Black and His Law Clerks." *Alabama Law Review* 15, no. 1 (Fall 1962): 57–63.

Meserve, Richard A. "A Tribute to Justice Harry A. Blackmun." *North Dakota Law Review* 71, no. 1 (1995): 21–24.

Messinger, I. Scott. "The Judge as Mentor: Oliver Wendell Holmes, Jr. and His Law Clerks." *Yale Journal of Law & The Humanities* 11, no. 1 (Winter 1999): 119–52.

Miller, Samuel. "Judicial Reforms." *The United States Jurist* 2 (Jan. 1872): 3.

Minow, Martha. "A Tribute to Justice Marshall." *Harvard Law Review* 105 (1991): 66–76.

Moe, Terry. "The New Economics of Organization." *American Journal of Political Science* 28 (1984): 739–78.

Moore, Karen Nelson. "In Memorium: Harry A. Blackmun." *Harvard Law Review* 113, no. 1 (Nov. 1999): 17–21.

Nesson, Charles. "Mr. Justice Harlan." *Harvard Law Review* 85, no. 1 (Nov. 1971): 390–91.

Newland, Chester A. "Personal Assistants to Supreme Court Justices: The Law Clerks." *Oregon Law Review* 40, no. 4 (June 1961): 299–317.

O'Neil, Robert. "Clerking for Justice Brennan." *Journal of Supreme Court History* (1961): 3–4.

Owens, John B. "The Clerk, the Thief, His Life as a Baker: Ashton Embry and the Supreme Court Leak Scandal of 1919." *Northwestern University Law Review* 95, no. 1 (Fall 2002): 271–308.

Painter, Richard W. "Matters of Ethics: Open Chambers?" *Michigan Law Review* 97, no. 6 (May 1999): 1430–71.

Parr, Henry L., Jr. "In Memoriam: Warren E. Burger: A Law Clerk's Reminiscences." *Texas Law Review* 74, no. 2 (Dec. 1995): 225–29.

Pearlstein, Deborah N. "The Power to Persuade: A Year in the Life of a Supreme Court Clerk." *NCJW Journal* (Oct. 31, 2000): 12–13, 15, 28.

Pickering, John H., Eugene Gressman, and T. L. Tolan, Jr. "Mr. Justice Murphy—A Note of Appreciation." *Michigan Law Review* 48, no. 6 (Apr. 1950): 742–44.

Posner, Richard A. 1990. "William J. Brennan, Jr." *Harvard Law Review* 104, no. 1 (Nov. 1990): 13–15.

Post, Robert. "The Supreme Court Opinion as Institutional Practice: Dissent, Legal Scholarship, and Decision-Making in the Taft Court." *Minnesota Law Review* 85, no. 5 (May 2001): 1267–390.

Proceedings of the Bar and Officers of the Supreme Court of the United States: In Memoriam, Honorable Hugo Lafayette Black. Apr. 18, 1972. Washington, D.C.

Proceedings of the Bar and Officers of the Supreme Court of the United States in Memory of Associate Justice Louis D. Brandeis. Dec. 21, 1942. Washington, D.C.

Proceedings of the Bar and Officers of the Supreme Court of the United States in Memory of David Josiah Brewer. Apr. 30, 1910. Washington, D.C.

Proceedings of the Bar and Officers of the Supreme Court of the United States in Memory of Harold H. Burton. May 24, 1965. Washington, D.C.

Proceedings of the Bar and Officers of the Supreme Court of the United States in Memory of Pierce Butler. Jan. 27, 1940. Washington, D.C.

Proceedings of the Bar and Officers of the Supreme Court of the United States in Memory of Benjamin Nathan Cardozo. Nov. 26, 1938. Washington, D.C.

Proceedings of the Bar and Officers of the Supreme Court of the United States in Memory of Felix Frankfurter. Oct. 25, 1965. Washington, D.C.

Proceedings of the Bar and Officers of the Supreme Court of the United States in Memory of Melville Weston Fuller. Dec. 10, 1910. Washington, D.C.

Proceedings of the Bar and Officers of the Supreme Court of the United States in Memory of Charles Evans Hughes. May 8, 1950. Washington, D.C.

Proceedings of the Bar and Officers of the Supreme Court of the United States in Memory of Robert Houghwout Jackson. Apr. 4, 1955. Washington, D.C.

Proceedings of the Bar and Officers of the Supreme Court of the United States in Memory of Joseph Rucker Lamar. May 27, 1916. Washington, D.C.

Proceedings of the Bar and Officers of the Supreme Court of the United States in Memory of James Clark McReynolds. Mar. 31, 1948. Washington, D.C.

Proceedings of the Bar and Officers of the Supreme Court of the United States in Memory of Rufus Wheeler Peckham, Dec. 18, 1909, 1910. Washington, D.C.

Proceedings of the Bar and Officers of the Supreme Court of the United States in Memory of Wiley Blount Rutledge. Apr. 10, 1951. Washington, D.C.

Proceedings of the Bar and Officers of the Supreme Court of the United States in Memory of Harlan Fiske Stone. Mar. 31, 1948. Washington, D.C.

Proceedings of the Bar and Officers of the Supreme Court of the United States in Memory of George Sutherland. Dec. 18, 1944. Washington, D.C.

Proceedings of the Bar and Officers of the Supreme Court of the United States in Memory of William Howard Taft. Dec. 13, 1930. Washington, D.C.

Proceedings of the Bar and Officers of the Supreme Court of the United States in Memory of Fred. M. Vinson. 1954. Washington, D.C.

Proceedings of the Bar and of the Supreme Judicial Court of Massachusetts in Memory of Horace Gray. Jan. 17, 1903.

Proceedings at the Meeting of the Essex Bar in the Supreme Judicial Court in Memory of Hon. William Henry Moody. Apr. 26, 1919. (Compiled for Essex Bar Association by Winfield S. Nevins)

Purcell, Richard J. "Mr. Justice Pierce Butler." *Catholic Educational Review* 42 (Apr. 1944): 193–215.

Rao, Radhika. "The Author of Roe." *Hastings Constitutional Law Quarterly* 26, no. 1 (Fall 1998): 21–40.

Rauh, Joseph L., Jr. "Historical Perspectives: An Unabashed Liberal Looks at a Half-

Century of the Supreme Court." *North Carolina Law Review* 69, no. 1 (Nov. 1990): 213–49.

Rauh, Joseph L., Jr., Melvin Siegel, Ambrose Doskow, and Alan M. Stroock. "A Personal View of Justice Benjamin N. Cardozo: Recollections of Four Cardozo Law Clerks." *Cardozo Law Review* 1 (Spring 1979): 5–22.

Ray, Laura K. "A Law Clerk and His Justice: What William Rehnquist Did Not Learn from Robert Jackson." *Indiana Law Review* 29 (1996): 535–92.

Rehnquist, William H. "Another View: Clerks Might 'Influence' Some Actions." *U.S. News & World Report*, Feb. 21, 1958.

———. "Who Writes Decisions of the Supreme Court. *U.S. News & World Report*, Dec. 13, 1957.

Rehnquist, William H., J. Harvie Wilkinson III, T. S. Ellis III, John C. Jeffries, Jr., Nina Totenberg, Christina B. Whitman. "In Memoriam: Lewis F. Powell, Jr." *Harvard Law Review* 112, no. 3 (Jan. 1999): 589–610.

"Remembering U.S. Supreme Court Justice Frank Murphy, '14." *Law Quadrangle News* (Winter 2005): 41–44.

Rhode, Deborah L. "A Tribute to Justice Thurgood Marshall: Letting the Law Catch Up." *Stanford Law Review* 44 (Summer 1992): 1259–65.

Rogers, William. "Do Law Clerks Wield Power in Supreme Court Cases." *U.S. News & World Report* (Feb. 21, 1958).

Rombauer, Edgar R., Jr. "Secretary to Justice Harlan—The Early Days." *The Supreme Court Historical Society Quarterly* 24, no. 1 (2003): 6–7, 16–17.

Rothfeld, Charles. "One Fried Egg and Rye Toast." *Legal Times* (Mar. 8, 1999): 11.

Sandalow, Terrance. "Potter Stewart." *Harvard Law Review* 95, no. 1 (Nov. 1981): 6–10.

Sappington, David E. M. "Incentives in Principal-Agent Relationships." *Journal of Economic Perspectives* 5, no. 2 (Spring 1991): 45–66.

Schneider, Mark. "Justice Blackmun: A Wise Man Walking the Corridors of Power, Gently." *Georgetown Law Journal* 83, no. 1 (Nov. 1994): 11–15.

Sexton, John Edward. "A Tribute to Chief Justice Warren E. Burger." *Harvard Law Review* 100, no. 5 (Mar. 1987): 979–84.

Smith, John Malcolm. "Mr. Justice Horace Gray of the United States Supreme Court." *South Dakota Law Review* 6, no. 2 (Fall 1961): 221–47.

Starr, Kenneth W. "The Man from Minnesota: A Remembrance from Things Past." *Texas Law Review* 74, no. 2 (Dec. 1995): 223–24.

Steiker, Jordan. "The Long Road Up From Barbarism: Thurgood Marshall and the Death Penalty." *Texas Law Review* 71, no. 6 (May 1993): 1131–64.

Stone, Lauson H. "My Father the Chief Justice." *Yearbook of the Supreme Court Historical Society* (1978): 7–17.

Stookey, John A., and Larry A. Hammond. "A Conversation Between Two Old Friends." *The Supreme Court Historical Society Quarterly* 18 (1997): 1, 4–5.

Strauss, Peter L. "In Memoriam: William J. Brennan, Jr." *Columbia Law Review* 97, no. 6 (Oct. 1997): 1609–11.

"Supreme Court: Memo from Rehnquist." *Newsweek* (Dec. 13, 1971).

Tribe, Laurence H. "Justice Stewart: A Tale of Two Portraits." *Yale Law Journal* 95, no. 7 (June 1986): 1328–33.

Tushnet, Mark. "The Jurisprudence of Thurgood Marshall." *University of Illinois Law Review*, no. 4 (1996): 1129–50.

———. "Thurgood Marshall and the Brethren." *Georgetown Law Journal* 80, no. 6 (Aug. 1992): 2109–30.

———. "What Really Happened in *Brown v. Board of Education*." *Columbia Law Review* 91, no. 8 (Dec. 1991): 1867–930.

Volling, James L. "Warren E. Burger: An Independent Pragmatist Remembered." *William Mitchell Law Review* 22, no. 1 (1996): 39–61.

Waite, Morrison R. "Remarks of Chief Justice Waite." *The Albany Law Journal* 36 (1887): 318.

Walker, Thomas G., Lee Epstein, and William J. Dixon. "On the Mysterious Demise of Consensual Norms in the United States Supreme Court." *Journal of Politics* 50 (May 1988): 361–89.

Weston, David. "Justice Powell and His Law Clerks." *Supreme Court Historical Society Yearbook* (1987): 16–19.

Williams, C. Dickerman. "The 1924 Term: Recollections of Chief Justice Taft's Law Clerk." *Yearbook of the Supreme Court Historical Society* (1989): 40–51.

Williams, Karen Hastie. "Humanizing the Legal Process: The Legacy of Thurgood Marshall." *Harvard Blackletter Journal* 6 (Spring 1989): 90–94.

Wood, Diane P. "Justice Harry A. Blackmun and the Responsibility of Judging." *Hastings Constitutional Law Quarterly* 26 (Fall 1998): 11–19.

———. "The Qualities of a Justice: Harry A. Blackmun." *Columbia Law Review* 99, no. 6 (Oct. 1999): 1409–12.

Worthen, Kevin J. "Shirt-Tales: Clerking for Byron White." *Brigham Young University Law Review* 2 (1994): 349–61.

Unpublished Sources

Atkinson, David N. "Mr. Justice Minton and the Supreme Court, 1949–1956." Ph.D. diss., University of Iowa, 1969.

Berry, Jennie. "Lucile Lomen."

Brown, Francis Joseph. "The Social and Economic Philosophy of Pierce Butler." Ph.D. diss., Catholic University, 1945.

Cole, Judith. "Mr. Justice Charles Evans Whittaker: A Case Study in Judicial Recruitment and Behavior." Master's thesis, University of Missouri-Kansas City, 1972.

Howard, James O'Brien. "Constitutional Doctrines of Mr. Justice Van Devanter." Master's thesis, State University of Iowa, 1937.

McCraw, John B. "Justice McReynolds and the Supreme Court: 1914–1941." Ph.D. diss., University of Texas, 1949.

Mitchell, Stephen Robert. "Mr. Justice Horace Gray" Ph.D. diss., University of Wisconsin, 1961.

Niznik, Monica Lynne. "Thomas G. Corcoran: The Public Service of Franklin Roosevelt's 'Tommy the Cork.'" Ph.D. diss., University of Notre Dame, 1981.

Rutherglen, George. "A Recollection of October Term, 1975." *Remembrances of William O. Douglas by His Friends and Associates*, special anniversary booklet (1989).

Smith, Craig Alan. "Charles Evans Whittaker, Associate Justice of the Supreme Court: A Thesis in History." Ph.D. diss., University of Missouri–Kansas City, 1997.

Sparrowe, Stanley. "W.O.D. and Me," *Remembrances of William O. Douglas by His Friends and Associates*, special anniversary booklet (1989).

Private Collections
Oaks, Dallin. *Personal Diary*.